THE WORKING WOMAN
SUCCESS BOOK

By The Editors of
Working Woman Magazine

With an Introduction
by Kate Rand Lloyd

ace books
A Division of Charter Communications Inc.
A GROSSET & DUNLAP COMPANY
51 Madison Avenue
New York, New York 10010

THE WORKING WOMAN SUCCESS BOOK

Copyright © 1981 by HAL Publications, Inc.

An Ace Book
First Ace Printing: October 1981

2 4 6 8 0 9 7 5 3 1
Manufactured in the United States of America

Table of Contents

VI THINKING AHEAD

Acknowledgement: We are grateful to all the editorial staff members, past and present, of *Working Woman* for their help in developing and shaping the material in this book and, in particular, to Jennifer Fortenbaugh, who took on the considerable task of assembling all the texts and of checking and clearing publication rights.

INTRODUCTION

by Kate Rand Lloyd, Editor-in-Chief

I wish this book had been around when I was starting my career. We just didn't have much like it then—nor was such basic, supportive help as *The Working Woman Success Book* provides thought to be necessary. After all, wasn't it a given that, after I had worked for a year or two (to justify my expensive education), I would retire to the suburbs with a nice husband and spend the rest of my life raising children and organizing cookouts?

Thanks be, it didn't work out that way. Husband, yes. Children, yes. Career, *yes*— that was the surprise. A surprise for which I and the rest of my generation were poorly prepared. We stumbled through years of hit-and-miss, carrying with us the baggage of mistaken notions that often disguised harsh realities. Here are a few notions and realities:

- By loyal to your company. (Hidden Meaning: Don't quit to get a better job.)
- Don't blow your own horn. (H.M.: Let others take credit for your work.)
- Remember the boss is always right. (H.M.: The boss wants no challenge from below.)
- Men should earn more than women; they have families to support. (H.M.: Pay discrimination saves the company money.)
- Be sweet and conscientious and your virtue will be rewarded. (H.M.: A pat on the head costs nothing.)

Those are just for starters.

The Working Woman Success Book is designed to help you get through these and other career traps quickly and painlessly. To help you advance as fast as is desirable (to help you advance faster then your skills are growing would do you no service). *The Working Woman Success Book* is filled with material tried and tested in *Working Woman*

magazine. As you will see, the book is organized in chapters around basic themes that have come up over and over again as areas of interest and concern to you, whether it's how to handle sexual harassment or how to update a résumé. These chapter heads are guides for your convenience, designed to get you to the heart of what you want to know.

This is not a book you need to sit down and read from cover to cover. Feel free to dip in wherever you choose. We believe you will find valuable ideas and information (as well as entertainment) on every page. We think you will want to read everything in the book, but you may want to do so in stages. Read a text or two. Mull it over. What questions does it raise? Give yourself time with the ideas it presents, then pick another text and absorb it.

I'm a great believer in the value of subliminal information. Of course, when I'm spouting facts and figures, I must know them exactly and get them precisely right. In many other areas, I have learned to rely on an accumulated body of experience, a sort of bouillabaisse of information that provides a framework within which I think and work.

At this time in our history, working women have a great need to alter and enlarge the body of reference material—the bouillabaisse—that directs their actions. Especially if their mothers did not work outside the home for pay. Especially if they still hold outdated ideas of where the safe jobs for women are (e.g. teaching, nursing). Especially if they have only recently noticed that they have ambition, skill and energy, and want to be rewarded by the work they do. Especially if they think of that work as a career and not just a job.

We need, in sum, a wised-up career mentality. We need to think within a framework that includes management techniques as well as supermarket strategies, office politics as well as family relations. We need to think effortlessly and automatically within the mindset of people who spend a third of their lives earning money in the market place, because that is who we are. This book is designed to help you to absorb that mindset until it becomes part of your built-in response system.

To accomplish this we have drawn on material originally published in *Working Woman* magazine. This material has been proved out in the real world: career women have read and responded to it. They have let the editors know what they needed and wanted and the editors have researched and presented the answers.

In its five years of publication, *Working Woman* has looked at the world of careers from a lot of angles. We have gone to experts for the best advice. We have listened to readers' questions and problems, and tried to give the best answers available. We have learned to recognize what are the common obstacles and dreams of working women at a time when they—we—are on the cutting edge of a social revolution that effects all of us, men and women. And we have heard of and addressed some very uncommon concerns as well.

We don't say we know it all. The world in which we work keeps on shifting and developing at a remarkable rate. Our charge as a magazine is to keep up with it and to keep you up to date each month.

But some things do not change. As women come newly into the work force, or return to it after years of raising a family, basic needs inevitably recur. How to start a business, for instance. Or handle an interview. How to negotiate a raise, or bob and weave successfully through the intricacies of the office power structure. Even those of us who continuously have been plugging away at our careers need reminders.

One reminder we sometimes need is how powerful we working women are as an eco-nomic force in this country. Right now more than half of all women in the United States work outside of the home full time or part time for pay. That's more than 45 million of us. We represent about 43 percent of the entire labor force and therefore are an indespensible and valuable asset to the productivity of the nation. We must not forget that! Sometimes when we are feeling slighted or underpaid or patronized we start to feel helpless, to downgrade our own worth. Don't let that occur. We have power we haven't even begun to use. It's time that we did. *The Working Woman Success Book* should help you to express your power as well at to enhance your skills.

I began by saying that I wish this book had been around when I was starting my career. It wasn't, so I had to learn my work lessons the slow, hard way. In closing, I want to share with you a few of the most important things I learned. Some of them may sound trivial. Believe me, they are not.

- Always spell people's names correctly; they're the very quick of who people are.
- Be exact about people's titles; there's a world of difference between a senior vice-president and a vice-president, between an editorial assistant and an assistant editor.
- Never badmouth anyone, even your enemies; you never know when an enemy may become the friend you need.
- Don't pick fights; if you are highly visible and successful, your enemies will make themselves—and they will be sufficient.
- Never promise anything you can't or won't deliver; your reputation for responsibility is career gold.
- Assume nothing; the times your assumptions are wrong can be crucial.
- Trust—check the facts, then trust; few people have the energy and ingenuity to remain successfully untrustworthy for long.
- Enjoy yourself; contrary to popular belief,

you don't have to hate your work to have it be good for you.

- Keep on learning; you're going to anyway, so you might as well make it positive and rewarding—as I hope your experience will be of reading this book.

Part One

Starting Up

Chapter One

Taking Stock

SURVIVING THE ENTRY-LEVEL BLAHS
by Lindsay Maracotta

Four years ago, I began my publishing career with a job as a researcher on a national magazine. My duties were routine and tedious, and trying to sustain myself on $100 a week was a problem in itself. But the job was a foot in the door of a highly competitive industry, and I felt lucky to have obtained it.

Soon I discovered the morale among my fellow researchers was not high. All of them had begun with the confident assumption that their talents would be quickly recognized and rewarded, but as months slipped by bringing no automatic promotions to editor, their enthusiasm gave way to a festering discontent. A dangerous pattern emerged: One by one, they began to come in later, leave earlier, grant only cursory attention to their work and develop a detached and cynical attitude toward the magazine.

Only about 25 percent of those who began in this "entry-level" job went on in publishing. Of the rest, some returned to school, some left to marry or begin again in another field, and others swelled the ranks of the unemployed for a time before deciding upon their next move. Watching the turnover, I realized that simply getting a foot in the door is not enough. In fact, once you have broken into an industry, the chasm between the entry-level job and a higher position can be almost unbridgeable.

"Someone with brains and some typing ability can get a job anywhere," said Bill Lewis, director of Career Blazers, an expanding New York employment agency. He encourages his clients to start with any kind of job in the field they are interested in: administrative assistant, secretary or "gal Friday." He warned: "The most difficult part is making that first jump. As you climb the ladder, it becomes increasingly competitive—the jobs are fewer and more desirable. As a result, I continually see people getting stuck where they began, simply because to go further is so difficult and takes a lot of strategy. In time, they begin to accept their positions—they convince themselves that it's really not so bad to be someone's secretary or assistant and they stay where they are."

Few of the employment and personnel experts I spoke to were willing to estimate how many women do manage to make the leap up from an entry-level position. According to personnel analyst Maryanne Smith, who has her own business—counseling companies and individuals, a woman's ability to move up can vary according to the field in which she is employed. "Companies connected

3

with some aspect of media generally offer good opportunities for mobility," she said. "You'll find that over half the women occupying high positions in such places as magazine publishing, the broadcasting networks and most book-publishing houses began as secretaries or the equivalent. Nonprofit organizations such as foundations or Government agencies also allow movement, as do such areas as advertising, personnel and public relations. These are all fields in which assistants are routinely trained in the duties of their superiors and are eventually qualified to assume them."

The drop-out rate among those who begin in these industries is high. "One of the major problems is money," said Smith. "Salaries for editorial assistants or publishing secretaries range from $125 to $150 a week; administrative assistants in nonprofit organizations can count on roughly $10–$20 more. After struggling for awhile on this, women are soon off in search of greener pastures." Another problem is summed up by a woman who spent a year and a half as a secretary-assistant in a major advertising firm before deciding to go back to law school: "Many of the secretaries were women who, like myself, had graduated with high grades from prestige colleges," she said. "We were grossly overqualified to do typing, filing, answering phones and got absolutely no satisfaction from it. I guess some of the ones who stuck it out did eventually land good copywriting jobs, but most of us soon fled back to school or into training programs of some sort."

For women entering the world of corporate industry, the financial opportunities are higher: Secretaries and administrative assistants start at about $150 to $225 a week; in managerial positions, salaries can soar as high as $50-to-$60,000 a year. But the difficulties in bridging the gap between the two levels are proportionately greater. Beverly Ibes, president of Womankind Executive Resources, said, "Frankly, I have to be negative; I don't see much of it happen-

ing. Most women who enter corporate hierarchies as secretaries remain secretaries." Ibes sees this as a response to the present state of the economy. "For a company to lift a secretary to manager, there has to be a lot of money around and more jobs than people to fill them. Right now, while jobs are scarce, the trend is to recruit women with MBAs for higher positions. Intuitively, I'm looking forward to a year from now when I think things will begin to open up and there'll be more action for women at the bottom."

The personnel director of one Fortune 500 company (firms whose published earnings bring them amongst the top 500 companies in the US) painted an equally disappointing picture. "One of our vice-presidents began with us as a secretary 20 years ago," he pointed out—but he agreed that she's an exceptional case. "Our management-trainee program draws almost exclusively from MBAs or business majors with high academic standings and business-oriented, extra-curricular activities. A secretary, even with a sound liberal arts background, seldom rises further than assistant to a top executive." Many women settle for less: A 1974 survey of one large corporation cited in sociologist Rosabeth Moss Kanter's *Men and Women of the Corporation* found that only 12 percent of the women who had worked for the company over 15 years had held more than three job levels; over half earned less than $11,000 despite their many years of service.

Ibes sees one exception to the corporate pattern: "I notice a few more companies beginning to post available jobs internally, to give those already in the company first crack at them. I'd advise women to exhaust every opportunity to get into such a company."

But even within those organizations that permit mobility, women often stagnate in entry-level jobs because they have formed no clear-cut goals to motivate them further. One woman, who for some years found herself in this position, is Carol Vance. She started at a New York book-publishing company right after college as an administrative assistant, with mostly secretarial duties, to the trade group. "My thought was that in six months I'd probably be married and moving to the suburbs anyway," she said. "But five and a half years later, I realized that not only had I no husband, I still had essentially the same job. I also realized that I needed to be much more financially independent. So for the first time I began planning, not just day to day, as I was accustomed to doing, but for years ahead."

Until then, Vance had perceived herself as a nine-to-five person and had seen her job in a limited way. She felt unqualified to offer ideas and was reluctant to speak up in meetings she felt she was attending in a secretarial role. Once having defined her goals, she was prepared to take more risks, even to the point of leaving the company if necessary.

"Luckily I had a boss who, as he became more successful himself, allowed me to acquire more and more responsibility," Vance continued. "I also took some career counseling, which showed me I enjoyed selling and helped direct me. I then went to my boss and explained that I wanted my own job, my own risks and responsibilities, and my own power—not just reflected power."

With the help of her boss, Vance secured a promotion, but before she actually assumed the duties of her new job, she got married and decided to work with her husband, Terence Wall, as director of marketing in his medical supply company. Looking back on her five and half years as a secretary as having been too long a time in one place, she said, "In retrospect I think that had I volunteered more and spoken up sooner, it would have hastened my transit."

Vivian Colnak, a California marketing consultant, began as a secretary, too, but encountered problems in moving up within the organization. "My first boss was extremely territorial," she recalled. "Any tasks I attempted to do on my own were considered an infringement on his territory and

earned me a good lecture and a warning." When it became obvious that she could go no further in the situation, Colnak began job-hunting. This time, while interviewing, she stressed her interest in growing in the job. After shopping around, she finally found an employer who welcomed someone who was eager to take on responsibilities. "In fact, I was actually sharing the job with my boss," she added," and eventually, I took it over when he moved up."

Among the professionals I interviewed, most were quick to point out the recent upsurge in the number of women seeking their advice on moving out of entry-level jobs. "Four or five years ago, these would have been the same women who were content to rise only as high as executive assistant," said Maryanne Smith. "Now they're asking themselves, 'Why shouldn't I be the executive?' And they're not hearing any good reasons why not."

For specific ways in which women can work to make the leap from a first job, I spoke to Sharon Bermon, head of the New York agency Counseling Women. Her suggestions:

1. Dress is extremely important. Never wear clothes that mark you as a secretary, such as casual pantsuits or platform wedgies. Instead, dress the way you'd want to look for the next job up—perhaps a little more expensively than you think you can afford. The object is to make superiors think of you as someone who should be moved up.

2. Don't put on track shoes at one minute to 5:00 PM; stay as long as it takes to get the job done. As an executive, you could be called upon to work 12 or 14 hours on occasion; by staying longer now, you make it clear you have a professional, rather than a secretarial, attitude.

3. Don't be negative and make an issue out of the things you don't want to do, such as fetching coffee. Instead, be positive about the things you do want to do. Spe-

cifically take on more responsibility and work on more diversified tasks.

4. Keep up with everything going on within the company; be as familiar as possible with all its functions. Read everything you can get your hands on—employees' manuals, annual reports. Make it well known that you have an interest in the company and wish to get involved.

5. Volunteer to do things, especially those duties that represent the next step up. Do it with the attitude that you're trying to be as helpful as possible to the organization, and not as if you are trying to move in on someone else's territory.

6. Become goal-oriented. Actually sit down and outline a plan for yourself. Define what you want to do and where you want to be five years from now; then list what skills you'll need to get there.

7. Take advantage of any company reimbursement policy for classes, training programs, etc. If the company won't pay, do it on your own. Make it your pol-

icy to pursue the skills you need through whatever means necessary.

8. Keep a copy of everything you do—if you write releases for your boss or help coordinate a sales program, keep some documentation in a portfolio of your own. This way you can prove to your boss or a prospective employer that you really have acquired the skills you claim to have.

9. Make a move quickly, within a year if possible. Move horizontally if necessary, but try to acquire another title—for instance, move from secretary to administrative assistant, or to "assistant to" an executive.

10. Look for midway jobs to move into—those that bridge the gap between secretary and executive. Right now, sales are probably your single best bet. Not only are many companies looking for women salespeople, it is the one position in which you may be aggressive and ambitious.

PRACTICAL ADVICE FROM PROS
by Ann Curran

Looking for a job under any circumstances can be a difficult and ego-shattering experience. Whether assaulting the job market for the first time or re-entering after a long or short absence, women often find that misinformation about why women seek employment can create added obstacles to an already difficult search.

The majority of women work because they must—for economic reasons. They are frequently the sole or major support of their families (as of March, 1975, one out of every eight families was headed by a woman); or their supplemental income is crucial to the livelihood of the family (half of the wives in

"intact" marriages now are part of the labor force); or they are single and self-supporting. Although many women seek employment because of a desire to achieve or to use their skills and abilities, this is more often coupled with economic realities.

How to avoid the common pitfalls of jobhunting? Following are tips from leading authorities in continuing education, career counseling and industry.

Developing and Pursuing Career Goals

Finding a job *is* your job until you have one. Crucial to the success of developing and

pursuing career goals are your attitude and your approach. Remember, there's no failure except ceasing to try."
—Anita Lands, Director, Programs for Women, Catalyst

1. Assess thoughtfully and thoroughly who you are and where you are. Take inventory of your skills, talents, strengths, weaknesses, interests, likes and dislikes, needs and values.
2. Don't overlook possible sources and resources. Be broad based at the beginning so you don't foreclose possibilities too early. You can't get a job in a field if you've never heard of it.
3. Be realistic without being limiting. Be goal-directed without being afraid to change direction, if appropriate.
4. If you have a problem getting started, attend a workshop, see a counselor, take a course, talk to people—whatever it takes to get the momentum going.
5. In researching job and career opportunities, aim for an information balance between printed sources and people.
6. Your résumé must create interest, present your major qualifications for the job—your education, work experience, activities, skills—and provoke positive reaction, positive enough to get you an interview. Length: two pages maximum. Make it easy to read (use short, concise sentences), and visually clear. Content: Make it accomplishment-oriented. Show how you've progressed. Use action words—initiated, instituted, implemented, presented, prepared, developed, conducted, designed, coordinated. Quantify where possible: the number of people you've supervised, the number of clients you've dealt with, the number of departments, associations and groups you've worked with.
7. Answer newspaper ads. Write or visit organizations on your own initiative. Use your contact network to arrange interviews. Consider creating your own job in an organization you know or have worked in.
8. Assemble letters of recommendation from both paid and unpaid positions.
9. Don't grab the first job unless it's really the one you want.
10. Find sources of information:

• *The Dictionary of Occupational Titles,* published by the Bureau of Labor Statistics; *Occupational Outlook Handbook,* published by the Women's Bureau of the Employment Standards Administration. (Check your local library.)
• Check the classified ads and financial sections in newspapers. Read articles describing jobs and careers.
• Business and professional publications; major business directories, company annual reports, college placement annuals.
• Catalyst publishes career booklets and résumé preparation manuals. Write: Catalyst, 14 East 60th Street, New York, NY 10022. (212) 759-9700. (Ask for booklet catalogue and price list).

Getting Your Credentials

"A college degree is no longer a golden key to opportunity. However, it still is an important credential, and for most professional careers, it is a prerequisite."
—Eileen Klapp, Director of Career Development, Marymount Manhattan College

1. Examine your career goals and determine what educational goals are required. Does the career you seek really require more education or simply catching up on current news in your field?
2. Look into interdisciplinary studies. For instance, if you're interested in management of the arts, combine a program in fine arts and business.

3. Go through the phone book or the library to find what resources in your area—women's centers, the YWCA, professional organizations, adult education courses at local high schools—offer career workshops and seminars.
4. Research the colleges in your area that have non-traditional class schedules—at night, on weekends.
5. Look into college programs that give "life experience" credit—credit for experience you already might have, combined with examination credits. Non-credit, non-degree programs are available at most universities.
6. Find out what companies sponsor college study programs for their employees.
7. Don't be intimidated by going back to school. Today more than 40 percent of college students are over 25.

Handling Interviews

"What is the number-one fear that Americans have? It's being interviewed or making a presentation."

—William Morin, President,
Drake-Beam & Associates

1. The phone rings. You're asked to come in for an interview. Be cool, don't overrespond.
2. Prepare for the interview, mentally and physically. The first things an interviewer will notice are your confidence and your appearance. To develop a perspective on things, ask yourself, "What is the worst thing that could result from this interview? I might not get the job. But it's not a life or death situation." Most corporations have a dress code, written or not; Try to find out what it is before the interview. Generally dark clothes carry more power impact. Wear conservative clothes in colors you feel are most appropriate. Don't try to dress younger than your are.
3. Sit on the front edge of the chair. (This will convey a high energy level.) Don't slouch.

4. Do not overelaborate. Answer the questions briefly and to the point. Do not put yourself down. Describe your attributes in businesslike terms. Be positive without being unrealistic.
5. Look directly at the interviewer. Adjust your style to her/his style. Keep in mind that interviews are almost purely subjective. It is often your personality that will determine how the interviewer will remember you.
6. Questions most interviewers ask:

- *Tell me about yourself.*
  Think of your life in four parts: early life (where you lived, school); formative years (education); work experience; where you are right now in terms of career goals. Keep it short!
- *What do you want to do? Where do you see yourself in ten years?*
  Keep your answer task-oriented, realistic and positive. Talk about the job you're applying for. Talk about what you can do for the company.
- *How much money do you want?*
  Try to answer that question with a question: Ask, "What is the range for this position?" If the interviewer insists on a figure, be prepared to give one decisively. (Do your homework: Talk to people to find out what the job is worth.)
- *Tell me some of your weaknesses and strengths.*
  Counteract a weakness with a strength. For instance, "I used to be somewhat disorganized, but I've improved my organizational skills, which has raised my job performance."
- *Who's going to take care of the kids?*
  By law, you do not have to answer, but the best way to handle it is to smile and say, "I've already made arrangements for child care."
- *I don't have any more questions for you, do you have any for me?*
  Yes! Be prepared with two or three, such as, "What are some of the growth plans for

this firm?" "Can you tell me more about the responsibilities of the position?"

The Superwoman Myth—How to Cope

"Anyone who opts for three such diverse roles as career woman, wife and mother, which are bound to conflict, has to expect a certain amount of craziness.'

—Carole Suplina, Director, Human Relations, Marymount Manhattan College

1. Let go of the "Superwoman Myth." Realize you cannot be everything all the time to everybody, including yourself. Set priorities.
2. Make one very good plan, then add two others as back-up plans.
3. Call people for help. One of the best sources of help for emergency child-care arrangements are other working mothers.
4. Ask yourself what you are trading off for your job. If you conclude the trade-offs are worth it, you've made a gigantic step toward self-fulfillment in a career.

"Identify your goals, prepare your family for change and enlist their help. Budget your time, but remember that the last two letters in the word 'time' are ME."

—Ann Diehl, Clairol Loving Care Scholarship winner, student, worker and divorced mother of seven.

1. Accept the fact that the changes you plan to make may not be met with enthusiasm by your spouse or children.
2. Have others in your household share home responsibilities. Each person, even the youngest, should have assigned tasks and accompanying privileges.
3. Draw up a time budget but make it flexible enough to provide for emergencies.
4. Substitute quality for quantity hours with your family. Brief periods on a one-to-one basis are often preferable to constant togetherness.
5. Accept your family members' accomplishments or failures as just that. Don't try to live your life through them. Your need for satisfaction and growth doesn't depend upon their achievements.

Editor's note: These experts were brought together during a workshop sponsored by the Clairol Loving Care Scholarship Program, Catalyst and Marymount Manhattan College in New York. For information on workshops planned across the country, and a list of educational financial aid programs available for women, write to:
Clairol Loving Care
Scholarship Program
Ellen Anderson, Administrator
345 Park Avenue
New York, NY 10022

FINDING OUT WHAT YOU'RE GOOD AT
A Do-It-Yourself Career Counseling Plan
By Sue Ries and Mary Jo Smrekar

"There's nothing I'm good at. . . ." "I'm interested in a lot of things, but none of them are job-related. . . ." "I'd like to change jobs, but I don't know where to begin. . . ."

If one of these statements is you talking, welcome to the club. Most women aren't really sure what they want to do with their working lives. Many waste time and energy in jobs for which they are neither well suited nor well paid. And very few know what to do about it.

Unfortunately, the traditional ways of finding a career are not very effective. One way has been "I've known since I was in high school that I would be a . . . ." The person who can say this may feel confident about her future direction, but she could wind up facing two serious problems. Often she has no realistic understanding of what the job behind the title is all about, and after years of preparation, finds that she's not very satisfied with or suited for the work once she has it. Secondly, there is nothing for her to fall back on if the "one right job" is not available. Especially with today's rapidly changing technology and economy, everyone has to have several job options in mind. If, instead of focusing only on one job title, we define career goals in terms of the interests and skills we want to use, we can usually identify dozens of different jobs which would be right.

A second common approach to career development has been to go to an expert for vocational interest testing. At best, such testing can serve only to confirm what a person already knows about herself—that she is interested in science, social service, health, or any one of a number of areas. This kind of information is too general to be of use as a specific career goal. Vocational testing also tends to oversimplify the complex process of career development and to encourage people to look at the working world in an unrealistic way.

"I'll leave myself open and apply for whatever's available in the job market" is the third common approach to personal career development. We all know people who just fall into the greatest job in the world. Many others, though, end up in jobs they can't stand. Unless it happens to be your turn with Lady Luck, this unfocused approach to career development has several disadvantages. First, it is impossible to get academic training or practical experience for a particular kind of work if you don't know what you're aiming for. Second, this method leaves you dependent on advertised job sources when you're looking for work, and advertised vacancies—in the want ads, employment agencies, placement offices, professional journals, etc.—cover only 15 to 20 percent of the potentially available jobs. You need to know what work you want in order to investigate sources in the hidden job market where the majority of jobs are to be found.

The traditional approaches to career development leave things pretty much to chance and to the advice of others. But only you should be making the decisions about your career—and you can learn to make good ones. It's simply a matter of know-how. First, you need to know how to analyze your own best skills, and important interests and values. Then you need to investigate career options which would relate to these—not with books or career counselors, but directly with people who are working in your field of interest.

Once you have gathered all the necessary information about yourself and the working world, you can develop a career goal statement, one which will give you direction and the flexibility to deal with changing conditions in the job market and your own lifestyle.

Action planning—to prepare yourself for attaining your goal—is the final step, after which you will be ready to actually look for a job.

Now for an outline of a do-it-yourself, inner-directed career counseling program.

Take a Different Look at the World of Work

Traditionally, we have viewed the working world as being made up of a number of occupational fields, each with its own set of separate and distinct jobs. We assume that jobs in the social service field, for example, are completely different from jobs in banking or international relations. However, the more realistic approach is to think in terms of functions: all jobs are simply functions which need to be done with people, data (verbal and numerical), and tangible things. Many of the same functions—research, budgeting, public relations, and training and supervising people, to name just a few—are necessary in a variety of occupational fields. They are simply performed with different people, subject matter, or objects.

If we take this functional approach to the working world, we recognize the importance of knowing what our skills are, since performing job functions requires a variety of specific skills. We usually know some of our skills, especially the more technical ones which we have acquired through formal or on-the-job training. It is much harder, however, for us to identify other skills which we have developed more informally, perhaps through volunteer activities or hobbies. Yet these are often our most important skills for two reasons: first, because they are our natural abilities (the easiest and most satisfactory for us to apply), and second, because these skills are usually more transferable from one work setting to another. For example, if you are good at coordinating and scheduling activities, you can do this as a conference planner, an executive secretary, a recreation leader, or in dozens of other positions, depending on what other skills and interests you have. Once you have inventoried your own transferable/functional skills, you can identify the whole range of possible career options.

Identify Your Transferable/Functional Skills

The first step in identifying your functional skills is to make a list of your achievements—the things you have done well, enjoyed doing, and done within a specific period of time. It does not matter whether you were paid or recognized by others for these achievements; you are the only judge. It may be helpful to divide your life into a number of time segments or events such as

high school or college, jobs you have held, places you have lived, and different roles you have played, as well as to consider homemaking and leisure pursuits. Some examples of achievements might include: planning and executing a backpacking trip; organizing a neighborhood play school; campaigning for a state senate candidate; planning a dinner party for sixteen guests; designing and crocheting a poncho without using a pattern.

After completing your list of achievements, select the seven which you consider most important. Describe each achievement on a separate piece of paper in a detailed chronological account. Include only what you, not others, actually did to make the achievement happen. For each step that you describe, try to identify the skills which you demonstrated. For example, if you had to convince others about an idea, you have shown persuasive speaking skills; if you found things around the house to use in a crafts project, you have demonstrated creative use of available resources; if you kept five kids occupied for three hours, you have shown ability to plan and conduct activities for children.

These skills—the ones you have used in your past achievements—are the functional skills that you would most likely want to use on a job.

Consider Important Interest Areas

After you have identified your best skills, you need to decide in what areas or occupational fields you would like to use them. There are many introspective exercises to help you recognize main interest areas.

Try an exercise called Twenty Satisfying Activites. Simply list up to twenty activities which you enjoy when you have free time. Do this rather spontaneously, without censoring any activities or concentrating too hard. Some examples might be: decorating a room, working in the garden, meeting new people, sewing, traveling, visiting museums, discussing politics, and writing.

After completing your list, consider the following questions:

1. Are most of your activities done alone or with other people?
2. How many involve working with ideas, information, or numbers?
3. How many involve working with tangible things?
4. Which of the categories—people, data, or things—do you seem to prefer?
5. Are there many physical activities on your list?
6. Which of these activities would you like to be work-related, if you could find such jobs?
7. Can you think of occupational areas which relate to your activities?
8. Overall, what can you discover about your most important interests from this exercise?

A second self-inventory exercise is called Career Daydreams. Here the idea is to list as many occupations as you can remember that you have ever considered, either seriously or as passing fancies.

After making your list, jot down any images these occupations bring to mind. For instance, social work might bring to mind helping kids and visiting homes; journalism might mean working on important assignments and meeting interesting people.

To analyze the daydreams, there are also a number of questions to answer:

1. Does this exercise confirm your people/data/thing orientation?
2. What occupational interest areas are indicated?
3. Is there emphasis on short-range tangible products or on open-ended, long-range goals?
4. Do you seem to want power and influence over others or approval from and affiliation with them?
5. Do the occupations involve risk taking or security?

6. What lifestyle/workstyle values are evident?
7. Are there any other patterns that you can identify?

One final introspective technique that helps clarify important interests is self-monitoring. Become more aware of what you read, discuss with others, watch on television, and do in your leisure time. Keep records of your activities in a special notebook for one or two weeks and then analyze them to see in what interest areas they seem to fall. You can also clip out anything that catches your interest in the newspapers or magazines for one month. Then try to categorize these articles. Again, what interest areas can you identify?

Clarify Important Lifestyle/Workstyle Values

Because your working life is so dramatically interwoven with your personal life, it is very important to consider the lifestyle/workstyle values which will contribute to your job satisfaction.

Most people find it easier to identify what they don't want in their work situation than to express what they do want. Another paper and pencil exercise, Things I Can't Stand, will help you identify some of the positive values behind any of your negative reactions to past work situations.

To do this exercise, imagine yourself in a past work, academic, or social setting. As you imagine that situation, list the things you can't stand about it. After completing your list, write the positive value implied by each negative. For example, "I can't stand routine" might be positively stated as "I value a job with a variety of functions." "I can't stand punching a time clock" implies "I value working for organizations that have flexible work hours."

Other issues you may have strong feelings about are level of job responsibility, pace of work, geographic location, professional growth possibilities, salary, characteristics of co-workers, status and recognition, fringe benefits, and day-care facilities. It is important to consider your stand on each issue. We suggest ranking your attitudes in order of their importance to you, so that you can clearly see which values you are willing to compromise and which you are not.

Begin Talking About What You Want

At this point, you need to develop a tentative statement about your ideal job in terms of the skills you would like to use, the interests and/or purposes you would like to pursue, and the personal values you would not want to compromise. A sample career goal statement might be:

I want to use my skills in educational program planning, research, and promotional writing in the area of consumer product safety or preventive health education. I want to work in a small- to moderate-sized organization where I can have a variety of functions and get to know my co-workers well.

Notice that this statement is based solely on you and does not mention specific job titles.

Understand How Personal Skills, Interests, and Values Relate to the Working World

Each of the major self-components which you have been analyzing relates to a particular aspect of the world of work and can be charted in the following way:

Self-Compo- nent	Related Component in the Working World
Skills	Work Functions (types of jobs)
Interests and/or purposes	Occupational Fields and Types of Organizations
Values	Specific Work Settings (e.g. co-workers, organizational policies, physical environment, benefits, etc.)

Use Information Interviewing to Connect with the Working World

Now you are ready to consider appropriate career options by investigating which types of jobs, occupational fields, and organizational settings relate to your skills, interests, and values. The best way to do this is to use the information interviewing process. Information interviewing means talking with people who work in jobs, fields, or organizations of interest, finding out exactly what they do in their jobs, and getting relevant, up-to-date information for your own career development. Information interviewing should not be confused with job interviewing, which comes later.

There are many information needs to cover when you conduct information interviews. In the initial decision-making stage of career development, you will be inquiring about the kinds of jobs that use your skills and interests. It is important to do enough information interviewing at this stage to get a sense of the variety of different job options and the realistic availability of these jobs. Knowing there's more than one job that's right for you is comforting.

Once you have discovered the kinds of jobs that appeal to you, your information needs will focus on the kinds of training and practical experience that are needed to prepare for such jobs. Don't assume that a certain degree or type of work experience will qualify you for any job; get the advice of people who are in hiring and supervising positions related to the work you want to do.

There are always two purposes involved in information interviewing: one is to get the information you are seeking, and the other is to develop more and more contacts among professionals in the career areas of interest to you. It's easiest to start information interviewing informally—with friends, relatives, or acquaintances who work, or know others who work, in jobs or fields which you want to explore. It is essential to obtain referrals to other people who can be helpful to you each time you do an information interview.

Later, when you are job seeking, you will have a built-in network of contacts to use as a result of your actions now.

When you have personal referrals to work with, you will have no problem getting in to see people for information interviews. If you can't think of anyone to help you get started, you can use area directories of organizations and businesses to identify appropriate organizations and people. These are usually available in the local library or college placement office. Your local chamber of commerce and the Yellow Pages are also excellent sources of information.

Some important points to keep in mind while conducting your interviews are:

1. Give each person enough information about your skills, interests, and values so that s/he can offer you relevant information.
2. Get an overview of the field, and not just information about a specific job or organization.
3. Ask open-ended questions, such as, "What are the ideal qualifications for someone in this job?"
4. Keep in contact with people who are helpful to you. Follow up with thank-you notes and a phone call or visit every once in a while.

Develop Plans for Action

Most of us have a tendency to do a lot of wishful thinking about the future. Action planning is a systematic way of turning our wishful thinking into reality. Five steps are involved in this process.

First, we need to state our goal and indicate the timing involved. A possible goal statement might read:

Goal: To change jobs from secretarial work to a public information job with an organization that is involved in protecting the natural environment. Time deadline: January, 1977.

The second and third steps in action planning are to brainstorm what needs to be done (the broad strategies) and how you will do it (the specific action steps). One broad strategy for the above goal might be: "Identify all the organizations in the area involved in environmental protection." When planning how to do this, your specific action steps could include:

Use area directories of organizations and businesses available in the library or a college placement office, and the Yellow Pages.

Contact the county or state government's department of environmental affairs.

Call the nearest university to see if they have an environmental science program. If so, ask for faculty members who could give information about environmental organizations in this area.

Set up information interviews with people in all of these organizations.

The fourth step in action planning is to rank your broad strategies and specific action steps in logical, situational order. Some of your broad strategies may involve large expenditures of time and money—getting an undergraduate degree for example—and cannot be undertaken right away. Some will be essential preliminary steps which must be done before taking other steps. You may also have to consider the needs of other significant people in your life, as well as your own time and energy, as you rank your items.

The final step in the action-planning process is to assign time deadlines to each of your plans. Be sure that you start with reasonable time goals, so that you can keep patting yourself on the back for your progress rather than kicking yourself elsewhere for not getting things done.

To help you follow through on your do-it-yourself career guidance program, you might consider forming a "career planning support group" with three or four friends or co-workers. It's a good idea for all of the group members to be at the same stage of career development so that their self-inventory, planning, and action needs are similar. Individual interests and career goals among group members can be widely different, however.

Whatever stage of career development you are at, there is always something that can be done today to decide on your goal, or to prepare for achieving it. As one do-it-yourselfer recently commented: "Before, I used to talk about how the right things never happened *for* me; now I realize that it's up to me to *make* them happen—and that I can!" So can you.

SUE RIES AND MARY JO SMREKAR *are co-founders of Creative Career Counseling and Consulting Services, a firm which specializes in both individual career counseling and consulting with Federal Government agencies, private organizations, and educational systems nationwide. They are affiliated with the American University in Washington, D.C.*

WILL YOUR JOB GROW WITH YOU?
Are You on a Real Career Track or Just Going Around in Circles? Take This Quiz and Find Out
By Mark J. Appleman

How much of a springboard is your job? How high can it take you? How fast? Unless you see your present position as the apex of your career and your ceiling for pay and satisfaction, these are questions to be reckoned with.

Apart from the critical luck element—which may or may not balance out over time—advancement begins with you and your capacity for growth. Rarely does it end there. Because a job is only as good as the organization of which it is a part, and because no firm is better than the people running it, your career path can be straightened out or twisted up by the quality of management.

What's more, since upward mobility is seldom a solo flight, competence—or even superiority of performance—can be far less rewarding than being needed, fitting in or just going along.

One independent and objective way to avoid getting stuck in a rut or being shelved at mid-career for reasons not entirely of your own making is to appraise your job's growth potential, psychic and monetary, from a realistically broad perspective. This quiz can help you do just that by testing the "give" of your company and your field and by helping you to determine whether the conditions you work under are conducive to growth.

Allow yourself enough time to choose the answers that most nearly describe your job environment—not as you think it ought to be, but as it is. Answer all of the questions, even those that seem to apply to an organization with a management style unlike that of your organization. Then score the results as indicated. The overall rating may not tell you what you deserve, but it should provide a quick measure of what you can expect.

1. *To find out more about job activity in your field, openings, salaries, etc., it's a good idea to:*
   a. check the want ads, both classified and display.
   b. read professional journals.

   c. become active in professional, trade or business societies.

   d. be patient and wait until you're told.

2. *It's informative to trace the career paths of other women at one or two levels above you. You do this by:*

   a. asking them how they got there.

   b. asking personnel to open their files.

   c. talking to their secretaries.

   d. checking public information, such as house organs and local papers.

3. *To see how you stack up against the competition, it helps to write out profiles, including age, seniority, length of time in present capacity, salary range, education and family situation of:*

   a. those at your present level.

   b. those at your present and next-higher level.

   c. top management.

   d. those at the level just below yours.

4. *If special study would qualify you for a higher position, you should:*

   a. do it on the quiet until you've mastered it.

   b. check it out to see if the company will pay all or part of the cost.

   c. do it only if the money and responsibility are worth the extra effort.

   d. do it if you're really excited about the subject.

5. *To impress your boss with your aptitude:*

   a. look around for things that he/she might do and suggest them.

   b. look around for a project that's sure to fail and suggest that the boss assign it to your closest competitor.

   c. look around for a project that turns you on and research the first step before discussing it with your boss.

   d. do something on your own and tell your boss about it when it's over and done.

6. *As matters stand in your organization, chances of being promoted will be determined mainly by:*

   a. ability plus experience or training.

   b. congeniality and cooperativeness.

   c. objective performance standards.

   d. cronyism.

   e. romantic or family relationship.

   f. expansion of the company's business.

7. *As far as you are concerned, your pay has not kept pace with your responsibility level because:*

   a. you don't come under an affirmative-action program.

   b. you lack seniority.

   c. someone else has an inside track.

   d. you haven't talked to your boss about the new things you're doing.

   e. of company policy or salary administration.

8. *In your company the way to find out what the next-highest position calls for is to:*

   a. keep your ear open in the ladies' room.

   b. observe your boss.

   c. ask your boss.

   d. make friends in the personnel department.

9. *In every sizable firm there's always more room at the bottom than at the top. What are you doing to protect yourself against the pyramid crunch? You're:*

   a. sticking to the "in" side of office politics.

   b. cultivating an influential sponsor.

   c. systematically broadening your knowledge of the field.

   d. putting on the charm for the VIPs.

10. *The last time you volunteered a suggestion for improving something, your boss:*

   a. accepted it as a matter of course.

   b. praised you for trying but didn't use your suggestion.

   c. pooh-poohed your suggestion, then used part of it.

d. rejected it but encouraged you to keep trying.

e. let you know that if there were suggestions to be made, he/she would make them.

11. *Your department or division:*
   a. is short of qualified help.
   b. keeps hiring people who don't stay.
   c. has enough people to get the job done.
   d. is a dumping ground for managers and supervisors who don't move up the ladder.

12. *As a rule:*
   a. you're asked to make suggestions about new work methods or procedures.
   b. you're invited to estimate budget or supply requirements for your area.
   c. instructions and quotas come down from above.
   d. you just go your own way.

13. *Your immediate boss is:*
   a. someone on the way up.
   b. running scared.
   c. underqualified.
   d. overqualified.
   e. in a rut.

14. *Because of technological changes being introduced by your company or the industry, your position is:*
   a. becoming obsolete.
   b. being upgraded.
   c. being combined with another job at the same level.
   d. being maintained only because of union rules, tradition or poor management.
   e. unaffected.

15. *On the basis of performance over the last five years—as shown in the annual report of every publicly owned company—your firm is:*
   a. growing.
   b. stagnating.
   c. slipping.
   d. up and down like a roller coaster.

16. *Frequent, unscheduled management turnover is a sign of poor morale and a warning of worse to come. In your company:*
   a. there's an ongoing game of musical chairs in the executive suite.
   b. the "old man" will never retire.
   c. the only way to move up the ladder is to tumble someone from the rung above.
   d. promotion and retirement of top management are quite orderly and fairly easy to anticipate.
   e. chips off the old block automatically head the executive parade.

17. *One-man rule is like a time bomb in a large modern corporation. In your company:*
   a. No. 1 earns more than twice as much as No. 2.
   b. No. 1's office makes No. 2's look like a broom closet.
   c. No. 2 does all the work, and No. 1 takes the bows.
   d. No. 1 and No. 2 are not far apart in pay and perks.

18. *The senior executives are:*
   a. whiz kids in their 30s or younger.
   b. a balance of ages across the board.
   c. all over 60.

19. *Your company is characterized by:*
   a. strong research and technical development.
   b. leadership in new styles or fads.
   c. a snail's pace approach to innovation.
   d. fast reactions to new challenges or opportunities.

20. *On the whole, management is:*
   a. slow to pay bills, quick to start lawsuits.
   b. likely to cut corners and duck unpleasant obligations.
   c. apt to place personal interests above those of the organization.
   d. scrupulously fair and honest.

RATING YOUR JOB'S GROWTH POTENTIAL

1. A-4 B-5 C-4 D-0	5. A-3 B-0 C-5 D-3	9. A-3 B-3 C-5 D-2	13. A-5 B-2 C-2 D-4 E-2	17 A-1 B-1 C-3 D-5
2. A-5 B-0 C-2 D-3	6. A-5 B-5 C-5 D-2 E-2	10. A-5 B-3 C-2 D-3	14. A-0 B-5 C-3 D-0 E-5	18. A-3 B-5 C-3
3. A-3 B-5 C-3 D-0	7. A-0 B-0 C-0 D-5	11. A-5 B-5 C-3 D-0	15. A-5 B-0 C-0 D-3	19. A-5 B-5 C-2 D-4
4. A-3 B-4 C-3 D-5	8. A-0 B-3 C-5 D-2	12. A-5 B-5 C-2 D-3	16. A-2 B-2 C-2 D-5 E-2	20. A-0 B-0 C-0 D-5

Point Total	Job Growth Potential
90 and over	Rocket to the Moon
70 to 89	Steady as She Goes
50 to 69	Mulepack up Grand Canyon
Below 50	Dead End

Mark Appleman *is a New York-based corporate management consultant and financial writer.*

HELEN YGLESIAS:
THOUGHTS ON STARTING, WORKING, RISKING

by Edith Baer

Helen Yglesias is the author of two highly acclaimed novels—How She Died and Family Feeling—and a third book, called Starting: Over, Fresh, Anew—Early and Late. Yglesias herself has been an undaunted starter through successive phases of her life—Depression-time jobs, two marriages, the mothering of three children, a hearing loss and several rounds of jobs, culminating in a rewarding career as a magazine editor.

At age 54, she quit her editing job to do what she really wanted to do—write a book. Here, she shares some thoughts on starting, working and risking.

"I was a working woman for quite some time before I became the working woman I wanted to be. The end of self-expression is not necessarily a job—it is doing the work you really want to do.

"There are so many women who stay in secretarial or assistant capacities who have every right, need and ability to be running the show. Not enough of them are demanding it or putting themselves to the risk of getting it. The same things are stopping them that stop the creative writer: 'I won't make it; I'll fail. I can't compete with men who've been in the field for so many years and are so successful at what they do.' These women know perfectly well in how many ways these men are failing and not doing the job they should be doing or not performing work at the level it could be performed."

Starting Isn't Easy

One of the reasons Yglesias decided to write a book on the topic of starting was her disagreement with those who insist that there is "some magic way of looking at yourself in the mirror one morning and turning your life around, simply by using the right device, whatever that may be." Yglesias holds out no such panacea. Starting, in her view, involves an "inner process" so profound that "outside gimmicks are totally irrelevant.

"At any age, the element of risk is a powerful deterrent to starting. There is the fear of failure, of switching tracks from an established career and the measure of security it provides. And the later you put it off, the harder it gets, because you develop patterns of behavior that become almost too difficult to break."

Excuses, Excuses

Yglesias touches on some of the excuses we make to ourselves—"being needed" is the one most frequently given by women. "It's much harder for women to start—not because they're constitutionally different, but because society has impressed upon them that they are present on the social scene in a nonselfish, nonaggressive way—and starting *is* aggressive and self-assertive. It *has* to be.

"Eventually, in any work that has any social contact, you've got to become aggressive in order to do what you want to do and be what you want to be. If you look upon yourself as a top person in your field, then you're willing to act that way and you're expected to act that way."

Overcoming Hurdles

Attitudes have begun to change since the 1950s, when women were expected to define themselves entirely in their roles as wives, mothers and homemakers. But Yglesias has found that the woman with young children still has hurdles to overcome before she can do what she wants to do.

"There is very little help out there. There are not enough day-care centers, not enough husbands who will share the full burden. These are *outer* problems but they reflect upon the *inner* problems in such a way that a woman who feels, 'Oh, I'm not good enough' can add these barriers to her inner hesitations and build an excuse for doing what is essentially easier."

For everyone, starting comes hard, but Yglesias is quick to point out that the rewards are great. "The resolution of the problem is immensely euphoric. We simply *feel* much better when we've made that start and entered on what we really want to do. Even if the going is rough, even if it's not entirely successful, even if you're meeting rejection and difficulties—it *is* a new life and it has that euphoria of accomplishment. I have found that everybody—really *everybody*—has this basic creative urge: to do what you have always wanted to do."

Chapter Two

Getting the Job

CONNECTIONS

by Sally Koslow

At a magazine where I once worked. I had a colleague named Wendy Greer. Greer was just another copywriter (albeit a very attractive one) until she married the publisher's chum and, sooner than you could say "connections," became our managing editor. Those of us still occupying the middle echelons from which Greer had so rapidly ascended were self-righteously indignant.

Use a contact to get a job? Not us, we said in underpaid unison. That's for people who expect shortcuts. We would *earn* our promotions the *hard* way.

The dumb way? Maybe. Surely, the slow way.

I tell Greer's story because she did, in fact, make a solid managing editor, as we who had begrudged her the job had to admit. As for our slurs about it paying to know people in high places . . . well, it does.

Observations over the years have taught us that a situation such as Greer's, rather than being the exception, is often a major factor in influencing who gets what job. It's who you know. It's connections.

Barbara Cohen's story is typical. She spent over a year trying unsuccessfully to switch from audio-visual production to book publishing. When answering newspaper ads or visiting personnel departments and employment agencies. Cohen was told again and again that her experience wasn't right for publishing and that she should stick to her field. Then, an acquaintance happened to mention Cohen's credentials to an executive in a major encyclopedia publishing firm that was relocating near Cohen's suburban home. "The same day I was going to call him, he called me," Cohen said, "and he practically hired me on the phone as a picture researcher." Rather than belittling her experience in a related field, he applauded its diversity. "Having a connection made all the difference. My skills were definitely transferable, but agencies and personnel departments couldn't see that."

20

Making contacts has long been part of the male repertoire. Meeting for drinks after work, sharing a tennis court, getting acquainted over lunches where the discussion is 10 percent business and 90 percent football—these are connection-building processes with which men feel comfortable and have been using to advantage for years.

We women are less clever than men in identifying and using connections because usually we have been taught to believe that: 1) Asking for help is a sign of weakness and/ or 2) Those who do ask for help become involved in a form of professional chess, requiring a finesse beyond our reach. It's time to erase these irrational assumptions and understand once and for all that it's okay to ask for help. Using connections is always advisable, often necessary, and it isn't hard to do.

Although contacts in and of themselves do not get you jobs, they do get your call past the secretary who is paid to screen you out. They get your résumé read, get you an interview with the right person, give you information on where job openings exist and get nice things said about you to the people who count. These kinds of boosts are, quite simply, an edge—and no small edge at that.

Through the use of contacts you often get an opportunity to sell yourself that you might otherwise never have. An advertising agency vice-president, who not only uses contacts herself but hires people through contacts, said, "If you get a note from the president of the company saying so-and-so wants a job, you *see* that person."

There is no field where contacts can't help you and many where, without them, you may as well forget all lofty aspirations. As a general rule, the smaller the industry or corner of an industry in which you operate, the more visible people are and, therefore, the greater the importance of contacts. Advertising, publishing, and textile and garment manufacturing are typical.

The textile and garment manufacturing industry, though it serves most of the coun-

try, essentially is a tiny, Manhattan-based profession crowded into an area literally only ten blocks long and wide. Occasionally, openings are advertised in *Women's Wear Daily*, the trade newspaper, but, said Sheri Horen, a showroom saleswoman who recently left one designer for another, "It's very hard for an outsider to come into our industry. Getting jobs depends on whom you know, and connections are the only way employers can decipher what a person's experience really has been. There's no doubt about it—people look at you more closely if they know somebody who recommends you. And when you utilize a connection, it shows a certain aggressiveness that is looked upon favorably."

One reason why connection-using makes sense is the advantages it offers employers. On the most basic level, having a qualified job candidate presented to you with someone else's blessing (even when the recommendation is as noncommittal as, "Look, Sam, the kid's my brother's daughter, and I'd like to see her get a break") simplifies the problem of filling a job because it helps the employer make up his mind. Most people, whatever their professional level, find it difficult to make decisions; they appreciate help. If all candidates are equal, there is no reason *not* to give a job to the one recommended. For an employer, it's a no-loss proposition.

An employer also stands to gain in a second way: By granting a favor, someone then owes him one. "Everything in business is a trade," explained a partner in a firm that specializes in international law. "It's natural to my industry, and I think it's true of business in general—you do things for people who can do things for you."

The president of a major executive-recruiting firm said: "Good jobs are prizes. Why give one away to a perfect stranger, no matter how qualified? What can they do for you? You're much better off giving a job to a person someone knows because then you can ask the middleman for something and, chances are, they will feel they can't turn you down. One hand washes the other."

Such barter is less ruthless than it appears. With good positions at a premium, most people genuinely would like to see them awarded to a worthy candidate, and someone who comes recommended by known, trusted sources has considerable appeal. It's important, therefore, to make sure you're the Someone someone knows.

We all know more people than we think we do. Connections can be your father, uncle or mother's friend. They don't have to be only your near and dear ones. They can be your current or former boss, the woman you met at a conference last week, an alumna of your college, a colleague at another firm. Connections are anyone who can help you get a job or promotion. There is no limit to how many you can have.

The obvious places to make helpful contacts are, of course, work-related environments—your own or other people's offices, meetings of associations in your field, conventions, workshops. Don't believe that the only time a worthy connection can be formed is when you're wearing your professional hat. Everyone is a potential connection. A dedicated connection-seeker is, in an inoffensive way, always on the prowl.

Leslie Warren, the director of publicity for the consumer product division of West Point Pepperell, a textile manufacturer, met an important contact at church. "We had met once at a business meeting," she explained, "but seeing this man every month or so with his wife allowed me to get to know him on a more personal level." She confided in him that she was ready for a change, in spite of a recent promotion. ("I had worked so closely with my boss that, when I got her job, my responsibilities didn't change much.")

When there was an opening in his firm, the contact she'd developed at church remembered Warren and got in touch with her. "It was a natural process, a very painless way to get a new job." Knowing one of her major interviewers allowed Warren to feel comfortable asking for a hefty salary increase. "They didn't give it to me right away, but with my first raise, they met my figure."

One of your best sources of potential contacts is the person who interviews you for a job you don't get. Even when your interviewer finds a more qualified candidate, if you develop a rapport, chances are you'll be remembered when future positions open.

This approach worked for Kalia Lulow, a writer of non-fiction books. For the first four years after her graduation from college, Lulow held a number of unrelated jobs that included managing a nightclub in Nashville, working as a social secretary to a contessa and waitressing—almost everything but what she wanted to do—write. Three years ago, she succeeded in becoming the production manager of a trade magazine. In that job, she was still only on the periphery of her chosen field, but job hunt as she might, she stayed in production.

A devotée of newspaper ads, Lulow one day spotted an ad that looked familiar—she was sure it was for a company whose owner had been particularly gracious in rejecting her earlier. She responded to the ad, interviewed and, again, was rejected. This time, her interviewer presented her with a counter-proposal—the chance to collaborate with her on an outside writing project.

Recently, Lulow completed the book and, through her mentor's agent—now Lulow's agent—is negotiating for a contract on a textbook.

"Don't say no to yourself," Lulow learned from her experience. "You don't get connections unless you put yourself in positions where they are likely to develop. Never be self-censoring."

Maxine Wineapple, co-director of New Options, a New York City program given by Catalyst designed to help women define goals and develop assertive behavior, encourages job-hunters to keep a workbook including a list of anyone who may be a connection. "Besides all your friends and personal contacts, your list should include your banker, insurance agent, attorney, accountant and stockbroker, as well as the names of people whom you may not necessarily know but who have the potential to help you," she said.

"People make the mistake of not realizing that it's okay to ask someone to call someone else for them so that, eventually, they get a hook into the person who's really going to be able to help. By the same token, if someone you thought might be helpful turns out not to be, always try to elicit from them another name to call. . . . Just make sure that when you finally hit on someone with whom you'd like an interview, you set up your appointment yourself. It's a far more assertive approach than having someone do this work for you."

"Women don't really take inventory of their sources," said Jean Showalter, an instructor for the Sales Executive Club, which sponsors classes in how to job hunt and market yourself. "Secretaries, for instance, frequently don't realize that their bosses' telephone contacts—those people they get to know so well over the phone—can be theirs, too, if they are smart enough to make use of them. . . . Also, women are hesitant to ask friends for help—we think it's an imposition."

People are more approachable than most of us think. "Keep in mind that it is flattering to be asked for help," advised Wineapple. "Top people, in particular, are rarely too busy to see you for a short time—because they're secure in their positions and don't feel threatened by you. So when pursuing connections, always aim for the highest-ranking person you can find. Seeing him first sets you up favorably with anyone else he may send you to. Because you come through a power channel, hiring authorities are predisposed to like you." That is, if during subsequent interviews you have the good sense not to name-drop or use any other heavy-handed technique that makes your interviewer feel leaned on.

Be sure, when you do secure the name of an important contact, that you speak to that person. (If you first get in touch by letter, always follow up with a call.) To get past the secretary when you call, you might try this frequently successful technique: Say, "This is Jane Doe. May I speak to Ms. Smith, please? Judy Jones, a friend of hers, suggested I call." If you say it in one breath, it will sound authoritative and usually will prevent a secretary from asking, "What is this in reference to?" If she does ask that annoying question, say it's a personal matter or that Ms. Smith is expecting your call. The idea is to reveal as little of your purpose as possible.

"If you must leave messages, use good psychology," said Showalter. "Rather than leave your phone number and wait for a response, keep leaving a message with only your name. You're not threatening someone by doing this. You're playing on natural curiosity. Sooner or later, most people will take your call."

Another approach in dealing with a secretary is to try to establish a rapport and enlist her support. Said Wineapple: "Ask her name and use it every time you call. You may even ask her to call you when she feels it is a good time to approach her boss." Best of all is to avoid secretaries altogether, which you can sometimes do by calling late or early in the day, when an executive may answer the telephone.

According to Showalter, "So much of the impression you make depends on your phone technique. You have to do on the phone what you do in person—smile. Someone can hear your self-confidence over the phone, but they can also hear tension and insecurity."

The higher your stakes, the more sense it makes to use connections. Even if you're a wunderkind with a job to match, it's not always easy to open doors. Anna Quindlen was something of a storybook success when, right out of Barnard College, she landed a job as a reporter for *The New York Post.* (How did she first get to *The Post?* Two reporters for whom she baby-sat were her contacts.) After two and a half years, Quindlen wanted to move on. And to where else but *The New York Times.* "I decided to use a connection," she said, "mostly because so many people had used me as a contact, and invoking my name seemed to work well for them. So I wrote a note to a former colleague asking to meet for a drink—which translated into 'I'm looking for a new job.' He set the wheels in motion . . . though I had to be interviewed by everybody but the janitor." Less than a year after joining *The Times*, Quindlen now occupies a job created for her, covering the effect of the Women's Movement on contemporary society—a subject of particular interest to her. She is 24.

"The Times literally gets mountains of letters and applications, and there are obvious pools from which such a newspaper can choose. It's not impossible to get a job there without connections, but the odds being what they are, you almost have to have more than a good letter and clips."

A thorough job-hunt is a sophisticated research project. You are at point A, sitting without a job or in one which you've outgrown. Point Z is your ideal job. A creative jobhunter is a detective trying to get from A to Z through the most efficient network possible. Contacts not only can speed your way, they can help to create a path for you. Use them well.

12 WAYS TO USE CONNECTIONS

1. Realize you have the right to ask for help.

2. Do your homework and have a clear idea of what you want before you approach a contact. "Women fall deplorably short in doing their thinking-through of goals," said Anne Hyde of Management Women, Inc. "You can't expect someone to second guess you."

3. Don't ignore your own parents as potential contacts. Who is more apt to help you?

4. Don't stay home. Meet people wherever you can. Go to a dull cocktail party now and then.

5. Suggest having lunch or a drink after work with someone who can help you, but always be upfront about your purpose. If you are looking for a job, say so. If you simply want to get to know the person better or exchange information, you should say that.

6. Try to create an informal old-girl network among your friends. The longer you work, the more you will find your college friends and former roommates now are in high places.

7. Avoid personnel departments. Instead, pursue connections with employees who already work in a department that interests you.

8. Always carry a business card and use it frequently. If you don't have one, print one at your own expense.

9. Join professional organizations in your community, such as Washington, DC's Women in Government or the local chapter of the American Society of Journalists and Authors.

10. Participate in and attend workshops and conventions.

11. Follow up the smallest bit of help someone gives you with a thank-you note. It will be appreciated.

12. Once you have succeeded in getting a job, don't stop pursuing connections. This is the time to cultivate a new batch.

JOB INTERVIEWS:

Coming Out a Winner

How do you feel about job interviews? If you're like most people, you're terrified of them! However, you *can* learn to sell yourself on one—and even win a job you're not sure you deserve. All it takes is practice and a little chutzpah.

Of course you're concerned about the negatives in your background—the lack of a college diploma, for example, or the fact that there's a missing year in your employment record. But instead of concentrating on your weaknesses (you've never sold ad space before), concentrate on your strengths (you did convince the Board of Education to set up an after-school, coed sports program). Instead of worrying about the fact that you're "too old" (any woman who's over twenty-one thinks she's too old!), think about all the wisdom and experience you can bring to a job which a younger person can't. Instead of worrying about the fact that you've been out of work for six months, concentrate on the good things you accomplished while you were working.

Here are more specific techniques to help you land the job you want.

Do Your Homework

Figure out what the employer wants.
Don't go into an interview "blind." Know the functions of the job you are applying for. You can find them out by talking to people in the field or by looking through some professional journals. Even a classified ad may help you because employers often describe job functions in their ads.

Know, too, what the organization does and where it stands with its competitors. Leafing through a copy of the firm's annual report which is often available upon request may be a good idea.

Even if the job functions seem obvious, write them all down, starting with the most important ones. Then, under each function, list two or three things you have done which relate to these functions. If a job calls for organizing ability, what have you organized? If the job calls for selling, what have you sold? Though men are likely to grow up thinking about which of their abilities are worth money on the labor market, too many women take their talents for granted.

This *functional analysis* of your skills is the best thing you can do to prepare for a job interview.

If you've never had a job before, dig into your background for any activities that can show off your talents—you wrote for the school newspaper, coordinated a talent night, interviewed students for a term paper. Along with your skills, you can stress your enthusiasm, commitment, and willingness to learn.

If you're changing jobs, or career fields, emphasize your skills, and not your job title. Many skills are *transferrable,* and what you must relate is how your skills can be transferred from one field to another. Transferrable skills include, among other things: selling; coordinating; writing and editing; speaking; organizing; managing; supervising; raising money.

If you're returning to the work world after a hiatus in the home, again, relate to transferrable job functions. You haven't sold real estate before, but you have sold community fund drive tickets. Once you know beforehand, in detail, how your experience and interests relate to the functions of the job you're seeking, you'll feel much more prepared and confident.

Stop thinking about your problems (you don't have quite the number of years of experience the ad calls for) and begin thinking about the employer's problems. What do you have to offer that can meet this employer's needs? The fact that you have already thought this through gives you a competitive advantage.

Look the Part

Looks do count.
Find out what people in your field wear—you may have to dress up more as a saleswoman than you would if you were a TV production assistant. When in doubt, dress up. Wear something you know looks terrific. Look professional rather than ultra-feminine.

Chances are that the interviewer, if he is a man, believes that he is firmly committed to equal opportunities for women. But his reaction to pretty, feminine women was conditioned a long time ago. Some women applicants may get dinner dates instead of jobs; some get offers for secretarial jobs; some get rejected because the interviewer is not completely sold, even though he may not know why.

Ask Questions

Establish a rapport with the interviewer. Try to spend the first few minutes breaking the ice. You can chat about a restaurant in the area, a book you notice on the interviewer's shelf. You don't have to prolong the chitchat—just a few remarks are all that's necessary to show that you're a friendly, confident person who can be at ease in a new environment.

As the interview progresses, don't be afraid to ask questions about the job. What is the day-to-day work like? Where did the person who had the job before you go? What are the possibilities for growth and advancement? When are the busiest times? What are the biggest problems? You can also be much more specific: "I notice your sales are up this year. Can you tell me why?" Or, "I notice your competitor has come out with a new wax. Does that affect you?" Showing your knowledge reveals commitment and interest.

Sell Your Abilities

Women often don't succeed on job interviews because they don't put themselves forward enough.
Many women have been brought up to be *overly* polite—to listen rather than speak, to be modest about their accomplishments. In a job interview, this kind of behavior can be disastrous.

All selling means is that you are in charge of what you want to communicate about yourself. You don't have to be pushy or aggressive to get your points across. Remember, the interviewer wants to hear your ideas, particularly if they will reveal the way you'll approach your job. If you are overly polite or modest, the interviewer may fail to notice what you have to offer, or may take your compliance for weakness. Therefore, speak up!

Be prepared for the question, "Tell me about yourself." The right answer is your best way to sell yourself—so have a two-minute *personal sales presentation* ready. The person hiring does not want to know *all* about you, so don't talk about your love of poetry, pottery, or stamp collecting. The interviewer wants to know the things about you that tell him whether you can do the job. Be specific about your skills and relate them to the functions of the job. For example, "Well, I've spent the last year as a photo representative for one of the best photographers in the business. During that time I opened many new accounts for him. I feel I'd bring sales ability to your firm."

Have well thought-out examples and stories to back you up. Don't say, "I'm a good communicator"—that's too vague. Say instead, "I convinced six organizations to back our community efforts to improve Lawrence Park, reducing the crime rate in the immediate area by 50 percent." Don't say, "I'm good at organizing"—that's too vague too. Say instead, "I initiated a series of lectures which increased membership in the Women's Political Caucus by 25 percent." That shows that you *do* have organizational skills. Anytime you can use a number or statistic, do.

When answering the very common question, "Why do you want this job?," frame your answer in terms of your *employer's* needs, and not your own. Don't begin by discussing your desire to make money, get out of the house, or meet new people. Talk about the job—what challenges it presents and why *you* are the person to handle it. Discuss your aspirations in terms of the company's growth. For example, "I plan to be a top saleswoman one day, and I believe this firm will offer me the opportunity to show what I can do."

Field the Tough Ones

Be prepared for the difficult questions.
An interviewer will usually zero in on your weak points. So be ready. Before the interview, list the questions you're most worried about. Don't repress the ones you hope won't come up—like "Why were you fired from your last job?" Write them all down.

Now, work on your answers. Practice out loud with friends. After a while, reverse the role-playing and see what answers *they* come up with. (Since they're not as emotionally involved, they may be more imaginative in their approaches and you may hear an answer you like.)

Here are some common difficult questions asked of many women today—and some approaches to help you.

Why should we hire you when you'll leave to get married or have a baby?

Geraldine, an art major who wanted to locate with an advertising firm, was asked this question—it's a common one asked of young women. And Geraldine reported that the question was causing her problems—not only because she wasn't sure how to answer it, but because she questioned whether a company *should* hire her since she might very well marry or have a child one day!

"I did lie twice and say I didn't want to have children," she said, "but one interviewer patronizingly told me he was sure I'd change my mind when I was a little older. And another began to ask me questions about why I *didn't* want children. He thought I was neurotic."

Geraldine's guilt and confusion are understandable—she is caught in a bind between being loyal to the company she'll work for and being loyal to herself. However, many men train for jobs at their company's expense, then later resign or relocate with little feeling of guilt or obligation. Geraldine need not feel guilty about wanting a personal life too.

What's the best answer to this kind of question? One might answer, "What I do with my personal life is not relevant." However, if the interviewer thinks it is, you may lose the job. You can suggest that it's an illegal, discriminatory question ("Would you ask that of a man?"), but that may cost you the job too. You have to decide whether you want to raise the interviewer's consciousness, put him in his place, or land the position.

The best kind of response will indicate that you are working out a reasonable structure for your life. You can say, "If I do marry and have children, I expect to have my career so well developed that I'll be earning enough money to have help. I've noticed that many successful women have done this and it makes sense to me."

We've never had a woman in this position before.

Your best approach is to prove that you are equally as competent as your male competitors. Contest the interviewer's prejudices with facts. If it's a job that requires selling ability, have examples ready that show your ability—"I sold more Avon products in my neighborhood than the last two saleswomen who preceded me." Moreover, if you want to answer the question directly; you can say, "Yes, many traditions are changing, and I'm delighted about it. This is the kind of job I've wanted for a long time and I'm happy that the opportunity is finally here." Don't be defensive. Be positive.

You're not experienced enough.

Men come up against this problem too, but not in quite the same way as women. It's more easily accepted that men will gain experience as they progress through the ranks, whereas a woman's "lack of experience" is often a good excuse to keep her in her place.

For example, a secretary may have coordinated programs, written captions, edited speeches, dealt with clients, but may still be stopped in her advancement because of her job title. A woman who's done outstanding community work may be blocked in getting a paid job because of the under-evaluation of her volunteer work.

The best way to fight this "lack of experience" catch-all is to *define yourself*, not through your job title but through your activities, accomplishments, and aspirations. ("Yes I have coordinated programs. Let me tell you about one of them.") When it comes to a weak area, compensate for quantity with quality. "I only coordinated one conference, but I outlined and implemented a publicity campaign that drew 1,000 participants as against a previous high of 500."

Learn to take credit for what you did. How many times have women complained, "I did all the work and he got all the credit." A job interview is *the* place to take credit, to tell a story or two which illustrate your ability to learn, to problem solve, to make things happen. Get the interviewer involved with the complexity of the problem and the ingenuity it took to solve it. ("I only had two weeks to get this conference set up, so here's what I did.")

You haven't worked for a long time.

An interviewer who says this really wants to know: Will you be able to handle the responsibility of a job? Will you tire of working and quit? Will your family interfere with your commitment? Your answer, therefore, should reassure—you can assume the discipline of a job and you have your family life under control.

You can say something like, "I'm the kind of person who takes my responsibilities seriously. When my children were young, I devoted myself to giving them the best care possible. Now that they're in school, I am making a commitment to working in a paid job which I'd planned to do when my children reached this age."

If you feel the interviewer is worried about your responsibilities at home (and this is especially true for divorced or separated women who have young children but who have to return to work), reassure him by saying something like, "I've arranged to have a housekeeper take care of my children, so I'm able to devote my full time and energy to my job when I'm on the job."

Why did you leave your last job?

If your last job was a dead end, and you left for that reason, don't simply say, "I wasn't getting anywhere and I decided to quit." That's too negative. Say something like, "I learned a lot at my last job, but I was prepared to risk the security of the job to find a position in which I can contribute more and use all of my talents and skills." That's presenting your need for a challenge in a positive light.

If you were fired, analyze why. In most cases, being fired doesn't mean that you are incompetent, but that the job you held just wasn't right for you. All of us have certain strengths and weaknesses, and it's important to work in a job that utilizes *your* particular strengths.

If asked why you were fired from your last job, you might say, "My strength lies in dealing with people, which was not needed for the job. My boss and I agreed the position should have been filled by someone with a scientific background."

However your last job ended, never, never, never knock a former employer in an interview.

Know how you are going to account for your time if you've been out of work for awhile. Were you taking time to explore various career fields? Were you investing in yourself by taking courses in your field? Doing volunteer work in your field? Running a family business or doing some consulting or free lance work? Don't put yourself down simply because you haven't been drawing a paycheck week in and week out. Instead, focus on presenting your strengths, accomplishments, and interests.

What's your biggest weakness?

This question comes up more often than you'd think. And you'd better be careful about the answer you give. For example, Joan would tell an interviewer that her biggest weakness was that she was "stubborn."

She felt stubbornness was a positive quality—it meant she didn't give up easily and was willing to stand by her own ideas, even in the face of other people's resistance. That being the case, it would be better if she said something like, "My biggest weakness is that I am persistent. I don't give up easily." The moral: Choose your words carefully.

Moreover, don't be self-destructive and confess to the interviewer that you have a hard time getting up in the morning, or that you're afraid to deal with people. Instead, think of "weaknesses" that are really strengths—you work too hard, you're too aggressive, you get so totally involved in solving office problems that you don't give enough time to your tennis game. Don't give an interviewer reasons not to hire you. And don't be shy about mentioning your strengths here too—even if you're not asked for them.

Show What You Can Do

Be prepared to take risks and show some chutzpah.
Laura was a secretary who wanted to be a fund-raiser. She went to a job interview with a stack of books on fund-raising. "Ask me anything about fund-raising," she told the interviewer as she put the books on his desk. "I've studied them all and feel I know the subject as well as anyone."

Come in with some proposals for the company, some ideas about what you would like to accomplish, and be willing to work on a trial basis.

Marsha wanted a job representing a group of craftspeople. They were hesitant about hiring her, because she had little sales experience. So she suggested that she try to sell some samples. When she came back two days later with an order, she was hired.

Keep Things Going

Don't let the interview sink.
If the interview isn't going well, your first reaction may be to leave as fast as you can, but

don't. If you really think the job might interest you, say to the interviewer, "I have a feeling I'm not coming across to you. Can you tell me why?" Then, *listen.* Perhaps the interviewer feels you've talked too much (and not let him make his points) or that he wants a more dominant personality. You won't know what's wrong unless you ask; once you know, you can think fast and try to salvage the situation.

When the interview is over, don't show that you're depressed, if indeed you are. Leave on a cordial, hopeful note. The more you can locate your self-esteem within yourself, the better off you'll be. Some people deliberately give high-stress interviews to see if you can take the heat.

Sum It All Up

Write the interviewer a note.
This is only polite. If you are hopeful and enthusiastic about the job, reiterate your feelings in your note. Condense some of the points you got out of the interview—what attracts you to the job. If you feel you've omitted a key fact that may help you land the job, now's the time to let him know about it. Shore up any weak points that emerged.

Do Better Next Time

Be prepared for rejections and don't take them personally.
Many interviewers hire unlikely candidates for all sorts of quirky reasons—because they're pretty or plain, or shy or aggressive, because they remind the interviewer of himself—or because they don't. The reasons may be irrational, but they're very human.

If you didn't get a job you wanted, analyze what went wrong. Go over the interview with a friend or job counselor. Could you have been more assertive? More sure of your own abilities? What should you do to prepare yourself for the next job interview?

Sometimes, you may find that you have to invest in yourself more before you can land the job you want—perhaps taking a course, or gaining experience through a well thought-out paid or volunteer commitment. Other times, you'll see that an effective sales presentation is all you need—whether you're just starting out, returning to the work world, or changing fields.

—*Victoria Pellegrino*

THE (REAL) REASON YOU DIDN'T GET THE JOB

by Ann Pringle Eliasberg

Since 1967—when the Age Discrimination in Employment Act was passed—it has been illegal to discriminate against or refuse to hire a person solely on the basis of age.

Illegal, perhaps—but not unheard of. Just recently, in fact, while studying the effects of hidden age prejudice on the working woman, I came upon these examples of ageism among people who either employ or refer women for employment:

- An interviewer at the Stanton Agency in New York City showed me a job order requesting a "cute, perky" secretary for a large broadcasting company. I asked if that sort of request was common and what it meant. "It's against the law for companies to discriminate," he said, "but let's face it, they do. There wouldn't be any point in sending a mature woman on that interview."
- A bank public-information specialist to whom I addressed an inquiry about job opportunities there for women over 40 said she couldn't think of any. The bank, she said, has a young staff, with many vice-presidents under 35. Its management-training program, famous in the banking community, is open only to young women. When I asked if there was any place where a mature woman might fit in, she replied that the bank had hired a lot of housewives as part-time computer-card processors.
- A professional colleague, learning of editorial openings from a major newspaper executive, suggested a woman journalist of 25 years' experience. He was told they were looking for someone younger.

Hearing on all sides about second careers and mid-life options, the woman who is over 40 and unwillingly jobless thinks there must be something wrong with *her*—especially since age discrimination, though widely practiced, is almost universally denied. No executive or personnel officer I spoke to saw himself or herself as prejudiced against hiring older women—though some conceded that other people might be. Most said they had no idea of the ages of the people they hired or that they were sure older people had as good a chance as younger ones.

But nationwide figures gathered by the US Employment Service reveal quite the contrary. In the fiscal year 1975–76, one out of every five applicants for work was over 40. Yet, of those placed in jobs, only *one out of every 11* was over 40. Put another way: If you are over 40 and looking for a job, your chance of finding one is less than half that of the average worker. And a woman in such a predicament almost undoubtedly faces greater odds than her male counterpart. USES figures do not show a male-female breakdown for over-40 placements, but they do show that about 44 percent of all job applicants are female.

In light of such figures, the commonly expressed view that private industry is looking for mature women to fill middle-management positions shows as a myth. So, too, does the claim that there are not enough qualified women to fill available jobs.

For example, Ruth W. (I've changed her

name but not her story), was laid off from a responsible job in a company she had been with for more than 20 years. She was unemployed for 22 months and frequently felt so enraged and discouraged that, had she been less determined, she would have given up. Employment agencies, she told me, wouldn't see her. Personnel interviewers blanched when they learned she had graduated from college by the time they were born. And Ruth couldn't fudge about her age, either, because 46 was hardly better than 51. Besides, one of her best selling points was that she had landed a good job straight from college and had kept moving up ever since.

Ruth finally found a job through a former colleague, and time has softened the memory of her ordeal. "I was always aware that my age was a handicap," she told me recently, "but if you ask me to pin down an occasion when I wasn't offered a job I would have been offered if I'd been younger—I don't know, it doesn't happen that way, there's usually another reason. . . ."

Though age may be the actual reason that you, as a mature woman, are not offered a job, the company—and you for that matter—can always think of another explanation. Job descriptions, for instance, may be tailored to fit only young applicants: "College grad, two to five years of experience" is a signal that a late-20s person is wanted, and news and trade papers are full of such ads. When a woman with 20 years of experience applies, she may be told that she is overqualified or underqualified, overspecialized or overgeneralized, or that she got her experience in the wrong place at the wrong time.

If the woman's experience is recent and relevant, other tactics may be used. One woman told me she was encouraged to apply for a much bigger job than the one she knew was open, and by the time she learned that the big job had been filled from within the company, she was out of the running for the lesser one.

Requiring an MBA is another way of ensuring a pool of youthful applicants, since women have been attending graduate business schools in large numbers only in recent years. Then, too, a suggested salary may be so low that only a young woman with no family responsibilities can afford to take it. In each of these instances, a company can say truthfully that the older applicant was not suitable; and she, in turn, may accept such a decision simply because she is unaware of the overall odds against which she is struggling.

Can a woman beat the odds? Not easily, since she faces two hurdles: anti-female and anti-age prejudice. And the second is perhaps worse than the first. Almost no one believes that Affirmative Action Programs for Equal Employment Opportunity have been spectacularly effective, but almost everyone agrees that they are more effective than the Age Discrimination Act, which sets no goals or timetables for the hiring of mature workers such as Affirmative Action sets for the hiring of minorities and women. Nor is an employer obliged to show that hiring a younger, rather than a mature, worker is a necessity, but only that it is justified according to his best business interest. Thus, mature workers are relatively unprotected in a competitive market.

Violations of the Age Discrimination Act are handled by the US Department of Labor's Wage and Hour Division. I asked Norman Bromberg, the division's New York-area director, how the system was working:

"Frankly," he said, "there are things wrong with the act. We've lost some cases we shouldn't have lost, and our funding pretty much limits us to responding to complaints. We investigate and follow up on those but there's always a backlog, and so, in general, we can't go out and look for violative situations."

"Isn't an individual complaint very hard to prove?" I queried.

"What we look for are patterns. Maybe the person who complains only suspects she's been discriminated against, but when we go in we may find that a lot of other older applicants for similar jobs were also turned down, and that, in fact, no one over 30 has been hired for that kind of job or in that department for over a year. That certainly looks like a violation. So anyone who even suspects age discrimination ought to complain, because we need that information."

"What would constitute a violative situation?"

"There's a violative situation whenever a company recruits exclusively on campus or at business schools and also has a promotion-from-within policy. The two together mean that an older person will amost never have access to employment in that company. And a lot of companies do that. There are big oil companies with more than 90 percent of their sales force under 32, and consumer-products companies with a sales force of 90 percent under 30. You don't get that kind of pattern without trying for it. And the big accounting firms—they ask for two to eight years of experience, so they aren't going to get a 45-year-old person."

"Then how do you make a company change its practices?" I wanted to know.

"We get a commitment from them to recruit from among the protected age group, 40–65, because recruitment is where discrimination begins. We follow up on that a year later, to see if there's been an improvement, and we make sure that the older people who are hired aren't being pushed into one type of job. But I personally feel that things aren't going to change drastically until people's attitudes change."

Since I know something about discriminatory hiring practices, I began to look for the attitudes that lie behind them, especially those toward mature women. I knew that NBC women had charged the network with sex discrimination in recruitment, hiring and promotion opportunities and benefits, and so I inquired about network policy toward hiring over-40 women.

But NBC's corporate mouth was closed.

Personnel officer Sue Ann Krakower said she couldn't reveal such information without the approval of Press Information. Press representative Natalie Tiranno said she couldn't discuss the matter without the approval of Personnel. I said Personnel had referred me to her. She said she would check with Personnel—and so it went for several telephone calls. In the end, Ms. Tiranno said she did not believe any information on the ages of women hired by NBC in the last year was available for publication. Besides, she said, "I don't think a woman over 40 likes to admit it."

I heard this kind of comment frequently, and have come to feel that the attitude it expresses—that maturity is something to deny or conceal—works strongly against older workers' receiving the recognition or jobs they deserve. The notion of age as an unmentionable secret allows companies to dodge questions of hiring policy and to disavow discriminatory practices that may in truth exist. A conversation I had with a personnel director at Babcock & Wilcox, a large industrial firm with many government contracts, was typical of others I had with executives in the private sector. I asked if he would care to tell me the number of over 40 women hired in the last year or two:

"No, I would not," he said. "I'd consider that private information. I'd say we have hired people from all categories, but I don't have statistics on age."

"I believe the Age Discrimination Act requires you to keep such statistics, and I am not asking out of personal curiosity. It sounds as if your record may not be too good," I ventured.

"That's your judgment. Someone else might judge differently. I am not required to give out this information."

Even executives who agreed that the figures might be of public interest said they would be too difficult or too expensive to compile, or that only informed estimates were available, or that if raw figures were provided, they must not be connected with the company's name. Actually, all the figures I collected, whether estimates or computations, proved similar to government figures—or worse. Heavy hirings of women occurred in low-level jobs among young workers, and as age categories rose, far fewer women than men were hired except at the lowest job levels.

Even there, young women get preference, as I learned through a small experiment I did with my 23-year-old daughter. She, armed with a résumé exactly like mine as to typing speed but indicating less administrative experience, was given a wide variety of referrals by agencies routinely used by large companies. On the other hand, I was told either that I was overqualified, that I should improve my typing speed or both.

As I grew more alert to the corporate attitude toward female maturity, I noticed that some of the men I spoke to never used the word "woman" at all:

"We've just appointed a new vice-president, a topnotch gal"; "I'll put you in touch with Alice, she's the girl in charge of that"; "We treat our older gals the same as your younger ones." Such remarks suggested that whatever age a woman may be, the man who hires or supervises her likes to feel she is a girl: an inferior, younger than he in rank and experience, if not in actual age.

Among mature female executives, surface cool sometimes cracks, revealing an underlying anxiety at the prospect of sharing the turf. I asked Dorothy Chappel, Human Resources vice-president at the Equitable Life Assurance Society, about Equitable's policy toward hiring older women.

"We don't discriminate in age or any other way," she explained. "I'm an example. I'd like to be able to say that I'm 30, but I'm not, I'm a mature woman myself. And I'm a company officer."

"Does Equitable make any effort to bring in mature women?" I asked.

"No. But we have an open-door policy. Anyone can walk in here and fill out a job-application form. But I'll tell you something.

An older woman has to have something to offer. Some of them expect it to be all laid out for them. I hired a secretary recently and I would have liked a mature woman, but I couldn't find one. They came in here with broad hips, wearing tight pants, V-necks, T-shirts. . . . Why, we went for job interviews wearing hats and white gloves. I don't expect that, but I expect a good appearance."

"Do you mean that you were unable to find any suitable mature women?" I asked.

"That's right."

Equitable, at least, addressed itself to the problems of mature female workers. Other companies—R. H. Macy, Colgate-Palmolive, IBM—either did not respond to questions or said they would check on available information, then did not call back. IBM's initial comment was that it had done very little hiring and almost no job training in the last year or two. And perhaps not. Certainly, in a recession, the less favored workers will go jobless.

One day, as I walked from 15th to 19th Street in New York City, I passed a tall young woman wearing the dark blue uniform of the telephone company and carrying what looked like repair equipment. In 1973, American Telephone & Telegraph entered into a consent agreement with the government that required the company to adjust pay inequities affecting female workers and to give females access to craft positions and fast-track management-development programs, almost exclusively male. This uniformed woman I saw held her job as a result of legal action. I considered that fact as I went on to keep my appointment at one of Pearl Knie's job-counseling sessions at the New York headquarters of the National Organization for Women.

Knie began by telling us some of the ways in which we are all unprepared for survival in a competitive job market: We grow up thinking we will be taken care of. We don't learn the techniques of aggression that our brothers learn on the athletic field. We value service over power. We don't know how to market ourselves. We do not build professional support-networks as men do. We meet a few successful female role models in the business world. Then, each woman in turn told of her experiences, feelings and problems. Knie offered occasional comments, concluding on the note: There *is* discrimination, there *are* obstacles. But each of us will have to solve it personally. . . . One of the ways that I know is to build a case to prove that this discrimination doesn't apply to you.

As I thought about Knie's advice, which in some respects was helpful and specific, I questioned the assumption that each individual woman could beat the general odds against her. For some years now, mature women have been trying to do that. If the strategy were successful, would the odds be so bad?

And what about Knie's portrait of the disadvantaged female? It didn't look like me at all. I was brought up in a deliberately nonprotective, Midwestern, Scots/Irish household in which I was expected to cope and achieve. I never willingly gave up my chance to be captain of the team. I had no special yen for service. I *was* taught not to brag, but so were my brothers, and all of us eventually learned enough self-sell for urban survival. I have a network of supportive colleagues and I have worked for female executives who were superb role models. So why did I accept a generalized, stereotyped portrait that neither fit me nor other women any better? Why did we all accept it?

Then I remembered the advertising axiom that in order to sell your product you must first create your market. In other words, women must first realize their plight before anything can be done to change it. Perhaps a step in the right direction is the proposed Displaced Homemakers' Act, which would serve certain unemployed women between 35 and 64. In addition to a variety of counseling programs offered at centers to be established throughout the country, the Act would explore the feasibility of including displaced homemakers in various Federal work programs and making them eligible for unemployment pay.

What is a displaced homemaker? According to the bill, it is a mature woman without a live-in husband or young children. In their presence she is a homemaker, in their absence she is a displaced homemaker. DH Centers would offer job training as well as counseling, but—and I quote the head of the Alliance for Displaced Homemakers, who has already established a pilot center in California—"We do not want to take jobs away from other people who need them." In her view, the jobs for which displaced homemakers are most likely to qualify are divorce counseling, one-to-one widow counseling, aging-programs-information specialist, money-management specialist and so on.

The Displaced Homemakers' Act projects a support system in which unemployed women will find employment counseling other unemployed women, a kind of perpetual care for the middle-aged female. The whole proposal, including its restriction of eligibility to spouseless females, reminded me of 19th-century schemes whereby spinsters who failed to find either a job or a husband would be helped to emigrate.

Legislators supporting this act constantly referred to displaced homemakers as "unskilled" and "untrained." But since nine out of ten American women do paid work at some stage in their lives, and another large group takes post-high-school training, those terms are not accurate. Realistically, most displaced homemakers are mature, unemployed women whose work experience happens to be less recent than that of other mature, unemployed women. Both groups face the common problem of age prejudice, and neither Pearl Knie's notion that each woman can beat the odds on her own nor a bureaucratic effort to divert women from the economic mainstream seems an acceptable solution.

What *is* the solution? The woman who told me about youth recruitment at Citibank also volunteered this opinion on women over 40: "They've got to get themselves a movement," she said. "There's no way they're going to make it otherwise."

Ann Pringle Eliasberg *learned first-hand of the employment discrimination problems of women*

over 40 when she began her search for a full-time job after 20 years as a free-lancer. Although her previous experience included working as a columnist and writer for a number of newspapers and magazines, she faced many hurdles before she found her present position as copywriter with Hoffmann-La Roche, a pharmaceutical company.

HELP-WANTED ADS

by Jane Trahey

Help-wanted ads often are exercises in euphemism. Jane Trahey attacks the classifieds with her **Handy Guide to Help Wanted Ads for Office Workers** (with helpful hints, clues and definitions of hidden meanings). So—whether you're an ad reader or an ad placer—this is the kind of language to watch out for.

"Work with minimum supervision"
(The office is your responsibility. Phones, files, customers and orders. The works. Boss checks in three times a day. 9 AM, 12:30 and 5 PM.)

"We're looking for someone who responds to variety"
(You'll be expected to do anything and everything.)

"Set up systems"
(The place is an utter mess.)

"Must have keen sense of PR"
(The boss has just left his wife for a new chick. Wife wants his unlisted phone number.)

"Receptionist. Busy office. Must have good appearance. Loads of meeting and greeting"
(Watch out for the hands.)

"Fee Paid"
(By whom?)

"Work with 5 partners in prestigious law firm and handle overflow"
(Is overflow another lawyer or is the toilet on the blink?)

"Secretary with bookkeeping knowledge"
(They're too cheap to hire a bookkeeper.)

"Close concentration abilities in busy office"
(Everyone shouts. It's an ulcer farm.)

"Cost-of-living and merit raises"
(What other kinds are there?)

"Work with several execs"
(But who decides which one comes first?)

"Must have confidential nature"
(You'll be in payroll.)

"Some light warehouse packing"
(Congratulations. You've just become the shipping clerk.)

"Handle our European office"
(Just remember the time change.)

"Medical terminology a plus"
(Whom are you treating?)

"Free tuition"
(Low pay.)

"Must be well above average"
(An MBA will do.)

"We offer top pay"
(A pit to work in.)

"Fantastic working conditions"
(Carpeting, Muzak and your own cubbyhole.)

"Must have driver's license"
(You're going to the airport a lot.)

"Must be well organized"
(They haven't filed since 1922.)

"Must think on your feet"
(Everything gets done at the very last second.)

"Challenging position"
(No one will show you anything.)

"Receptions in glamorous fashion world. Discount on clothes"
(You'll owe the company store.)

"Interfacing with clients a must"
(Define interfacing.)

"Lots of customer contact!"
(You'll help sell, but without sales commissions.)

"Need experienced receptionist for South Side office. Call Annie, 555-7777"
(You now know how they feel about women.)

"We need a 'people' person!"
(No one gets along.)

"We're seeking an energetic individual to pick up mail. Other duties include serving lunch, setting tables, cleaning area, washing dishes, setting up conference room with coffee and snack trays, cleaning up"
(Forget the mail! Get a maid!)

"Candidate must have ability to communicate with people at all levels of organization"
(Dad hates his son-in-law. Bud won't speak to Harry. Mother is bookkeeper.)

"Convenient location"
(Depends on where you live.)

"Work on temporary assignments"
(No unemployment, no insurance, no hospitalization, no paid holidays, no Christmas bonus, no nothing.)

"Supper money and overtime"
(Bad news)

YOUR FIRST JOB: HOW TO FIND A GOOD ONE

by Miriam Markus

It happened in a sociology class in a small college. The vice-president of a local company finished his guest lecture. Members of the class asked a few questions then drifted out of the room. One woman approached the speaker. "I'm graduating next month. I enjoy people. I think I have the imagination and persistence to be a good sales representa-tive, and I'm interested in a job like that with a company like yours."

The v-p took out his business card. "Write to me. Remind me of your qualifications and that you met me here. I'll set up an inter-view."

After graduation, five students who had heard the v-p speak tried for sales-rep positions with his company. Naturally, they applied through the personnel department. That summer the company hired only one new sales rep—the woman who had spoken to the v-p. With a base salary of $13,200, plus commission, she earned nearly $17,000 her first year after college. And she began accumulating experience with an excellent company that could lead to better positions in the years ahead.

There are jobs. And, yes, there are *good* jobs.

The Basic Steps

This woman won her *good* job by following basic "start here" job-hunting rules:

1. She directly approached (either by speaking or writing) the person **who had the power to hire her.** Except for low-level jobs, personnel departments rarely can hire. They screen applications and send "suitable" candidates to those who make the decisions.
2. She didn't let her lack of experience defeat her. She talked about her **relevant abilities:** "I like people . . . I have imagination . . . persistence . . ."
3. When she followed through and wrote to him, the v-p set up an interview with himself. She came prepared to discuss **how she had used her people skills, her imagination,** etc., to succeed with school and personal projects. She also could have offered relevant volunteer experiences.
4. By using the above job-hunting points, **the woman helped the v-p create a job expecially for her.** The company had no openings for sales representatives and those who applied through personnel were told, "Not hiring." But the student's initiative in speaking to the v-p had impressed him. Companies always are seeking intelligence and initiative. At the interview the v-p realized that this woman did have the makings of an effective salesperson. His automatic thought

was, "How can the company use her?" He remembered an idea he'd never been able to act on.

"Would you be interested in opening a new type of sales territory?" he asked her. "We've never approached supermarkets."

"Certainly," the woman replied.

"OK. It's all yours."

In this case, the sales job created for the woman was the type of work she had applied for, but very often the created job is different from the applicant's original goal. As an employer recognizes ability and searches for ways to use it, excellent jobs materialize— because the need existed in the company but was never acted upon.

The offered position may be better than the applicant's original goal. For example, a middle-aged East Coast woman applied at a neighborhood senior citizens center for a part-time job as a social director. No such job had been advertised, but she thought there might be a need. (Applying where you think a job may exist is another great job-getting technique because it makes you the only applicant.) This woman's experiences consisted of 20 years of varied volunteer work. The executive director listened, appraised her and invented a job: assistant director for the entire center—a job and salary far better than the one the woman had sought.

The women at the college and at the senior-citizens center were smart not to concentrate on ads or agencies. Employment experts believe that between 64 percent and 80 percent of all *good* jobs never are advertised. Because they are good, they are filled quickly by personal contacts. Furthermore, say the experts, three out of ten of these jobs *do not exist* until the right person arrives and the job is created for that person.

Pyramiding

Wait! Don't say, "I don't have contacts." Everyone does. The trick is realizing it and then approaching them properly.

Career-counseling services call it the "pyramid approach" to job hunting. You speak and write to people you know— in clubs you belong to, in your church, synagogue, your dentist—anyone who can suggest employers who might be able to use you. Don't pressure by asking for a job. Ask only for advice—"I have such and such skills. What jobs might I use my abilities for? Who could use my abilities?"

People are flattered to be asked for advice. They think about your problem. Sometimes they realize you can solve *their* business problems. They offer you a job. Other times they make no job offer but suggest an employer in another company.

Now you are equipped to bypass the personnel department in the new company and can approach the person with the power to hire. You have a magic opening because of your mutual friend/acquaintance: "Susan Jones suggested I make an appointment with you." With the personal introduction from Jones you almost certainly will get an interview.

Interview Smarts

At the interview not only should you talk, you should listen. People will give you insights into your potential that never might have occurred to you. You may go in looking for an administrative job and come out realizing that you have the ability to succeed at public relations. If the interview doesn't lead to a job offer, "pyramid" your contacts by asking for suggestions of other employers. Eventually—and often quickly—someone's "advice" will be, "We've been needing someone to do such and such. Are you interested?" And there you are—another person with a good job.

FOR MORE INFORMATION

From Kitchen to Career: How Any Woman Can Skip Low-Level Jobs and Start in the Middle or at the Top, by Shirley Sloan Fader, Stein & Day, $4.95.

Re-Entering: Successful Back-to-Work Strategies for Women Seeking a Fresh Start, by Eleanor Berman, Crown, $8.95.

Where Do I Go from Here with My Life?, by John C. Crystal and Richard N. Bolles, Ten Speed Press, $7.95.

THE ANSWERS TO TOUGH INTERVIEW QUESTIONS
by Shirley Sloan Fader

You may think the tension at the job interview is all yours. Not true. Interviewers know they must choose people who will do well on the job—or *they* will be labeled incompetent by *their* superiors. If the interviewer also is the boss, she must choose the proper applicant or later struggle with an unsatisfactory employee.

Interviewers tend to use certain questions to relieve their anxieties about whether you will do the job competently and whether you have the necessary temperament—stability, flexibility, dependability, etc.—to fit into the work team.

When you relieve the interviewer of these worries, she relaxes. At last, here is someone she safely can choose for the job! "Most jobs are filled by people who meet only *some* of the job's specifications," says employment expert Richard K. Irish, author of *Go Hire Yourself an Employer* (Anchor Press/Doubleday). But that successful candidate has made the interviewer feel "safe": "Yes, this person can handle the job well."

Following are some of the most frequently asked job-interview questions with the appropriate answers that will project your competence.

• **What are your major strengths?** This really means: "Tell me how your abilities fit what's needed for this job."

Suppose the position you're applying for requires initiative. (You figured this out beforehand by analyzing characteristics needed for this type of work and by analyzing their job description.) Instead of simply stating, "I'm definitely a self-starter," be prepared with examples. To illustrate your initiative you might be able to say, "My present boss travels almost 40 percent of the time. I have to deal on my own with problems in customer service, scheduling, expediting, numerous day-to-day plans."

You also can project competence by quoting others. "My bosses/teachers often say I'm unusually quick to learn and am accurate. For instance . . ." Or, "I've been told I'm very good at winning cooperation from people I supervise."

• **What are your biggest weaknesses?** If you insist you have none, you'll lose out as having no insight into yourself. Instead, choose an appropriate strength and be prepared to report it as a "weakness."

Perhaps for this job, system is essential. You might confess you can't stand work done on a piecemeal, what's-today's-crisis basis. You like to plan ahead, to foresee and prevent problems. Just the "weakness" needed for the position.

• **What can you do for us?** This really means: "Why would you be the best applicant to hire?" Thomas L. Weck in his book on executive job hunting techniques, *Moving Up Quickly* (John Wiley & Sons), suggests that if you can offer it, a facts-and-figures answer is one of the best. For instance: "I can develop a well-run department with satisfied employees. When I started my present job, my department was paying about 20 hours overtime weekly. Now the department workload has risen 15 percent, and I've organized things so efficiently that there's almost no overtime. And there's very little employee turnover."

Another excellent reply discusses new business you can bring into the company. (Many women entering the work force after years of homemaking find this approach useful.) The bottom line for all business is customers. When you can provide new ones, you are almost irresistible as an employee. One woman used the new-business potential of her wide social circle to obtain a travel-agency job. Another created a part-time job selling newspaper advertising by drawing on her wide volunteer contacts as her I-can-bring-new-ads reply to this question.

• **What do you see yourself working at three to five years from now?** This really means: "If we hire you, are you likely to stay for a while?" You can crowd considerable reassurance for the interviewer into this question. Although questions about marriage, babies, child care are illegal, if you've completed your family or do not expect to start one for some years or have good child-care arrangements, strengthen your appeal by volunteering the information. You reply you know you'll stay and grow with the job because . . .

Most career experts warn against naming a specific future job you hope to hold lest it mark you as too narrow or inflexible. Rather, indicate that you are mature and realistic in your thinking by discussing areas within this company where you can grow based on your expertise and contributions. If you dream of becoming a state assemblywoman or opening your own business, this is not the place to mention it.

• **Tell me about yourself.** This really means: "Are you well adjusted, able to work well with others? Do your outside interests add to or conflict with the job?"

Don't pour out your whole biography; just enough to reassure the interviewer you will fit in well. "I enjoy people and they seem to like me." "I work well under pressure."

• **What starting salary do you expect?** Deal with this only near the end of the interview, preferably after the interviewer has made you an offer. If he or she inquires earlier, reply you'd like to explore the dimensions of the job before considering salary. But do ask the salary range. This saves you from sabotaging yourself by requesting less than the company expected to pay.

Resist the temptation to inflate your current salary. It can be checked easily. Achieve the same highsounding results honestly by replying, "With salary and benefits together, my present income package comes to . . ." The US Chamber of Commerce's latest survey indicates that, on the average, American jobs pay benefits worth $5,560 annually. Compute the monetary value of your company-paid health and life insurance; tuition plans, etc.

When you do discuss salary, try at first for the top amount you think possible. If necessary, you can accept less—"Because the position looks so promising"—and leave the company feeling it's won a good bargain. If you quickly agree to the first salary suggested, you make them wonder why you're so eager.

FOR MORE INFORMATION

For a free, excellent eight-page booklet discussing *Getting Chosen: The Job Interview and Before,* write: Bureau of Labor Statistics, Inquiries Branch, Washington, DC 20212.

Part Two

Keep Moving

Chapter Three

Stepping Ahead

HOW TO GET WHAT YOU WANT ON THE JOB

A growing number of women moving up in the work world are finding that strategy, not talent, is the deciding factor in moving toward higher, better-paid positions. These women plan strategies for their companies' progress, but they may not be investing the same kind of time and energy into planning their careers.

Many professional women aren't aware of the simple rules of maneuvering on the job. Furthermore, the women who are least likely to seek advice on career moves are the ones most likely to benefit from it, according to Marcia P. Kleiman, codirector of Options for Women, a Philadelphia corporation that was one of the first career-advisory and business-consulting services created to contend with the issues women face in the work world.

Special Problems

"Most professional and managerial women see themselves as special," said Kleiman, "with problems so special that if they can't solve them themselves, no one else can help them." The male-oriented atmosphere in which professional women work causes them to feel that way, as does their relative isolation.

"A woman needs to be better than equal to receive a promotion," said Vicki W. Kramer, Options' other codirector and its affirmative-action consultant. Faced with such pressure to perform, a woman becomes exceedingly self-critical and fearful of disapproval. "She is made to feel that she can't afford to fail or to have questions or weaknesses," added Kramer. "Seeking assistance is not a weakness, but women sometimes perceive it that way."

For these reasons, a woman may need to look outside the company for the support and advice that male executives traditionally get from the company's old-boy network. This is where a career-advisory organization comes in for middle-management women. It's like having an expert friend to give guidance, and it is a service of considerable help to professionals who feel they cannot afford to show any chinks in their on-the-job armor.

The Questions Women Executives Ask

The questions most often asked of Options for Women concern getting raises, getting

43

recognition, getting ahead. Some of Options' advice:

To negotiate successfully for a raise, first stop believing that your company can't stretch its salary scale for a deserving talent. It can. It does it all the time—for men.

Next, find out what you really are worth:

- Break down and itemize your skills and responsibilities.
- Identify what's special about the skills you bring to your job.
- Figure out how your skills save your company money.
- Write it all down.

The third step is to find out what others in your position are paid. You can find out comparable salaries by:

- Joining a professional organization and talking with other members.
- Developing relationships with people in your company who have similar levels of responsibility and discussing salaries with them.
- Noting the salaries for similar jobs advertised in the want ads of newspapers and business publications.
- Researching what the American Management Association has published as the going salary for your kind of job. This information should be available from your company's personnel department.

Write up and document all you can about the typical salaries in your field. If you are underpaid, you can negotiate successfully for more money when armed with this information. During the discussion for a raise, be clear about how much money you expect. Remember that you are making a business agreement about your professional worth in your present position, not about your personal value. What you get you get because you demanded it and deserve it, so don't be *too* grateful.

Getting Credit Where Credit's Due

In their eagerness to get approval by being helpful, many women in management forget that they ought to get something in return for their additional efforts.

To get the recognition you deserve on the job, Options advises that you plan a strategy that will bring your ideas and extra work to the attention of your superiors. You should document, in writing, not only your clear job responsibilities, but also the areas in which you have assumed added responsibilities and how your efforts benefit the organization. Use this documentation to show your worth at performance-appraisal time.

Make sure that the person whom you keep informed about what you are doing has the power to assist you in furthering your career. If that person does not help you, find someone else. If the superiors in your department are not supportive, you can try to establish an understanding by explaining your goals for growth to them. Ask for concrete commitments on what they will do to support your goals. If no one around is willing to offer help, you may have to face a decision about changing departments or companies.

In order to succeed, getting what you want in your job must become part of your job.

PROSPER: GET THE DEGREE THAT EARNS YOU MORE MONEY

by Jean Murray

I'm cashing a check at the bank and I overhear a man at the next window: "My wife has a BA, but she keeps going for more degrees. She says she has to. She's in guidance and the field is dead."

A colleague is worrying about her daughter: "She'll have her BA next year and she wants to go to graduate school. She isn't sure why. She just isn't ready to look for work."

I'm reading the paper and come across an increasingly familiar feature: the one about Jane Smith who received a bachelor's in biology, dropped out to raise four terrific kids to maturity, and is now enrolled for a master's in social work.

My divorced friend with the fine-arts degree is complaining: "I can't get a job. I keep hearing I'm overeducated for what I want to do—for making money in any ordinary way."

These are the "overeducated": women who are aimlessly collecting degrees as protective coating for the job world; women who are reentering or who are stymied and are back in school for a confidence fix and salable new skills; women who are "buying" degrees as though they were magical springboards to glamour jobs; women who are tracked into expensive credential mills for the traditionally female, low-paying careers; women who are educated to join the idle rich but must, after the divorce, quickly join the gainfully employed.

Of course, a woman who's into the pursuit of learning, apart from her career prospects, is never called overeducated. And the education of a bright, ambitious 21-year-old woman who is thinking about banking is likely to be considered just right.

"Today *that* woman is better off than her male counterpart," explained Gail Parker, the former president of Bennington College and co-author of the recently published *College on Your Own* (Bantam Books). "She's something they are looking for, while he is swimming upstream with the rest of the competition."

But Parker suspects that wherever the decision to hire or promote a woman is controversial, an (unrequired) advanced degree improves her chances. "Credentials can take the employer off the hook," said Parker. "I'm sure there are plenty of instances in which employers are genuinely relieved to be able to defend their choices by saying, 'You might say she's a woman, but she's also a master's degree.' "

According to Patricia Kosinar, who runs the Middle Management Program at Simmons College in Boston, "Women starting out in business often have the same education as their male counterparts. But the man is a known quantity. His boss has seen plenty of these 21-year-old hotshots and knows that if he puts the kid in a sales-training program, he'll get results. He doesn't have enough experience with women to know if they will produce. So a woman who wants to rise in the company becomes credible to him only if she gets an MBA. After all, that means she's passed 15 marketing courses."

Obviously, whose education is over- or undercooked has a lot to do with expediency and diehard double standards. When I asked Bernice Sandler, director of the Washington, DC-based Project on the Status and Education of Women (of the Association of American Colleges), if she thought women were overeducated, she was indignant: "Women aren't overeducated, they're underemployed. Their educations don't pay off. The average income of women with bachelor's degrees who are working full time is about the same as that of men who are high-school dropouts. Women tend to be attracted to the 'female' fields where salaries are low. The problem for women is occupational segregation."

On the bright side, the millions of women now pouring into the work force are beginning to put pressure on the old double standards. Today only one woman in 25 considers herself a full-time homemaker and the number of married women working has tripled in the last generation. Because of inflation, few couples can make it on just one income, and more women are taking only two to three years off for childrearing. Now the reentry women is as likely to be in her late 20s as she is in her late 40s. As a result, the traditional obstacles that have hampered women's preparation for and experience in the working world are going the way of the dinosaur.

"When I was starting out 22 years ago," said Sandler, "work was something a woman did if things went bad—if you didn't get married, were widowed or divorced, after your kids left the nest. We know that attitude has changed. Because women are now looking at work as a major commitment in their lives, we are seeing more practical choices, more vocational planning among undergraduates."

More colleges now offer work/study programs. To encourage students to plan ahead, Smith College invites its alumnae back to tell them what it's like out there. There are substantial increases in the numbers of women entering medical, law, veterinary and architecture schools. Percentages are up for women enrolling in graduate programs in mathematics, environmental design, journalism and the physical sciences.

The community and junior colleges, whose emphasis is occupational and whose enrollments of mostly women account for one-third of all undergraduates in higher education, are under attack. A Carnegie Corporation-funded study-in-progress by The Center for Women's Opportunities (of the American Association of Women in Community and Junior Colleges) is finding that these institutions, which are now enrolling many women returning to school after a break, are not providing the kinds of programs students will need if they are to break out of stereotyped occupations. The CWO survey, having pinpointed a recent rise in the number of women entering "neutral" fields—accounting, data processing, personnel management—is recommending these skills be taught as electives in the more traditional programs.

While these efforts are encouraging and one day may make a woman's education and her job a perfect fit, there still isn't much comfort for the women in no-win situations. Even women who have the motivation and the educational opportunities to enter the better-paying, male-dominated fields may find themselves in the ironic situation of having their breakthroughs depress the salaries and prestige in those fields. And the woman who has had to interrupt her work life or has been unable to stay in her field may just be stuck for now.

"Many of these women have to go after jobs for which they seem over-educated," Sandler pointed out. "Often, they're turned down as overqualified. But what we're noticing lately is, as jobs get scarcer, more men are applying for clerical work. And no one's confronting them as overeducated."

LEARN: HOW FURTHER EDUCATION HELPS YOU GET AHEAD

by Wendy Schuman

Not too long ago, it was assumed that education was the private preserve of the young, and anyone caught in graduate school after 25 had better have a good excuse (getting an MD) or risk being labelled a "professional student."

Never mind that many people were locked stepped into the wrong career or, lacking a degree, stuck at a lower level than their potential warranted. Once you were an adult, it was, "Never look back."

Times have changed emphatically. "Today we recognize learning as a lifelong experience," said Pat Koch Thaler, director of the

Continuing Education Division of Marymount College in New York. "We realize that continuous education is essential, both for keeping up skills and for personal gratification."

The number of older students attending college has risen dramatically. Forty-eight percent of college students are over 21, and 10 percent are over 35. The number of older students has increased three times as fast as those of traditional college age. And these figures don't include the explosion of noncredit and nondegree courses and programs.

Faced with a dwindling pool of younger students, colleges and universities have begun to recruit the older student and to offer flexible programs to meet the special needs and problems of adults—especially adult women. For one startling fact emerges—the majority of these older students are women.

"The normal pattern of women's lives has always been disruptive to their education," noted Jean Campbell, director of the University of Michigan's Center for the Continuing Education of Women, "but now, women are returning to school much earlier than they did in the 1950s and '60s." Many are single, aspiring to higher job levels, or they're divorced heads of households. If married, they tend to have fewer children, which makes going back easier.

Campbell added: "Schools must adapt to the patterns of women instead of penalizing them for not being like traditional male students."

Change is already in evidence. A report of the Women's Bureau of the US Department of Labor noted that in the early 1960s, programs geared specifically to women emphasized assisting housewives in reentering the work force. Today, new courses help employed women with their career development.

Another form of institutional response is the granting of "life experience" credit. "We're helping women translate their experience into workskills and trying to convince

universities that such skills are accreditable," said Marlaine Lockheed, PhD, of the Educational Testing Service in Princeton, NJ. She is coauthor of *How to Get College Credit for What You've Learned as a Homemaker-Volunteer*, available for $3 from ETS.

Continuing Education: What It Is, Where It Is

To some educators, continuing education is a broad rubric for any course or program outside the traditional, full-time, on-campus bachelor's program. Others relate it to age—any student older than 22 is "continuing her education." Such courses can be found in universities, colleges, high schools, museums, professional associations, the local "Y," churches and synagogues, business schools and in the newly developing educational exchanges. At universities, continuing education can be called graduate school, night school, evening program, adult education, part-time study or university extension.

In general, continuing education courses are aimed at either personal development or career development; often there is overlap. Personal development courses (anything from assertiveness training to flower arranging) are usually noncredit. Career courses sometimes carry academic credit or, if taken in sequence, may culminate in a diploma or certificate. If no credit is involved, the cost is often nominal, but Thaler advises paying the extra amount for credits if you might want a degree.

Courses geared to adults may be different from standard classes. "Our courses have more specific goals, whether it be basic reading improvement or a highly specialized area of tax law," said Dean Ann Marcus, of the School of Continuing Education at NYU. The career courses there are taught by practitioners in the field rather than professors. Other schools offer the same courses undergraduates take, but at a later hour.

From such an array of possibilities, how should you choose? Time pressures, proximity to home or work, flexibility of the program, financial aid and quality of education are some factors to consider. Many students cite the prestige of the institution as important to employers.

Whatever you choose, try to start small, with a sample course or two, before investing in a longer program.

Why Return to School?

In returning to school for career purposes, it's important to be clear about your goals—and whether school is the best route to them.

First, make an honest examination of your values, interests, skills, aptitudes and goals, and what you enjoy and dislike doing. Some helpful aids are the Self-Guidance Series and the Education Opportunities Series of booklets from Catalyst, 14 East 60th Street, New York, NY 10022.

Next, get some idea of what the job market for your skills will be when your training is done—and be flexible enough to consider a backup career. One woman in New York pursued a long and costly PhD in philosophy, then, predictably, could not find a teaching job. She retrained as a paralegal and found work.

To get a sense of the job market, talk to professionals in your chosen field, especially those who do the hiring. And check the *Occupational Outlook Handbook* (US Dept. of Labor) in your library for an idea of the future of some 700 occupations.

Find out if your proposed educational plan is the right training for your goal. Janet Klein (profiled below) found she might have used her evenings better by getting a BA than by taking noncredit professional courses. A talk with your personnel director or a top person in your department may help you decide how to move up.

Above all, seek counseling. Nearly all schools offer some kind of educational, career and personal counseling. "Careful counseling is essential," said Campbell. "You don't have to do it alone."

Common problems include clarifying goals and fields of study, managing a wife-mother-student role, dealing with the pressures of being a single parent, putting together credits from various colleges toward a degree and transferring credits. The most pervasive problem, according to a University of Michigan Center report, is "lack of self-confidence, uncertainty about self-definition and about aims."

Many women find returning to school a different experience from the first time around. "Going to school is not my primary job," said a candidate for a Master's in healthcare management, who has one child and expects another. "I put it into perspective and I'm not overcome by the little successes and failures. There is no time to agonize."

The motivation of mature students is legendary among educators. "Adults are hungry to learn what's relevant to their needs," said one. Adults take school seriously; they feel the pressures of time and money—and don't want to waste either.

Does Continuing Education Help Professionally?

Lacking hard statistics, several educators and many students feel that it does help—depending on a host of individual factors. "Degrees and certificates are fine," noted Denis Sinclair Philipps, associate dean of the School of Continuing Education at NYU, "but what a company wants to know is: 'Can you do the job?' It's up to the individual to prove she can."

Several women said their extra training did not help them find jobs or raise their salaries—but they were glad they had it anyway. "I was glad I made my first mistakes in school rather than on the job," said one.

Generally speaking, a college degree is an important credential. A college graduate is currently estimated to earn 30 to 50 percent more during her lifetime than a high school graduate. Beyond that, it is difficult to predict if you will really get the job you trained for. As Lenz and Shaevitz point out in *So You Want to Go Back to School* (McGraw-Hill, 1977): ". . . the uncertainties of the economy make job expectations risky, which is why adult students are advised to cultivate as much flexibility and versatility as possible. . . ."

The women profiled below all felt benefited by continuing education—although each made her own sacrifices of time, money, energy and personal relationships.

Can a former pianist find happiness as a certified public accountant? Joan Walsh thinks so. Many years have passed between her Master's degree in music and the Master's in business administration she is getting from Columbia University. After a brief period of teaching piano and performing, Walsh spent the next 13 years as an educational administrative assistant at two small colleges in Manhattan. "I worked in the business office of Marymount and used accounting heavily—I learned it on the job," she said. "At Mannes, I assisted the academic dean."

In 1976, Walsh enrolled in the Business Management Certificate Program at Marymount to brush up her work skills. "I felt the need to apply a formal system to my work instead of going at it instinctively," she said. Walsh's program took 15 months and led to 30 undergraduate credits in business subjects. Because of an agreement with the school she worked in, her tuition was free.

"The course I took in personnel management made me think about returning to graduate school," Walsh said. Of all the work she had done, she preferred accounting. "Accounting is like music," she said. "There is a sense of balance and measure. In fact, analyzing a consolidated financial form requires similar skills to playing a Brahms quartet. You have to deal with highly complex material without losing sight of the whole."

Walsh began at Columbia right after Marymount (she had quit her job in between)—and has been going to school full

time ever since. She is financing her degree with savings, loans and scholarships.

Thanks to mid-year interviews on campus, Walsh has found a position with a major accounting firm, but her studying will continue—for her certified public accounting exams. "I'm looking forward to playing the piano again—it's been nothing but a bookshelf for months."

Six years ago, Terry Bohrer led a comfortably balanced life in suburban Maryland—wife of a busy doctor, mother of four little girls and part-time nurse at a local hospital. But something gnawed at her: "After 13 years of nursing, I wanted to get involved in health-care reform, in making policy. Without a college diploma, I was at a dead end."

In 1959, when she had graduated from a three-year hospital program, Bachelors' degrees were not offered. If she returned to nursing school now, her previous training would count for nothing—it was ten years old. "I couldn't do the same thing again," she said. "Also, I needed new skills for the kind of work I wanted." At 33, she enrolled as a freshman social-work major at Bowie State College, a former black teachers' college that was expanding its courses to attract housewives returning to school.

"Frankly, I picked it because it was ten minutes from the house," said Bohrer. "I was scared. I had been out of school for 13 years and I had so many responsibilities." Her children soon learned to ask other people for rides and to keep their own appointments. "I had been the memory bank for six people, and the first few weeks, everyone forgot everything."

Bohrer found school rather easy but enormously time-consuming. "It's true I was much more concerned with academic excellence than the younger students. They were into socializing and just getting by. I was always conscious that this was my big opportunity."

She had something of a struggle convincing the school to accept some of her previous nursing credits but succeeded at last and graduated magna cum laude in three and a half years. She is now finishing her Master's in social work at the University of Maryland and doing 60 hours a week of school-related work.

"Next, I'll have to face job-hunting, and at 39, it's scary. When I was a nurse, I could just walk into a hospital and they were thrilled. I've never had to sell myself before."

During field placement, she obtained a $37,000 Federal grant for her county corrections department and also worked as a community organizer in a mental-health center. Good experience, but the social-service market is tight.

"I hope the degree I've been coveting all these years won't turn out to be a disappointment," she mused. "I don't feel like going for a PhD."

Janet Klein is a pseudonym for a woman on the public-relations staff of a huge, conservative multinational corporation that markets its own manufactured products. As a publicist, she finds it safer to keep her own personality deep in the background, away from the spotlight of the client she is paid to promote. Even behind the veil of anonymity, she is ill at ease revealing her upward struggle through the company.

Klein is 38. She joined the company 17 years ago, fresh out of secretarial school, certain she would leave in a few years as someone's wife. Ten years later, at the age of 30, she realized, "I'm going to be supporting myself. I've got to get serious about a career. And I've got to start now."

By that time, Klein had become a research assistant for a corporate economist but was unable to move into a management grade in her department. (This company has enough employee grades to rival the Federal Government.) There was scarcely a woman in management, then or now, and Klein knew that the largely male competition for the few available management positions was fierce.

When she learned that the editor of the company newsletter was retiring, she seized her opportunity. His was a management-grade job in corporate public relations, an area that the young MBAs didn't care about and top management didn't know much about. To Klein, it seemed a good spot to carve her own niche away from the hungry, better-educated competition. She was allowed to train for the job and three months later, she got it.

Klein immediately signed up for night courses at the Publicity Club of New York. "I took everything they had—writing, photography, editing, how to make press contacts—about ten courses in all."

In class, she worked on problems she was actually facing at work. "I wanted to make changes in our in-house publications, and these courses gave me a practical basis for doing it," she said. "I felt much more secure about initiating changes when I saw these ideas right there in text books."

Because it's part of her job to keep an eye on all developments in the company, she's enrolled herself in all company training programs—from sales to operations—and sits in on high-level management seminars. She even took the Dale Carnegie ("How to win friends . . .") course when it was offered to the sales department.

Despite her self-determined course of study, she hasn't reached the level—in management grade or salary—she wants to achieve. "I'm going to have to get that degree," she said, somewhat wearily. "In any promotion situation, degrees are noted by personnel. I'm sure it's knocked me out of the ballgame a number of times.

"I hope I can get some credit for life experience and my professional courses. Today they're giving Master's credits for the courses I took six years ago at the Publicity Club.

"If I had it to do over again, I'd get the degree first," she said. "In a large corporation, it's the only way."

Anita Allen, tired but animated, was eating a Sunday brunch of eggs and megavitamins washed down with milk. "Business is so active, I sometimes don't have time to eat during the week. In real estate, when there's wind, you have to sail." She is a vice-president and broker with L.B. Kaye Associates, Ltd., a New York real-estate firm, and one of the few women around specializing in property sales. It's an uncertain, gut-wrenching business in which you can make a $10,000 commission in one day—or nothing for months. Allen loves it—and a good thing. For the last five years she has done little else. "I can't even sit through a play—it's so passive. I'm always anxious to get back to work."

Now in her 30s, Allen had been married directly out of high school and spent the next few years working for medical schools as an administrative assistant.

After her divorce, she found herself, as she put it, conditioned by society to search for a new husband who would change her life and make her a complete person. "One day, I realized no one could do it for me. If I was going to make money and gain satisfaction, it would have to come from me."

But what was open to a woman with no profession and neither the time nor money to study full time? She finally narrowed her options to the stock market, opening a small business, or real estate.

A free real-estate seminar at New York University confirmed her inclination to go into sales. (Three years later, she was a guest speaker at that same seminar.)

At the time Allen entered real estate, jobs for beginners, particularly women, were scarce and were offered on a straight-commission basis only. "I expected to make very little or nothing," she recalled. In exchange for lesser commissions, she negotiated a $100 per week salary and hoped that in combination with savings, it would sustain her through the first year.

The next step was signing up for courses at NYU's Real Estate Institute at the School of Continuing Education toward a certificate in real-estate studies and a license.

In an area where the attrition of new salespeople can be as high as 80 percent, Allen earned $25,000 her first year. Her income now, five years later, is in the six-figure range. Allen attributes her success to a number of factors—her personal drive, working for a person whom she liked and who believed in her and the good luck of finding work she truly loves: "It's a continuing kaleidoscope of new people, properties and events."

Returning to school was not as difficult as she had expected; the subjects she took in the evening tied in directly to her work during the day. They were on a lecture basis, with no additional homework. Many evenings when she was too exhausted to pay close attention, she taped the lectures for later review.

Allen found among the advantages of a professional school the many friends and business contacts she made. Her instructors were practicing realtors, and many of her classmates were in related fields.

Two years ago, Allen changed firms and remarried. Her husband, who is in real estate, was originally a business contact. "When we met, I was trying to sell him a building," recalled Allen, smiling. "The deal fell through. . . ."

MBA: THE FANTASY AND THE REALITY

by Laurie Werner

A master's degree in business administration represents a set of skills in much the same way that a medical degree does. According to Marlene Deverell-Van Meter, former editor of *MBA* magazine (which recently ceased publication), these skills include "facility with the language of the business community, the ability to analyze data from an integrated perspective and the ability to make conscientious and responsible business decisions."

Corporate and government employers, moreover, generally see an MBA as a step forward on the fast track. "It means that you can fit into a company quickly and productively," said Joan Motyka, editor of the *MBA Executive*, the monthly newsletter of the Association of MBA Executives in New York. "Your skills can be applied," she said, "almost directly, with a minimum amount of training from the company." To Marian Kellogg, vice-president of the General Electric Company in Connecticut, MBAs are simply "one of the best sources of potential managers and are ideal passports to consulting work."

What precisely does an MBA degree mean for those who are candidates for one? It means opportunity; it means money. Although starting salaries vary according to school, region (Northeast, West, Midwest and South, in descending order), personal experience and MBA specialty (consulting is high, accounting is lower), median starting salaries range from $16,500 to $28,000, several thousand dollars above what they were a few years ago, according to the Association of MBA Executives' 1978–79 salary survey.

An MBA can be especially important to an aspiring manager if she is young and a business-world novice. Deborah Thomas, 23, who has a BA in economics and a 1979 MBA from Northwestern University, explained: "I've heard that an MBA represents ten years of experience in two years—it's true. An MBA gives you new ways of analyzing and solving problems, and that largely makes up for your lack of experience." Upon graduation, Thomas expected to move directly into a management-trainee position in a bank, at a minimum of $21,000 a year, and within five years, to move into management and make $40,000.

"In the most basic sense, an MBA means credibility," said Lawton Wehle Fitt, 25, a Brown University (European history) graduate who received her MBA from the University of Virginia in 1979 and who plans to go into product management or management consulting at a minimum salary of $23,000 a year. "Men still look across the board room with a 'What is she doing here?' expression on their faces. A woman with an MBA is able to say, 'I'm committed to my career. I'm serious. I wouldn't have worked this hard, kept myself out of the salary-paying job and accumulated massive debts [the cost of an MBA varies from $800 at a state university to $20,000 at a private one] if I wasn't serious.' "

For other women, the MBA provides a chance to sharpen already acquired skills and to move higher and faster in the fields that employ them than they could through standard promotions. One example is Susan Klieman, 33, a New York University BA and 1979 New York University MBA. A former senior assistant buyer for New York's Bonwit Teller department store, she wanted to advance quickly, "to be president of a company." So, a few years ago, she began her own recruiting campaign: "interviewing personnel people, vice-presidents, anyone who would talk to me, and asking them, 'What would I need to do to sit in your chair? " Nine out of ten said get an MBA. So she applied to business schools.

Now, the results are a "200 percent leap in self-confidence, an integrated way of solving problems and a sense of the realities of the business world." Klieman expected, prior to graduation, because of the degree and her exerience, to start at a salary around $25,000 and to skip stages in the eventual company's hierarchy easily.

Still other women who have found themselves dead-ended or restless in one field are using the MBA to switch—at a respectable level—to another.

Lennie Copeland, 33, a psychology BA at Vassar and social-service planning MA at Boston University and a Stanford University 1979 MBA, is an example of this. She had worked for ten years in social service before deciding that what she really wanted was "a challenge in the man's world of business" and to combine two loves: movies and marketing. She went to Stanford to gain the skills she needed. Copeland works as the director of planning and development for the Ocean Trust Foundation, a nonprofit organization devoted to scientific research in underwater film making.

Of course, hopes and expectations among recent graduates naturally run high. But they aren't altogether unrealistic; many earlier MBAs have done very well for themselves.

Donna Ecton, for example, 31 years old and, like Thomas, an economics BA (Wellesley) who went directly to business school (Harvard, class of 1971) and then to work as a management trainee in a bank (Chemical Bank in New York), has found the route upward relatively smooth. She was told she would be made a vice-president ("if I did a super job") in five years' time. "But I was made a vice-president in four," she said. She also was told that she'd be managing a district of banks within seven or eight years; "it took four and a half." Her salary, although by choice undisclosed, has increased to over four times her starting salary within six and a half years. Now a vice-president and area director for Citibank, she supervises 350 people within a group of major midtown New York branches. She expects eventually to run a company, either her own or a New York bank.

Vivienne Vare-Armonas, 27, a New York University financial BS and 1975 MBA, has had a similarly effortless route. "It was very easy for qualified women to get in" when she joined CBS, Inc., as a marketing analyst after graduation and "to move up." She became a marketing specialist (responsible for analyzing national advertising campaigns for companies) one year later and the director of national marketing services last year.

Marian Adams, 30, a psychology BA from Northwestern and a 1973 Stanford MBA, also has progressed upward easily. "I went after my MBA during the recessionary period in the winter of 1970. Job mobility, at that time, was limited for persons with my undergraduate major and lack of other job experience." After graduation, she entered Blyth Eastman Dillon & Company, Inc., an investment banking firm as an associate, planning municipal bond issues. She became an assistant vice-president one year later.

In a more unusual case, but by no means a rare one, Maryellie Moore, a Stanford business BA and 1976 MBA, has advanced apace. Twenty years ago, she dropped out of Radcliffe College to get married and raise five children; she was 40 by the time she got her MBA—a good ten years older than most of her classmates. But right after graduation she joined the Matson Navigation Company, a shipping firm with over $200 million in revenues; two years later the company appointed her treasurer. "It was due in large part to the MBA," she claimed.

In addition to their MBAs, Moore, Copeland and other women who succeed in business usually have special talents and skills that propel them: They are bright and focused and naturally proficient managers. Moore and Ecton entered the work force at a time when affirmative action was beginning to have a powerful effect on hiring and advancement policies and the company rosters were not yet clogged with MBAs.

In the last few years, the number of women MBAs has swelled: 4,974 women earned MBAs in 1976 (ten times the number of ten years previous), 6,681 a year later and an estimated 10,000 in 1979. Between 1971 and 1976, the enrollment of women in business schools tripled; and in the more than 535 graduate business schools around the country today, an estimated 20 to 35 percent of all MBA candidates are women.

Today, experts agree, women have to be even more focused on themselves and their goals. One reason is that as the number of

MBAs has increased in recent years, so have specialties within the degree and expectations and misconceptions about it. It is now possible—and in many schools compulsory—to concentrate in specialized subjects: accounting, management consulting, financial consulting and marketing, for example. It is also possible to specialize within the problems of an *industry.* Because of this, and because a new mystique has sprung up around the degree, "Some companies, mostly small ones, expect MBAs to be *wunderkinds,* to come in and solve all problems instantly," said Deverell-Van Meter. "Some students think that an MBA is the equivalent of the divine right of kings," said one corporate recruiter—"that it gives everyone who holds it license to take over the show within two years' time." This has *not* been the experience of a great number of recent graduates, in spite of the startling successes of many. To set the record straight, here are some of the possible limitations on the overall value of the MBA degree.

An MBA Does Not Guarantee a Job

In most cases, an MBA *is* a big help in getting a job. Industries traditionally indifferent to MBAs (such as public relations, advertising, travel) now are hiring MBAs, often in order to facilitate contact with clients who themselves are MBAs. And industries that always were interested—banks, accounting firms, manufacturers and government agencies— are currently even more so. According to Motyka, these industries are becoming ever more sophisticated in their financial and management policies, and they want to hire employees who have finely honed business skills.

Not surprisingly, graduates from the very top schools (especially Stanford and Harvard, the top two according to *MBA* magazine) are practically guaranteed several job offers and high starting salaries. But for graduates of schools in the middle and lower range, job placement is less assured. Here, a candidate's personal characteristics take on much greater importance to potential employers. Among these characteristics is initiative. "Our graduates go to the top companies in the country," said Edward Beckett, director of placement for Ohio University, a middle school on the *MBA* magazine list; but in some cases, students pursued those companies—researching their products, requesting interviews, following up—rather than the other way around. "Companies do respond well to motivation and enthusiasm," Beckett said.

On the other hand, New York University's dean of the Office of Career Development, Fred Siegel, has found that "although we have a 99 percent placement rate, there are a few people who, no matter how good their grades, are impossible to place. These few have the personality of a stuck zipper. They don't know how to dress, can't interview and can't present a credible business image." Others, and this is especially important, seemed unfocused and uncertain in a highly focused world, where a sense of direction is crucial.

"They may have looked at the degree as just another stripe to pick up," said Mike Miles, assistant professor at the University of North Carolina Business School. "They don't really know why they are there or what they want from it," except, perhaps, a job when they graduate. If they specialize in the wrong area and can't project confidence, they may find it difficult to get one.

Sometimes the very way in which you regard your MBA can work against you. "Employers resent a certain arrogance we've been seeing lately," explained Antoinette Leonard, personnel manager of Ted Bates and Company, a New York advertising firm, which screened hundreds of applicants last year for positions that were filled equally with BAs and MBAs. The rationale: "If we see an exceptional MBA, there's no question; but if we're comparing an average MBA who expects the job and an exceptional BA who can be trained and has enthusiasm, we probably will hire the BA. With a salary difference—it doesn't make sense to do otherwise."

Another obstacle to hiring might be age or life situation. "It's unfortunate," said a placement official from a large Northeast university, "but if a woman takes time off to raise her family and goes back to school in her 40s, she may have experience, yes, but the company hires an MBA as an investment and expects a return from it in both effort and years. With an older woman, they know they can lop off ten to 15 years from her work life, which they don't like to have to do." A smaller company may be the solution in that case; a major company with intense competition for jobs would be out of the question.

An MBA Does Not Guarantee Job and Field Satisfaction

"There is absolutely no way of knowing before hand what it's like out there," explained Nina Mosely, 33, a 1973 Stanford MBA, who went from a trainee spot in international banking to account management at an advertising agency in just over five years. "You do get a sense of the rigors of the business world in school—the hours, the workload, the pressures they put you through—but not necessarily of the nature of the field you choose. In fact, you may hate it."

Even graduates of the venerable Harvard Business School make mistakes, according to Roderic C. Hodgins, former director of the Office of Career Development there. "Some may have heavy debts to repay," he said, "and so they grab the top dollar in glamorous industries that are buying a lot of MBAs. But they may be disappointed." The reason, according to *MBA* magazine's Deverell-Van Meter, is largely the result of heightened expectations: "Harvard trains its people to be chief executive officers of Fortune 500 companies," she said. "They think they're on a fast track, but there are only so many of those jobs around. It's no accident that there are so many Harvard MBAs driving cabs."

An MBA Does Not Guarantee Future Promotions

Lillian Lincoln, 39, a Howard University BA and Harvard MBA, class of 1969, is now president of Centenial One in Crofton, Maryland, her own company dealing in custodial services (with sales of $2.5 million a year). She well remembers being passed over for a promotion in her first job, even though she was obviously the next in line. Harvard MBA notwithstanding, "They never even considered me," she recalled. "Instead, the company decided to ship in a man from another one of our offices."

Admittedly, that was nearly ten years ago; but for Harvard's more recent MBAs, the situation, surprisingly, has not improved very much. In a study conducted by Harvard Assistant Professor Anne Harlan, it was found that among men and women who had been out of Harvard and into the business world for a period of from one to five years, the men earned an average of $6,000 to $12,000 a year more than the women did and were twice as likely to reach upper-level management positions within that time. Moreover, in a separate study of the class of 1973 (the first class in which women were enrolled in significant numbers), men and women were found to start work at the same salary levels; but after three years, the men's salaries had zoomed and the women's had not. Of the handful of 1973 graduates earning more that $36,000, every one was male.

Harvard MBAs are far from being alone in this. "There is less and less incidence of access discrimination," said Deverell-Van Meter, "but women just don't seem to be promoted at a rate comparable with men." This is borne out by *MBA* magazine's 1978 salary survey, in which younger female managers (under 26) were shown to earn $1,000 more than men at the very beginning of their careers but were left in the dust years later. "I think it has a great deal to do with the lack of mentors," said Deverell-Van Meter. "The women who could encourage and train other women are still largely in middle management themselves." Another reason is lingering discrimination: Some men still choke, said Motyka, on the thought of a $30,000-plus salary for a woman.

Future Worth

With an average of 30 business schools opening each year to accommodate students' demands, experts in the field fear that the "1983 glut" of MBAs predicted two years ago by Laurance Fouraker, dean of Harvard Business School, may in fact come sooner—supply simply will outpace demand. And when it does, according to New York University's Siegel, there will be two results: "Companies still will recruit, but they'll go to fewer schools—only the top ones. Degrees from those schools will take on more value, whereas the MBA, on the whole, will take on less. It will become what the bachelor's de-gree became several years ago—a requirement, not a credential." Even—affirmative action notwithstanding—for women.

How, then, to guard against the coming glut? Specialization within the MBA and/or an unusual combination of degrees, say the experts, will be the key. Engineering BAs combined with MBAs will open doors for women with manufacturers, according to Ohio University's Beckett, Deverell-Van Meter noted the potential of combining graduate degrees, such as business and law.

The best prospects still are for women who are focused, clear and present a good image of themselves.

IS IT TIME TO QUIT YOUR JOB?
This Quiz Will Help You Decide

by Mary Coeli Meyer

Try this on for size. It's possible that your low resistance to colds and flu is caused, not by the "bug," but by an organizational germ called DEMOTIVATION. Affecting both men and women, it accounts for that blah, headachy feeling, lowered productivity and errors . . . not to mention a "why bother" attitude. To date, most companies are focusing on "how to motivate" people rather than using the motivation an employee comes with. That being the case, the employee—you—has the responsibility to diagnose her own situation and take corrective action.

To acquaint you with the symptoms of demotivation, a questionnaire has been provided. When answering, consider the last two or three weeks *only,* and respond to each question as honestly as possible.

If you scored fewer than 15 points in each of the six categories, take an aspirin for your headache and read no further. You're feeling fine about your job and you're free, at least, of any organizational germ. If, on the other hand, you scored 15 points or more in any of the six groups, pills and bed rest won't help. For a cure to what ails you, you'll need stronger medicine.

There are six phases to the demotivation process. Every person who ends up at Departure has passed through the preceding five phases. She may pause for a while when organizational feedback becomes positive, but if it returns to negative, she will reenter the process at the same, or at an earlier, phase.

Confusion

When a person is confused, she is really saying, "What the hell is going on around here? I thought I understood what was required, but apparently my hearing is on the fritz. I can't seem to get my act together!" Generally, this reaction results from mixed messages generated either from the company, the supervisor or the employee herself. What is being said or done is not in line with what the person wants to perceive, and thus, the message is confused. For example: "Sure I like female employees, but you and I both know some have shortcomings." That could mean at least two different things depending upon what you were listening for: 1) This particular individual has a hang-up about all women; 2) In general, he likes female employees but some of the ones he's encountered have had shortcomings.

Confusion is not limited to messages alone; actions also can confuse. When we experience confusion, we seek to clarify the information and get reassurance that we're hearing correctly. To do this, we take time away from work to talk with persons "in-the-know," which means, of course, that our productivity goes down. The less productive we are, the more stressful we feel. When neither we nor the suprvisor takes correc-

---

DEMOTIVATION QUESTIONNAIRE

		never	rarely	sometimes	often	always
1.	How often do you seek reassurance or ask questions regarding your work?	1	2	3	4	5
2.	Do you find your disposition friendly one moment and angry the next?	1	2	3	4	5
3.	Are you defensive when the boss gives you feedback?	1	2	3	4	5
4.	Do you chat with other employees on office time more often than would be considered satisfactory?	1	2	3	4	5
5.	Do you find fault with the department or the organization?	1	2	3	4	5
6.	Are you cynical and sarcastic in your interactions?	1	2	3	4	5
7.	Are you exhibiting nervous behavior?	1	2	3	4	5
8.	Do you fluctuate between openness and introspection?	1	2	3	4	5
9.	Are you withholding important information from the boss until the last minute?	1	2	3	4	5
10.	Are you involved with departmental "politics"?	1	2	3	4	5
11.	Do you openly show dislike for the boss or the boss's practices?	1	2	3	4	5
12.	Do you avoid socializing with co-workers?	1	2	3	4	5
13.	Do you spend a lot of time working out your role and responsibilities?	1	2	3	4	5
14.	Are you a workaholic?	1	2	3	4	5
15.	Does your response to the supervisor vary to the point that it could be understood as a mixed message?	1	2	3	4	5
16.	Are you spending less time in your work area?	1	2	3	4	5
17.	Are you disregarding office rules and procedures?	1	2	3	4	5
18.	Are you indifferent about your work and the company?	1	2	3	4	5
19.	Do you feel you're losing self-confidence?	1	2	3	4	5
20.	How often do you "turn off" the boss when you are being given instructions?	1	2	3	4	5
21.	How often do you pretend not to understand directions?	1	2	3	4	5
22.	Have you been seeking information on company policy and rules?	1	2	3	4	5
23.	How often do you express your discontentment to the boss?	1	2	3	4	5
24.	How often are you unresponsive to the influence of the supervisor?	1	2	3	4	5
25.	Are you hesitant to take on new responsibilities and assignments?	1	2	3	4	5
26.	How often do you chose to work alone?	1	2	3	4	5
27.	To what extent are you getting along with everyone but the supervisor?	1	2	3	4	5

DEMOTIVATION QUESTIONNAIRE

		never	rarely	sometimes	often	always
28.	Have you ever thought about or asked for a transfer or new assignment at work?	1	2	3	4	5
29.	Have you verbally or silently said, "It's not my job!"	1	2	3	4	5
30.	Are you apathetic toward work?	1	2	3	4	5

ANSWER KEY

Instructions: Each stage has been assigned five questions. Enter the number you circled on the questionnaire in the space opposite the question. Then add up the numbers in each of the six categories.

Confusion	**Anger**	**Subconscious Hope**
1_____	2_____	3_____
7_____	8_____	9_____
13_____	14_____	15_____
19_____	20_____	21_____
25_____	26_____	27_____
Total_____	Total_____	Total_____

Disillusionment	**Uncooperativeness**	**Departure**
4_____	5_____	6_____
10_____	11_____	12_____
16_____	17_____	18_____
22_____	23_____	24_____
28_____	29_____	30_____
Total_____	Total_____	Total_____

Circle the total that is largest. That is where you are now. Check to see if the next largest number is before or after the circled number. If it is before, you are just moving into the phase circled. If it is after, you are in an advanced stage of the circled number.

tive action, the demotivation process begins. We assume the confusion is our fault. We are so ready to accept blame that often we don't seek a solution. One thing leads to another, and our dissatisfaction continues to grow.

How do you get rid of confusion? At the first sign of it, you must arrange to talk privately with the supervisor. You should choose a casual environment for the conversation, perhaps over coffee. It makes no difference if you are a vice-president or a file clerk, the person who has the answer is the boss. She has half the information, while you have the other half. For example: Last week, your boss decided there would be a staff meeting the following Thursday and assigned you to take care of the arrangements and coordinate the agenda. As you are informing Annette of the meeting, she tells you she already knows about it but, "Thanks anyway." "That's funny," you think, "I was supposed to pull this meeting together. . . ."

This is the type of situation that causes

confusion, and it is precisely because it seems insignificant that corrective action isn't taken. Only when such incidents accumulate do we recognize that we have had enough.

At your informal meeting with the boss, don't take the offensive; you're simply trying to sort things out. You might broach the subject this way: "You know, Martha, in the past two weeks I've felt terribly confused. I thought I was supposed to arrange the meeting for Thursday, but someone was helping me. Then, at the Tuesday meeting, when I was prepared to make the financial presentation for our new 'Z' product, Harold stood up and made it. These are only two examples, but I can't seem to see *the source* of the confusion. Do you have any ideas?"

Having calmly thought the situation through prior to the meeting, presented it rationally and solicited assistance, you can reasonably expect Martha either to explain her part in the situation or to offer to help in clarifying the irregularities. At that point, plans for new action and communication can be negotiated, and the demotivation process is nipped in the bud.

Anger

If you have progressed beyond the confusion stage, you are probably angry at yourself for not having controlled the situation better. Suppose you have taken the initiative in your job, worked extra hard to accomplish your goals but now find yourself feeling like a stressful workaholic. You haven't time for your family anymore; people, generally, get in your way; you are coming early to the office and leaving late and you can't depend on your disposition—one moment you're friendly, the next moment, abrupt. You may fear your feelings are those of the proverbial "emotional female" but even if true, they are also accurately reporting the reality of the situation. It seems that the entire socialization of women has been directed toward promoting the correctness of everyone but ourselves. Rationally, we know that assumption can't always be true, yet we are inclined to go along passively accepting our role.

Before inflicting more anger on yourself, take an objective look at what's happening. First of all, working like a maniac probably isn't going to get you the recognition you think it will. Secondly, your erratic behavior gains you no empathy from other people. Therefore, the pain you're suffering is useless; it offers no redeeming rewards. Your first action is to understand that you can gain control over the situation; are not cornered. Perhaps you have been upstaged inadvertantly, perhaps on purpose. Confront the possibilities calmly. The important thing is *to assume responsibility* for your own feelings. You have the problem and the problem is that you are angry. Why? Because you can't seem to get control of your environment.

Schedule a formal appointment with the supervisor to express your viewpoint and solicit assistance. Don't expect any easy solutions. Instead, listen carefully to what is being offered. If it's insufficient, make some decisions as to what your future in the job is likely to be and what you want to do about it.

Subconscious Hope

If you have moved on to the subconscious hope phase, your anger from Phase 2, which was self-directed, has now shifted toward the supervisor. You have expected her to notice your distress and perhaps ask, "What's bothering you? You haven't been yourself lately. Is there something I can help you with?" but that did not occur. Now you're mad at the boss for being so insensitive.

You are probably avoiding her whenever possible and focusing instead on repairing the weaknesses of the department you work in. Your productivity is no longer at a workaholic pace, but you, nonetheless, take work home with you. Inside, you feel like Vesuvius about to erupt but you don't let it show on the job. You take your stress home, too, and brood all night about your job problems. You can't seem to get them off your mind, even while watching TV, reading a book or playing chess. Friends think you're obsessed with work and you have become a bore to yourself.

To understand how one arrives at Phase 3, consider what we do when we enter the work force. We expect that we will do our job and the company will appreciate us. Those expectations are part of a psychological contract that develops from the moment of the interview, through the orientation process and into the actual job. Everyone has psychological contracts, and frequently they include many unspoken expectations. The company has its expectations and so does the boss. Thus, there are at least three of you with information no one else has.

The company says: "We offer growth, support, an excellent benefits package and, furthermore, this organization cares about its employees! We are looking for someone who can make decisions, rise to challenges, use her mind and solve problems creatively." You hear that and say to yourself, "Boy! That's me. I work hard, I'm creative, well-educated and I do like challenges. If you offer me the right salary, I'm yours!" All that was up front, but what about the unspoken dialogue that takes place?

The interviewer, who respresents the company, is saying to herself, "This person fits the job. She seems stable, knows the business and won't make waves." In your mind, the paneled office, the significant raises, the staff of 20 working under you come into view. The problems you are now encountering can be traced directly to that initial communications gap. At this point, you feel your efforts to achieve are being frustrated, thereby diminishing the possibility of your moving up in the company. You may feel like saying: "Look, Boss, this job was supposed to be challenging, but it is so political I can't even make a decision without playing games with the in-group. And it seems you don't really want me to be decisive. You ask for written feedback but you weigh more heavily the input from one phone call from an in-group member than you do the 50 answers on the feedback form. If only you would let me do my thing, I could work wonders for you."

What's needed is the establishment of a new, valid psychological contract with the boss, the department and the organization that will allow you to contribute to your full capacity.

First, you must think back and recall exactly what was offered to you at the job interview. What did the interviewer say? What did your supervisor say? What did you say? And what things did you think at the time? List these in separate columns so that you can identify the disparity, not only in the information the company provided, but also, in your own expectations.

You may find that you did not ask enough questions, or the right questions. This should be discussed with the supervisor—that your expectations were not addressed in the interview because of your failure to articulate them. If there is a disparity between what was actually offered and what is now occurring, this needs to be discussed as well.

Remember, during this phase, you are really hoping the situation can be clarified without further anxiety to you. Thus, when you make your appointment with the boss, bring your fact sheet with you, but leave the emotional contents at home. This is the time to discuss business. The way to the top is by producing profits for the organization, and that is where you should focus your attention. You need to point out subtly to the supervisor that if she helps you to help her, she will appear more successful. Your best chance to convince her of that is to communicate with her as openly and honestly as possible. What you're seeking is a solution—not redress from all the "wrongs" you've been dealt. You should arrange a formal meeting with a planned agenda of which the boss has been informed ahead of time.

Disillusionment

"Why bother, it won't make any difference anyhow because no one really gives a damn whether I succeed or not. Everyone is interested only in protecting her own skin, making a fast buck and doing as little as possible!" This could be you in Phase 4. You have probably considered three options already: 1) a transfer; 2) giving in to the system and producing the minimum required to keep your job; or 3) quitting. About this time, you are starting to check out the feelings of other employees to make sure "it isn't you alone" who is suffering the injustices of the system.

To your colleagues, you probably don't identify who is causing you difficulty and you soft-pedal the specifics of your troubles. You are avoiding the supervisor because she causes you pain; seeing her reminds you of what you are capable of, what you were dreaming of and what died for want of use. Your productivity is down.

If you are a highly active, self-confident person, with a clearly defined set of values, you have written your résumé. If you are not quite so brave, you are probably checking out transfer possibilities within the organization. You might also be fighting an internal war about whether you are able to sit down and shut up without suffering personal anguish. You really don't want to stay, but you may feel either that you've already invested too much time in this organization to leave now or that change is too spooky to confront.

Those who have written their résumés are helping themselves toward a solution. Those lacking self-confidence need to understand that no matter what you want, it requires effort. Everyone else feels the same way you do. Whether we appear confident or not, none of us likes to change jobs, nor do we like settling for contributing less than we can. That knowledge may not inspire your confidence, but consider what will happen if you *don't* take action: Your life and your dreams will be blown out the window, and you will be the one who chose to let it happen. Consider that a week from now, the situation will undoubtedly be unchanged, and there are still two more phases of demotivation to go.

The feeling that you have right now is not pleasant, so why continue to endure it? There is a wonderful freshness to assuming command of your life. And if you look at it as an adventure in exploring yourself and your abilities, the scariness of change subsides. Consider the time you spend looking for an apartment, buying a car or planning a vacation. Is your own well-being worth less? No? Then why not invest in yourself? Take the bull by the horns, see the supervisor and tell her what is on your mind. Tell her you're disillusioned and why.

Remember, it is you who are disillusioned, you who have the problem, so don't project it onto her; ask only for her insights and assistance. If assistance is not forthcoming, consider your next alternative. You can seek further help by discussing your problem with personnel or you can request a transfer. If those alternatives don't seem reasonable, you can write your résumé and start looking for a job. Be decisive. If you have trouble being decisive, just ask, "What's the worst thing that could happen?" If the answer is getting fired, then continue to play the organizational game while looking for new work. If unemployment isn't a financial burden, then take the responsibility for yourself and openly confront your situation.

Uncooperativeness

"That's not my job!" Are you thinking or saying it? If you're in Phase 5, you're experiencing that feeling. It is the only way you know to protect your dignity, assert yourself and feel like a person who still has some control. To demonstrate your attitude, you arrive at work on the dot of 9:00 AM (or slightly later to assert yourself) and you leave on the dot of 5:00 PM. Talking with colleagues takes a new twist now. When they agree with you that "Thelma" is the one who has a problem, not you, that they have experienced the same thing, you are reassured. Their agreement satisfies your need to belong, if not to the organizational team, then at least to the malcontents group.

(If everyone in the department agrees that Thelma has a problem, then probably she does. It's an organizational problem that can generate widespread discontent, lowered productivity, higher costs, grievances, turnover, absenteeism, etc.)

Meanwhile, you are not about to do anything that wasn't "psychologically contracted" when you took this job. "It doesn't make any difference, anyhow." CAREFUL! These negative actions *can* make a difference. You may not get the raise you'd anticipated, or the promotion. Too, you just might get fired and although that doesn't happen too frequently, for the same reasons that demotivation isn't resolved, you could be caught by surprise. If you're going to be fired, it's much better to make the boss dream up a reason for it.

If the supervisor hasn't responded to you by now and she is aware of your dissatisfaction, the time has come to pack your bags and leave. You have only one other choice: to stay and become the deadwood of the organization. Taking that alternative benefits neither you nor the organization. Disregarding the organization's welfare, why should *you* sacrifice yourself and your abilities for the remainder of your working years? If you are doing the "Deadwood Drudge," that is,

showing up for work, doing what is necessary, collecting your paycheck and going home, you are wasting eight precious hours each day of your life, doing someting that doesn't satisfy you. Think about that.

If, by chance, you have a new supervisor, you can use the same approach to solving your problem as you did in Phase 4. But be sure to be very clear about what is your responsibility, what is her responsibility, what is the organization's responsibility? If these can be determined, then periodically follow up with the supervisor to assure continued communication and clarity.

Departure

At this stage, you have either physically or mentally retired from the organization. Those who have done so know it. For those of you who haven't yet but are curious, it means that your colleagues didn't agree with you in Phase 5 and don't share your dissatisfactions. Feeling alone, you mingle with only those longtime friends who have joined you in the "giving up." You drag through the day and go home at night. The rut has become so deep you are buried in it.

You have chosen to live this way, but you can un-choose it. You have the opportunity to leave the organization, and if you have elected not to, don't complain. It can't be all that bad or you would have done something about it. Still, it's never too late to make a plan, write your résumé and start afresh on a new adventure to reestablish your abilities, earning power and self-confidence. Whatever your choice—to stay, transfer or leave—remember, you made it.

Chapter Four

Office Politics

OFFICE POLITICS: RUNNING A CLEAN CAMPAIGN

by Victoria Pellegrino

It was an ineradicable gaff, a mistake with consequences. A naive move had escalated to war: enemies were made, humiliation endured, trust shaken. And all because of a memo.

The cause of the memo was simple enough. Several years ago, when I was running a department in a large corporation, I believed I wasn't receiving the cooperation I needed from our company's publicity department. I wrote the company president a memo, complaining about the publicity department's lassitude.

To my astonishment, several days later I received a call from Al, the head of the publicity department, who said that *he* had been given my memo, and that he felt his department *was* doing a competent job, thank you.

The phone call concluded with a few pauses, some low moans, and a smattering of stutters. I was on Al's slow boat to China list from then on.

At the time, I was as sophisticated about office politics as a two-year-old. But live and learn. I was young . . . I grew older. Soon, I too had mastered the art (and it is an art) of office politics, learning enough to survive and even flourish. Today, in fact, embarked upon a new career I run career workshops and teach women the ins and outs of the business world.

Office politics: the unwitting, uninitiated woman must beware. She is a sitting duck for master gameplayers who roam through corporate offices looking for, well . . . sitting ducks. Knowledge of office politics is crucial for the woman who wants to advance, not to mention the woman who simply wants to keep breathing the same desk-space air year after year.

What exactly does office politics mean? It doesn't mean killing people so that you rise to the top, bruised but triumphant. It *can* mean the Machiavellian manipulations of others, but it can also simply mean good human relations. Most of all, knowledge of office politics implies an awareness that office life is different from personal life, that one doesn't operate on feelings alone, but also on strategy. When in doubt, study chess. An astute office politician recognizes that her relationships with people are as crucial to her success as her productivity and creativity.

For example, let's analyze my memo fiasco. Where had I gone wrong? Well, first I didn't calculate that my charming boss might show the memo to Al. (Always know your risks before you toss your dice.) Second, I trusted my boss not to show Al the memo. (An office is no place for blind trust—in anyone). Third, I incautiously put my true feelings in writing. (When in doubt, throw the memo out.) Four, by appealing for help, I demonstrated a lack of independence. (Fight your own battles.) Five, I was blunt about my feelings towards Al's department. (Undiluted honesty is not always the best office policy.) The result: I lost a potential ally and made an enemy instead. Not very political of me, for allies are as important in the business world as tipsters are in the gambling world.

I would have been a more astute gameplayer, and won a gold star rather than a slap on the wrist, if I had appealed to Al in terms of *his* interests, suggesting to him how helping me would actually help him. If his department was still intractable (which is doubtful, given the chance to do itself some good), I could always have enlisted my president's support in a more subtle way, by perhaps scheduling a planning meeting with the public relations department and then inviting my boss or one of his assistants to sit in.

Women are often more naive than men about office politics. (The main reasons: discrimination, social conditioning, lack of role models.) Women therefore sometimes bring a domestic set of values (honesty, openness, and trust) to the corporate world, and while there is a place for these qualities, reality dictates that they be tempered by business

ethics (competition, aggressiveness, productivity, winning). I have seen women get knifed in the back, lose out to inferior men, and be frustrated in dead-end positions because they didn't know how to put themselves forward, counteract prejudice, recognize the perfidy of others, and assess political situations.

However . . . our time has come! No longer business virgins, no longer living in a Jamesian world of innocents, we now realize that we must learn to hold our own. Let me tell you a few things I know.

First, make as many allies and contacts as you can, in your organization and in your field. Allies can tell you what's happening below the surface of things, who has a sister married to the chairman of the board, why your department is losing clout, when and where a better job beckons. If the people in your own department are reluctant to disclose the institutional gossip because they feel they are in competition with you, outside contacts become imperative. Everybody needs a Deep Throat.

Making allies can be more difficult for a woman, since her contact resources are more limited than a man's: men may take the commuter train home together, make deals over golf or drinks at an all-male athletic club. But clever women have learned to maneuver in other ways. Clara, a space saleswoman, says she gives extra attention to her clients' needs. "One of my clients' daughters likes stamps so I take an interest in stamps," she says. "He's delighted to have a woman account executive now, although he wasn't in the beginning, because he knows I'll work harder for him than any man since I'm out to prove myself. I have also learned to talk sports with the guys—believe me, this is a big help in business." Irene, a cash flow specialist, who is single and prefers to live in the city rather than in the suburbs, fights the commuter old-boy network by lavish entertaining. "I put time, thought, and money into my parties," she says. "Many executives have wives who do this, but I have to do it for myself. I make sure my parties are better than anyone else's." Charlotte, a stockbroker, says, "My boss gets to the office at eight-thirty, so that's when I'm there. Often we chat over coffee for a couple of minutes and that's an advantageous time for me to put in points for myself. If I don't do p.r. for me, nobody else will."

When making allies, the good manners you should have learned at your mother's knee are still appropos. For instance, try to remember people's names; as Dale Carnegie said, there is no sweeter sound in the English language than the sound of a person's own name. And treat people the way *you* would like to be treated—with courtesy, sympathy, and an understanding of their needs, problems, and aspirations. This genuine, positive kind of human contact is so important I can't emphasize it enough.

Sometimes, of course, more sophisticated strategy is called for, especially today when many women are facing a common problem—gaining entry into an all-male network. In such cases, the newcomer is likely to find herself facing male resentment, hostility, and even ostracism.

Why do some men behave this way and what can women do about it? Psychiatrist Carol Mann of the University of Pennsylvania and Hal Frank, assistant professor of group dynamics on psychiatry at Penn's School of Medicine, studied the lone woman working among a group of men and observed that, by and large, men tended to reject the lone woman's attempts to take an active role in the group. If the woman reacted with anger or emotion, they dismissed her either as a woman's liberation bitch or as a typically neurotic female.

The researchers found that the men behaved this way because the presence of a woman interferes with the mechanisms by which all-male groups usually function. ("The men lose their hunting group atmosphere and must mourn their loss.") The men have to deal with their hostility to women, the researchers went on to say, "but to ex-

press it openly would be taboo." Moreover, the men are afraid that the woman will act weak and demand that they take care of her, "violating the norm of independence and toughness." Or, the men fear that she will compete successfully with them, "violating the norm that women are seen as objects and thus threatening their masculinity." In addition, they say, the men fear the woman will "stir up sexual rivalry among them, disrupting their friendship and violating the norm that sexual feelings are taboo."

The researchers felt that only the ploy of "poor little me" seemed to work to allow the woman to gain entry. However, there's room for disagreement here. In my opinion, it would be far better for a woman to build alliances with a few individuals and to establish herself as a competent member of the team, than to play Victim. Compliant, helpless behavior doesn't win promotions.

Joan, a tax lawyer, found that her three male colleagues often lunched together and made business decisions at those lunches. Because Joan was a woman and a newcomer, the men were reluctant to have her along. "I felt like the wallflower at the high school prom," she told me. She finally solved her problem by inviting one of her colleagues (the most accessible one) to lunch. "I took him to the most expensive French restaurant I knew and fed him like a king," she says. "We broke the ice over that lunch." Joan's approach was the old one of divide and conquer.

Carol had to use a different tactic. She was the first woman hired in the computer department of a Wall Street firm. Her coworkers resented the fact that she had "taken away a man's job" and that she "didn't need to work" because she was married. Without their help, she wasn't learning her job and was afraid of being fired. So, without complaining about her co-workers, she asked her boss to appoint one man in the office to train her. She suggested that the three of them meet every so often to see how she was doing. Larry, who was appointed to teach her, had little choice but to help or look incompetent. Carol also told Larry, "You were chosen to teach me because you're the best." Flattery never hurts.

Joanne Tyhken, in a study she did for Public Communication Research, wanted to determine whether professional business-women elicited more positive responses from their male colleagues with aggressive messages than with non-aggressive ones. She had a female speaker deliver a message in a pleasant, non-aggressive undemanding manner; in the second instance, the speaker's manner was aggressive, forceful, and a bit pushy. The non-aggressive message used words like, "You should think about" and "You probably are" whereas the aggressive message said, "You must" and "You undoubtedly are." The results were that the aggressive message received a response ten times higher than the non-aggressive one in terms of readiness to act. The men rated the aggressive speaker ten times higher in competence and twenty times higher as far as her ability to hold attention.

This study makes it clear that women must assert themselves. Too often, women do not move actively enough in their own behalf. Yet one must. You cannot wait to be noticed, to be included, to be helped, to be respected.

In fact, the assertive strategic move is central to the concept of office politics. Take May. A systems analyst, she has made friends in other departments and tries to keep abreast of what's happening in her company. She had an instinct that the man she was working for was a "dead man"— that is, a man who wasn't going anywhere. When she heard that a department head in another section was going to be granted an exciting project, she decided to toss some dice. She knew her boss would be furious if she asked for a transfer, and she was rightly afraid of going over his head. Instead, she did some research on the new project, and found a few relevant books and articles. She

said, "I then wrote this department head a memo, and told him I'd heard of his new project and that I knew of some books and articles he might find helpful. Would he like to have a cup of coffee and talk? We had a nice chat and I gave him the information without asking for anything in return. I continued to show interest in the project. When the project was ready to begin, he asked me to work on it. I had made myself part of a winning team."

Here's another example. Ray, a TV production assistant, wanted to become a writer. Instead of simply asking for a transfer, which might have labeled her a discontented employee, she wrote a profile of her boss and the new series he was working on, and sold it to his hometown newspaper. Part of her piece was later picked up for the company newsletter. By doing this, Ray not only established herself as a writer (following another piece of good advice which is: Define your own identity and work on the level where you want to be), but also proved herself a loyal employee. When a writing job became available, a grateful and impressed boss advanced her.

Strategically, it also pays to be in the know about what the other person is up to. Rita, for instance, had "a fantastic job" working for a large corporation. She says, "I had opened up a job that didn't exist before and I was moving along. At this company, they have a unique system of supervisions and reports. Everyone is evaluated after six months, and then re-evaluated every year. You do the job description yourself and naturally try to make yourself look as good as possible. The form then goes to your supervisor, who writes an evaluation of the work you said you do. The form goes back to you. You can rebut your supervisor's evaluation if you don't think it's fair, but the rebuttal is then given back to your supervisor, so this may be a Catch-22 situation.

"I had received two glowing evaluations, but going into my second year, the head of the department felt, I think, that I was beginning to do too well and get too much attention. And so his attitude towards me changed radically.

"I was thrown by his hostility because I hadn't done anything. He made me report in writing whenever I was leaving the office, even though my job called for me to be out frequently. I began receiving a steady stream of memos which said things like, 'I am concerned that you have not complied with my latest request . . . and 'We spoke about your problem yesterday. . . .'

"I was being harassed to death. I didn't know what was going on. Finally, I told my immediate supervisor, who looked very wise and told me that the department head was compiling a dossier on me in order to get me out. 'That's what people do here,' he told me. 'But there is a way of dealing back. You have to answer his charges in writing. If you think you are being treated unfairly, moreover, you can write a dated memo to yourself and file a copy with a third party.' I did that right away—after all, if you can't stand the heat, get out of the kitchen. When this department head finally presented the powers that be with his dossier, I had a dossier of my own. I still could have been fired, but he'd tried to do this to people before and the big guns were out to get him. So they let him practically hang me before they cut my noose and hanged him instead."

Rita received good advice, acted in a clear-headed and systematic manner, and her story had a happy ending. Faye wasn't so lucky. When Jeb became the president of a multi-million-dollar book company, he brought Faye with him. She was a young, aggressive, fantastically hard-working woman with whom he'd worked in his last position. He made her the executive editor, even though she'd previously only been an associate editor. She was a tough woman who would work twenty-four hours a day if she had to. However, he hired Joe to be his editor-in-chief.

The war between Faye and Joe raged eloquently. Jeb would tell Joe, "You're the editor. You make the decisions around here." He would then tell Faye, "Joe's an ass. Just do what you want to do. You don't have to clear things with him." The favorite quote around the office was that "Jeb had given Faye the keys to the kingdom of heaven, but then changed the lock."

Finally, "made crazy" by the situation, Faye went over Jeb's head to the head of the conglomerate and threatened to leave for another position if she weren't made editor. The result was predictable. The conglomerate head notified Jeb, and Faye was forced out faster than you can say Mary Hartman.

The moral of this sad tail: don't go over your boss's head. (Or, to thine own boss be true.) It's one thing to "get noticed" by your boss's supervisors. It's quite another to bite the hand that feeds you.

Another point: work at building up a rapport with your boss—not only is it simple, good human relations, it really pays off in terms of your job. Lila, for example, who was in one of my career workshops, was both furious and puzzled when Harry secured the product manager promotion: she believed she was better qualified. However, Harry ran an occasional errand for Bill, their boss, boosted Bill's stock at company parties, and covered for Bill when his lunches stretched into late afternoon tête-à-têtes. Was Harry an ass kisser? Perhaps. He was also the new product manager.

Bosses, as a general rule, are human. They promote people who are loyal and enthusiastic, people on whom they can depend and with whom they feel comfortable. Lila's attitude that she wanted to be rewarded for her work and her work only was, unfortunately, a naive one.

An ally, moreover, can become a mentor, just as a mentor can be one's most ardent ally. Jane's colleagues thought she was foolish for doing much of her boss's work without receiving the credit. Yet when Carl moved up, he brought Jane up along with him. At the right time, Jane will have to sever the umbilical cord; for now, her relationship with Carl is in her best interests.

As a last word (need I point it out?), overt competition with a supervisor is not good politics. A competent supervisor will only respond to influence which is noncompetitive. If you come on as a rival (or are antagonistic) you may have to be crushed!

Another thing I've learned: it's important to attend key meetings and become part of the action. If you're not totally entitled to participate, you can either request to attend a meeting or convince someone who has been invited to take you along. Attempt to ascertain beforehand why a meeting has been called, where colleagues stand on the issues, and what your own agenda will be. Make sure that you talk up at a meeting. (At least ask an intelligent question—not speaking up at a meeting is like not dancing at a wedding.) And keep in mind that it's considered "bad form" to show anger or competitive behavior at meetings. While there may be myriad underground power moves taking place, the form calls for a show of cooperation. As Joseph Heller jokes in *Something Happened,* by far the best American novel ever written on office politics, "We are all on a cordial, first-name basis, especially with people we loathe." While this may seem two-faced, it's actually based on a sound principle: people who happen to inhabit the same turf from nine to five do not have to love each other, but they do have to swallow their feelings in order to get the work done. Then, after five o'clock, they can go home and kick their dogs.

What I've found to be most significant in office politics is this: if you don't like your script, change it yourself. There are few rescue squads in business, fewer knights in shining armor. In the office, you do have to be your own best friend. For example, Ginny, a secretary, complains that she and another woman do most of the work while Deborah, the office queen bee, flourishes like a hothouse plant under the admiring eyes of the law partners. Yet Ginny and her co-worker Nancy allow this situation to continue by their silent although resentful acquiescence to the unwritten rules in that office, to the status quo. For while they can't change Deborah, they can change their own behavior. Ginny feels abused and angry, yet she continues to type Deborah's work and answer three phones at once (if only she were an octopus!) while Deborah rummages through her drawers for paper clips, looks helpless, and gets the men coffee with a smile. Ginny's self-effacement, partly the result of her powerlessness in that office, is also the result of her own "good girl" upbringing. And only she can change her own script.

Women often relate to their co-workers in the same way they've related to family members. Sarah, for instance, became furious whenever Carla received a plum—a business trip, a prestigious assignment. Carla handled Sarah's envy and rage by withdrawing. She didn't demand much in the office, but was quiet and did her work. This is the same way she handled her elder sister's jealousy, by trying to fade into the woodwork so as not to arouse jealousy in the first place.

The kind of woman, like Carla, who withdraws from a fight, is more than likely a resigned woman who isn't able to "rock the boat" without becoming extremely anxious. In an office, she is crippled by her inability to fight and win. The self-effacing woman too, who is more typical in our culture, must always take a subordinate position to others, is compulsively humble, and needs a great deal of approval. She is not prone to risk-taking, or to taking an independent stand which may alienate others. Because of this, she too is inhibited in getting ahead. The compulsively domineering woman, on the other hand, who is competitive and aggressive, is more likely to succeed. She may alienate others, however, unless she shows some tolerance for other people's perhaps lesser abilities and can "get along." Getting along is mandatory. If your colleagues don't respect you and like to work with you, you are in trouble. Please note that I didn't say that your colleagues had to love you, but that they had to like working with you. There's a difference. Too many women worry too much about being "loved" in an office, and this interferes with their ability to give orders, compete effectively, reprimand when necessary.

To sum up some other important tips: Work like a demon. (As long as you're not in a dead-end job. If you are, get out.) Work harder than the men around you. Work harder than the women around you. Expand your allies and your base of operations. Don't turn the other cheek; use your wits and fight back. Lastly, plan where you want to go: You and nobody else have to be in charge of your career.

The final question: can you run a clean office politics campaign? Of course you can. As in a bridge game, you don't have to cheat someone to outsmart him. And you *can* be competitive without being ruthless. Politics is not a four-letter word.

THE MYTH OF FEMALE COMPETITION

by Norma Klein

My husband and I and some friends were having a drink together after the theatre one night. I don't remember how, but we got onto the subject of competition and envy and other such feelings that one often tends to shove under the carpet rather than discuss. I do recall that I announced that if my husband (who is a scientist) were to win the Nobel Prize, although it might not make me want to kill myself, I would feel definite and fierce negative feelings. My husband, who is used to my expressing such sentiments, looked nonplussed. The other couple were both amazed. "But you're a writer," they said. "Why should you feel so competitive toward someone not even in your own field? And your husband!" At that point the husband of this particular couple, who is a professor, announced that he would feel only pleasure if his wife won the Nobel Prize. And his wife said that not only would she feel similarly toward her husband, but she would feel pleasure if I or any of her close friends were so honored.

Probably I felt free to say what I did because I've been married thirteen years and feel secure enough about my love for my husband and my supportive feelings toward him to realize it would be judged in that perspective. Still, when you express a feeling which *you* take for granted, but everyone around you regards it as downright peculiar, it does make you a little uneasy. It started me thinking about some of the myths about competition that exist in our society at present, particularly competitive feelings of women.

One myth about female competition is that it has to exclude or stand opposed to friendly feelings. In the dictionary, competition is linked to rivalry, and the antithesis of rivalry is partnership. In short, it seems an anomaly to feel a sense of partnership, friendship, or love and still be competitive with someone. It's probably always been hard to see that seemingly opposed feelings can and usually do exist within the same breast toward the same individual. Yet we accept that one can love and hate, that toward the people to whom we feel closest these deepest of emotions are somehow intertwined.

Society has always made it harder for women to admit to having competitive feelings, to wanting to outdo someone, and until recently women were not thought to be naturally aggressive. When they expressed or experienced feelings of aggression, they were punished or felt guilty. This led to the kind of deviousness many of us displayed in our personal relations.

That sense of constraint, which many of us in our thirties or forties felt, is, if not completely vanishing, at least diminishing. But the fact remains that to admit one feels competitive, as a woman, still has a negative cast. I don't think a man who admits to feeling competitive thinks he is admitting to some deep, dark secret. He might even say it with a little bit of pride, implying that he wouldn't be as successful as he is, in sports or business or even with women, if he weren't competitive. For a woman to announce that she feels competitive toward men is to invite accusations of being castrating. Yet curiously there is no word with anything like the same overtones about a man who feels competitive toward a woman. Clearly as more women go into the various professions, more of us will be engaged in competition with men, whether we will handle this in precisely the same way men have traditionally handled it or not. And unless we can begin to handle and accept a sense of competition calmly, without a sense of guilt, we will surely be disadvantaged by others who can.

It used to be said that women's sense of competition was directed mainly toward the area women traditionally cared most about—catching a man. Women, so the theory went, could become ardent if competing for a man; society had decided that this was woman's given arena. From this theory arose the feeling that women couldn't be friends because in the back of their minds, from teen years on, would lurk the fear that their best friend might be after their boy friend or spouse. Then came the women's movement and suddenly articles began appearing right and left about how *now* women could be friends, could be supportive of one

another, didn't have to feel that getting a man was so all important that it need violate a friendship with another woman.

I have to admit that I personally was puzzled by all of this. I can't remember a single experience—at anytime—when I felt pitted against another woman in an effort to gain the attention or affection of a particular man. It always seemed to me that if a man decided to like or love you, it usually had very little to do with any conscious effort you made to gain this love, but rather with qualities of which you were probably unconscious. In short, I always felt a particular man was drawn to a particular woman rather than to the woman standing beside her, not because one of the two women made a greater effort to smile or talk or flirt, but because of some intrinsic, inexplicable chemistry.

I do agree, however, that for most people—men or women—competitive feelings are felt most keenly in the area which matters most to them. When I was a mother with preschool children and would go to the playground, I would find a ferocious sense of competition among the mothers sitting on the park benches. It would all be centered on the children—which child was doing what first, who was walking first, talking first, being toilet-trained first. But what this seemed to indicate was just that competitiveness can arise within any given arena. For women the arena previously has been more restricted to nonwork situations, and in these nonwork situations the competition tended to be only among other women. I'm sure if men and women had shared equally in responsibilities for preschool children, competition about areas such as who was walking first would have existed across sex lines. But since they didn't, women tended to feel competitive toward other women more often than they felt competitive toward men.

The other thing which has puzzled me about the new, movement emphasis on how women ought to be friends is the implication that somehow up until the 1970s they hadn't been. My own recollection was that from first grade on—even from nursery school on—little girls always sought each other out, always confided and talked openly together. I think women at any age tend to have several close women friends to whom they enjoy feeling they can confide anything. These friendships usually endure for decades, often through marriages, divorces, moves to other parts of the country. But what if, as in my own case and I believe in the case of many women, these same close friends happen to be in the same field? Will the ugly head of competition threaten the friendship? Certainly it's probably easier in some ways for a woman writer to be friendly with a woman lawyer, say, because their professional goals are different enough so that competition is harder to feel in any direct sense. And in fact, most of us have among our friends women who are successful but in areas where we don't feel personally threatened by that success.

In my own case I happen to have at least two close friends, writers like myself, who, during the course of our friendship, made huge sums of money and whose names became, in effect, household words in America. I remember when one of these friends called to tell me about a giant paperback sale for one of her books. Her voice was so low I could barely hear what she was saying. Between every breath came phrases like, "I don't see why they bid so much . . . a little book like this . . . they must be crazy." Of course, what she was really saying through all this was: "Please don't hate me, please still be my friend even though right at this moment you must feel like killing me." And I was! I *was* feeling like killing her, even though she had done nothing except had the good fortune to write a book which had done well financially. That was several years ago. We have stayed friends, we are just as close, and probably we are that much closer for having ridden through what was a difficult moment for both of us.

For some reason it's always much harder to understand why other people should feel competitive toward you than to understand why you feel competitive toward other people. If I sell paperback rights to a book for a large sum, some part of me, weirdly naive though this is, genuinely expects everyone, other writers included, to feel warmly toward me because of it and is genuinely amazed when they display precisely the same feelings of hostility and resentment that I would feel if the situation were reversed.

It's true one could avoid having friends in the same field and therefore only have friendships with women where such competitive feelings would not arise so easily. But I think most of us enjoy the special pleasure of having close friends in the same profession. As a writer, for instance, with whom else but another novelist could I spend an hour discussing the merits of the third person over the first person? Who else really cares as deeply whether the opening of a particular novel worked in a certain way? Without friends who are writers, I would miss that special pleasure I get when I read a novel by a friend and see certain traits of hers, certain opinions, certain habits appearing here and there so that the novel becomes almost like a letter, written just for me. Who else but a friend who is a writer will call you up and say, "Listen, let me read you this terrific review you got in *Publishers Weekly*" or will call long distance to pass on some nice comment that was overheard about one's work? I think we would all make life easier for each other if we realized that feelings of competition can and almost always do coexist with feelings of warmth, love, tenderness and all the other complex emotions that come under the word "friendship."

There was probably a natural but exaggerated idealism in the idea started by the women's movement that friendship among women was so precious that it was going to preclude competitive feelings. We were all, supposedly, going to love each other, admire each other, stand by each other through thick and thin. Then, when this proved unfeasible, there was a recoil: maybe friendship between women was impossible after all. I think it certainly is possible—not only possible, but crucial—but only if we define friendship more realistically. Most of us don't decide our feelings for our children are worthless if we feel angry at them for a day or a week. We don't give up on our husbands because we have a fight occasionally. Similarly, if at the same time we were feeling competitive toward a friend, we could stand back and say: "okay, but that's only part of the picture," we would prevent ourselves from overreacting to a momentary spasm of envy.

Not everyone is equally competitive. I don't think competition is a sex-linked trait. I think men have expressed it more openly than women, but not necessarily felt it more keenly. I have women friends and men friends who I genuinely feel are noncompetitive and I certainly think there are enormous gradations in the extent to which people—men *and* women—are prone to competitive feelings. In the case of my husband and myself, it's always been clear that I am by far the more competitive of the two of us. In fact, I find his relative lack of competitiveness one of his more appealing traits, incomprehensible as it sometimes appears to me.

Once we were in Copenhagen, where my husband was giving a talk at a scientific conference. While we were there, a younger colleague of his, five or ten years younger, won the Nobel Prize. His wife, who was also giving a talk at the conference, gave a party for him. At the party, watching my husband cheerfully chat with various people, I was mystified at his genial good mood. Finally, when we were alone together, I confronted him: "But don't you somewhere deep down feel suicidally depressed?" "Why should I?" he replied. "Out of wishing it was you and not him?" "But what does he have to do with me?" my husband answered. This was not the first occasion on which I had noted that my husband is singularly—and to me blessedly—unaffected by the success of other people in his field. And he is not the only such person I know.

Presumably there should be many writers with this attitude, since it is said that in the arts there *is* no such thing as direct competition. Give ten writers the very same theme to write about, and they will come up with ten different books. There is, at least in fiction, no such thing as being "scooped" by another writer. And yet it doesn't seem that writers are basically any less competitive than scientists, who are realistically in constant danger of being scooped by their colleagues.

Frankly, I would like to be less competitive. I don't feel it's an especially appealing trait, though I think I do accept it in myself with a certain equanimity. I'm sure it has something to do with being a firstborn child. I do think firstborn children fight throughout life to maintain the edge they had originally over their siblings and that this competitive feeling which starts so early never entirely dies out. I think growing up in a big city where there is a certain atmosphere of dog-eat-dog seems to make people more competitive. The least competitive people I've known have grown up in small towns where, perhaps, there was less to compete for, or at least the stakes were lower. I think people who grow up on the "wrong side of the tracks" also tend to be more competitive—men or women who know that only by dint of their own efforts will they manage to cross over into the comforts of another social class. Probably basically it's a matter of the old "Is life a ladder or a garden?" philosophy, which in most people seems to be intrinsic. If you're a competitive person, man or woman, you see it as a ladder and you start climbing early on and keep on climbing, or trying to. If you're not, you relax and lie down under the cork tree and smell the flowers, like Ferdinand the Bull in the children's story by Munro Leaf.

This option is one I think we need to preserve, even in an age which seems to be making competition into a cardinal virtue. It's possible that now that women are being encouraged to admit competitive feelings—which I take as a healthy phenomenon—there are some who will feel guilty about not being competitive *enough*. We go so quickly from regarding a trait as horrible and socially undesirable to hailing it as necessary and essential. Many mothers now are almost more eager for their little girls to grow up assertive, strong and competitive than they are for their sons to have these same traits. They feel they grew up not being allowed to act a certain way and want to make sure their daughters are not similarly hampered. All this is well and good, but it would be a pity if little girls felt that being competitive was a necessary component of success. Surely it is, but only in the broadest sense of trying to achieve the best of which one is personally capable, not in the narrow sense of there being only one slice of pie to go around for which dozens must grapple.

By accepting that friendship can contain competitive feelings, I don't think one is giving up on the ideal of women being supportive to one another, particularly in a work situation. Recently there was a note in the paper that Governor Ella Grasso of Connecticut was being accused by a woman's group of not having selected a sufficient number of women to fill various posts. I don't know if this allegation is true, but I do feel that it's been an unfortunate fact that when women do attain high positions, do manage to compete successfully with men as well as women and reach the top, they do not necessarily regard it as a primary goal to help the women around them rise, they do not always lend a helping hand to those on the way up. In the past this was because women who succeeded felt, often truthfully, that there was only room for one of them, the "token" woman, or that they, by making it, had proved themselves to be such an exception that any identification with other women

was unnecessary. More deeply, I think many women felt, and unfortunately still feel, that women as a group are less capable; therefore their own instincts moved them to exclude other women. Perhaps it was also simply more enjoyable to be the only woman at the top rather than one of several.

For whatever reason, I think one can understand these feelings, especially as they applied to earlier decades, yet appreciate the need to move beyond them. I am always pleased, for instance, when a woman writer who has "made it" makes a point of writing appreciative comments about a younger or less successful woman writer's work or writes a recommendation that will enable another woman writer to win a particular fellowship. All of us remember the older and more successful women who lent us this kind of helping hand when we were on the way up, whether it was a teacher, or a boss, or a fellow employee. Men traditionally got a certain psychological boost out of being supported emotionally by their mothers, who, deprived of the ability to compete professionally, lived vicariously through their sons. Fewer women got similar emotional support from their mothers, and therefore other female role models in their lives played an even greater role. I hope that women will recognize competitive feelings in themselves as being natural and healthy, but will not allow these feelings to grow into fear, the kind of fear that says: if *she* succeeds, I won't. It stands to reason that just as men have over the ages supported each other professionally because in the end it was in their interests to do so, women will form similar professional bonds.

One need not regard oneself as a feminist in any ideological sense to realize deep down that friendship is one of the better things life has to offer all of us. Maybe a few of us can make it by ourselves, but I believe the great majority of women will always need someone of their own sex to whom they can talk freely, with whom they can share laughter, tears, worries. If we can accept the competitive side of female friendship without letting it corrode the supportive,

warm, helping side, we'll all be better off and, most important, less alone.

ONE OF THE GANG . . . BUT NOT ONE OF THE BOYS

by Sheila Mary Eby

This is a great time for women to be in business, or so current opinion would have it. Corporations are beginning to hire and promote women to positions of real consequence. But what happens to women once they get those jobs? It is difficult to be the only woman—or one of the few—on a formerly all male executive staff?

What's it like to work with men who wonder whether you've earned your stripes legitimately or simply are a "token," hired to fill an affirmative-action quota? What's it like to be excluded from everyday office banter, from friendly lunches and informal meetings over drinks? To know that, despite all the *pro forma* rhetoric, management continues to place ceilings on your advancement?

"That's just the way the world is," said an oil-company executive, echoing the words of many other women. It's a crooked game, but it's the only game in town. And how well women play it is becoming a vital question, according to Syracuse University social psychologist Judith Long Laws, PhD, author of *The Psychology of Tokenism:* "If women are going to be allowed into the highest business ranks, they'll be accepted in a trickle."

How do companies feel about women entering traditionally male dominated areas? They want them to succeed, according to a leading search firm. Long-range business planners see executive women as good role models for younger women. (In 20 years, when the drop in the birth rate has an effect,

there won't be enough men to fill all the managerial positions.) "These women are not being hired for show," a spokeswoman for the search firm continued. "No one pays upward of $70,000 a year for window dressing."

To be sure, virtually all executive women take top-notch skills to their traditionally male posts. And many of the female recruits operate professionally with the utmost aplomb. But others encounter real problems. In *Men and Women of the Corporation*, Rosabeth Moss Kanter wrote of the experiences of management women in the upper strata of a company she called Indsco. "Their turnover and 'failure rate,' " she said, "were known to be much higher than those of men in entry and early-grade positions; in the sales function, women's turnover was twice that of men. What happened around Indsco women resembled other reports of the experiences of women in politics, law, medicine or management who have been the few among many men." The skewed proportion of women to men creates dynamics that can make it tough for women to succeed.

Facing the Limelight

First of all, management women stand out. Like the lone black among whites or the few foreigners among natives, their very scarcity singles them out. In a system where success is tied to becoming well known, this can be an advantage. "Whenever I spoke, all the men sat straight and listened," said the only female participant in a recent seminar in Las Vegas. "It makes me feel great to be the only woman in a room full of executives."

The unsolicited spotlight often can bring problems. "The men I work with were terribly attentive when I first started this job," said the only female merchandising executive at a major film company. "Their attitude seemed to be, 'I'll say yes to anything.' It took me a while to realize that they were just treating me like a daughter. What they really meant was, 'I won't do it, but I'll say yes.'"

"The men you work with may make a big fuss over you," said Laws. "They may like you a lot, but they don't like all of you, and because they can't see your professional skills, they shoot you down. Being singled out as the only girl-person initially makes many female executives feel special, but that feeling usually vanishes after the woman misses her first promotion."

Undue attention can make ordinary office competition more bitter. "One of the biggest problems I've had here is that I'm written up in a lot of professional journals," said the manager of stockholder relations of one of the nation's largest companies. "Editors like to run my picture, I think, for no reason other than that I'm an attractive blonde in an otherwise all-male field. My boss, who happens to be jealous of my education, gets resentful whenever this happens, and I feel the heat for days afterward. And if you want to know what else the corporate limelight brings," she added, "wait until you make your first big mistake."

In fact, veteran women executives groaned when the subject of attention arose. Men, they reported, were more curious about their personal lives and physical appearance than interested in the quality of the work. (Who hasn't heard a businessman evaluate a female co-worker in terms of the prettiness of her face, the seductiveness of her dress and the sweetness of her personality?) It's easy for management women to be noticed, these women said, but difficult to get their achievements recognized.

When scrutiny extends to personal business, everyday habits, styles of dress and supposed sexual activity, all become grist for the gossip mills. "A woman swore in an elevator in an Atlanta hotel while going to have drinks with colleagues," Kanter reported, "and it was known all over Chicago a few days later that she was a 'radical.'" Many women said that they regularly paused in the course of business conversations to deflect such questions as, "When are you going to get married and have a baby?" and "That's quite a pattern on your panty hose—does it go all the way up?" Since women saw these questions as undermining their authority, they soon tried to divulge as little as possible about their personal lives.

Isolation in High Places

Men, on the other hand, are reluctant to discuss *business* with their female counterparts. "My boss will always talk to my colleagues first and deal with me only when he can't avoid it," said an executive in the governmental-affairs department of a major US firm.

The consequences of this isolation can be great. Was the woman quoted above earning money on a par with men at her level? She didn't know. Being divorced from casual networks can hurt women in other ways, too. They miss the warnings, advice and training most men receive from their peers, and they miss feedback from higher management, too. "There were instances in which women trainees did not get direct criticism in time to improve their performance," Kanter stated in her book, "and did not know they were the subjects of criticism in the company until told to find jobs in other divisions. . . . (One man put quite simply how he felt about giving negative feedback to a woman: 'I'm chicken.')."

Men have set notions about how a woman should act and how an effective manager should behave," said Betty Lehan Harragan, author of *Games Mother Never Taught You*, "and they don't see the two stereotypes mixing. As far as a lot of men are concerned, executive women are just anomalies.

"A feeling that you can't trust these ambitious women prevails among men," Harragan continued, and she pointed out that some of their distrust is well grounded. "Lots of women are blind and deaf to unwritten business understandings," she said. They complain to their supervisors the minute they're crossed and get furious when bosses rightfully claim credit for their work. Sticklers for spelled-out rules, many women display arrogant conviction that they're above office politicks. "These women represent a real threat to men who are out to protect their jobs," the author continued, "and the men consequently don't want to go near them."

Of course, executive women signal another kind of threat, too: Lots of men think female advancement, mandated by law, wipes out their own chance for promotion. "When I first reached the sales department of my company," one woman said, "the feeling was basically, 'She's here, she's going to be promoted, but let's not make it easy for her.' " Other women have found men in their departments actively sabotaging their work, often in insultingly obvious ways. "For a couple of months after I started my last position," one woman said, "two of my subordinates—who had wanted my job—gave me reports that were incorrectly drawn up. They thought I'd pass the reports, errors and all, on to my boss." Plenty of other women went through the same kind of hazing. "It's always a struggle to make guys realize that you're not just a token," said an executive with a major utility company.

Will Talent Out?

Men who beef about affirmative-action recruiting argue that talent speaks for itself. Performance, they say, should be the sole criterion for advancement.

Many believe that if women and minorities produced good work, they wouldn't need the government to act in their behalf. But these assumptions rest on an image of the business community as a meritocracy—a place where people with the greatest skills reach top positions. Today, most people laugh at such a notion. Indeed, one of the greatest clichés of the work place is, "It's not what you know, but *who* you know, that counts."

Studies show that performance is evaluated in highly subjective ways. In a number of experiments, bosses were asked to evaluate projects that they'd been told women had produced. Later, they were asked to assess the same work—only this time they were told that men had executed it. Men judged the work attributed to men more favorably.

The men's performance typically is attributed to their skill, whereas the women's good work is written off to luck or dogged determination. "This is very important," said New York University psychologist Madeline Heilman, PhD, who conducted the experiment that resulted in this finding. "When people decide whom to promote, they go for the person with skills, not for the lucky person or the drudge."

In another study, Heilman found that attractive women are thought to be less suited to managerial roles than their plainer counterparts. "An attractive female apparently seems less decisive, less tough," said the researcher, who published her findings in a study called *When Beauty Is Beastly.* And Laws pointed to another stumbling block women may face: "A guy climbs up the corporate ladder under the mentorship of another man, who takes his protégé to lunches, meetings and trips out of town. The younger man thus becomes known as a promising young professional. But a woman in the same position gets a lot of raised eyebrows turned her way."

"Whenever you have to evaluate someone," Laws pointed out, "you put yourself out on a limb, and the tendency is to be conservative." Supervisors, therefore, give high ratings to workers who already enjoy everyone's esteem. Here, too, assessment is less than objective.

How far can affirmative action really take anyone? One woman said she felt absolutely dead-ended in her position. "I'd like another promotion, and I've told my boss so. But he just shrugs and tells me there's nothing he can do, unless I sue the company. There's just no precedent for promoting a woman to a position higher than the one I'm holding."

Another woman who blazed trails for her sex into management—now a vice-president at a major New York bank—feels pretty much the same way. Watching men younger and less experienced than herself being groomed for presidency, she feels that, be-cause she is a woman, she's gone as far as she can. To be sure, she said, the ceilings for women's corporate advancement have been raised—but they still exist.

Women executives aren't hired to fail (al-though many of their co-workers undoubt-edly wish they would). They do face prob-lems that make it harder for them to succeed—and harder for others to believe that their success is earned. But things are changing fast. After all, it is sheer num-bers—the proportion of men to women in the corporation—that set a lot of the prob-lems in motion. And as women study, scram-ble and sue their way to the top, they're turning those proportions around.

LOOK BEFORE YOU LEAP:

Some companies deal more fairly with women executives than do others. For the sake of your sanity—and your success—it's worth asking a few leading questions in the interview stage.

- Do women occupy good positions in at least a few departments? If so, have they been promoted? Or has there been a procession of females in and out of the company—or the position—you're considering?
- Do your prospective colleagues or superiors have wives or daughters who are committed to their careers? These men are apt to be easier to work with.
- Does your prospective boss seem to be a strong, self-confident supervisor, willing to support your authority and go to bat for you?

THAT WAS NO LADY, THAT WAS MY BOSS
by Rita Jacobs

You have two attractive job offers. The sala-ries are comparable, so are the work de-mands. The career potential looks good in both positions. The only apparent difference is that in one job your immediate superior is male, in the other, female. How do you choose?

Of course, you say to yourself, gender is no criterion for prejudging a boss. Then again, you've never worked for a woman. You've worked *with* women, but never *for* a woman. Women who formerly have given you direction come to mind—your mother, an older sister, teachers, a bossy friend. Vis-ual images of the kind of boss a woman might be begin to form on your mental screen. . . .

The Motherly Boss

She's warm, generous, but constantly de-manding. She creates an environment that is simultaneously nurturing and guilt ridden. There is hurt, along with compassion, in her voice when she corrects her woman subor- .

dinate (her "daughter"). Her directions are fraught with personal as well as professional demands: "It would please me if . . . " "It would be good for you if . . . ." She wants you to trust her and only her. She will be good to you as long as you do.

The Sibling Boss

She's like an older sister, with all the potential for jealousy that relationship might involve. She is a few years older than her woman employee, newly successful and apparently welcoming of new talent. Her openness makes it easy to confide in her, and confidences extend outside the work situation. When the woman subordinate starts growing, perhaps into the Sibling Boss's job, the help stops and the rivalry begins. Work is monitored more closely; personal confessions become ammunition in the struggle for power; and superiors regularly are informed that the subordinate's contributions were made possible only through Sibling Boss's guidance and advice.

The Dean-of-Women Boss

She's the sorority housemother whose job depends on a certain number of people being coeds. She struggles to be fair and tries not to single out anyone for particular attention. All of her female workers are encouraged to come to her with problems, personal and professional. She wears sensible clothes, encourages team efforts and has a "we've all got to pitch in" philosophy. She's been around longer than any of her co-workers and has seen it all. Her caring is apt to be institutional rather than personal, and it's hard to imagine moving out from under her wing without leaving her particular school.

The Insecure Bosses

1. **The Nit-picker**—This woman has to find something wrong with each of her subordinate's assignments, otherwise she can't exercise her "boss-ness." Her comments always include a "but" clause:

"This is a fine piece of work, but. . . ." She never allows a worker to please her completely because to do so would threaten her existence as "the boss." She is careful not to hire anyone who might vie for her job.

2. **The Buck Passer**—She seems to be saying, "I'm only here thanks to the grace of God and Management." She's not really willing to admit she's the boss, at least not directly. Her "I'm just the same as you are" posture is seductive. A woman worker feels comforted by this boss's accessibility and openness. The trouble comes when she finds there is no one giving direction or taking ultimate responsibility. The buck doesn't stop anywhere in this office. It just keeps spiraling upward until a top manager steps in and demands to know what's going on. The Buck Passer is rarely fired; her workers often are.

Boss Lady

A terror, she's ruthlessly successful, totally demanding. She feels that she made it on her own in a man's world and she's tough—tougher than any woman who comes to work for her. She rewards hard work, runs a tight ship and usually incites a great deal of backroom complaining. No one would *dare* complain to her face. She often sends her professional women workers on petty errands and thinks nothing of asking her executive assistant to pick up her cleaning or order her groceries. She is the 1940s Hollywood version of the woman boss, with none of Rosalind Russell's redeeming qualities.

The Perfect Boss

She's a brisk, efficient woman who contributes to her workers' success, confident that it won't eclipse her own. She does her work and trusts others to do theirs. She doesn't panic or run guilt trips. She stands up for her beliefs and respects those of others. She wants her workers to grow and, through teaching and understanding, helps them do the best job possible.

All of these boss-types are caricatures, exaggerated stereotypes that no more define women bosses than they do any other group of individuals. Although some of us feel that we know at least one person who fits neatly into one of the above categories, no one is ever so one dimensional. Obviously, in actual work situations, characteristics from several categories often are combined in one woman boss.

Dealing with any boss, male or female, may be problematic. We do know that women face special problems in working for other women. Since competition between women often is not openly acknowledged, it tends to express itself in a kind of covert jockeying for position. Traditionally, women's sensitivities have been trained to manipulate and please males, both at work and at home; the relationships among women have been left to sort themselves out. Although these social conventions are changing, there still are a great many women in the work force who have been raised under them. Even Hennig and Jardim, coauthors of *The Managerial Woman,* concentrate primarily on the woman who works for a man. In their book, little, if any, attention is given to the woman who has a woman boss. The best advice available on working for women comes directly from women who do it.

Among the women we interviewed on the subject, the predominant view seemed to be that working for a woman is a mixed blessing. The women's names have been changed to protect their working relationships.

Learning from Your Boss

Barbara is a young scientist with a PhD who works in a research laboratory. Her boss, a woman old enough to be her mother, is a well-known research scientist who commands a good deal of respect in professional circles. Barbara's previous boss—a man— warned her that although this woman's work was excellent, she was very emotional. Barbara considered the source of the comment

and took the job. She is quite happy in her new environment, although there are some aspects of working for a woman that surprise her.

Perhaps the fact that women are in the minority in the scientific world accounts for the professional identification that goes on among them. There is no doubt in Barbara's mind that she chose to work for a role model. She did not choose to work for her mother. When she was interviewed for the job, Barbara was struck by the number of personal questions and the interest shown in her answers. The personal inquiry continued after Barbara was employed. At first, she was pleased by it, but recently Barbara not only has pulled away from her boss's maternal concern, she has attempted to guide her boss into a different way of dealing with her.

To some extent this shift has worked, although the noted scientist's last resort is to employ tears. Barbara emphasizes the word "employ" because she feels the tears often are used to manipulate. Manipulation occurs in other ways as well—for instance, expecting the lab workers, all but one of whom are women, to relay messages of criticism. The boss complains to one worker about another and, as in a family, expects her indirect message to get delivered.

On the other hand, this woman boss is very intelligent. She cares a great deal about her work and her workers and tries hard to be a mentor. In fact, Barbara thinks she is being groomed to take over the lab, and owns up to some of the responsibility for establishing the mother/daughter relationship. Looking back on her several years in this job, she feels that some of her most valuable experience has been in learning how to be a boss—which she recently became. In hiring and working with her new lab assistant, Barbara has made a conscious effort not to pursue personal topics. She has tried to be consistent rather than arbitrary or manipulative. She has tried to nurture and teach (something she feels she did learn from her own boss); and she is trying not to overidentify with whatever errors her lab assistant makes, to understand that they are not personal attacks on Barbara's own abilities.

Fighting with Your Boss

Karen, 32, worked until recently as assistant personnel manager in a large real-estate firm. Her immediate supervisor was the 36-year-old director of personnel. Karen deliberately chose to work for a woman whose personality was different from her own, someone she felt was even-tempered and relaxed. At first, the two women responded to each other as friends, sharing confidences and occasionally having an after-work drink together. But, when Karen began making it clear that she wanted to move up in the firm and that the first step up would be her boss's job, the relationship suffered.

There is a standard routine on the job-interview circuit that encourages the use of this technique to illustrate one's ambition and drive. Question: "Where do you want to be in five years?" Answer: "In your job." In Karen's case, it backfired.

Karen's boss was not confident about her own competence and didn't feel secure in her position. If she had been more secure, Karen might not have been considered a threat. The boss hired Karen, knowing she was hiring someone with skill and ambition—and then found that the possible threat such an aggressive woman presented was more than she could handle. Karen increased the ill feeling by trying to establish her own relationship with her boss's boss. In response, Karen's boss began to monitor her work like a hawk, used past personal confidences against her and stopped sharing information.

Karen's frustration and anger escalated, as did her criticism of her boss. She felt she was being watched and judged by someone less competent than she. Her advice to anyone planning to work for a woman: "Do everything you can to check out your potential boss's competence and, once hired,

don't reveal yourself personally as though you were making a new friend!"

Karen is right; bosses are not peers. Not only do they judge employees, they also have the power to hire and fire. Karen was fired shortly after her boss's new boss arrived at the company. Karen had played her hand too openly. Because she felt that her boss was incompetent, she was quick to dismiss her boss's power. But even an incompetent boss—most especially an incompetent boss—will act strongly to rid herself of competition. Karen is now investigating new ways of presenting her desire to succeed. In the future, she will not deny her ambitions, but she certainly will choose her next boss more carefully and will enter her next job without planning so blatantly to take over.

Leaving Your Boss

Rosalind, in her early 30s, has had several women bosses. Currently, she works for a female vice-president in the television industry, but Rosalind feels it was her previous job that taught her how to handle working for a woman. She acknowledges the fact that it's easier for her to be direct with male bosses; with a woman, she's sensitive to the possibility of stepping on toes. "You are more wary of the innuendoes the small hurts and the possibility of bitchiness." This is indeed what happened in Rosalind's former job. The more competent Rosalind became, the more her boss, an older woman with recognition in her field, began to slight her. In one instance, when Rosalind was being considered for membership in a prestigious organization, her boss, already a member, did not choose to nominate her. When confronted, she said it hadn't occurred to her that Rosalind would be eligible.

Rosalind's boss was nurturing up to a point, but when Rosalind wanted to grow professionally, she had to move on. Now that Rosalind is working elsewhere, she and her former boss communicate frequently, share information and experiences. No longer competitors within the same organization, they have become friends.

Now, herself a boss, Rosalind works *with* her subordinates, allowing them to establish their own styles. She tries to be direct in expressing dissatisfaction, which, she admits, is a struggle. By inclination she would like to be everyone's friend.

Loving Your Boss

Anne is in her mid-30s, and one of two female vice-presidents in a large public-relations firm. The other is her boss. Anne has almost nothing but praise for her boss and feels that, along with her own hard work, her boss's interest and ability to help Anne develop her skills have contributed greatly to her success. In the beginning, her boss took the time to sit down with Anne and go over copy and press releases line by line. The relationship, which Anne describes in mentor/protégé terms, has helped foster her own sense of responsibility toward women who are coming up through the ranks. She sees the managerial role as a teaching one, and has spent a good deal of time speaking to women's groups about succeeding in the world of work.

Anne feels that women tend to "jump into the fray without having watched and evaluated others' behavior first." She also thinks that the personal element that is so important to the woman boss's humanity can be a double-edged sword: "If the personal gets in the way of her professionalism, the woman executive may lose respect."

Anne's advice: Work for secure people. Only a woman who feels secure in herself can work well with another woman, who may be brighter or smarter than she is. Anne has learned that she can't be every place at once. She has confidence in her staff and delegates responsibility. She has seen other women fail to get things done because they want to control every piece of work and consequently can't delegate effectively.

We all carry with us baggage from our pasts, both familial and social, that burdens us with preconceptions about dealing with other women. If we stoop under this burden, then working for a woman is oppressive. If we become conscious of the often covert interactions among women, we can begin to use these insights to make our working relationships strong and productive. It may not be fruitful to discuss these issues with your woman boss. Nonetheless, your own conscious realization of qualities such as empathy, sensitivity to innuendo, and your sense of the fragility of power can strengthen your ability to deal with other women in work situations. Working for a woman is different from working for a man, and it should be. But there's no reason why it can't be just as rewarding.

HOW TO BE/CHOOSE A GOOD WOMAN BOSS

Rosalind's rules for being a good boss:
- Delegate responsibility.
- Set up specific timetables for work completion.
- Be aware of the political and strategic situations in your office. (For example, know who gets copies of work or memos.)
- Ask for clear, concise reports from those under you and, in turn, make good reports to your supervisor.
- Be alert to situations in which discipline is called for.
- Avoid gossip.

For the woman who works for a woman, Rosalind lists these danger signals:
- New restrictions are placed upon your work.
- The information flow stops or slows down significantly.

- You're not invited to meetings.

These are the signals the indirect boss sends out. If you are the target, your best move is to ask for direct criticism. In any work situation, the most important thing is to know what you can do. Rosalind's advice: "Don't let the nit-picker shake your self-confidence."

Anne's advice for working women:
- Develop your own style.
- Meet challenges and conflicts head on.
- Set goals for yourself. (Anne sits down every January 1 and writes goals for the year on index cards that she checks periodically.)
- Have a sense of humor.
- Work "smarter" rather than harder.
- Listen and observe and, when you take action, don't shoot from the hip.

Everyone we talked to offered some version of the following cautions to women who work for women:
- Be careful about personal confessions, revelations, etc.
- Don't try to establish personal rapport by gossiping about co-workers.
- Be conscious of your boss's place in the hierarchy and don't step on her toes or go over her head.
- Keep her informed of your work activities and progress.
- Know thyself!

RITA JACOBS *teaches college, writes and works for a woman boss, who is not included in the article.*

9 TO 5
THE MOVIE: Hollywood Goes to the Office
THE MOVEMENT: Women Office Workers Organize
THE MANAGEMENT: Union Busters Target Women

Who would have thought that the mundane world of nine to five would become 1980's hot topic? But such is the case. Not only do we have a major movie from Twentieth Century-Fox called *Nine to Five* (a comedy in which Jane Fonda, Lily Tomlin and Dolly Parton play oppressed secretaries), but we have a related campaign for better conditions in offices launched by Working Women: National Association of Office Workers. Then, behind the scenes, we find there's big interest on the part of unions in organizing women office workers, and just as serious intent by hired professionals to counter any attempts at unionizing women.

Women who work in offices have long been aware of the realities—that in many cases women's jobs need to be upgraded and wages and conditions improved. Most important, women workers need to be awarded their due respect as professionals. A $2 million movie and a well-organized pressure group are only part of what's stirring up some serious issues for the 80s: The giant issue of office automation is forcing a reassessment of the role of office support personnel; at the same time, liberation forces secretaries to assess their "office wife" roles, and management is looking with alarm at the falling productivity and the estimated billions of dollars it would cost to change the status of women office workers. These three articles look at the aspects of this issue, from the frivolous to the fundamental. . . .

THE MOVIE . . .

by Kathy Mackay

About two years ago, Jane Fonda, who, as one of America's most bankable actresses, is able to command two million dollars per film, became concerned about women working in offices after hearing about their on-the-job problems. She then met with some office workers and became determined to call attention to their usually unpublicized plight.

By now, American movie audiences know that when Fonda finds an issue she thinks the world should be aware of, she goes ahead and makes an enormously successful movie about it. Past projects have been both timely and intelligent, without being too intellectual. Her films, though, have in the past been heavy on the dramatic aspects of a subject—obviously, Fonda found nothing hilarious about Vietnam or nuclear meltdown. Why, then, has Fonda made a comedy based on the lives of women office workers? Are secretaries a laugh a minute?

Recently, Fonda explained: "We wanted to make a movie that Joe Blow will go see—as far as he's concerned, it'll be a really funny movie. But, if a secretary goes to see the movie, she's going to identify with it. She's going to laugh and at the same time say, 'Hey! This is a movie about me!' The movie has to entertain. There's a problem with a lot of labor movies—they hold up a mirror to the blue-collar situation. Art shouldn't be a mirror to life; art should recreate life in such a way that it elevates, teaches and allows you to go behind your present consciousness. And I think laughter is the greatest

way of all. You can go much further through farce."

"In fact," adds Bruce Gilbert, Fonda's partner and producer, "the stories we heard from secretaries were often so outrageous that no one would believe them if they were played as straight drama."

The movie, called *Nine to Five*, was, from the beginning, conceived for three stars—Jane Fonda, Lily Tomlin and Dolly Parton. Dolly Parton? "One day," Fonda recalls, "I was driving down the freeway, listening to one of my favorite singers—Dolly Parton—and I looked at the cover of the tape. I said, 'Boy, does she ever look like everybody's idea of a secretary.'"

But the catalyst for *Nine to Five* was a group of women office workers in Cleveland. According to Karen Nussbaum, a friend of Fonda's from the antiwar movement and now director of Working Women: National Association of Office Workers, "Jane and I started having discussions about her doing a movie on secretaries when she came to Cleveland to open *Coming Home* as a benefit for us. We talked about the makings of a good plot and about the problems faced by office workers."

Says Fonda, "One out of every three women in America works in an office, almost 20 to 30 million women. You're talking about the majority of women who work, and most do so because they have to. It is an absolute necessity that they are paid decent wages. If the [economic] crisis gets worse—which it will—if they are going to be frozen into those low-paying jobs, it's going to be a calamity for them."

Fonda feels that organizing is the only way for secretaries to improve their situation. "They become extremely vulnerable if just one of them stands up and makes a demand," she says. She and Gilbert hope they have made a movie that will effect subtle changes in people's attitudes toward secretaries, just as *Coming Home* and *The China Syndrome* forced viewers to reassess the Vietnam war and nuclear power.

Comedy writer Patricia Resnick, who previously had examined the lives of waitresses at work in "Ladies in Waiting," for PBS, wrote the first draft of the *Nine to Five* screenplay. She did her on-the-job research by working undercover at a large insurance company. Paula Weinstein of Twentieth Century-Fox then chose Colin Higgins to rework the script and direct the movie.

Higgins (*Harold and Maude, Silver Streak, Foul Play*) needed a clearer focus on the overall issue, so he and Fonda returned to Cleveland and met with 40 Working Women members. The women talked of their mistreatment, of how they felt about their employers and what they fantasized trying to change, including the recurring dream of killing the boss. Much of the movie is based on these discussions—the "death to the tyrant" theme, along with the problems of low pay, lack of promotion and sexual harassment.

In the plot of *Nine to Five*, three secretaries, played by Fonda, Tomlin and Parton, work for the same outfit, Consolidated Companies, Inc. They dream of the demise of their lecherous boss (by means of rat poison and/or an elephant gun in the men's room). To their amazement, their demise wish is granted. The entire organization rejoices the end of the evil boss, and, of course, runs far better without him.

Is *Nine to Five* making a political statement about power in the office? "It's about women who are not getting promoted and who want respect," according to Fonda.

"These women work hard. They do skilled work and know the offices as well as or better than the bosses do, and they deserve justice. That has to be reflected in the way they're treated, in their wages and in their right to be promoted. The movie shouldn't be taken as an antiboss sort of thing."

Gilbert and Higgins, and even Fonda, seem to have been surprised by how much office workers resented the lack of respect with which they were treated on the job. Not so Tomlin, who described her own office experiences, from back in the days when she was breaking into comedy in New York.

"I used to alternate between being a waitress and an office temp. You'd go a little berserk being a waitress, then you'd go back to being an office temp, then you'd go berserk, so you'd go back to being a waitress. But you made more as a waitress, and that's why you'd go back.

"I would do office work for two or three days and then black out. I would say I was going to the john and not come back."

Tomlin even recalled the physical realities of life in the office 18 years ago: "It's grinding to sit all day, and the lighting and air are awful. Those sealed offices would drain away my energy. Not to mention the lights over the mirrors in the ladies' rooms. I knew I would get into a terrible physical and mental state working there."

Parton, who spent 16 years working her way to the top of the country-music field, also believes she has experiences in common with the women in the movie.

"I could relate to my role in *Nine to Five*. I started my career as a song-writer when I was 18 years old. I went to Nashville and started my own publishing company—I had hundreds of songs—with my best girl friend, Judy Ogle. For years we ran the office ourselves."

Parton's words summarize the movie's overall theme: Little is going to change overnight, but mutual support and the willingness of women to help one another can make a difference.

As Fonda puts it, "You have to realize: 'I have the *right* to ask more from the people with whom and for whom I work.' It's hard to do it by yourself. That's the importance of the women's movement—and of this movement for secretaries."

THE MOVEMENT

by Victoria Boughton

Appropriately enough, the movement behind the movie will reap the benefits of the *Nine to Five* New York premiere on December 14. Working Women: National Association for Office Workers was formed four years ago, when five local groups of fed-up women office workers united to form a national organization with Karen Nussbaum at the head. Today there are 12 local chapters, 10,000 members across the country and three national offices (in Cleveland, Boston and Washington, DC). Two Boston members, above.

According to *Business Week*, WW has a paid staff of 50 and an annual budget of $700,000. Pivotal points of the organization's Action Campaign are: higher pay for women office workers, fair employment in banks, job rights for older women workers. WW already has helped secure millions of dollars in back pay for working women, persuaded larger employers to institute training programs and job postings and, of course, is responsible for the Pettiest Office Procedure Contest and the Scrooge of the Year Award.

Working Women is a tax-exempt group. It gets funding any way it can—from foundations, the church and now, promotional fund-raising tied in with the upcoming Fonda movie.

Anne Hill, national organizer, stresses the fact "that we are an activist organization. Our members do more than pay dues . . . they help on all levels: running seminars, organizing benefits and money-raising events, staffing local offices. Each of our national offices has only three or four full-time people, which means that the national committee is made up of no more than 12 women. Local offices have permanent staffs of anywhere from two people to eight, although members are in and out helping with things that need to be done."

In Cleveland, Nussbaum explained the reason for Working Women's existence and continuing growth: "Women office workers—that is, all nonmanagement women— have a tough time winning respect on the job. Their problems are universal: low pay, lack of upward mobility, treatment as second-class citizens, sexual harassment. And, of course, because so often you can still get two women workers for the price of one male worker, there are a lot of women working within this unfair system of employment."

And a lot of women working to change it. The national headquarters of Working Women, which moved three years ago from Boston to Cleveland ("Cleveland is more centrally located and better represents the typical American city," says Nussbaum), coordinates the activities of the national offices and makes sure their affiliates are aware of important issues across the country. The Washington, DC, office keeps an eye on legislation coming out of the Capitol. Regional affiliates rely on networking to keep in constant touch. As Nussbaum puts it, "Our power comes from our ability to organize."

And organize they do. "We can tell women who call us with problems that they're not alone. Chances are, whatever the situation, we've dealt with it before," says Janice Blood, national publicist based in the Boston office. "We let the caller know we're behind her and that we've handled similar situations. We encourage a meeting between the caller and one of our staff to discuss things further, and often we put the caller in touch with others who've dealt with a given problem effectively and can offer advice."

What of the company that creates dissatisfaction? Blood continues: "It's quite common for our staff to receive a number of calls from the same place. We handle each complaint on a personal basis, and when we meet for our regular staff sessions, we may decide to take action against the company's overall policy on a particular issue. We exert pressure, and management becomes aware of the workers' dissatisfaction. We've had some impressive successes."

WW's newsletters are informative and professional. Its flyers and abstracts are well written and thoughtful. Its policies and positions make perfect sense.

Does Working Women represent the beginning of a union; is unionization the next logical step? According to Nussbaum, yes and no. "Like a union, this is a support group. We exist to lend support to women office workers. We point out problems and potential problems in an effort to make management aware of them. Sometimes, depending on the issue, management takes action." Sometimes, it doesn't. Do unions then take over, supplanting the original organization?

"When certain problems are resolved, yet there is still profound dissatisfaction, that's when union organization would come about," says Nussbaum. "In areas where unions form, we see ourselves as continuing to formulate policy and prescribe courses of action given a certain set of circumstances," says Blood. "We may not have the legal edge, but management, we find, is less likely to try to get away with something when they learn that a worker is a member of Working Women."

For information on Working Women offices in your area, write: Working Women: National Association for Office Workers, 1124 Huron Road, Cleveland, OH 44115.

THE MANAGEMENT

by Anne Field

- Nurses at White Plains Hospital in suburban White Plains, New York, were forced to postpone holding a union election when their organizing campaign failed to gain support.
- The mostly female staff of the Catholic Charities of the Archdiocese of Chicago lost an election after waging a six-month campaign to form a union.
- Unionized employees of the Eden Park Nursing Home in Poughkeepsie, New York—largely female—have been on

strike for 15 months and, as this issue went to press, management still had refused to negotiate a contract.

What do all these union failures have in common? Employers who have brought in a new breed of consultant, members of one of the country's newest and most thriving management specialties: union-busting.

"The consultants specialize in the manipulation of women," says Robert Meulenkamp, director of organizing for New York's

District 1199 National Union of Hospital and Health Care Employees, a 60,000-member union. "It's no accident they don't work very often in heavy industry; steelworkers would kill them." Active primarily in the clerical and service sectors, which employ mostly women, the consultants use tactics aimed at the fears and insecurities peculiar to women workers—that women don't trust one another, have a need to please and are more afraid of violence than men, for example.

"A man would punch them [the consultants] out, while a woman would listen and take it," says Henrietta Doar, an organizer for District 1199 and a former registered nurse. "I don't think they'd intimidate men the way they intimidate women."

"They understand that women can be real patsies," says Mary Beth Guinan, executive vice-president and former organizer for local 372 of the Service Employees International Union in Chicago, which tried unsuccessfully to organize the workers at the Catholic Archdiocese.

Union-Busting: A Growth Industry

With over 2,000 consultants across the country employed by firms that charge per diem fees of $500 to $800 for their advice, the union-busters have become expert in a unique approach to keeping unions out of unorganized companies and decertifying existing unions. Their method: a sophisticated mixture of industrial relations and behavioral psychology.

"It's the daily use of behavior modification, using rewards and punishments to change people's attitudes," said Mike Rifkin, an administrative organizer for District 1199. The tactics seem to work—Modern Management Methods, a 70-person Illinois consulting firm, boasts a 98 percent success record.

It's hard to find figures that connect the two situations, but we do know that, in recent years, the use of consultants has soared and unions have been defeated in increasing numbers of situations.

Ten years ago, unions won 57 percent of their representation elections; today, they're winning 46 percent. At the same time, decertification elections—attempts to remove existing unions—have risen 400 percent over the past ten years; unions have lost 75 percent of these elections. Unfair labor practice complaints have increased by an eye-opening 250 percent from a total of 18,651 in 1969 to 41,259 in 1979. Charges by unions against companies during organizing campaigns, including accusations of illegal surveillance of union sympathizers, discrimination against employees and refusal by the company to bargain, have increased from 13,036 in 1969 to 31,167 in 1979.

Meantime, in 1978, the US Labor Department reported the involvement of consultants in 159 labor disputes, which is a 127 percent increase since 1975.

Unfair Manipulators or Employee Relations Counselors?

The unions say that the consultants' successes are achieved unfairly. "When you lose an election, someone's been hired to do some manipulating," says Arthur Lewandowski, director of organizing for the Office and Professional Employees Union, which represents 15,000 New York white-collar workers.

The consultants disagree. "God didn't create unions. In a normal situation, there aren't any," says Alfred T. DeMaria, a New York attorney who calls himself the "father of decertification" and has written a book on the subject. Twelve times a year, DeMaria teaches a special $275-per-person course on decertification for Executive Enterprises, one of the two most popular firms that offer seminars to executives on keeping unions out. Both organizations are headquartered in New York and work in association with law firms that specialize in the field.

The traveling seminars are as profitable as the actual on-site consulting work. With costs ranging from $275 to $550 per person, the seminars instruct executives in the theory behind the union-busting practice, as well as a step-by-step approach to union avoidance.

"Companies systematically send whole platoons of their people through the seminars," says Lewis Abrams, president of Executive Enterprises.

Consultants take issue with the term "anti-union," preferring to call themselves "employee relations counselors." They assert that their role is one of peacemaker between worker and management.

In the spacious Manhattan offices of Advanced Management Research, Inc., Executive Enterprises' major competitor, staff member Thomas L. Kenyon describes the consultants as "a pro-human resource. We teach management to remain union free. We try to understand the feelings of workers, why they're unhappy," he says. "Maybe it's because of a small thing like management not having created enough parking spaces. We teach management to listen."

"Treat your employees properly, and you can make unions unnecessary," advises DeMaria. "Unions come between the employee and management; they create a we-they philosophy. We're just fulfilling our responsibility to our client to communicate its position without violating the labor laws."

"If unions came to us, we'd be happy to do a seminar for them as well," says Abrams.

The "Plum and Cactus" Approach

When the consultants do the real thing— their on-the-scene campaigning—they follow the scenario sketched out in the seminars.

The basic plan, according to most observers, is what has been called the "plum and cactus" approach. District 1199's Meulenkamp says, "They do what they have to do to win. They'll show you that without a union life will be OK, and that joining a union will lead to trouble. The combination of approaches is what they work on."

Crucial to the method throughout is the clandestine role of the consultant, who never confronts the workers directly. The "undercover use of psychology," as one labor lawyer described it, is a brand-new experience for the employee who is never told that the company has hired outside advisers and is not prepared to deal with them.

Stage One: Drag It Out

Anti-union campaigns are waged in stages, increasing in intensity as the election date draws near. The first tactic is to delay; the longer the time between the initiation of an organizing drive and the actual vote, the less interested and more discouraged the employee may become.

Delays are brought about by manipulation of the legal process. Permission to hold a union election must be granted at National Labor Relations Board (NLRB) hearings. The pattern is clear: Drag out the NLRB proceedings and force the union to appeal to Washington.

Marge Albert, an organizer for District 65 of the Distributive Workers' Union in New York City, has been trying to organize secretaries at Stroock and Stroock and Lavin, a Wall Street corporate law firm, for almost a year and a half. The union has been waiting six months for a decision from the NLRB in Washington. According to Albert, the company has hired the law firm of Jackson, Lewis, Schnitzler and Krupman to advise them on how to keep the union out.

Lewis Cole, an attorney with Stroock and Stroock and Lavin, holds that the company has acted in good faith. "A union is not in the best interest of the employee or the company," he says.

A major element in this strategy is the employer's refusal to agree on which workers are entitled to take part in the election; a squabble over the appropriate bargaining unit can drag on for months.

Stage Two: Pressure the Supervisors

The burden of the company campaign rests on the shoulders of the supervisors who meet with employees to discuss the cons of union organizing. Supervisors are not protected by the National Labor Relations Act and can be fired at any time. Many labor officials argue that the threat of losing their jobs is the main reason for the supervisors' cooperation.

"From a management standpoint, either you're on their team or you're not," says Executive Enterprises' Abrams. "If supervisors can't live up to their responsibilities, maybe they shouldn't have that job."

Supervisors attend intensive training sessions in which consultants teach them the art of one-to-one persuasion. Lessons include quizzes on what management can and cannot say legally to employees. The employer, for instance, cannot tell an employee not to join a union or ask whether the employee wants to become a member. Supervisors also hear detailed descriptions of their week-by-week duties and receive handbooks for future referral.

One nurse who was active in District 1199's seven-month attempt to organize registered nurses at White Plains Hospital remembers, "Our supervisors, the head nurses, would disappear for hours a day to attend meetings. And they were pulled out of their beds at night for more sessions. They would be briefed at night before they went to work the next day." White Plains officials refused to comment on this situation.

Supervisors also are made to feel responsible for pro-union sympathy among employees. "The company gave the nurses a guilt complex," says the White Plains nurse. "They said it would be all their fault if the union won."

By the end of the campaign, supervisors have had about 25 meetings with each employee. Armed with letters, pamphlets and diagrams designed by the consultants, supervisors determine where each worker's sympathies lie, paying most attention to the "fence-sitters." They also keep careful notes of their conversations, recording the current status of every employee.

Organizers say that the constant meet-ings, which last up to an hour, create an atmosphere of suspicion. Employees distrust not only union representatives, but one another. "People wouldn't talk to each other because they didn't know where it would go back," says Liz Giger, a District 1199 organizer, who was involved in the White Plains organizing effort. "Before, they'd had a cohesive team approach; that is gone."

"The consultants know how to break down trust between women," says SEIU, local 372 organizer Guinan. "They get the women to break each other down."

According to Guinan, supervisors would lead "encounter groups" in which employees would gang up against a union sympathizer. "It's a typical technique used against women," she says. "The worst thing you can say to a woman is that she's not a nice person."

Many women also turn anti-union because they sympathize with the plight of the supervisor. "The supervisor goes through a horrible time and finally, she'll break down and cry on the shoulder of the worker, who may also be her friend," says Guinan. "By the time of the election, I had my own people saying, 'Look, this is really ugly; let's try to work this out without a union.' They play on the woman's tendency to be supportive."

Stage Three: You May Be Permanently Replaced

As the date of the election approaches, the tone of the literature and of the meetings changes. In the beginning, the letters, which always are signed by the company's top administrator, convey a message of understanding and cooperation. Letters begin "Dear Fellow Employee" and end "Please feel free to ask questions of me." Supervisors also include messages in paychecks saying, "Union dues would make this check less."

Later, supervisors change their tune. Letters and visits increase in frequency as the new twist is added to the campaign: the threat of a strike. Supervisors enclose a different message in employees' paychecks: "When you strike, your pay stops." Carrying letters warning that unions inevitably create long and violent work stoppages, supervisors indicate that the striking employee will be "permanently replaced."

"Posters are plastered from ceiling to floor with pictures of cops beating up strikers," says 1199's Meulenkamp. "The consultants play on the insecurities that workers, especially women, have. Women and men react differently to the threat of violence."

"The employer has the responsibility to the employee to bring up the prospect of a strike," consultant DeMaria counters. "It's a tactic specifically designed to induce the person to vote against a union. Then everyone picks up on this and says it's so unfair."

The campaign reaches a crescendo on election day. "They'll have cops all over the place. When union organizers go into the room to count the ballots, there will be a swarm of security guards who'll surround them so people who are voting will see them," says Meulenkamp. Often, the poll is near an administrator's office.

Even if the union wins, the campaign does not end. Employers revive the delay approach and refuse to negotiate, forcing the union to take them to court. "The process can go on for years," says one lawyer who has represented many unions in cases before the NLRB. "By that time, the whole complexion of the employees has changed. They've had a bad experience with union organizing. People become timid."

Labor: Slow to Counterattack

Organized labor has not responded quickly to the threat posed by the new consulting industry. It was not until 1977 that the late George Meany formed an AFL-CIO National Organizing Committee to develop counterstrategies. A staff, based in Washington, DC, collects information, designs defensive tactics and issues a newsletter.

Union officials admit that they still are in the early stages of their counterattack. "We haven't gotten very sophisticated in exposing the industry," says Sondra Clark, director of the League of Registered Nurses and executive vice-president of District 1199. "It's hard to know what to do to fight them. There are no road maps."

Organizers are unsure of how to guard women employees against the tactics designed to play on their insecurities. "In general, we just try to involve people in every phase of the campaign," explains Meulenkamp. "You rely on the strengths that many women have, like much closer personal relationships and support networks."

Meanwhile, labor leaders are attempting to pass legislation restricting the consultants' activities. Some protective legislation exists already. The 1959 Landrum-Griffin Act obligates companies to report to the Department of Labor when they use outside consultants in an anti-union campaign. Last year, only 31 such reports were filed. Most companies, it seems, take advantage of loopholes in the law to get out of making such reports. For example, many consultants will use the employer's name and letterhead rather than their own, or will avoid direct contact with employees. A Labor Department campaign, spear-headed by William P. Hobgood, assistant secretary of labor for management-labor relations, is investigating over 250 cases in which management consultants have been accused by union officials of failure to file reports with the Department of Labor.

But the Landrum-Griffin Act does not protect employees against another tactic recommended by consultants—employee organizations quietly funded by management that then are presented to employees as alternatives to a union. Since December 1977, Representatives Theodore Weiss (D-NY) and Frank Thompson (D-NJ) have been trying to get Congress to pass a bill revising the Landrum-Griffin Act to require that employee organizations disclose the sources of their funding. The idea is to prevent attempts to present employee organizations as worker sponsored and financed when they are not.

The success of the proposed legislation is doubtful, though. Many observers of the labor scene point to the failure of the 1978 Labor Law Reform Bill as an ominous sign that Congress is in no mood to pass laws favorable to unions. The bill would have increased penalties on companies that do not comply with NLRB decisions. Although organized labor spent over $1 million on its lobbying campaign, and although the bill was backed by President Carter, the business community was able to mobilize its considerable resources and the legislation was defeated in a Senate filibuster.

Why Working Women Are Crucial

Organized labor has lost its strength in the eyes not only of the Senate, but of the rest of the country. Only 22 percent of the US work force is unionized today, compared to 34 percent in 1955. Many experts place the blame for labor's declining ranks on its failure until recently to organize service industry and clerical workers, who make up about 50 percent of the nation's labor force, but only 16.5 percent of total union membership. Yet these are the very job categories the Department of Labor predicts will increase most in the 1980s—service and clerical jobs are expected to account for over two-thirds of all job increases in the next decade.

According to some union officials, the largely female work force in these fields has made organizing more difficult. "Part of our problem is that the health industry is 84 percent female," said 1199's Sondra Clark. "The women's liberation movement hasn't had that much of an impact in these areas. The majority of women don't see themselves as having any rights in the home, so why should they think of it in the work place?"

Others say that working women have been harder to organize than men because they often have more responsibilities at home, and have even less time to spare for outside activities. They also cite the woman's tendency to overidentify with her boss and to see union sympathy as a test of her loyalty to her employer.

Giger of 1199 sees "professionalism" as another major obstacle to organizing women. "A lot of nurses think they're above unions," she says. "They forget they have to clock in just like everyone else."

Yet, the future of organized labor may rest on getting more working women into unions. Forty-five percent of the labor force is female while only 25 percent of union members are women.

"Organizing women will mean developing new techniques," says Ellen Gruzinski, executive director of the Coalition of Labor Union Women (CLUW). "It means education, and it may mean a slow process."

Gruzinski believes that labor will adapt to the changing times. She points to the formation of CLUW, which was started in 1974 to push for women's issues in the AFL-CIO, to CLUW's role in convincing the AFL-CIO to back the Equal Rights Amendment and to an AFL-CIO national conference on unionizing unorganized women held last January in Washington, DC. And last August, Joyce Miller, head of CLUW, became the first woman to be appointed a member of the AFL-CIO Executive Board.

Unions also believe that the more the public knows about the latest threat to their existence—the union-busting business—the easier it will be for women trying to organize a union. The more publicity, the more women will wake up," says Guinan.

Chapter Five

Sex in the Office

YOUR WORK AND YOUR SEX LIFE FOR BETTER OR WORSE

by Bernice Kanner Mosesson

Caution; Working may be hazardous to your sex life, and your sex life may hinder your work.

Then again, work may add dimension and sparkle to your sexual relationships, and a good sex life can brighten your career prospects.

The two are mutually affective and *how* they affect you is up to you, say today's sex therapists. But that, and the existence of a bond between work and sex may be the only points concerning sexuality and the working woman upon which the experts agree.

There is no firm data to support either view because no one has yet investigated the connection between work and sex—though volumes have been written on sex and teenagers, sex and older women, sex and widows and sex and men in all stages of their lives.

This, despite the fact that almost half of all women in this country work, and the incidences of reported sexual dysfunctions are sharply on the rise.

According to pioneer sexologists, William Masters, MD, and Virginia Johnson, whose book *Human Sexual Inadequacy* fired the national sexual consciousness when it was published in 1970, 50 percent of married couples have sexual problems. Their more recent, yet unpublished, study probed the sexual lives of 100 Pittsburgh couples and revealed that 48 percent of the female subjects have trouble getting aroused; 32 percent have trouble staying aroused, and 47 percent have trouble reaching orgasm.

In these surveys, as well as in clinical programs and private sex counseling across the country, working women are proportion-

92

ately represented—though again, few therapists can quote any figures. One, Martin Weisberg, MD, a Philadelphia obstetrician-gynecologist turned sex therapist, has taken a recent survey of his patients: he reports that 40 percent of his female patients work.

Of course, sexual problems affect nonworking women and their mates, too. But while they are often the same Big Three—failure to reach orgasm, impotence and premature ejaculation, as well as a host of supporting complaints—that plague dual-career couples, they are triggered by different experiences and arrive by different routes.

According to Carroll M. Brodsky, MD, professor of psychiatry at the University of California School of Medicine in San Francisco, a person's work life is often at the root of psychological problems that manifest themselves in sexual problems.

"You carry your job experience and the way it affects you—your anger or resentment or your bloated ego, depending on the way superiors, coworkers and customers treat you—into the bedroom. In addition, what goes on in the bedroom affects what goes on in the office, store or factory. You can also project the problems you have at work onto your sex partner, making him sexually undesirable or unacceptable. You may be subject to a number of tensions at work that make it difficult to relax—or to enjoy a satisfactory sex act."

Unfortunately, the reverse isn't necessarily true for employees who are happy at work, Brodsky adds. "When work is pleasant and enjoyable and provides ample ego gratification, some workers look forward to going to work—and regret having to go home." They see domestic responsibilities, including love-making, as "duty," and they can become resentful.

Anger and resentment aren't the only fare on the take-home menu. Seeds of depression, which has been labeled a major cause of sexual dysfunction, are also sown in disappointing or unpleasant work situations: when an employee is passed over for promotion, a raise or a plum assignment, when one's work is criticized or when one is bored on the job.

Although data are still sketchy, sex therapists have noticed over the years that certain patterns of sexual problems have emerged. Those typical of the working woman are:

- **The Workaholic Syndrome.** In the movie *Network*, Faye Dunaway, a beautiful programming-executive-on-the-rise, sacrifices her love relationships for her job. She is a classic workaholic, says Robert Taylor Segraves, MD, co-director of the Sex and Marital Therapy Clinic at the University of Chicago Medical School, too fascinated with her job and the political manipulations it requires to make a go of her personal life. Because workaholics are goal-oriented, they can't enjoy sex as a pleasureful time in itself.

- **The "I'm Too Tired" Syndrome.** Although wives have been traditionally widowed by late office conferences, long business trips and homework-bound husbands, the increasing number of women working and their expanding responsibilities may change this pattern. Love and love-making take energy. So does work. When all or a large part of one's energies are channeled into work, there's little left for sex.

- **The Anxiety Syndrome.** New opportunities create new problems, say the therapists, and working women often experience conflict in one form or another. They may not be sure it's all right to leave their families for a job. They may be worried that they are not handling their business and domestic responsibilities adequately. And they may be torn between traditional, passive home values and more liberated, aggressive business ones.

According to Helen Singer Kaplan, MD, head of the Human Sexuality Program at New York Hospital-Cornell Medical Center in New York City, "There's only one cause for inhibited sexual desire, and that is anxiety. Anxiety can cause a diminution of sexual desire, or it can cause a person to engage in compulsive sexual behavior."

- **Assertiveness Fallout Syndrome.** For many women, working becomes an assertiveness training course of sorts: While learning to speak up, they may become overzealous. "Sometimes a woman practices what she learns on her partner, except, instead of being assertive, she becomes aggressive," says Weisberg.

- **The Role Reversal Syndrome.** Some men feel threatened by independent, aggressive working women. The result may be impotence, warns Arnold L. Gilberg, MD, assistant professor of psychiatry at the University of California School of Medicine. An estimated half of all men in this country have at some time experienced transient secondary impotence. According to Gilberg, "Impotence shows the male is troubled by rage at the world and women in particular. The woman who feels more complete becomes a frightening object to these males, and the only way they can cope is to become more distant."

- **The Grass Is Always Greener Syndrome.** Working women, with greater opportunities to meet people and discover the embodiments of their sexual fantasies, may have a hard time dealing with the reality of their real mates, says Brodsky. Faced with a wide range of partner possibilities, they wonder what life would have been like had they waited. They often feel cheated and dissatisfied. And they also probably take more extra-relationship lovers than nonworking women, hypothesizes Weisberg.

Some working women never experience any of these sexual syndromes or problems: A job outside the home is all the therapy they need to feel complete and strong in their sexual identity and relationships. Indeed, Brodsky speculates that many dual-career couples may work through to more adult relationships. Although he emphasizes that no survey, article or research has been done to support his theory, he thinks working couples develop a greater respect for each other; that theirs are more peer relationships than dominant subordinate ones. Of course, nonworking women may also feel successful in their occupation, but a paycheck carries ego clout in today's society— and can reinforce one's feelings of self-worth.

R. Clay Burchell, MD, director of obstetrics and gynecology at Hartford Hospital in Connecticut, goes a step further: "Low self-esteem weakens the basis of the relationship; high self-esteem provides a foundation for risk-taking and growth that is nurturing in any relationship." Achieving sexual fulfillment by working through sexual problems takes personal fortitude. Women with high esteem are more apt to chance learning about themselves, to allow themselves to feel pain and pleasure and to share their feelings with their partners. According to Burchell, they progress rapidly, while for those with low self-esteem, growth may not even be possible.

If women learn how to please themselves sexually and take responsibility for their sexual pleasure, the myth of the male as sexually omniscient will soon shatter. According to Lonnie Barbach, PhD, author of *For Yourself: The Fulfillment of Female Sexuality* and adviser at the University of California Human Sexuality Program, most women look to men as experts in sex. "They wait silently hoping their partners will discover the techniques that suit them best. Men also accept this burdensome authority and blame themselves when things don't work out right." Sharing, on the other hand, assures a better chance of sexual pleasure.

Many men find aware women who are their equals far more appealing than passive, subordinate women, says Robert Gould, MD, professor of psychiatry at New York Medical College. These men welcome a sexually assertive woman and lose nothing of themselves in relating to her. "On the contrary, a man gains the promise of a more fulfilling sexual experience since his partner's behavior is not compromised or distorted by pretense, holding back, false modesty or by playing a prescribed, culturally induced, passive game," Gould adds. Men also gain by not having to guess what the woman wants. The old notion, "If he loved me he would know what I want," belongs to a romantic age that should be recognized for what it is: a myth that has little to do with the business of living or loving.

According to the latest figures from the Kinsey Institute, Americans care a lot about sex, and most of them enjoy it regularly. American women average two to three episodes a week. Most culminate in orgasm. Seventy-eight percent of 16-20 year olds regularly achieve orgasm. Orgasms per sexual episode peak for the 30-36-year olds at more than 90 percent and dip only slightly to 82 percent for those over 60.

There are, of course, factors other than work that affect a woman's sex life, age and relationship status being high on the list. Statistics indicate that sexual activity drops to an average of once every two weeks for women over 60 and for those not involved in relationships. Then, too, one's general metabolic level (the lower the metabolism, the more sluggish one is in responding sexually) and nutritional health (undernourished or obese women have less sexual drive) are vitally important.

There are no clear-cut definitions of what is normal and what constitutes sexual dysfunction. Nor are there pat solutions. "Sex therapy is not cook-bookery," warns Weis-

berg. "If something works for you, do it."

Despite the glut of self-help books available, it's difficult for a couple to solve their own sexual problems, says Dr. Robert T. Segraves. "We're more than just a cheering section. We give couples hope of improving their relationships. The patients know we've seen similar problems to what they're experiencing and that, for the most part, these problems can be solved."

But beware in your search for a suitable therapist: The field is crowded with quacks. Dr. William Masters estimates the number of self-proclaimed experts at 3,500. So where should you look? Many major teaching hospitals and university hospitals have sex counseling clinics or human sexuality programs. Any professor, not necessarily a doctor, associated with such a program or trained by such a program is probably well-trained and ethical.

In addition, a number of professional organizations have emerged recently. Among them, the American Association of Sex Educators, Counselors and Therapists (AASECT) is the oldest and biggest. It shares the field with the Eastern Association of Sex Therapists and the Society for the Scientific Study of Sex. AASECT offers a state-by-state listing of more than 600 persons in this country, Canada and abroad who have been certified under their guidelines. The register is available for $3 from AASECT, 5010 Wisconsin Avenue NW, Suite 304, Washington D.C. 20016.

BERNICE KANNER MOSESSON *is rounds editor of* Medical Dimensions Magazine. *In her research for this article, she was surprised to find that working women have as many sexual problems as they do, and that a woman who is happy at work is not necessarily happy in her sex life. Now that she's assured that age may actually enhance a woman's sexual life, she's not a bit worried about getting older.*

WORKING WITH THE MAN YOU LOVE

by Sally Koslow

The Cast

MaryEllen and William Brennan—partners in The Brennans, an agency specializing in marketing, advertising and public relations

Bernadette Evangelist and Robert Anthony—partners in Robert Anthony, Inc., a graphic-design firm

Dale and David Ginsburg, MD—office manager and practicing physician

Patricia McBride and Jean-Pierre Bonnefous—principal dancers with The New York City Ballet

Regina and Shep Porter—partners in Porterhouse, a manufacturer of women's sportswear

If you've ever entertained the notion of working with a man you love, you know: It is a rich and colorful fantasy. If you take for granted that working is as basic as loving, working together would seem to tie up the package of your life, neatly, romantically.

Some women dismiss such a fantasy out of hand. Maybe they're half of a couple who argues over everything, even how to poach an egg. Maybe they know they need their own space, or that their career choices are too divergent. For the rest of us, working together can be a tender concept. Like all realities, it often falls short of the ideal. Rewarding, stimulating, enriching, yes; but "working together as a romantic idea just doesn't pan out," said psychiatrist Alexandra Symonds, MD. "The very nature of work involves friction and bad times; it isn't romantic at all."

By most accounts, the problems of working with the man/woman you love are numerous, if solvable, with the negatives and positives curiously intertwined. For example, in a joint enterprise, work often becomes so compelling that it fills every cranny of one's life, crowding out all other interests.

"Sometimes we can't cut it off," agreed MaryEllen Brennan. Bill Brennan sees this seeming "minus" as "more a disadvantage for us than for our clients," who benefit from the Brennans' total consumption by their projects.

Jean-Pierre Bonnefous recalled that for the first two or three years he and Patricia McBride danced together, "If something went wrong in rehearsal, we would spend the whole evening talking about it—it can ruin your life." A one-dimensional, albeit passionate, commitment, which seems invigorating at first, ultimately can become a trap. "Being together all the time creates stress," Symonds said. "I think most people absolutely need time apart. We all need chances to draw on ourselves spontaneously. Men tend to go overboard in this direction, wanting to be alone too much; women often have trouble being alone at all. This is a cultural phenomenon, not biological."

For eight years, Regina and Shep Porter have shared an airy office with "his and hers" desks and a harmonious business partnership. Yet Shep admitted that there is a "big disadvantage in being with the same person 24 hours a day. Sometimes I want to get lost. It's important to be able to tune the other person out, which Regina does better than I."

The Porters' primary relief from constant, overwhelming togetherness comes through the psychological separation of divided responsibilities. She designs the sportswear line and administers the manufacturing end; he oversees sales, production and financing.

When couples share an office *and* similar responsibilities, as Robert Anthony and Bernadette Evangelist do in their graphic-design firm, knowing where personal life begins and professional life ends can be a problem. Although they try to maintain a 9:00-to-6:00 business day, frequently it stretches until 10:00 PM. The tightness of a partnership can pinch when there is reason to disagree. When arguments are unresolved, Evangelist said, "Neither of us sulks or stops working; we get very formal with each other."

Two people involved together only in their personal lives are free to fight at will. In a working environment, married or living-together partners discipline themselves, putting their fights on hold for hours—sometimes days.

"You have to be mature enough to handle it," said Dale Ginsburg. "There have been times when we haven't spoken to each other in the office; we go home and talk things out." This self-imposed time lag occasionally acts as a tranquilizer; at the end of the long business day, neither partner wants to heat up a leftover argument.

Although most couples are willing to thrash out *business* problems in the office, they make strict rules about private matters. "I think it's fair to say we're professionals," said Bill Brennan. "If we have something to do, we do it. I don't think we've ever let a personal argument get in the way of our work. Conversely, we have had professional disagreements that spilled over into off hours."

The intimacy of a working couple also presents certain hurdles. "Because they know each other so well, couples tend to neglect a lot of the formalities that are assumed in most business relationships," said Marilyn Landis Hauser, PhD, who, with her husband Frederick, is part of a behavioral scientist twosome.

One of the most frequently forgotten courtesies is the softening of criticism. Couples often come right out and say, "You know, you really screwed up again."

"When Jean-Pierre joined the City Ballet in 1970, I was in my 11th year there," said Patricia McBride: "I knew the repertoire and I was used to telling my partners what to do. I found that it's hard for a wife to instruct her husband, and it was difficult for me to take directions from him." It took Bonnefous and McBride some time to iron out the problem. How long is something they still don't agree on: McBride said "several months," while Bonnefous thought "two or three years."

Bestowing praise seems as difficult for most couples as dishing out criticism is easy. Bernadette Evangelist began at Robert Anthony, Inc., in 1968 as business manager, then shifted her role to designer as she acquired technical expertise. Even now, an experienced artist, she is hungry for her husband's tributes. "He is a hard person to please," she said. "I've had to earn my pats on the back."

A lover or spouse can be excessively honest in assessing his/her partner's every verbal, physical or artistic stroke. "I think we're more critical than we would be if we weren't emotionally involved. We expect more of each other than we would of someone else," said Regina Porter. "It can get kind of sticky to point out that one of us has made a mistake."

If a couple harbors secret insecurities, the backlash—especially in dealing with criticism—can mushroom into bitter competition. A couple may not even realize they are competitive until they begin to work together and one starts closing in on the other's activities. The best working relationships seem to be those in which the partners bring together equal but different strengths.

"I think for two people to be able to work together," said Frederick Hauser, PhD, "they have to be reasonably autonomous, independent people. Two semi-cripples can't hold each other up. Each has to be able to make it on his own. . . . My hunch is that the teams that produce the best work are those who compete not against each other but against 'the guys out there.' In a partnership, anything that isn't equal is phony. . . ."

Part and parcel of the issue of competition is the question of Who's Boss. In the past, women assumed subordinate positions when working with men, avoiding that conflict. Dale and David Ginsburg have followed the traditional pattern. When David opened his private medical practice a little over a year ago, Dale left her homemaker role to manage his typing, billing, bookkeeping, etc. Dale sees her work with David as primarily a support function, which suits her fine. "But when he wants to make me mad, he starts calling me a secretary."

For those who have more or less equal experience, the expectation of having to defer to a ringleader can breed tension. For maximum satisfaction, "both parties have to be able to play the submissive role," said Marilyn Hauser.

"There is no boss at Porterhouse," said Regina Porter. Shep added, "We discuss and argue, then come to a decision." When possible, they try to compromise. "A lot of the time you can't compromise," he said, "because there's either a right way or a wrong way, and you have to convince the other person that your way is right."

The success of many coupled working relationships depends on maintaining a delicate balance: equal responsibility, equal pay, equal recognition. If one party surges ahead in any of these areas, the symmetry can be spoiled. Flexibility and mutual respect give a couple insurance against any such imbalance, as McBride and Bonnefous prove. Her name is much more a household word in America than his, yet . . . "I feel we're totally equal," McBride said. "When we go to France, everyone there knows Jean Pierre and no one knows me." Bonnefous has a slightly different view of their uneven

celebrity. "Patricia *is* more well known," he said. "Her name is more important than mine. But I think we deal with that really well." For him, it is not that big an issue. Her work is exclusively dancing; his involves less dancing and more teaching and choreography.

Who gets credit for mutual projects is another competition-linked issue. "Women are so timid about asking for credit," Symonds said. "They say it doesn't matter. But it does matter—to them."

Several years ago, a successful husband/wife graphic-design team broke up, partly because the woman—who entered the business as its manager and evolved into an impressive creative talent—was not given credit for her award-winning work. "My husband wasn't confident enough to give me credit," she said. "I know now that I am too competitive to be involved in a work situation with the man I love."

Without flexibility, the same problems might have arisen at Robert Anthony, Inc. Initially, Evangelist resisted asking for credit. "I thought art directors were looking for Bob's personal touch," she said, "and would be disappointed to learn that what they thought was an Anthony original was actually an Evangelist." Then art directors who were familiar with her work began encouraging her to put her name on her designs. Evangelist is giving in.

Recently, she became a partner in the firm: "I screamed and hollered— I felt it was time for recognition." Anthony, who married her several years after they started the business, was slow to grant her that foothold. "I'm not proud of it," he said. "It was one gesture that, for some lousy reason, I was holding back."

Anythony and Evangelist have nothing in their contract allowing for the possibility of a split in their personal relationship—a precaution that attorneys advise and most couples ignore. "Our feeling—and it may be unrealistic—is that we would sell each other our shares in the business if we were divorced," Anthony said. "But if there ever were real craziness, one of us could write a check for everything in the business account!"

Shep and Regina Porter protected themselves against such a catastrophe when they drew up their corporate plans. The Brennans have no such provision. "We've never thought about it because we assume we'll be together forever," Bill said. Dale and David Ginsburg also have no legal contract covering their mutual work. "If you think about what would happen if you got divorced, you have no business working together," he maintained. "You have to be sure you have a profound relationship before you begin."

Sharon Bermon, a career counselor at Counseling Women in New York City, disagreed. "Any woman who is considering going into business with her mate should discuss and define responsibilities, time commitments and areas of expertise before she starts. Just because you're going into partnership with someone you love doesn't mean that you should be unbusinesslike about it. In any business venture you need legal protection. This is no exception."

Whether couples follow Bermon's suggestion or let their feelings guide them, one norm prevails: Most couples become involved in each other's professional lives because they feel they have an important relationship. Despite the hazards, the couples who succeed find their relationships are enriched.

"I never expected to marry a dancer," said McBride. "Jean-Pierre was the first one I had ever dated. . . . It was a shock for both of us and, at first, hard working together. But we have found a way of doing it in complete harmony. We had lived together before we married and we both were established in our field."

The last factor seems to be especially critical to maintaining a strong, gratifying union. Just as the commitment to each other on an intimate level must be deep, so must the commitment to one's own career.

"With so many women wanting to enter the labor market, there is a tendency for them to latch on to a husband or lover already established in business," said Marilyn Hauser. "This can be very dangerous. First, the woman can become too dependent, rather than developing her own abilities. Second, if the woman does start to grow, she may become a threat and the relationship may crumble."

Far better is for lovers to join forces as experienced, mature working people. When they pool their talents, they make a whole that is greater than the sum of the parts.

Both Brennans spent many years in large corporations before they formed their business. "We had freelanced together, which proved to us we could work together," said Bill. "Our abilities and experience were very sympatico. When we began, I thought Mary Ellen would be our creative department, but she's better in all areas than I'd realized. I know that anything we do is going to be thought out on the highest level in a disciplined way. If I didn't have it before, I've gained confidence from seeing her produce."

Since people generally behave differently in each sphere of their lives, introducing a personal relationship into a work setting—or vice versa—can be illuminating. "For some couples, the experience may expose inadequacies; they begin to see each other in an uncomplimentary light," Symonds said. The reverse is true as well.

"Through dancing with her, I have discovered that Pat is one of the strongest people I know," Bonnefous said. "I have more respect for Regina's business sense now," admitted Shep Porter.

Many couples speak of advantages such as trust and loyalty, qualities often in short supply in an ordinary business relationship. "With Dale in the office, I can confine my attention to patients, not business decisions,"

Ginsburg said. Particularly important to couples whose work is creative is the dynamic way in which they spark each other. "In a large agency, a copywriter and art director work together." Bill Brenan said. "this process is all the more exciting when it's us together with our deep relationship, coming up with ideas. There's an added kick."

Perhaps the most glowing positive of all in working together is what brings most couples to the decision in the first place—they enjoy each other's company.

"Ninety percent of the people we know say, 'I would never work with my spouse.'" Dale Ginsburg said. For a lucky few, working with the one you love works.

Sally Koslow *is a free-lance writer specializing in women's careers and behavior.*

SHOP TALK ABOUT SHOP SEX: A QUIZ

by Joyce Dudney Fleming, PhD

Sex is a fact of life.

For working women, it's a fact of business life as well. Employment experts argue over how many women run into sexual harassment on the job (current guesses range from an ultraconservative 10 percent to an incredible 88 percent), but no one contends that sex does not put in an appearance at many a workplace. We all know it's there. Few of us know what to do about it.

When we're not aware of our choices or don't comprehend their consequences, we often feel damned if we do and damned if we don't. WORKING WOMAN asked me to put together this set of exercises as a little shop talk on shop sex. I hope they'll help you to understand how to deal effectively with ordinary, nine-to-five sexual situations while maintaining pleasant and productive relationships at work.

Here are four situations you may run into. See if you can spot the best way to handle each.

1. Principal's Wandering Hands

Janet, an elementary-school teacher, gets a little nervous every time the principal comes into her classroom. He's never done anything wrong, but he often touches her hands or shoulders or back while they discuss school matters. This habit annoys Janet, because she always wonders if he's going to make a pass at her someday. Janet should say:

A. Nothing at all, because, in light of her own standards, he hasn't behaved improperly. Why should she start trouble when she can avoid it?

B. "I really feel uncomfortable when you touch me, because I don't believe that such personal familiarity is an appropriate part of professional relationships."

C. "You shouldn't touch me because I don't want you to. You may enjoy it, but I don't."

D. "A person in your position should know better than to touch me like that. It's unethical and unprofessional."

Check Janet's solution below.

Ah, yes, the laying on of hands—perhaps the most common form of quasisexual behavior a working woman confronts. Sometimes it's a friendly gesture. Sometimes it's too friendly. Here's an easy way to tell the difference. If both sexes feel free to be initiators and terminators of casual touching, then you probably have little to worry about.

There's apt to be more camaraderie than conquest in such a touch. When men are the touchers and women the touchees, these contacts signal unhealthy circumstances for females. Reciprocity is the key.

This does not mean that Janet should ignore a colleague's habits when they interfere with her job.

A. **Wrong.** Janet feels uneasy about some aspect of her work environment. Pretending that she doesn't damages her self-confidence and undermines her dealings with her boss. Avoidance may seem to be an effective strategy, but it's not. Because it magnifies the importance of the problem, it decreases your ability to see simple solutions.

B. **Right.** Janet accurately expresses her feelings and the reasons behind them, without making any assumptions about the principal's unknown intentions. She meets her own need to stop his behavior while showing respect for him. This approach helps to establish and maintain good working relationships.

C. **Wrong.** This response may meet Janet's needs, but it also demonstrates a lack of concern for the principal's feelings. Although he probably will stop touching her, he also is apt to feel uncomfortable about working with her—a result that will harm their future interactions.

D. **Wrong.** Janet makes two mistakes here. First, she doesn't tell her boss how she feels. Second, she makes judgmental statements about his behavior. Such statements blame or hurt others, damaging the good feelings between the two parties.

2. "My Wife Doesn't Understand Me . . ."

Jack and Mary are friendly co-workers who joke and talk while they operate adjoining stations on an assembly line. One evening as Mary is hurrying to leave for an exercise class, Jack asks her to go have a cup of coffee with him. He says he needs someone to talk to, since his wife won't listen and he likes Mary so much. The prospect of such a conversation upsets Mary because she's not sure what Jack really wants. She should say:

A. "Okay, Jack, I'll have a cup of coffee and talk with you for a few minutes, but then I really have to go."

B. "Gee, I'm sorry, Jack. I'd like to, but I can't tonight because I have to go to my exercise class."

C. "No, Jack, I don't want to. I get very anxious when someone tries to tell me things he really wants to tell his wife."

D. "No, I won't go, because you should be home talking to your wife instead of trying to solve your problems this way. This won't help."

Here's How to Handle Jack.

"My spouse doesn't understand me" and similar statements ("won't listen to me") have launched more extramarital affairs than mere romantic murmurings ever have. Whether the speaker is aware of it or not, these words identify the search for a spouse substitute. What type of surrogate—emotional, intellectual, sexual—is hard to tell, but once these words are spoken, the search is on.

Since you have no intention of providing an end to that quest, you need to make your feelings clear before you find yourself deeply involved in someone else's divorce, dissolution or disappointment.

A. **Wrong.** Mary is trying to be nice and considerate of Jack's feelings because she values his friendship. But when she refuses to be honest about her reaction to his request, she creates circumstances that are almost certain to hurt his feelings and their friendship, too, later on.

B. **Wrong.** When Mary says she'd like to but can't tonight, Jack has good reason to believe that she would like to on some other night. A repeat invitation is a near certainty. By the time Jack realizes what her excuses really mean, their friendship will have been severely damaged by her lies.

C. **Right.** Mary tells Jack how she feels and why she feels that way. Since it is difficult to argue with decisions based on another's feelings, he probably will accept her explanation and drop the subject. Then he and Mary can still be friends, regardless of whether he continues his search.

D. **Wrong.** Here Mary repeats Janet's mistake in exercise 1-D. No one wants to hear unsolicited opinions about his behavior. Telling Jack what she thinks he should do isn't likely to change his behavior, and it is certain to cause bad feelings between them.

3. When the Client Has Something to Sell

Linda sells real estate in an area where the competition among realtors is intense. Sometimes her male clients suggest that they discuss a prospective sale over drinks or dinner. If she doesn't go, she's afraid she'll lose the sale. If she agrees, she's afraid that more intimate requests will follow, and that she'll refuse and lose the sale anyway. She should say:

A. "Sure, I'll go along if you promise to talk business and not try to turn this into a party."

B. "That sounds fine to me, and I think Carol should come along so that we can work really hard on finding the best property for you. She has some listings that may be just what you want."

C. "I won't do that, but I am willing to meet you for lunch later this week. That should give us plenty of time to discuss the properties I have listed."

D. "No, it's not right to mix business with pleasure. You shouldn't ask me to do it, and I won't let you talk me into it."

How to Stay on Top.

Prospective clients hold substantial power over the people they might choose to work with. Unequal power in business relationships invites abuse, just as it does in all types of interpersonal interactions. It may be a company official who asks a female employee to "entertain" a client or it may be the client himself. Either way, businesswomen have to face these dilemmas and make decisions about them.

Although no strategy is effective in all cases, rejecting the possibility that you might use subtle—or not so subtle—sexual enticements to influence a client usually maximizes your chances of getting the client while you keep your self-respect and your job. I'm not suggesting that women cannot handle sexually aggressive men in semisocial situations. Many can, but their methods may cause them to lose the client. In order to avoid the potential problems, you must refuse to allow work relationships to be converted into personal ones or even to be nudged in that direction.

A. **Wrong.** Linda is trying to set limits on the kinds of interactions that will occur. It's a good idea, but it rarely works. Most clients readily consent to such proposals beforehand and then blithely ignore them later, assuming that if you agree to one kind of social interaction, you will agree to other kinds as well.

B. **Wrong.** Here Linda tries another limit-setting approach. If the client accepts the presence of a third party, this strategy could work. Unfortunately, it carries with it the false implication that Linda cannot do this job by herself. Another drawback: The third party may end up with the commission Linda was after.

C. **Right.** By firmly rejecting the client's suggestion and offering a simple time-limited alternative (lunches can't turn into all-nighters like dinners and after-work drinks can), Linda plays her best shot. This effective approach tells the client exactly how she feels without putting him down. It also forces him to drop the pretense that he's primarily interested in doing business, if that is not the case.

D. **Wrong.** Linda's aggressive accusation will embarrass the client and make him feel hostile toward her. In all probability, she'll lose the sale.

4. Extra-Secretarial Services

When Andrea took the job as executive secretary to the president of a small manufacturing firm, she knew her duties included many personal services for her boss. She didn't know that he would try to extend her duties to include sexual services as well. When he told her what he wanted, she didn't know what to do. Since he owned the company, she couldn't complain to his boss. Although he did not threaten to fire her, she felt that her job would be in jeopardy if she refused. At her request, he agreed to let her think about it overnight. When Andrea talks to him the next day, she should say:

A. "I won't have intercourse with you because it's against my principles. If that's the kind of secretary you want, you should have said so when you interviewed me for the job."

B. "I won't, and if you ask me again, I'll tell your wife and everyone who works here. If you don't mention it again, I won't either. It's up to you."

C. "I can't, even though I like you a lot, because I'm not attracted to you and I never get involved with men unless they turn me on."

D. "I won't because I know that sex would harm the good working relationship we have. I take pride in my work and would not knowingly do anything that would interfere with it."

Andrea's Best Chance.

When your boss asks for sexual favors, there's no easy way out. The unequal power I mentioned earlier is even more lopsided here. In most cases your boss has complete control over your job, while you have virtually no influence over his.

Yet even under these extreme circumstances, some responses are more effective than others. Since incidents of sexual harassment are a little like automobile accidents (they happen only to other people), they often take us by surprise. If you can't answer immediately, say that you need some time to think it over, and then use that time to plan and rehearse your reply. Knowing exactly what you want to say and how you want to say it will make you less anxious. An outward appearance of calm control will help to defuse an emotionally explosive situation and show that you handle business matters in a professional way.

A. **Wrong.** Although each word of this statement may be completely true, it's not going to help Andrea to keep her job. Her boss probably will do exactly what she suggests: start looking for her replacement and tell the candidates that intercourse comes with the paycheck.

B. **Wrong.** By threatening her boss, Andrea may win the battle, but almost certainly will lose the war, and her job. While this response may buy her some time (which she will spend looking for other employment if she's smart), it is unlikely to do more than that. Most people respond to threats with retaliation, and there's no reason to think her boss is different from the rest of us.

C. **Wrong.** Here, again, Andrea is trying to postpone the highly probable pink slip. But many men would read her words as an open invitation to courtship—"Well, maybe if we got to know each other better . . ."—and proceed accordingly. Then, Andrea would have to face her boss's attempt to increase her sexual interest in him, in addition to her worry over losing her job.

D. **Right.** Although no response, including legal action, can protect Andrea from being fired, this one generates several good consequences. First, it makes Andrea feel good about herself. Second, it presents her decision as a business-related one instead of a personal putdown. Third, it shows her boss that she's more interested in getting the job done than in name-calling, threatening or playing games. Positive results are far from guaranteed, but it is possible that her boss will decide to keep such a professional employee and turn his sexual attentions elsewhere.

Backfiring Alternative.

You may be wondering why my recommendations didn't include quitting the job, registering a formal complaint with some higher authority or taking legal action. Since these women did nothing wrong, why should they put up with offensive behavior? That's a perfectly logical question about some perfectly logical alternatives. I did not recommend them for these reasons:

Quitting—Very few of us can get by without our paychecks, and unemployment compensation for women who have quit or lost their jobs because of sexual harassment is rare in liberal states and nonexistent in the others. If you can afford to quit, then you should when you think that's the best option. Most of us simply cannot leave one job until we have another.

Complaining—Complaints administered through a company's proper channels bring mixed results. Since you're the one who knows how your organization operates, you'll have to judge this option for yourself. If you decide to complain, speak discreetly with some of your female colleagues first. Any man who approached you probably has approached other women, too. A complaint will carry more weight if it comes from several workers. The major problem with protests is that they tend to backfire. For example, you may discover that the higher authority would rather get rid of you—an obvious troublemaker—than rock the company boat by confronting the guilty party. A union may help, but don't be surprised to find a male-dominated organization unsympathetic to your plight.

Suing—According to the project director of Working Woman United Institute (WWUI), Karen Sauvigné, none of the situations described in this article has been judged unlawful by US courts. You can sue under Title VII of the Civil Rights Act (the section prohibiting discrimination in employment on the basis of race, sex, etc.) *only* when it is certain that your continued employment is dependent upon sexual activity. Because of this ridiculously narrow definition, many women who encounter offensive sex on the job would be better off to support WWUI (593 Park Avenue, New York, NY 10021) than to spend money on a lawyer who probably won't be able to get their cases into court. WWUI is the only national institute dedicated to providing research and resources on the sexual harassment of working women.

I hope I've offered some useful suggestions. If you understand what to do but don't believe you can carry it off, I have another suggestion: Effectiveness Training for Women (ETW). Don't confuse ETW with the many assertiveness seminars that show women how to stand up for their rights (particularly in impersonal settings, such as gas stations and restaurants). This inexpensive course—about $100 for 30 hours of instruction and experience—teaches women how to be effective in all kinds of interpersonal relationships, how to meet their needs and respect others at the same time. This national program operates in many locations. To find the one nearest you, write to Effectiveness Training, Inc., 531 Stevens Avenue, Solano Beach, CA 92075.

One final suggestion about those truly rare cases when an intense and mutual attraction tempts you to mix business with pleasure. Don't do it! Business affairs can be grand, while they last. Afterwards, the soot left behind by the dying flame blackens your weekdays. Working with a person you used to love is the pits. There's only one reliable way to prevent such dark days: Keep your sex life out of your shop.

JOYCE DUDNEY FLEMING, *a Ph.D. in psychology, owns a California-based editorial consulting service, WORD'SWORTH. "Nothing ends a good working relationship faster than ambivalence," Fleming says. "It really opens up a rat's nest."*

Chapter Six

Travel

WORKING WOMEN ON THE ROAD

by Patricia Beard

Two women are seated next to each other on a flight from Tucson, Arizona, to New York City. One has opened her business case and is reading reports. The other has a notebook on her lap and is writing. Suddenly, the plane runs into turbulence and a cup of hot tea spills into the lap of the woman in the window seat. She rings for the stewardess. After a few minutes, she rings again. The woman with the briefcase puts down her papers and looks at her soaked seatmate. "Traveling on business?" she asks. "Yes. I'm a journalist," is the reply. "Have you ever noticed how hard it is for a woman business traveler to get a stewardess's attention?" her companion remarks. The women agree that the question hardly needs to be answered.

On that day in 1979, according to United Airlines, these two women represented two out of ten business travelers, a remarkable surge from 1970, when the women traveling on business didn't appear on United's com-

puters at all. In 1977, women accounted for 16 percent of United's market. By fall 1978, travel by businesswomen on United had increased 54 percent over the same period in 1977. At Hertz, 12 percent of all business travelers renting cars are women. Air New England said that the increase in women business travelers from fall 1978 to summer 1979 was double the increase in total passenger travel.

Who's Traveling?

What's more, the woman business traveler now has a profile. According to *Career Travel*, a newsletter for traveling businesswomen, she's about 38 (her male counterpart is 41); her family income is about $25,000; she takes ten round trips a year (male business flyers take 18); 39 percent of the time she's flying to attend conventions; she stays away from home seven nights a year, as compared to a man's average of five nights; there's a 63 percent chance that

106

she's married (as compared with 84 percent for male business flyers); and she's an executive or professional.

Along with the changing statistics, attitudes have changed. In 1967, United ran an advertising campaign in which a homemaker pleaded with her husband to "take me along" on a business trip. The man in the ad replied, "I love you, little cutie, but the office is my duty." United's Fred Heckel, vice-president of advertising and promotion, pointed out that the campaign was one of the most successful in airline history. Women across the nation wrote "take me along" on the bottoms of coffee cups they raised as they sat across from their husbands at breakfast. They stuck the words on beer cans in refrigerators. United's 1978 campaign showed a woman stockbroker.

Managing the Social Aspects of Business

Women have plenty of problems on business trips, problems that don't affect men—uncooperative stewardesses are the least of them. Most of the difficulties center around the social aspects of doing business. An executive woman meeting with clients in her office is surrounded with the paraphernalia that proclaim her status—a secretary; a corner office; a board room in which she controls meetings from the head of the table; a charge account at a restaurant, making it unnecessary to negotiate over who pays the check. On the road, she has to create an aura of authority with no more props than her clothes and her briefcase. Especially if she's young, she runs the risk of not being taken as a "heavy" and even invoking the client's indignation at not being sent a "more important" executive. To compound her problems, a woman is likely to get worse service at hotels and restaurants than a man gets and to have more trouble commanding special services, such as a stenographer or a slide projector.

If a businesswoman is attractive, she may have to field passes by a client who assumes

that a woman free enough to travel alone is free in other ways, too. She may find herself stuck late at night after a business dinner with the choice of waiting for a cab on a deserted corner or being taken to her hotel by a man with unbusinesslike intentions.

Evaluating the problems you may encounter as a woman traveling on business is a first step toward coping with them. As for the solutions, if you're good enough at your job to be sent to Japan or Paris or Houston to represent your company, you're smart enough to figure out how to pay the restaurant check without stepping on your client's cultural taboos.

Maintaining a Professional Image

The first question is how to establish yourself as an authoritative business person while on the road. A lawyer who often has meetings with her clients in the living room of her hotel suite reports that when she checks into a hotel, she introduces herself to the manager and generously tips the concierge, the headwaiter in the hotel restaurant and the room-service waiter. What's more, she stays in the best hotel in town and entertains there, where the staff knows her, and lunch and dinner checks are charged to her hotel bill. She never has a problem with men who want to take her home—because she is home.

When a purchasing agent for a big steamship company visits steel mills where there are no executive women, she usually travels with a male associate, who is her junior. She noticed that the men in the mill addressed most of their comments to her subordinate. She often had to interrupt to make a point or ask a question. Now, when she visits suppliers, she makes the introductions. "I'm Marilyn Craw," she says, "and I'd like you to meet my associate, Bob Applegarth." The client gets the message.

A retail-store vice-president reported that evading passes usually has more to do with knowing when to leave a business party than how you look and act. There's a point when even the most formal business evening begins to loosen its metaphorical tie. That's when she goes home. There's nothing to be gained by staying at a party when a client's had too much to drink or is flirting with you. In fact, there's a lot to lose because he'll probably be embarrassed the next day.

Keeping in Touch with the Home Front

All of these techniques are reminders that a woman traveling on business has to be more careful and more professional than a man.

While doing business away from home is likely to be more difficult for a woman than for a man, being away from home is surely harder for a woman. If she's single and travels frequently, she'll find that she gets out of touch with men and women friends who have found her "out of town" so often that they stop calling. If she's married, her husband is likely to complain that he has all the disadvantages of being single (principally, the lack of companionship) with none of the freedom. And when a man goes away and leaves his wife alone, is he likely to stock the freezer with prepared meals that need only to be heated? If she has children, she'll find that parents' visiting days at school and childhood diseases seem to be synchronized with her business trips. Have you ever known a father setting off on a business trip to leave a list of menus and emergency phone numbers? The worst option of all probably is the mother who is either divorced or widowed and can't count on even a begrudging husband to fill in the gaps.

Every businesswoman we spoke with reported that when it comes to covering the home front, the telephone is her best friend. Most mothers call their children before bedtime every night. An investment banker with two toddlers sings lullabies from phone booths or requests the use of a private office to make a phone call if a meeting is still going on at 6:00 PM. She reports that even though her children miss her, they know she'll call every night.

A journalist who leaves her husband for a week or more at least once a month says her trips have been the catalyst for a series of wonderful weekends when her husband meets her on location or at a place between the site of her assignment and home. Because her plane fare is paid for, they can afford to go away together more often than if she didn't travel.

A fashion model, who may be in the Canary Islands one week and Jamaica the next, leaves precise information with her answering service as to her planned date of return. She's asked her service to tell callers she'll be phoning in for her messages—and even if she's at a remote location, she checks in and returns calls.

All of this may seem like a lot of extra work for a busy executive, but, as the 36-year-old woman president of a cosmetics company commented, "Men have been traveling on business since they put sails on ships. Women have only started. It's not surprising that it's more difficult for us. But it's so exciting to take on new responsibilities that it's worth the effort to work out a system."

. . . SMOOTH GOING FOR BUSINESS TRIPS . . .

by Elizabeth Elliot

"Women, you know, Sir, are considered domestic beings, and although they inherit an equal share of curiosity with the other sex . . . the natural tenderness and delicacy of our constitutions, added to the many dangers we are subject to from your sex, renders it almost impossible for a single lady to travel without injury to her character."

Over 200 years ago, Abigail Adams wrote those words to a male friend. Although outwardly frail and delicate, Abigail raised five children, and, for long periods of time when her husband was away, she ran the family farm and did much of the physical work. Fascinated with books and adventure, she read and wrote almost as much as her husband did. Yet she hardly ever traveled alone. For the lone female traveler, conditions were impossible.

Change came slowly. Only a few years ago, a woman traveling by herself for business or pleasure was ignored by busy hotel desk-clerks (and occasionally refused a room, particularly if she was carrying only a small overnight case); found herself seated behind the potted palms or next to the kitchen door in a popular restaurant; and had her financial reliability triple-checked before being granted a credit card that a man might have obtained with little difficulty.

But now, after all those years as a second-class traveling citizen, she's finally in the catbird seat. The travel industry has discovered that businesswomen are among its best customers. A recent survey by the trade journal *Hotel and Motel Management* disclosed that, conservatively estimated, businesswomen represent about 11 million per-person nights a year for hotels and motels. Airlines have noted similar statistics. So, instead of ignoring women or regarding them as appendages to a husband or a male boss, the travel industry is now actively wooing the businesswoman.

Symbolic of this development is a drastic change in advertising tactics. Only two years ago, a TV commercial featured a sexy, short-skirted stewardess breathlessly announcing to (presumably) male customers: "I'm Nancy . . . fly me." Today's advertising messages are different. An ad for Eastern Airlines, for instance, now shows an efficient, attractive young woman carrying a briefcase

being served by a male cabin attendant. A TV voice-over says something like: "You're the boss . . . it's you we aim to please."

Many of the new special services have been designed by airline and hotel customer-relations specialists clearly with the traveling woman in mind. Take airline meals. Traditional in-flight meals are meant for the meat-and-potatoes man . . . especially the one who couldn't care less about counting calories. Of course, for some years low-cholesterol, low-sodium or kosher meals have been available if they were ordered ahead of departure time. But American Airlines has now added a new wrinkle: Instead of Beef Bourguignon or Chicken Paprikash, you can order a fresh fruit salad, a chef's salad or the "Mariner's Seafood Plate." The last is a particularly delicious, low-calorie, high-protein combination of fresh shrimp, crabmeat and lobster. Order your salad when you make your plane reservation, either through your travel agent or the airline's reservation desk.

Lufthansa and Scandinavian Airlines Systems added another method to keep passengers slim and fit . . . instruction in isometric and other exercises that can be done in your seat. On many of their trans-oceanic flights, you dial a special headset-channel and listen to an exercise specialist instruct you to tense, relax and stretch. Besides keeping you in shape and helping you to relax even on a bumpy trip, all of this should also minimize jet lag.

Those special airport clubs, which formerly seemed like all-male enclaves, are also changing. Eastern actually solicits female membership in its Ionosphere Club through a special publication published several times a year called *Eastern's Businesswoman: Travel and Times for Women On-The-Go*. This brochure is well worth ordering for its valuable information and can be obtained free by writing to Eastern's Businesswoman, PO Box 530, Radio City Station, New York, NY 10019.) The Ionosphere Clubs offer complimentary coffee, tea and newspapers, and cocktails at a slight charge; but most importantly, desk areas with phones, and, if requested ahead of time, meeting rooms for private conferences. Clubs are situated in airports in Atlanta, Boston, Chicago, Houston, Miami, Montreal, Newark, New York, Orlando, San Juan, Tampa and Washington, DC. The membership fee is $25 a year (tax deductible as a business expense) and is well worth it if you spend a lot of time traveling between US cities.

Pan American Airlines' Clipper Club, with facilities throughout the world, offers complimentary cocktails, hot and cold drinks, private sitting areas, local newspapers, advice on overnight accommodations by friendly, English-speaking personnel and other useful amenities. The cost is $40 per year, but frequent travelers may be eligible to join free-of-charge. Application forms can be obtained from your travel agent or the nearest Pan Am office. Clipper Club members also receive special baggage tags designed to expedite handling of suitcases, and they are entitled to sit in a special section of the plane where there are no movies and no small children so they can work in peace. Other airlines offer similar special services. Ask your travel agent.

Hotels and motels are also beginning to think about the special needs of traveling businesswomen. (There was a time when the management's concern amounted to little more than offering free bobby pins, hairnets or sewing kits.) For instance, since it's difficult for a woman to invite a male colleague to her room for a private business conference, some hotel chains are now offering "convertible" rooms, in which the bed can easily be turned into a sofa. There's also a businesslike desk and table with chairs for conferences. Some of the larger chains—including Marriott, Hyatt House, Hilton and Sheraton—have discarded sofa beds in convertible rooms and are using wall beds that pull up or go down with a very light touch. When concealed, they give no evidence to the uninformed that they are even in the room.

In Washington, DC; Alexandria, Virginia; Greensboro, North Carolina and Atlanta, Georgia, a new chain called "Guest Quarters" works on an even more revolutionary principle; for a price comparable to a first-class hotel room, "Guest Quarters" provides the traveler with a living room, bedroom and kitchenette. These "Guest Quarters" establishments don't have elaborate restaurants and meeting rooms, nor large lobbies; they look more like apartment houses than hotels. But Continental breakfasts are available, and it is possible to make arrangements to have business luncheons or dinners catered in your suite. If you want, you can cook, too. Reservations can be made through your travel agent or by calling the facility directly.

Women who spend a day or more on business in a town they don't know well may need secretarial services, typewriters, dictating or duplicating equipment, etc. Although few hotels have such facilities available on their own, the management often can arrange for these needs before the guest arrives. Let them know what you need when you make a reservation. If the hotel is not able to supply it directly, they should be able to put you in touch with firms or individuals who can.

Now for some of the problems that still may beset the lone woman traveling on business. She may, in a few places, have to put up with what seems like discriminatory treatment. A hotel may ask a woman to prepay her room if she does not have a credit card or has forgotten to bring it. If that same hotel does not make similar requests of male guests under the same circumstances, it's breaking both Federal and State Fair Accommodations Laws. Usually, a reminder of that fact may change the reservation clerk's or manager's mind.

Some of the older hotels still have health clubs and other sports facilities that cater only to male guests. The reason most frequently given for this is that there are no dressing rooms for women. This, too, may be illegal, but usually it's hardly worth a major hassle. If a woman feels strongly about this, a letter to the State Tourist Office may change the situation, eventually.

Yet women travelers today are in a situation that Abigail Adams as well as their own mothers (and even older sisters) might well envy.

TRAVELING ALONE

by Margaret Zellers

Traveling alone doesn't have to be lonely. I haven't found it to be so—and am convinced that a sure cure for shedding the "blahs" is travel. It is essential to leave the mental baggage of fear at home—along with as much of the rest of your baggage as possible. (You'll be carrying what you *do* take yourself.)

Look ahead, and expect the adventure to be fun. Don't get "meandering" mixed up with "men." Traveling alone can be exciting. Being alone and wanting to be half of two is not.

First Day Out

Setting out alone the first morning in a new city can be terrifying (like the days when setting out from your own home seems more than you can handle). Pull yourself together, push yourself out the door (one of the problems with traveling alone is that there's no one else to do the pushing) and sign on for at least a half-day tour—where you relax in a seat on a bus and are talked to. This has two advantages: 1) You can get your bearings and figure out which places to return to, and 2) you may strike up a conversation with someone and arrange to do some touring or wandering together later.

Evening hours can be the longest part of the day under any circumstances. Solutions for filling the time when you're traveling in a foreign city are tickets for a show or concert, easily arranged through the hotel activities desk. If you're on a Caribbean island, lingering over dinner is your best bet or—as I have done more than once—turn in early (some-times even before dinner, if I've had a big, late lunch) and wake with the dawn to get out and do some early wandering when the local streets have some action.

Eating Alone

Dining alone terrifies people. Why? You have a perfect right to dine alone and like it—to savor your food or to people-watch, as you wish. I've found that tucking a paperback book, or postcards to send, into my pocketbook takes care of waiting time; others meditate before mealtime or use the time to make a list for tomorrow.

For trying out fancy restaurants, you have a choice. Go for lunch, on your own and leisurely. Or, if you are near a restaurant known for its evening ambiance or show, stop at the place mid-afternoon (at the end of the late-lunch surge) and talk with the maitre d'. Ask when they start serving dinner, tell him you will be coming back alone and would like a nice table out of the way but where you can see the show (if there is one) and ask what time would be best. Chances are, when you return at the hour he's suggested, you'll be treated like visiting royalty, taken to your table and kept watch over by a staff alerted to your special status.

Where to Go

The place you choose to travel to alone is all-important. Until you've become a confirmed, happy loner, try one of the following:

- London, where there are plenty of shows to see and some of the most civilized sights to track down, and you speak the language.

- A special-interest tour, nonrestricted by age or sex, such as those offered through the Smithsonian.
- A foreign-study course—in cooking, language, handicraft or some sport. Government tourist offices can provide a list of specific courses that may interest you. (All governments have representatives for tourism in New York and often in other cities.)
- The Caribbean, because of the climate and the sea breeze, is romantic and usually thought of for two. I have traveled every inch of that area alone. There are plenty of places for one—and that one does not have to be a hermit. Choose an inn in downtown St. Thomas or at Christiansted, St. Croix, where you can walk to shops and restaurants and where the atmosphere is casual.

More than once, I have caved in on a quiet beach, happy to be alone, to languish in the warm sun and sea, secure in the knowledge that there are other people around . . . but relaxed in knowing that none of them is my responsibility. If that appeals, try Grand Cayman's Holiday Inn—known as the Grand Caymanian—or Cerromar, on Puerto Rico's north coast. If sports are your thing (or could be), sign on for a scuba, sailing or tennis week. Above all, whether you live your life alone or just want to travel alone, there's a lot to be said for sampling the rest of the world first-hand and unfettered.

TRAVEL ABROAD

by Jane E. Lasky

There's a lot to know in the world of international travel, and women who are planning business trips to foreign countries don't always have the time or resources to keep up with the details. Obtaining visas is one area that may present difficulties, and so you may want to employ the services of a visa agency—a professional service run by experienced personnel who will do the running around for you.

Visa agencies offer a number of travel services from processing visas and securing passports to more specialized services, such as arranging for the Arabic translations needed to obtain a Libyan visa or the State Department documentation required for legal authentication. These organizations will duplicate forms when necessary and arrange for fast delivery service by express mail or air freight.

Visa agency fees vary according to the kind of service done, but are usually minimal. One company, called Visa Advisors, which is now doing a $200,000-a-year business as a visa liaison in Washington, DC, charges from $7 to $15 for securing a visa, depending on the difficulty of procurement, plus the consular fee charged by the issuing country, if any; $30 for Arabic translations; $7 to get additional passport pages; and $15 for pickup and delivery at Washington's National Airport.

Elizabeth F. Wallace, Visa Advisors' 26-year-old president, pointed out, "Using a visa service can sometimes mean saving days or weeks avoiding red-tape situations. While women don't have more trouble than men in being granted visas to most countries, sometimes they do confront special trouble spots that don't always seem fair or logical.

"Every time you apply for a visa to a particular area of the world, you are subject to that country's customs, mores and attitudes," said Wallace. "The rules and regulations for securing visas are not always decided upon during bilateral agreements between the US and foreign countries. Each visa application is subject to the particular idiosyncrasies of individual embassy personnel."

The Embassy of Afghanistan, for instance, requires that one of the three required photos for application must be *paper clipped to the center of the first form sheet*, or the application will be rejected—not a detail that a person applying for a visa for the first time is likely to know.

Certain countries will not grant you a visa or allow you to enter with a valid visa if there is evidence on your passport of a visa or airport stamp from a country they are not on friendly terms with. Several Middle Eastern countries, for example, will not grant a visa when an Israeli airport entry or exit stamp appears on the passport. Travelers can't enter the People's Republic of China if they have a visa from Taiwan on their passports.

To solve this particular problem, you must apply for a second, restricted passport, valid only for the countries of South Africa, Israel and either Taiwan or the People's Republic of China. If evidence of travel to South Africa, Taiwan or Israel is already on the passport, simply have the old passport restricted for travel to those countries only, and have a new passport issued for travel to all other countries.

Other factors, such as unexpected bad weather conditions or national holidays particular to a foreign country, can cause a temporary shutdown of embassy operations, which in turn causes a slowdown on visa issuance. Visa agencies, which often have special contacts, are in the best position to skirt catastrophes of this sort.

Besides the dozen or so visa agencies in Washington, DC, there are others located in most major US cities, including Boston, New York, Chicago, Los Angeles, San Francisco,

Seattle and Houston. But the Washington agencies handle the bulk of the business, either directly or from work passed, for expediency's sake, from agencies in other cities. Many visas can be issued only from an embassy, not from a consulate operating in other areas, so Washington is the only place where travelers can get visas to the following countries: Bulgaria, Czechoslovakia, Malaysia, Sri Lanka, Thailand, Romania, United Arab Emirates, Cameroon, Iraq, Libya and the People's Republic of China.

Be careful in selecting a visa agency—the employees of these services, like travel agents, are not legally required to undergo an official licensing program. Get the names of several recommended visa companies from your travel agent or look for visa agencies listed in the Yellow Pages. Call each one and request the necessary documents for the visas you need. Those that respond promptly and efficiently are probably reliable. As a further check, call the embassy in question and confirm whether or not the agency you intend to use is indeed reliable and efficient.

Passports

- Applications for a first passport are available from passport agencies in 15 offices across the country. Completed applications are accepted in person at 195 US district courts, 2,747 state courts, 798 post offices.
- Required in addition to the application are: two identical, frontview, full-face photographs (taken within the past six months, either black and white or color, and no larger than two inches by two inches); a $14 application fee; proof of identity (birth or naturalization certificate, driver's license or government or municipal ID pass).
- Standard passports have 24 pages; frequent travelers should request a 48-page passport. Additional pages can be added free at any passport office.
- Passports must be renewed every five

years. Renewal can be done through the mail by sending the current passport (it must have been issued within the last eight years), a $10 fee, new photos and an appropriate, completed application form to the nearest passport agency.

Inoculations

● One, two, or three types of inoculation may be required: cholera, smallpox and/or yellow fever.

● A single shot does it for smallpox and yellow fever; for cholera you need to get two shots, ten days apart. A yellow-fever shot can't be taken within ten days of a smallpox or cholera shot.

● Smallpox vaccinations are good for three years; yellow fever for ten years; cholera for six months.

● Most doctors have up-to-date information on the recommended vaccinations for each country, supplied by the World Health Organization. If yours doesn't, contact your state or local health department or call the US Public Health Service. Crosscheck with embassy requirements. Sometimes WHO recommendations and embassy requirements differ, so compare the combined information.

● A record of shots must be entered on an International Certificate of Vaccination, available from doctors, passport offices, travel agents and airlines. Any licensed physician can give the shots, but only doctors with an official health department stamp can validate the vaccination. If the doctor does not have this stamp, have the shots validated at city hall or at a county or state health department. You can get yellow-fever vaccinations only at yellow-fever vaccination centers in major US cities.

● When getting shots, keep your travel itinerary in mind—some countries require vaccination only if you arrive from an infected area.

The following countries require a business visa but not a tourist visa:

Dominican Republic	Philippines
Jamaica	Sri Lanka
Mexico	Trinidad/Tobago
Pakistan	Venezuela

As of June 1979, the following countries do *not* require a business or tourist visa for entry:

Argentina	Ecuador	Israel	Paraguay
Austria	El Salvador	Italy	Peru
Bahamas	Fiji	Lesotho	Panama
Barbados	Finland	Luxembourg	Portugal
Belgium	France	Malawi	Singapore
Botswana	Great Britain	Malaysia	Spain
Canada	Greece	Malta	Surinam
Chile	Grenada	Morocco	Sweden
Colombia	Guyana	Netherlands	Switzerland
Costa Rica	Haiti	New Zealand	Tunisia
Cyprus	Iceland	Nicaragua	Turkey
Denmark	Ireland	Norway	Uruguay
			West Germany

WHAT BUSINESSWOMEN LOOK FOR IN HOTELS

by Tania Grossinger

One out of every six business travelers in the United States today is a woman, and the number of women traveling for business reasons is increasing at a rate three times faster than that of men. In 1977 over three million women spent more than $12 billion for 32 million nights on the road. Yet it is only now, finally, that the hotel business is beginning to wake up and acknowledge and even encourage its new and very lucrative market among working women.

What does a businesswoman want from a hotel? Ideally, of course, she wants to live as well there as she lives at home, perhaps even a little better. At the very least, she wants a room that is safe, clean, comfortable, reasonably priced and located conveniently to the place where she'll be doing business. She also wants to be treated as a professional person whose time is too valuable to be spent reconfirming reservations or chasing after telephone messages. The attitude of the hotel staff and management toward her is important; she expects to be treated with respect, efficiency and courtesy; she does not want to be patronized.

Which Hotel?

Most businesswomen prefer to stay in chain hotels with a national reputation and a familiar name: Hilton, Marriott, Sheraton, Holiday Inn, Western International. Because time is at a premium, traveling women usually prefer hotels that offer full services: same-day valet and laundry service, self-service refrigerator/bars in the rooms, restaurant, cocktail lounge, newspaper stand, beauty salon, drugstore, car-rental desk, sightseeing and ticket counters on premises, dictating and secretarial services, typewriters, conference rooms, 24-hour doormen and desk attendants.

Security is uppermost in the minds of many women. They look for hotels in neighborhoods where it is safe to come and go, if need be, late at night. They look for internal security measures, too: a busy lobby, well-lighted hallways, attended elevators and strong locks on hotel-room doors.

Safety in a Hotel

Once you've checked into a hotel, there are steps you can take to ensure your safety:

- Have a bellhop escort you to your room. Have him inspect the closets and bathroom to be sure that no one is loitering.
- Try not to let people around you see or hear your name when you are at the front desk. The easiest method is to hand over your business card as you check in. This relieves you of the necessity of announcing yourself, establishes your authority as a business traveler, and puts your business address rather than your home address on record.
- Ask for a room near the elevators. It may be a noisy area, but it will be well lighted and safe.
- If you can help it, never take a room in the motel section of a hotel. These rooms are the most isolated and also the easiest to break into.
- Don't travel with any jewelry you can't wear all the time.
- Lock your suitcases whenever you leave your room.
- Don't display your room key in public. Do not leave it on restaurant tables or in other places where it might be stolen easily.
- To deter robberies, consider leaving a radio or television on when you leave your room.
- Don't display large amounts of cash when making purchases.
- If you hear strange noises when you open the door to your room, do not enter. Close

the door, lock it and report what you've heard to the front desk immediately.

- If you come in late and the corridors are deserted, don't hesitate to have someone from the front desk or hotel security personnel escort you to your room.
- Double lock the door and bolt the chain before retiring.

Dining Out

Harvard magazine recently cited a survey that noted that "a majority of women rated eating alone in a restaurant more unpleasant than asking for a loan or having a gynecological examination." Considering the way women often are treated when they enter a restaurant or hotel dining room alone, it's no wonder they sometimes prefer room service or even a fast-food parlor. No woman likes to be treated as an unpresentable, second-class citizen, to be told that there will be an hour's wait when there are empty tables visible, to be seated behind a pole next to the kitchen or to be handed a check along with the main course.

What Hotels Are Doing for Women

Some hotels are taking steps to counteract traditional staff prejudice against single women diners. The Kansas City Marriott, for example, has inaugurated a Captain's Table in its Kings Wharf restaurant — inspired by a standard dining procedure on cruise ships—which single diners of both sexes are invited to join. The Carlton House in Pittsburgh has a VIP table exclusively for women who would like to share one another's company at dinner. And at Western International hotels (including the Plaza in New York City), waiters are instructed that if a man and woman are dining together and it can't be determined who is the host, the waiter should place the check equidistant from both diners rather than to hand it to the man.

One sure way for hotels to attract women

travelers is to offer special amenities to make them feel welcome. The Whitehall Hotel in Chicago provides skirt hangers, well-lighted makeup mirrors, a bathroom clothesline, shoe horns, terry-cloth robes, selected toiletries and two female concierges who do everything from arranging for the use of meeting rooms to running personal errands. The Carlton House in Pittsburgh gives every female guest an Ultrasuede pouch containing a razor, hand cream, shampoo, a shower cap, a sewing kit and information about how to get hair dryers, irons and ironing boards from the hotel. The Berkshire Hotel in midtown Manhattan employs a female concierge who will answer questions about night life and transportation.

In addition, hotels should:

- Make sure that telephone messages are delivered *when they are received*.
- Provide more convenient electrical outlets for hair dryers, irons and other appliances and reliable room service at breakfast time.
- Offer a complimentary cocktail or after-dinner drink to women in order to make single women feel welcome in the dining room.
- Make sure that part of the cocktail lounge is well lighted. A woman inviting a colleague for a drink to discuss business prefers a living-room atmosphere to that of a boudoir.
- Make sure that there is a desk in the room with adequate lighting as well as a good bed light.
- Never permit a female guest to be addressed as dear, honey or by her first name by anyone on the staff.
- Make sure that someone at the front desk knows where outside services such as copy machines, printers and audio-visual rental equipment are available.
- Prominently display a notice in each room regarding whom to call if there is a problem or a question.

Making Your Stay More Agreeable

Hospitality is a two-way street, and there are things every traveler can do to avoid uncomfortable situations.

- Make sure that your reservation confirmation is in writing and that you bring it with you.
- If you are going to be late checking in, call beforehand to announce your time of arrival. If you have to stay past the posted checkout hour or for an extra day, notify the front desk as soon as you can.
- If you have special requirements—meeting room, typewriter, secretarial help—make them known when you make your reservation or as soon after your arrival as possible. If you need an iron, ironing board or hair dryer, ask for it when you check in. The supply may be limited.
- Make sure you have single dollar bills or change available for tips. Know in advance how much service people should receive. Do *not* overtip. (Western International publishes this information in a booklet, *Tips for the Woman Business Traveler.* For a free copy write: Western International Hotels, PO Box 12640, Seattle, WA 98111.)
- If you are planning to entertain a business associate at dinner, let the maitre d' know before hand and arrange for the check to be presented to you. Better yet, ask him to add the standard tips (15 percent for the waiter and 5 percent for the captain if he has been especially helpful) and have the whole bill charged to your room number.
- If you have a complaint, make it on the spot. Don't be intimidated. If it is a serious matter, note the names of the staff members involved and send a letter to the manager or the president of the hotel chain, explaining exactly why you will not return and why you are suggesting to your company that it take its travel business elsewhere.

Business travel can be an interesting and broadening experience. The more sophisticated you become about it, the more you will look forward to and relish it.

Part Three

Making Work
Work for You

Chapter Seven

Your Paycheck

SALARIES:
HOW TO GET PAID WHAT YOU'RE WORTH

by David J. McLaughlin

If you are one of the 80 million people who work for a salary in this country, you may well be suffering from a crippling disease that isn't listed in the medical books—*ignoratio compensationis* (ignorance about compensation, from here on known as I.C.). Physically painless but psychologically and economically devastating, it can shrivel both the ego and the earning power of its victims, costing tens of thousands of dollars in lost income over the course of a career. For many of its victims, a job and a career are high priorities. Why are they suffering? Why is a third of the work force, in my experience, not paid what it's worth?

One reason is that pay has become an extremely complex matter. Most of us are paid in at least a dozen ways—salaries, overtime or cash bonuses, disability insurance, medical coverage, life insurance, pension plans, profit sharing and savings plans, credit unions, employee cafeterias, employee discounts and privileges, stock purchases or

other investment plans. Today, your salary is just the tip of the iceberg.

And even salaries are complex. Most large companies have a whole staff of personnel professionals who make pay surveys, analyze results, build elaborate salary systems, administer job-classification plans and develop budgets and increase policies. It takes effort and knowledge to stay on top of even the simplest element of your pay.

Find Out Where You Stand

In order to move forward, you have to understand where you are—and this might take some work.

Start by really getting to know your company's salary system. Most well-run companies have a salary structure consisting of a number of grades, each of which has a beginning (or minimum) salary, a control point (usually spoken of as the midpoint of the range) and a maximum. The range spread, that is, the percentage difference between the *minimum* and *maximum*, is usually about 40 percent. For example, if the minimum starting salary for your position is $20,000, the maximum is probably about $28,000. (The range is narrower for entry-level jobs, broader for executives.)

In many companies, you'll be able to get the salary range for your position from your boss (ask him or her first, *then* the personnel department). In others, you may regularly get this information during your performance review. If these straightforward approaches don't work for you, you can either: (a) ask your colleagues what *they* make, and deduce a range from their answers, *or* (b) work from your own salary and tenure, assuming the 40 percent standard spread, and remembering that in most companies it takes a new hire, without previous experience, three to five years to progress to the mid-point of her range. Once you've gotten a range estimate this way, try bouncing the numbers off your boss—he may be more willing to tell you whether you're in the ballpark than to give you the figures outright.

If you know your present range and its midpoint, you know a lot: (a) you know how your position is valued in the internal hierarchy, (b) you know, in general, how *you* are doing (are you progressing up the pay scale as quickly as you should be?) and (c) you also know what the company thinks the job is worth competitively, since most salary midpoints are set to match the average competitive pay level for jobs ranked in that category. Don't assume that the midpoint is a static figure, however. These days most companies are increasing their salary ranges every 12 to 18 months because of inflation and increases in competitive pay levels. Today's midpoint may well be 15 to 20 percent higher in three years. Of course, watching how the range itself changes will tell you a lot about a company's philosophy toward business prospects, as well as its philosophy toward employees.

Two other elements of the salary system that any informed woman needs to know are the policies and rules under which salaries are adjusted. Some key questions here include: What is the size of the average increase? How do increases vary with performance and current salary (the two variables that affect most "merit" increases)? Today, most sophisticated companies use a merit increase matrix, with target or guideline increases that vary with five to seven categories of performance and three to five categories of current salaries (i.e., bottom, middle or top third of the range).

What if you discover that there are no formal ranges or guidelines? First, recognize that your immediate boss (or the owner of a small, privately held company) is going to be operating more or less on gut feel, supplemented by informal exchanges with other businesspeople. But make no mistake about it, there is a range for your job, even if it's in your boss's head. Ferret it out if you can. The greater the degree of informality, the greater the need for you to be informed and *to be a good negotiator.*

Know what your present job is worth in the labor market. Understandably, most companies do not publish the results of their competitive salary surveys in the company newsletter. But other information is plentiful—in fact, there are probably over 200 regular surveys covering managerial jobs and two or three times that number for lower-level positions. Broadly based surveys such as the American Management Association reports (*Top Management Report, Middle Management Report, Professional and Scientific Report, Administrative and Technical Report, Office Personnel Report, Sales Personnel Report* and *Supervisory Management Report*) or the local Chamber of Commerce surveys are good places to start. These are often available in the local library. Government surveys are also useful, as are data published by most industry associations and possibly even your own university (check the placement office or alumni association). And general business magazines are providing more and more information on pay levels. With so many data available, it's easy to be overwhelmed by statistics; so let me offer three pieces of advice:

- Pay levels vary by industry, location and size of company. While precise comparisons take an expert's analysis, you can get a reasonably accurate feel for whether you are in a high-paying or low-paying industry and/or part of the country just by checking the general Government statistics and talking with people.
- If you can't find the data for your particular job in your particular region, you can reconstruct it. Suppose you are in the South, in a specialized middle-management job for which there are no local statistics. Find jobs at about the same level for which there *are* both national and local statistics, and see how the local "going rate" compares with the national average. If, for example, you find that the rate for those jobs is 12 percent lower in your area, you can calculate a range for your own job by reducing the national average by 4 percent.
- Finally, it's important to keep in mind that despite the many statistics, compensation levels for a given job still vary widely—so don't try for too much detail when you look at the figures. What you want to know is *roughly* where you stand: Is your pay clearly low? Is it in the general ballpark (give or take 10 percent)? Or are you lucky enough to be working with a company that pays a premium?

Pay attention to the non-cash benefits and compensation extras. Every two years, the US Chamber of Commerce does a survey of benefits. The latest survey includes a section tracking 152 companies since 1955 and shows that, in those companies, for every dollar of salary there is now an average of 45 cents of additional compensation. Some forms of non-cash compensation are fairly standard, such as paid time off and Government programs such as social security. But there is more variation in the remaining benefits—pensions, insurance and other extras—and they can easily add 20 to 25 percent to your salary.

A detailed analysis of benefits is beyond the scope of this article, but I can offer several general guidelines:

- Be familiar with your existing coverage. Under the present law, companies have to provide written descriptions of plans, and while the technical jargon makes for hard sledding, you should make an effort to understand it. If necessary, ask somebody in the personnel department to explain the finer points.
- Try to get your existing coverage expressed in dollars-and-cents terms. Sophisticated companies will be able to give you a breakdown by plan quite easily. In fact, some companies automatically send each employee annual benefit statements, showing both employee and company contributions, as well as the amounts of coverage by plan. Where this is not available, don't hesitate to ask for estimates.
- Focus on those plans of particular interest to you. At the very least, you should study your medical coverage and disability insurance plans. If you are concerned about whether your coverage is adequate, or if you want a professional explanation, ask an insurance agent to review the company coverage you have, evaluate it, and suggest supplemental coverage if necessary.
- Pay particular attention to any coverage that requires investment decisions by you—as most savings plans or profit-sharing plans do. Here again, you can sometimes get advice from professionals—e.g., ask a stockbroker to evaluate the investment record of your company's fund and advise you about supplementary personal investments.
- Finally, be sure you know the vesting pro-

visions of the pension, profit-sharing or thrift plans—that is, when you are entitled to the benefits you have earned even if you leave the company's employ. This can be a major factor in making career changes or negotiating with a new employer.

Learn How the Economy Affects You

Inflation and the tax laws probably affect your standard of living as much as your company's compensation policies do. One reason I.C. victims have trouble managing their economic lives is that they don't really understand these external factors. The next steps in the prescription should help:

Develop some expertise on taxes. Some forms of pay are taxed currently (salaries); some are provided with no tax consequence (medical insurance); some are not taxed until they are paid out—and then under special rules (pension plans); and some company benefits and perquisites may (or may not) be tax-free (such as a company car, or payment of club dues). These distinctions should influence the decisions you make as an employee. For example, you may be working for a company that matches part of the dollars it deducts from your pay for a savings plan. Or you may be making voluntary contributions to a profit-sharing plan. You cannot participate intelligently in plans like these unless you know:

- the tax consequences of investing money in what is in essence a tax-sheltered trust;
- the tax rules governing voluntary withdrawals.

If you are working for a company that doesn't offer a pension plan, it is up to you to set up your own. Under the 1974 tax law, persons not covered by a company retirement plan can put up to 15 percent of their cash compensation (currently limited to $1,500) in individual retirement accounts (IRAs). IRA deposits are considered a deductible item in calculating personal taxes.

Track your real salary (or total cash pay,

if you get commissions or bonuses). Have a good idea of what is happening to your net income, *after taxes and inflation,* and remember that these factors will cause the value of your salary dollars to erode over time. Three things to keep in mind are: a) we have a progressive income-tax structure; b) social security taxes are scheduled to increase threefold over the next ten years to over $3,000; and c) inflation will probably continue at a high rate. (It has averaged 7.7 percent over the last five years.)

It's obvious from the above example that state and local taxes can seriously affect your real income—so they become especially important if you find yourself having to make an intelligent trade-off, say, between a job for Xerox in Stamford and a comparable job for Citicorp in New York City.

How will this affect your *real* salary? That depends partly on where you live: Ignoring state and local taxes and assuming a 7 percent inflation rate, if you earn $25,000 a year now, your pay will have to go up 8.6 percent a year over the next decade *just for you to stay even.* If you live in New York City, the tax structure there will force your break-even figure up to 9.5 percent. Your salary increases will have to be much greater than these percentages if you are to achieve real income growth.

Make Plans Based on Your Priorities

Any estimate of how much pay you are worth must include an estimate of how hard, and where, you are willing to work for it. To be a good negotiator, you must know not only compensation, but yourself. The next steps in your recovery will require looking inward.

Know what you want from your current job. Since pay levels do vary by size of company, industry and location, it is often helpful to use compensation implications to face up to some highly personal trade-offs: Are you willing to work for a large company? To live in a major city? To work in certain industries? Possibly more important, how much pressure can you stand? How much uncertainty are you comfortable with? Here, too, there are trade-offs: In general, the more the pressure, or the higher the risks, the higher the rewards. If security is important, you are likely to prefer a large company to a small, new one. You are also more likely to find security in utilities, insurance companies or banks than in, say, consumer goods marketing companies or conglomerates. But remember that in a "secure" company the cash pay levels will probably not be so high as elsewhere and the mix of compensation will be tilted toward benefits.

Set career goals. Now you consider your priorities in a longer-term context. Bearing in mind the trade-offs I've already mentioned, consider any other relevant personal variables. For example: Do you intend to take some time from your career to have children? Are you interested in additional education? You should know the compensation implications of a given company's policies in these areas. How difficult will it be to resume your position after a maternity leave? Is there a tuition refund plan?

Then, in light of your personal decisions, examine your professional priorities. If your career goals are fuzzy, your pay will ultimately level off, even if you know all about compensation. Virtually every successful executive has deliberately made short-term "experience versus reward" trade-offs once or twice, and there is nothing wrong with taking a lower-paid job or accepting a lateral move to further one's long-range career. What *is* inexcusable is not knowing the compensation implications of your career decisions and taking less when you don't have to.

Set personal pay goals. If you have defined your career path and learned about compensation and the economy, you can set pay goals realistically. Try to think in terms of at least a five-year program, and develop two kinds of financial goals: First, set annual compensation targets, including estimates of your net earnings for each year. Then, set

a longer-range net-worth (assets less liabilities) target. While personal investment decisions will influence your net worth, company plans are the easiest, and often the most viable, way to build it. Company stock purchase, savings or profit-sharing plans provide a clear opportunity to save, of course. But when you calculate your net worth, don't forget to count the retirement plan as an asset—even though you may not intend to work for another 20 years. The lump sum value of a $20,000 pension, for example, is over $300,000.

Remember One Basic Rule

If you have come this far, you are almost ready to do something about your pay. But bear this in mind:

Recognize that promotions are the key to rapid pay progress. Time is money, particularly in the early years of your career, and the only way to really beat escalating taxes and inflation is through promotions. If you have a job you like in a good company, be aware that if you stay there without being promoted, you are drastically reducing your earning potential. How serious can this damage be? A couple of years ago, I did a study of over 1,000 graduates of one of the largest business schools in the country, tracking the incomes of those who had graduated ten and 15 years ago. *Promotional increases accounted for roughly two-thirds of their total pay progress during the intervening years.*

Be careful, though, to get a *real* promotion. Make sure that you move up to a job with more responsibility, a more elevated grade, and a higher salary range. Don't rely on titles—they can be misleading because some organizations use them in lieu of salary. A few other facts to keep in mind about promotions and pay:

● In a well-run company, promotional increases should be much larger than normal "merit" increases—in fact, the rule of thumb among professionals is that the average promotional increase should about double the average merit increase. In other words, if the average merit increase for someone who is staying in the same job is 7 percent, the promotional increase should be 14 percent.

- Getting a promotion and the accompanying increase should not penalize you by delaying your normal salary review. To make sure that you get everything you deserve, let your boss know that you understand the details of compensation—but don't complain about the size of your "promotion" raise if it seems low. Rather, mention that you still expect to be eligible for a merit review shortly.
- Compensation in most companies is hierarchical. Your pay takes a quantum leap when you become eligible for special executive extras such as incentive bonus plans, stock options and the like. Participation in these plans varies by company, however. If you are considering changing jobs or companies, be sure to find out beforehand the extras you would be eligible for.

Get Ready to Move

No matter how much you know, you'll continue to suffer from I.C. if you clutch when changing jobs or considering an internal transfer, so the final phase of the cure is action-oriented:

Learn how to negotiate pay. For some general guidelines on negotiating, you can refer to books such as Gerald Nierenberg's *The Art of Negotiating,* but there are some special caveats in negotiating pay.

If you're considering a new company, make sure the job *really* is a promotion by arming yourself with facts, figures, and caution:

- Find out as much as possible about the pay plans involved. A frequently overlooked source of information is the company's annual proxy statement, which lists top-executive pay levels and gives details on most bonus, stock option, pension and savings plans.
- If the benefits and other extras differ from those you're used to, compare the two plans carefully yourself, or have the offering company do a point-by-point lay-person comparison for you.
- Develop a baseline figure, using your current compensation and your next likely increase to forecast what you'd be earning in a year if you stayed in your present job. Any true promotion should top this. In today's environment, if you are not offered 25 to 30 percent above your current pay, you may not be stepping up.
- Finally, recognize that there is a lot of counterfeit coin offered: "We don't have a bonus plan, but we're going to develop one." . . . "You won't be eligible immediately for a stock option, but in a year or two . . ." "The pension plan is being liberalized." . . , etc. If any of these extras are major factors in your decision, get the commitment in writing. The smaller the company, the more important this protection can be.

When you negotiate pay in your present company, you need another set of guidelines, of course, and possibly more resourcefulness:

- If you are being considered for a transfer or a promotion, be sure to get the pay clearly spelled out beforehand. Few companies expect someone to agree automatically to a move these days, so you usually have negotiating room.
- If a change in location is involved, be sure to check out the real income consequences of local taxes and costs of living.
- Finally (and this is a real danger) if you are stuck on a pay plateau in a job and company you really like, be doubly careful, because months can stretch into years. Sometimes developing your own competitive pay data will help jar loose an increase, particularly in smaller companies. Another useful technique, and one any

boss will find it hard to argue with, is to stress that you are not asking for an *immediate* raise. Say something like, "I know we're under budget constraints (or profit pressures or whatever) now, but can we discuss what might be reasonable next year?" At a minimum this will give you a go/no-go date that will force your boss, and you, to assess your real value.

The incidence of *ignoratio compensationis* among women is decreasing as the business climate changes, but each victim—male or female—is still responsible for his or her own cure. If you are not being paid what you are worth, you have three choices: you can say nothing and seethe inwardly, or complain loudly and get nowhere, or take what I believe will be the most productive and least frustrating approach—treat the disease (rather than the symptoms) by following this plan for recovery.

DAVID J. McLAUGHLIN *is a consultant and author. As a principal in the general management-consulting firm of McKinsey and Co., he heads their compensation and personal management practice. His book,* The Executive Money Map, *was published by McGraw-Hill in 1975.*

WHEN IT COMES TO EXPENSE ACCOUNTS, WHY DO MEN GET THE GRAVY?

by Fran Hawthorne

When Mildred Herschler remembers the first time she used an expense account, five years ago, she smiles at her naiveté. It was less than a year after she'd started working, and her company had sent her to a convention in Las Vegas to develop clients for the newsletter she edited. "You know all the terrific restaurants in Las Vegas? I ate in coffee shops. I had money to spend on entertainment, and all I did was buy some man an ice cream. When I came back and told people, they laughed at me."

Ask almost any women in business, and she'll probably tell a similar story. As advertising manager for the Sales Executive Club of New York, Herschler still sees women who are afraid to use expense accounts for valid business activities. By failing to do so, women can hurt their careers.

Expense accounts are not fringe benefits or "perks," such as a turkey at Thanksgiving or a key to the corporate sauna. They're not incentives or bonuses, either. Expense accounts are the way companies pay for the necessary, ordinary, accepted costs involved in conducting business. Business people spend from these accounts. The Internal Revenue Service acknowledges them. Yet many women don't know how to use their accounts.

Although there are few statistics on the ways in which males and females employ their expense accounts (neither the IRS nor most companies keep records by sex), members of the business world say that they generally find women to be shyer with expenses than men are.

Boston management consultant Pat Kosinar remembered attending a publishing convention where every male delegate had his own hotel room, while the women, to save money, shared rooms. Milton Stohl, owner of a Connecticut consulting firm, said that when he worked with a public-relations company owned and operated by an all-female staff, "Their expenses were considerably lower than other public-relations firms we employed." Among the 600 members of the New York Society of Association Executives—65 percent of them men—a full 90 percent charge their society dues to their companies. Only about half of the 300 members of the Financial Women's Association of New York charge their dues.

Although males and females in similar jobs usually cite the same kinds of expense-account charges (especially meals, transportation and hotels), their attitudes toward price can be starkly different. Consider the advice of two vice-presidents. Kay Breakstone of Burson-Marsteller, the second largest public-relations firm in the country, follows this policy: "If you have a choice of hotels, it's not a good idea to go to the best hotel." On the other hand, the male vice-president of a top US hotel chain said, "There's only one way to do business when you're in a first-class business, as we are—that's in a first-class way."

The reasons that women pinch expense-account pennies are tied in with the reasons they may be paid less or promoted less—they are less experienced in business than men are.

"It's a defense mechanism," said Breakstone. "It has to do with the whole cultural problem of women in business. Women don't want to appear too aggressive. Spending less makes them less visible and less vulnerable." Stohl thinks women have good reason to keep a low visibility. Because women are new to business, Stohl said, some companies scrutinize their expenses more closely than males'.

Without experience, women may not know the unwritten codes of the business world and may be scared of breaking them inadvertently. What kinds of expenses can they charge to the firm? How much can they spend?

Director of corporate relations at CBS Paula Gottschalk, who now has no qualms about using her expense account, remembered starting in network sales 12 years ago. "I was scared to ask my boss to reimburse me, so I spent my own money. I wasn't sure of the procedures. I wasn't sure of myself."

Men, too, may be ignorant of the codes when they first enter the business world. But, unlike women, they usually are not fettered by a background of balancing household budgets—a background that is totally wrong for business. Kosinar pointed out: "The role of money in the home is a very concrete one. You have so much to spend; you save for what you want. In the household budget, you can't use money to make money; in business, you must. Money is seen as a tool in the business world."

A common example of that homebred attitude is the businesswoman who takes a bus instead of a taxi to her appointments, on the mistaken assumption that she's helping her company's budget. "It doesn't save the company money if the bus takes extra time that you could be spending meeting people," one consultant pointed out. "It doesn't help the company if you arrive frazzled."

In such industries as sales, communications and publishing, managers worry when they see low expense accounts. They assume that a saleswoman with few expenses just isn't hustling clients. After listening to a saleswoman talk about her expense account, Gottschalk said, "I realized she wasn't using it enough. She wasn't doing her job well. Part of her role is to cultivate suppliers. But she didn't travel, she didn't go out to lunch."

It's not only how often an expense account is used, it's also where it's spent that's important. As the hotel-chain executive put it, "I'm not going to talk about a multimillion-dollar deal at McDonald's." While it's not a good idea for the potential associate to think your firm wastes money, it's just as bad to appear cheap.

Using the expense account as a tool is not, of course, the same as padding an account. Expenses must be related to business and they must be documented. The IRS allows meals to be tax deductible, whether or not specific business deals are discussed. Under the Revenue Act of 1962, food and cocktails need only be consumed under circumstances "of a type generally considered to be conducive to a business discussion." The idea is that people in business may lunch together to establish a rapport that could lead to deals later.

Old-fashioned male chauvinism contributes to keeping women's expense accounts low: Men sometimes find it hard to accept the fact that a woman is picking up the tab. Usually, the man will give in after a protest or two, once he realizes the woman's firm, not her pocketbook, is footing the bill. Some women resort to subterfuges, such as pretending to go to the bathroom in order to pay the check; others call the maitre d' before hand to arrange payment. If the man insists on paying, most women agree with Melinda Lloyd, president of the Financial Women's Association of New York: "I don't press the issue. The essence of good manners is to make others feel comfortable."

Women who want to take the mystery out of expense accounts won't find any easy, general guidelines. Of the people interviewed for this story, one had an expense account of $3,300, while another had $13,225. The IRS sets no limit on the maximum deduction it will allow for an employee's business expenses, as long as all claims are documented. There's no such thing as a typical expense account, not even for a particular job level. A saleswoman who flies coast to coast every week to meet clients will spend more than one whose clients are nearby; both may spend more than their boss, who doesn't meet the public at all. Furthermore, as a spokesman for E.I. Du Pont de Nemours & Co. pointed out, "Motels in New York City are more expensive than motels in Biloxi."

About the only guideline that can be offered is that the size and use of an expense account depend mainly on the type of business, type of job, location of business, location of places visited and company policy. The best way to determine policy is to ask.

Some companies make it easy by setting written standards. The book of guidelines at Young & Rubicam International Inc., one of the largest advertising agencies in the US, spells out the maximum hotel rates allowed in each city where employees travel. (The yardstick in Los Angeles is the $56-a-day Century Plaza, a moderately expensive hotel.) At Burson-Marsteller, according to Breakstone, the company's manual clearly specifies who may and may not fly first class.

Gottschalk said she and her supervisor worked out her expense budget by calculating how much she spent the previous year, what she would be doing the next year, and how much CBS could afford. Employees in most firms—especially those in lower-level positions—don't get a set account to draw from. Instead, they are simply reimbursed for whatever valid expenses they claim.

It is possible to be too extravagant. For one thing, President Carter's scalpel still hovers over the three-martini lunch and other splurges. For another, there is a hierarchy of spending, depending on one's level in the corporation. But being aggressive doesn't have to mean being extravagant. Said CBS's Gottschalk, "The women I know who are successful in business use their expense accounts exactly as men do. A woman in sales has to be an aggressive, forceful woman. If you've got what it takes to get a closing on an order, then you should be able to say to your boss, 'I need bread.'"

EXPENSE ACCOUNTS: WHAT'S LEGIT, WHAT'S NOT

Just what kinds of expenses—and how much—can you bill to your expense account? Check your company's policy first, but here are some common expenses that most firms reimburse:

- **Meals at which business is discussed, and transportation to those meals and other meetings; tips; also, transportation, hotels and meals while attending to business away from home.** These expenses are by far the most common. How much you can spend on these items varies with location and company. For lunch for two in a nice Manhattan restaurant, $25 to $28 with tip is reasonable. According to a 1976 survey by *Sales and Marketing Management Magazine*, 96 percent of the 218 sales firms polled usually pay only for coach tickets on airplanes.

- **Other entertainment, such as taking a client to the theater or a sports event.** While the IRS keeps a wary eye on this kind of deduction, many companies will pay under special circumstances. The same is true for country-club dues.
- **Membership in professional organizations and subscriptions to professional journals.**
- **Travel insurance.**
- **Airline charges for excess baggage.**
- **Business expenses, other than entertaining, while away from the home office.** For instance, 85 percent of the firms in the S&MMM survey will pay for renting office equipment, and 63 percent will pay for a temporary secretary, depending on the situation.
- **Travel expenses for a spouse.** Seventy percent of the companies polled by S&MMM said they would pay a spouse's plane fare when she or he accompanied a sales employee to a convention.

And what if your best friend works for a company that just completed a major business deal with your firm—can you take her out to lunch at company expense? That might be pushing things, but: If you think your lunch could augment the business side of your friendship and lead to future deals, under the IRS guidelines for meals it could be a valid expense.

FRAN HAWTHORNE, a New York based freelance writer, doesn't worry about expense accounts. While a reporter, she "was hesitant to put in for lunches—I'd be braver now!"

HOW MUCH MONEY DO YOU EARN?

by Lynn Sherr

Like most people I know who work for a living, I have always hidden my paycheck stubs. Back in the days when I was a reporter and sat in a big open news room with everyone else and received my weekly pay in a plain brown envelope from the bookkeeper who made the rounds every Friday morning, it was tricky. Somehow I worked out a system whereby I could slit open the flap, peer inside to make sure nothing unusual had been deducted, and slip it into my handbag (zipper compartment) without allowing any alien eyeball to make contact. My desk might accumulate two months' growth of old letters, articles, and out-of-town newspapers, but never among the debris would anyone find a stray paycheck stub. Not mine.

Most of my colleagues operated the same way, because we all succumbed early to one of the most prevalent of American occupational diseases: Don't Let Anyone Know How Much Money You Earn. The reasons for this taboo vary as widely as the incomes themselves. Some people are embarrassed because they think they earn too much; others becuse they earn too little. Some are avoiding increases in alimony payments; others are trying to ward off the tax collector or less visible burglars. It is a way to protect social status, and to preserve something considerably less tangible.

"It's perfectly natural that you wouldn't want everyone to know how much you make," insists a professional financial consultant who wouldn't tell me how much she earned. "It's like your name. It's a target, something to shoot at. It puts you in a spot. I think of it as a personal question—as personal as, 'Are you sleeping with anyone now?' "

More personal. In an age when sleeping habits are flaunted on the front pages, financial matters are still primly tucked away in the bedroom. According to Dee Dee Ahern, who conducts money management workshops for women across the country and wrote *The Economics of Being a Woman,* "Money has replaced sex as the source of our most powerful hang-ups. Like sex, money means many different things to each of us; and each of its meanings is charged with such awesome emotions as greed, fear, envy, and guilt. We desire money as a means to material comfort, power, freedom, prestige, even love and beauty. . . . But at the same time we desire money, we fear it."

Or, as reporter Nancy Collins put it during a panel on gossip at a journalism convention last fall, "Celebrities will tell you everything and anything about their sex lives, but it's a different story when you ask them how much they make."

The same diffidence seems to be true of less famous workers, like those encountered on the lecture circuit by a psychologist dealing with people's reactions to money. His request that they tell what they earn was constantly greeted with silence, distinct lack of comfort, and then nervous laughter.

When I asked people how much money they earn in the course of preparing this article, I generally encountered a less evasive response. "It's none of your business," they all said. And they all said it with hostility.

There are, of course, individuals whose income becomes known because of a sudden success or a sudden windfall, like a bestselling novel that earns six-figure sums for paperback and movie rights. The figures in one case I know of were $360,000 and $250,000, and even after agents' fees and partnership payoffs, it left a tidy balance for the author. But he told me gently, still pleading for anonymity, "It's embarrassing when your friends read in the paper how much you've made. You walk into a gin mill and get

kidded. I'm not a particularly secretive person, but I do like to keep my business personal."

Some working people have no choice in the matter, since their salaries are made public by law, or by policy, or by dogged investigation. Members of trade unions know where their colleagues fit on the wage scale. The salaries of government officials, from office clerks to commission heads, are on the public record, as are those of the military or Civil Service. If you know someone's rank, military or civilian, you can find out his wages. And more and more, as we close the barn door after Watergate, public officials are being persuaded or legislated into holding up their bankbooks for public scrutiny before they attain the public trust. The best example is Jimmy Carter, who, as President-elect, insisted that Cabinet members and several thousand other policy-making members of his administration make full public disclosure of their financial worth.

A number of local governments have issued their own guidelines, like the District of Columbia which this January expanded the number of city workers who must disclose their financial interests from six hundred to about fifteen hundred. The point, according to one D.C. Council member who voted the change: "to help discourage any suggestion that city employees might profit illegally from something they do."

Private business also has its disclosure rules. The Securities and Exchange Commission requires a salary rundown of each of the directors and the top three officers of a corporation earning more than $40,000 a year. This information must be included in the proxy material sent out to stockholders, and it is on file at regional SEC offices on the annual 10-K financial statement. It's a public document, and you are entitled to look at it.

But if you're like me, you aren't in any of those categories. You may work for a large corporation or a small grocery store. You may sell cosmetics door-to-door or anchor the evening news on television. You may be female or male, single, married, or the parent of several children. But I'd bet that no one you work with, or compete with, or go to parties with, knows how much money you make.

As it turns out, the taboo on such talk may be hurting working people. If you don't know how much your colleagues make, you don't know if you're being paid fairly. This is doubly important for working women, in view of the rampant salary discrimination between men and women. The latest figures from the Women's Bureau of the Employment Standards Administration, U.S. Department of Labor, show that the earnings gap between men and women has nearly doubled in the last two decades.

"It's not uncommon for employees at all levels to be told not to discuss their salaries, but it's particularly true at the managerial level," says Professor Edward E. Lawler III, of the University of Michigan, who has been doing research in the behavioral-psychological aspects of "reward systems" (i.e., pay) since 1962. "The admonition goes, 'Gentlemen don't talk about pay. That's BAD! That's not good form.' " The real reason? "My own view is that it's something we're educated to believe, the idea that proper middle-class people don't talk about salary. In our culture we tie money and salary into a person's worth. No one wants to expose their worth. It's also that with secrecy a manager has more freedom to behave the way he or she wishes, because he isn't held as accountable for decisions as he would be if his salary were public knowledge." I asked Lawler if in his view secrecy is really encouraged to protect the company. "I think it is, but usually the company will say it's a favor for the employees."

Some favor. In test after test, Lawler has found that in terms of salary, most people "perceive themselves as worse off than they really are." In one survey of seven different organizations in different cities, lower-level managers tended to overestimate the pay of people of their own and subordinate levels

from $200 to $1,000 a year. Lawler calls this one of the hidden costs of salary secrecy, and wrote several years ago that employees' tendency to underestimate their salaries in relation to others in the company "apparently is related to dissatisfaction with their own pay, underestimation of the organization's evaluation of their own worth, and a belief that their job performance is relatively unimportant in determining their pay."

Lawler, whose own $38,000 salary at Michigan's Institute of Social Research is public information, believes employees ought to share such information. Especially when asking for a raise. "It would improve their bargaining position," he told me. "Basically it's an extension of the philosophy of the people's right to know. I just feel that people have the right to know that information, so they can plan their own career, have some idea how they're being treated by the organization, and put the whole thing in perspective. Without comparative information, you can't do that."

"Many people don't really want that kind of information," he said. "That's another side. People who haven't experienced open systems are afraid of them. You really would like to know, but if it turns out you are lowly paid compared to others, there are some pretty serious implications."

They are most serious if you are a woman or a member of a minority group. Salary secrecy, Lawler said, "aids and abets discrimination."

Even putting aside the question of discrimination, women seem to have special problems with money, problems that don't hinder men's financial achievements. "Why are women of all classes so ignorant of money?" ask authors Phyllis Chesler and Emily Jane Goodman in *Women, Money & Power*. "Why are so many women almost *against* money? Or afraid of knowing too much about it? When pressed, why do women say that money is 'not really important' and paradoxically, that 'money is evil'? . . . Why do so many women seem almost proud of their ignorance, as if economic ignorance, like sexual innocence, or timidity, is somehow a moral and economic asset?"

Why, indeed, in view of the fact that it can lead to disastrous consequences. "Women are poor negotiators about their salary levels," says a woman—call her Dorothea—who works as an "executive search," someone who unites people and executive jobs. She deals with situations in fashion-related industries in New York. "Women will often take a high base and a low percentage of the profits as opposed to a low base and a high percentage of the profits," Dorothea scolded. "That means that up front Uncle Sam gets a whole lot more."

When she tries to get women hired into executive spots, Dorothea is generous about salary. "I generally pad it," she says matter-of-factly. "Because I know in other companies a man with that job is making more than they're willing to pay. So even if they knock me down some, she'll still get more than they originally offered."

Dorothea is able to make such gestures because she knows what people get paid. Salaries are not secret to an executive search (also called a head-hunter), which is why, she says, one of the best ways to find out how your paycheck compares with others' is to consult an executive search.

There's another way, but it's limited at the moment. That is, go to work somewhere where salary disclosure is company policy. At Graphic Controls Corporation in Buffalo, the salaries of two dozen top executives, from president ($73,000) to a division management group level job ($25,000) are discussed openly. It all started about five years ago, when the company, which produces scientific instrument charts and data processing forms, established a bonus incentive plan based on annual pay. Since they were all participating in developing the plan, they realized they had to learn each other's salaries to work it out. "Initially there was some

resistance," recalls Lyman Randall, vice-president for human resources and planning. "People said, 'This is a very private thing, it will only create problems.' But the large majority view was, 'Do it. There is a reason for doing it. Let's get on with developing the incentive plan.' So it was done. And now in retrospect, some look back and say, 'How silly that we hesitated.' "

In the process of sharing the sensitive financial data, only one executive was shocked, according to Randall. "He had a job with no counterpart anywhere else, it was a unique job. And he thought he was underpaid compared to some of the others. The group re-evaluating his salary range agreed with him, and as a result he got a raise, and he feels good."

If you're one of Graphic Controls' other eight hundred employees around the country, you don't know specific salaries, but you know the range, both above and below you. Range sheets, showing the salary perimeters of all other jobs, are published and easily available. By finding your own dot on a big chart, you can get some idea of your relative value.

Lyman Randall is the first to admit that his company is a pioneer. "It's a part of management lore," he says, "that if people know what others are making, they will all queue up in long lines to ask for more money, and that will create a lot of grief for their supervisors. But if supervisors really motivate people, that won't happen," he insists. "When there's a closer ratio between performance contribution and salary increase, it's better for the organization because the organization gets results from its employees. It's also better for the employees, because they will feel more fairly treated and satisfied."

As for the drawbacks: "If you use this open approach, no question about it, there are going to be more hours spent with people talking about pay. Now the assumption is, that's a bad thing. But I think it's good because then people are part of an employee's motivational environment."

Randall was remarkably cool about the possibility of sex discrimination suits and other problems as pay levels become known in the company (where only one of the top dozen executives is a woman). "I think we're beginning to see the top of the iceberg, where gals are starting to ask, 'How come I'm here and so-and-so is there? And is it because I'm a woman?' I think they're becoming more comfortable in asking, and I think that's a healthy thing. My view is, companies that get suits filed against them are probably companies that try to lock up problems rather than solve them. I think if you have a willingness to look at the problem candidly and try to solve it, you're not likely to get a lawsuit."

Professor Lawler, who told me about Graphic Controls, was equally optimistic about the progress of salary disclosure. "It's

happening slowly, it's happening as people are changing their basic philosophy and attitudes toward authority," he said. "We're moving toward a less autocratic, more open—some would say chaotic—society, where we'll have more emphasis on disclosure and people's right to know. You see it already in the younger MBAs, who say, 'Keep the pay secret? Why?' "

Think about this: if companies can change, can we? As workers, I suppose we owe it to each other to stop pretending we make more, or less, than we really do. As women workers, we probably have a special obligation to liberate our paychecks from societal taboos. But I think it will be difficult. I had planned to end this article by telling you how much I am getting paid to write it. I have changed my mind. I'm not there yet. I'm afraid I really think it's none of your business.

HOW TO FIND OUT WHAT OTHERS ARE EARNING

1. Ask. Ask your colleagues at work, your supervisor, your subordinates. Ask people at other companies with equivalent jobs. Be prepared to tell what you earn in exchange.
2. If your colleagues seem intrigued but reluctant, try Professor Lawler's idea: put a batch of paycheck stubs (or anonymous pieces of paper with weekly salaries written on each) in a hat, then add up the total and figure out the average.
3. Find an executive search organization and consult with them when looking for a job. There are hundreds around the country, and their fees are paid by companies, not individuals.
4. If you suspect that you are the victim of sex discrimination in salary, check with your local Wage and Hours Division officer or Equal Employment Opportunity commissioner.
5. As one veteran of salary research told me, "The only way to find out is to come around and look." So, again—Ask.

THE WORKING WOMAN'S GUIDE TO PERKS

by Jamie Laughridge

As if by osmosis, men have absorbed information about those things called "perks"—special rewards that invisibly fatten paychecks or make life at the top of the corporate ladder just a bit more appealing. Now that more women are moving into the executive suite, it stands to reason that their

need for information about perks has increased, too.

Varied Meanings

The term "perk," short for perquisite, encompasses extras as diverse as free medical examinations, stock options and office-decorating allowances. Depending on its nature, a perk may be desirable because it eases a tax burden, helps to build an estate or demonstrates a position of superiority within the corporate structure.

During the gray-flannel-suit era, perks were prized for the corporate status they suggested. Eager young managers sought the key to the executive washroom as confirmation that their careers indeed had been launched.

Today, although people still compare perk ratings, the focus has shifted somewhat. People realize that such perks as company cars, club memberships and low-cost loans mean money in the pocket and that this part of the package carries more than psychological value.

Financial Value

"Most perks we talk about today have real cash value," said Helen J. McLane, vice-president of the management-consulting and executive-selection firm Heidrick and Struggles, Inc., in Chicago. "That includes stock options, extraordinary insurance coverage and even a stock-purchase plan if it's not available to everyone in the company. Automobiles, financial and legal counseling and low-coast loans are valuable perks, although some are offered only at the higher echelons of management.

"Sometimes women desire perks, but often they're not realistic about whether perks are available at their level of what they are," McLane cautioned. "When looking at the perk package, women should remember that the availability of perks depends on the industry, job level and functional area."

Who Gets Them?

Is it logical, then, for women below executive level to expect some perks to be offered? "Yes," said Joseph P. Tajcnar, associate director of the American Management Associations' Executive Compensation Service, "although certainly not to the extent or value of those offered at the top. Middle management is generally recognized as the entry level to perks. Depending on the company and industry, a middle manager might receive a company car, goods or services at a discount or special business-travel accident insurance."

Experts emphasize that the pattern of perk distribution is influenced by factors other than company and industry. Harriette A. Weiss, senior principal and consultant on total reward compensation for Hay Associates in New York, elaborated. "Perks are usually paid to positions rather than to individuals. Think of the club membership as one example. It's really the *job* of, say, national sales manager or chief lending officer that receives this perk, because the nature of the position requires it."

What's Out There

Regardless of their present level or position, women in business need to know about the range of cash-value perks that may be offered—or negotiated for—at some point in their careers. Availability of these coveted extras varies, but the list that follows covers categories of possibilities.

Interview and relocation costs: When a firm asks a job candidate to travel a considerable distance for an interview, the firm ordinarily picks up the tab for transportation and lodging costs. Some people believe this constitutes a "pre-hire" perk.

If the interviewee subsequently accepts the job offer, the firm will most likely pay her moving and relocation costs. According to Katharine H. Eley, vice-president of the executive search firm Management Woman Inc., "It's a given" that companies will pay to relocate a management level woman.

Depending on a number of other factors, including the employee's worth in the marketplace, the company may add on interim accommodations, pay closing costs on houses being vacated or moved into and even buy the house from the woman they're relocating and sell it themselves—sparing her the trouble.

Expense accounts: Because expense accounts provide those who have them with greater financial freedom and easier access to certain restaurants, hotels and other places they might not ordinarily visit, expense accounts are often thought of as perks. In some industries, notably advertising, public relations, publishing and entertainment, liberal expense accounts may be viewed as necessary to accomplishing the job.

Club memberships: Companies often pay an employee's dues in business and professional organizations, especially if a demonstrable relationship exists between membership and the employee's ability to perform her job effectively. Similarly, athletic- or country-club membership may go to those with jobs that require a positive community image or extensive customer contact. In an effort to encourage fitness, some companies enroll key executives in fitness programs.

Company cars: In its 1979 *Report on Executive Perquisites*, AMA's Executive Compensation Service stated, "Providing executives with the use of a company-owned or -leased automobile is a perk common in all industries, with 83.8 percent of 907 survey participants granting the benefit." If the company lets an employee use the car for personal driving as well, a monthly fee or per-mile charge is generally assessed.

In a large number of sales jobs, cars "come with the territory," a pharmaceutical sales representative in the South explained. "When I was thinking about taking this job—and I was very happy in the job I had—I analyzed all the benefits the new company offered. And the car was definitely a major consideration."

A corollary of the company-car perk is often the vehicle's size and luxury level or whether the company eventually will sell it to the employee at a reduced rate. In some areas, having a reserved parking space counts as a key perk.

Travel-related luxuries: This category covers everything from being able to hop a ride on the company jet to having your employer pay for membership in an airline courtesy club. How you value such perks, notes Tajcnar of the Executive Compensation Service, often depends on how much you travel. "If you're on the road 60 percent of the time, first-class air travel and admittance to the VIP club at the airport can mean a lot. The intention of these perks is to make travel a little less stressful."

Goods or services at a discount: The value of these perks depends largely on the industry and the employee's personal situation. Women who work for a full-service department store may enjoy a sizable merchandise discount, just as airline employees may find their travel discounts almost as desirable as their salaries.

Medical examinations: Optional free medical examinations were reported to be the single most prevalent perk by both AMA's Report on *Executive Perquisites* and Heidrick and Struggles' 1978 *Profile of a Woman Officer*. Some companies require executives to visit the in-house physician for this exam; others will reimburse them for examinations conducted by the physician of their choice.

Extra insurance plans or increased coverage: Additional benefits may be granted in the form of extraordinary coverage for health care, life insurance or dental services. Sometimes the perk extends coverage to an employee's spouse or children, but often it is a larger-than-average policy on the woman herself that constitutes the perk. Insurance plans covering job-related liabilities are perks, too.

Extra vacation benefits: In recent years, more companies have begun to grant extra vacation and sabbatical privileges and to allow employees the option of combining business with pleasure trips (or vice versa). Being able to take a spouse, friend or child along on a trip is a variation.

Educational assistance: Some employers pay all or part tuition costs for an employee who wishes to advance her education while working. Additionally, low-cost loans to help pay for an executive's children's education may be granted.

Financial and legal counseling: To aid busy executives, firms sometimes offer free or low-cost financial and legal counseling as a perk. This may include help in preparing tax returns, writing wills or formulating long-term financial plans.

Stock options: Stock options give employees the right to purchase company stock within a specified future time period, at a rate that most likely will be lower than the selling rate at that future date. According to Heidrick and Struggles, 44.5 percent of the women officers surveyed in their 1978 profile received this perk.

Reduced-interest loans: Although this perk is usually limited to members of top management, the granting of loans at interest levels below the current rate is common in some industries, particularly in banking. In most cases, the company sets up specific terms for the loan's use and repayment. A common reason for granting such a loan is to allow an executive to exercise a stock option.

Savings or thrift plans: In these plans, an employee contributes a certain percentage of her salary to a fund; the employer matches her contribution or a portion of it. Usually, the employee forfeits the employer's contribution if she leaves the company before a specified time period.

Deferred-compensation plans: Ferne R. Goldman, principal with the accounting firm of Coopers & Lybrand in New York and an expert in benefits and compensation, explained why people value these plans. "Generally, the advantage of deferred compensation is that the company agrees to pay you some money at a later date, so that you are not currently taxed on it. By the time you do collect it, you'll be in a lower tax bracket."

Research Is Key

With possibilities as wide ranging as flexible hours and company cars, how can a woman determine which perks may be available in any given job? "Do some research," advised Eley of Management Woman. "If you have access to any kind of network, this is the time to use it. If you have peers in other companies, find out what kinds of perks they have and what they know about the job you're considering."

Once the woman has a general idea of the perks that may be generally available, should she discuss her expectations with an interviewer? "Certainly not until she knows about the job and its substance and is sure that there's interest on both sides," said Eley's colleague Janet Jones-Parker, chairman of Management Woman. "And once she broaches the subject, it's important to depersonalize it. When she removes herself from the phrasing, she can ask such questions as 'What kinds of benefits are available to *management* in this company?' This gives her the information without creating the impression that she's interested only in perks."

The Total Picture

With perk information in hand, the woman faces a task of personal evaluation. "The real things to look at," said Weiss of Hay Associates, "is a combination of all those things that make up the total reward for the job. You can't focus entirely on any individual component, that is, on the salary or the perks or the noncash benefits. You have to concentrate on what the whole compensation package is worth to you in your situation."

Management Woman's Jones-Parker went further. "Women should look first at the quality of the work life and the content of the job. Remember that if your job doesn't provide growth and opportunity, all the perks in the world won't make it satisfying."

Chapter Eight

Career Strategies

DO YOU KNOW WHERE YOUR CAREER IS GOING?

by Linda Downs

Too many women still look only at the *now*. They do a superb job from day to day and hope to be discovered in the future. Career planning doesn't apply only to those who want to fight for the jobs at the top. Not everyone wants to chair the board of NBC, or even be vice-president in charge of engineering, but the wrong job at any level can fill every workday with drudgery instead of offering a challenge.

To know where your career is going, you have to decide where *you* want to go—and where you are. You have to be brutally honest with yourself about your interests, accomplishments and failures, about whether you'd rather be a specialist or a manager. You have to be realistic about the length of time you've been in your current job, whether it is a job that might lead logically to a higher position and about the kind of relationship you have with your superiors.

If you feel your current job is marching nowhere at a death-drum pace, perhaps you need a change. You might begin your planning for it by taking a few quiet hours to come mind-to-mind with yourself. Don't just think about your future in general. Take a pad and pen and force yourself to write out specific evaluations. The exercise should help focus your attention on the questions.

List everything (tasks, people and situations) you like about your present job. Then everything you dislike. In addition, list:

1. Household chores and social activities you most enjoy. Those you hate.
2. *All* your accomplishments of the past year—social, at home, on the job— everything large or small that gives you a feeling of satisfaction when you remember it.
3. All your failures.

Dream a Little

Now write down the highest or most important job you think you'd want, and at the bottom of that page, write your utmost fantasy job. Be completely free: "If I could be or do anything in the world, I would . . ." Such fantasies can provide invaluable clues to the most satisfying career path, said New York vocational counselor Ruth Shapiro. Look at your dream job: Is it one in which you are the center of attention, such as "movie star"? Is it one that is contemplative, a solitary type of work? Is it one that indicates you would like to be of service to others? Is it one in which recognition comes primarily through talent and personality or through professional skills?

Once you've come to grips with *the kind of work* your fantasy represents, look for patterns in your other answers. Do the "like" lists deal with people, objects, data or ideas? Do you enjoy polishing silver (handling fine objects) but hate washing clothes (an ordinary task)? Do you like the type of work you do but feel unrecognized and ignored by your present employer? Carefully look for similarities in all your likes and dislikes, your abilities and successes.

Chart a Course for Yourself

With these appraisals done, write again the job or career goal you think you'd like to aim for—it may or may not be the same one you wrote down before. Now add a brief paragraph on the prerequisites for that job. Do you need to take refresher courses or specialized training? Does it require a knowledge of management practices? Should you concentrate on gaining visibility or on gaining experience? Only you can decide where you want to go—and what steps to take next.

Two books that might offer you some practical assistance are: *28 Days to a Better Job* by Tom Jackson (Hawthorn Books, $6.95) and *Out of Work—the Complete Job Hunters Guide* by Lyn Taetzsch and Enid Littman (Henry Regnery Co., $4.95). Both have some good tests to take and job-hunting guidelines to follow. Also see *Developing New Horizons for Women* by Ruth Helm Osborn (McGraw-Hill Book Co., $11.95), which is styled as a correspondence course or classroom text.

Before embarking on an all-out job-change program, you should ask yourself two important questions:

1. *Am I planning a major change when a minor one would benefit me more?* Arthur A. Witkin, PhD, chief psychologist for the Personnel Sciences Center in New York, advises that you "avoid changing a career when you should be changing a job. Usually, it is preferable to make a small change rather than a big one, since in that way, you keep the market value you've gained through experience."
2. *Are there changes I can make in myself that could transform my current job from one of stagnation to one of movement and challenge?* In his book *Confronting Nonpromotability* (AMACOM, $12.95), Edward Roseman has devised a test, which he calls an "Early Warning System," for spotting those tendencies that too often lead one to the unrewarding state of nonpromotability.

Whether you have resolved to make large changes in your work situation or smaller changes that could reap large benefits, checking yourself against Roseman's "Early Warning System for Nonpromotability" (see below) should help sharpen your awareness of where you are now and encourage you to remove whatever stumbling blocks are hindering your progress.

Using the System*

Each area of nonpromotability is challenged and rated as a positive, negative or neutral.

---

*Early warning system and guide reprinted by permission of the publisher from "Confronting Nonpromotability, How to Manage a Stalled Career," by Edward Roseman. © 1977 by AMACOM, a Division of American Management Associations. All Rights Reserved.

If you feel very positive about a specific item, a + 3 is recorded in the space next to the item. Lesser degrees of positiveness are recorded as +2 or +1 ratings. Similarly, if you feel very negative about an item, record a −3 rating. For lesser feelings of negativism, rate a −2 or a −1. If you are neither negative nor positive about an item, or if you are uncertain, record a neutral score of 0.

The following explanation of the questions listed in the second column of the worksheet will help you to use the system properly.

- **Time:** How does your *age* compare with that of other people with the same job title in your own company and in other companies? If you're younger, record a positive score. If you're older, record a negative score. If you're about the same age, record a neutral score. How long have you been in the same job in comparison with others in similar jobs? How do you feel about the length of *time* you have been in that job? As in the first item, record your degree of positive or negative feelings, using a +3 to −3 scale.
- **Acceptance:** Do you accept your rate of advancement *submissively*, or do you question it regularly? If you accept it, record a negative score. If you question it, record a positive score. How *realistic* are your feelings about your rate of advancement? If you strive for attainable goals, record a positive score. If you tend to wish for unattainable goals, score negatively.
- **Awareness:** Do you *question* your own motives, feelings and behavior and observe them in others? If you do, score positively. If you're relatively unaware of yourself and others, score negatively. How *perceptive* are you? If you're usually on target, score positively. If you're often mistaken, score negatively.
- **Family:** How are your intimate *relationships?* Do you have a happy home? Are there any problems with your family relationships that might interfere with your job? If your family is a source of strength,

score positively. If it presents problems, score negatively. What kinds of *responsibilities* do you have? Is there any reason why you can't relocate, such as sick parents? If family responsibilities do not block your forward progress, score positively. If they do, score negatively.
- **Competitive differences:** How do you compare with others in terms of *intelligence?* Are you smarter? Not as smart? What about your *personality traits*, especially your needs for achievement, autonomy and dominance? How resistant are you to change? What is your need for approval from friends and superiors? To what degree are you influenced by the need to belong to the peer group? How strong is your ability to keep at a job until it is finished? In other words, does your personality work for you or against you? How much *self-confidence* and *self-esteem* do you have? Do you do things because you believe in them or because you are trying to please others? If you are self-confident and have a good opinion of yourself, score positively. If not, negatively. How do you compare with your peers in managerial ability? Technical ability? What's required for your next career step, and how well do your *abilities* match those requirements? If they match well, score positively. If not, score negatively. How strong are your *drive* and *aspirations?* Do you want to advance? How hard are you willing to work for advancement? What sacrifices are you willing to make? If you feel you will work harder than your competitors and are willing to pay the price for advancement, score positively. If not, negatively. How do your *attitudes*, particularly toward change, responsibility and failure, help or hinder your progress? If you accept change, face the unknown with courage, are resilient, score positively.
- **Education:** Do you have a college degree? Were your studies pertinent to your current job? Do you have *advanced degrees?* Will advanced degrees help you with a fu-

ture job? How much *technical training* have you had? If your educational background matches your future job needs, score positively.

- **Work history:** How many *job changes* have you made in your career? If you have not made any or have had fewer than most of your colleagues, is it because you are afraid to make a change in order to advance yourself? If you've made a great many job changes, did each contribute to your advancement? Too few or too many job changes can both be negatives, depending on circumstances. Of particular importance is whether you had valid *rea-*

NONPROMOTABILITY: THE EARLY WARNING SYSTEM				
+3 Very positive +2 Positive +1 Somewhat positive	0 Neutral	−3 Very negative −2 Negative −1 Somewhat negative		
Areas	**Questions**	+	−	0
Time	Age, related to title?			
	Time in same job?			
Acceptance	Submissive?			
	Realistic?			
Awareness	Self-questioning?			
	Perceptive?			
Family	Relationships?			
	Responsibilities?			
Competitive differences	Intelligence?			
	Personality traits?			
	Self-confidence and self-esteem?			
	Abilities?			
	Drive and aspirations?			
	Attitudes?			
Education	Number of degrees?			
	Technical?			
Work history	Job changes?			
	Reason for changing jobs?			
	Accomplishments and performance?			
Interpersonal relationships	Important others?			
	Peers?			
Development	Self?			
	By others?			
Opportunity	Short-term?			
	Foreseeable future?			
Stability	Financial?			
	Adaptability?			
	Self-discipline?			
	Total			

sons for making the moves. In each of your jobs, what *performance* ratings did you receive? Did you have outstanding *accomplishments?* If you were rated well and had outstanding accomplishments, score positively.

- **Interpersonal relationships:** How do you get along with people, particularly with *important others,* like your boss or those who are in positions to affect your job advancement? How do you get along with *peers?* Although peers do not have direct bearing on your advancement, their feelings about you are indirectly reflected upward, thereby affecting the attitudes of those in important positions. If you get along well with others, score positively.

- **Development:** Have you taken the initiative in your personal growth by attending postgraduate-education courses, reading, participating in *self-improvement* projects? To what extent have *others* assisted you with your personal development? Do you have a mentor who has served as a model in giving you helpful counseling? If you have an active self-development program and are being carefully groomed by others, score positively.

- **Opportunity:** Are there many job openings within your present company? Is the rate of growth of the company rapid, creating new promotional opportunities? Do you expect to reach your next career step in less than two years? If you don't expect *short-term* advancement, do you expect it in the *foreseeable future,* say in three to five years?

- **Stability:** How well do you manage your *financial* situation? Do you have strong financial needs? Although the pressure for more money can sometimes be a spur to advancement, it also can force you to rush your career and make wrong job decisions. If you have a reasonable desire for financial advancement but are not pressured by financial considerations, score positively. How *adaptable* are you? If you reach what appears to be a career impasse, can you change directions? Are you resilient enough to bounce back from failure? If you are adaptable, score positively. Finally, how much *self-discipline* do you have? Are you likely to cop out when the going gets rough? Will you be able to make the extra effort when necessary, and can you do so for sustained periods of time? If you have demonstrated self-discipline in the past, it's likely that it will serve you well in the future.

DON'T BE A CAREER LOSER. THINK WIN!

Many people have disappointing careers because they lack essential skills. Far more common, said Arthur A. Witkin. PhD, is "a naive attitude, unsound strategy in career planning or a total lack of planning, particularly by employees who think they're winners but are doomed to disappointment." Witkin divides career losers into four types:

- **The Jumpers**—who've "turned over jobs like hot cakes." They have histories of rapid job change *without growth,* which could make employers think they might soon be gone again.
- **The Pollyannas**—optimistic and unrealistic about their careers, who refuse to accept the fact that promotions may actually have been lateral transfers, or don't sense a problem if they have had no increase in responsibilities for three years.
- **The Dray Horses**—who work harder than anybody else, chain themselves to their desks until late at night, can be counted on to meet a schedule and follow the book. "They're popular with everyone and as loyal as your mother," Witkin added. "But hard work, reliability and a systematic approach don't always add up to productivity. There's a limited demand for people who roll up their sleeves and get the job done; far more valuable are those who can motivate others to roll up their sleeves."

- **The Revolutionists**—who often have excellent ideas but put them into action without getting management's approval, or they try for approval with a lecture or a hard sell. They fail to get their changes accepted and become known as malcontents in the process.

To be a career winner, Witkin concluded, "You must plan to be successful. Most people give as much thought to planning their careers as they do to ordering their lunches."

THE SEVEN TOUGHEST QUESTIONS YOU'LL EVER HAVE TO FACE
Compare notes with working women who've been there
by Jacqueline C. Warsaw

The Deep Seven: They're between-the-eyes questions you can't finesse. They come up mid-career, not necessarily mid-life, and, in a sense, you don't really answer them. You commit to them. The decisions you make depend on how much honesty and strategy, compromise and determination you bring to the effort. The women we interviewed (for a closer look at who they are and what they do, turn to the next two pages) did their homework and their soul-searching. They struggled for priorities and stuck by them. You'll find common denominators and advice here. Above all, you'll see a pattern of first steps taken. They include:

- Getting a clear idea about how you operate
- Deciding what it is you need in life and how hard you're willing to work for it
- Taking responsibility for yourself and what you want
- Analyzing the trade-offs
- Assessing the total picture
- Setting goals and sticking to them

1
SHOULD I GET MARRIED?

Jewell Jackson McCabe

Marriage is a very important part of a successful career for me. The drain of work ne-

cessitates a process of rejuvenation. Some people do that by going on a retreat. I do it through a healthy, viable marriage and family life. It's ego gratifying. It builds a sense of security and involves a friend you can bounce your ideas off. It's truly a sense of having a partner who isn't working in the same, everyday competitive arena. Of course, I offer the same kind of support to my husband. When he and I are working on projects together, it's as a unit. We strategize together, discuss problems together, support each other. It's like a sanctuary. Unless you have some very solid relationships, the working world can make you feel paranoid and insecure. The most important relationship for me is the one I have with my husband.

Linda Grant

I'm trying to decide whether or not to get married again. Certainly I've come full circle in my thinking about marriage and children. When I was young, I thought both were prisons women had to break out of, and I was determined not to get trapped. I don't feel that way now. In fact, I think both are probably essential if you're going to keep your emotional balance, given the special stresses of the business world. I want the emotional support and feedback of a marriage. You know, men don't ever have to make the choice. It's assumed they'll have their marriage, their children and their career. And when you look at the support systems successful executive men have, you see the best thing going for them is their wives. Can you imagine coming home after a hectic business day to a gourmet meal, a clean house and all that lovely ego stroking? . . . If you're working really hard, I don't know how you have the time and energy to date. Marriage removes that problem. I think it's a very lonely experience to have success without a family to share it. There are studies showing that women who put all of their energies into their careers usually falter around the age of 35.

Andrea Velletri

A major marriage problem with double-career couples is time. I have a 45-hour-a-week, full-time job, plus a private practice, plus some teaching commitments, plus a husband. There isn't much time left. At some point, you have to ask yourself about your own ambition. I cannot be a leading psychologist and have a marriage that has to come first. One of them has to go and that's a very hard trade-off. Ambition is hard to let go of once you've found it. Women are going to have to do a lot more thinking about themselves and focus less on the views others have of them. Wheaton College had a panel on this subject, and the women on the panel were talking about how they managed their careers and families and how all of it was "peachy keen." It was my feeling that nobody there was talking about the fact that she would never be president of IBM—not for as long as she attempted to maintain that balance. If you want to compete at that level, you work 15 to 18 hours a day, seven days a week. Let's not kid ourselves with the idea that if we want both, we can have both. We cannot.

2
SHOULD I CHANGE MY NAME?

Andrea Velletri

When I first married, I was in graduate school and I changed my last name to my husband's. I got my master's degree in my maiden name and my doctorate in both married and maiden names. But even during that process of trying to decide, it was a big issue. Now I'm coming to use my maiden name, Velletri, more and more in everything social and professional. In my profession, my name is my reputation. In the event of divorce or the death of my husband, I couldn't have a name that would then change. I have to have continuity and that means using my maiden name. It's a very pragmatic decision.

Dona MacDonald

I just got married last year and I chose to keep my maiden name, although my husband and I both adopted each other's last names as our middle names. From a career standpoint, I've established a professional reputation with my name and that continuity is important to me. Even if I didn't have a professional base, I would have chosen to keep my own name. It's something I'm familiar with and it's my identity.

Jewell Jackson McCabe

Jackson is my maiden name. McCabe is my married name. I'm Jewell Jackson because that's who I am, but I'm a McCabe, too, because I'm part of my husband. I feel that strongly. It's as simple as that.

Linda Grant

I went back to my maiden name after my divorce, and I wish I had never changed it in the first place. If you're going to have a byline, it's better to have it always in the same name. Also, it makes it difficult to renew business acquaintances when you suddenly have a different name. When I'm dealing with a chief executive officer of a Fortune

500 company, the last thing I want him to be thinking about is my personal life. When you have a new name, the comment is: "Oh, you got married." And I have to say, "No, I got un-married." This is a whole issue I don't like to introduce.

3
SHOULD I HAVE CHILDREN?

Jewell Jackson McCabe

I'm actively interested in having a family. I come from a tradition of middle-class black women who worked and raised children, so this is not such a major question for me as it might be for my white counterparts. My dilemma has to do with timing. Every time I'm about to start a family, I get a promotion and another kind of career challenge. It becomes very perplexing deciding which way to go. I get a lot of satisfaction out of work. Accomplishment stimulates me. Even though the commitment I make to my work is total, I do get paid back for it. It's the same kind of satisfaction a successful family would give me. But the challenge of a family still is very intriguing.

Andrea Velletri

Success is terribly appetizing to me. We've thought about starting a family, and it's still up in the air. The problem is not a financial one. It's that I'd want to be the child's mother. In order to do that, you have to invest a great deal of psychic energy as well as time. You do that because you want the experience of motherhood. On the other hand, all of that energy and time is taken away from something else, probably a career. I'm not sure where I am with that. It's really a three-part question. You're going to sacrifice your ambition and career, definitely. You're going to sacrifice your marital relationship, for sure. And you're going to add a new relationship, which may or may not balance it all out.

If you decide you can't do it, you might have a bitter taste in your mouth afterward.

If you go ahead but without giving up time from your career, your kid's in trouble. I think the notion that someone else can raise your children for you will get women into a great deal of trouble. I'm into early-childhood experience and the effect of the first five years of a child's life upon her/his future development. When working mothers look for nurses, we tend to want a carbon copy of ourselves. And that's impossible. We start compromising down. There are variables you can't test for when you interview a nurse. Variables such as the way she picks up the child, the way she tells the child not to do something, the quality of her emotional life and that it will influence the rest of that child's life.

Carole Beller

Everyone expects that if you're a woman, you'll be a wife, a mother, and a combination thereof, and that your career is always secondary. Having just had a child, I find the best way to talk about it really has to do with how you develop as a person in your career.

Biologically, there's a point in a woman's life when the answer to the question of having a child changes from "maybe" to "no." So you're always racing against time. I feel that it takes a woman a good ten years to get acclimated in business. To get her strength, her footing and to build a foundation. That puts her in her 30s. By that time she's getting very comfortable with her life style and she likes her freedom. Everything you do in a motherhood role begins to impinge upon that freedom. What usually happens is a shift in work style to accommodate the new life style.

In my situation, I've found some men who simply won't ask me about my child because they want to treat me like a man and accept me in a man's role. They absolutely pretend it doesn't exist. Others will talk about my child in terms of their own children, sort of buddy-to-buddy. A few are totally embarrassed by talking to a woman about her family. Most men have seen childbearing situations only in very traditional, average life styles such as those of their wives and mothers. They never have seen businesswomen in the role of being pregnant, and it's uncomfortable for them. In the past, most working women who got pregnant were secretaries. They'd work until the eighth month, leave to have the child and never come back. So men haven't learned the vocabulary of working with women who are mothers and executives.

I think working women mother differently, too. Where our parents read Dr. Spock for guidelines, a working mother today reads ten books and interviews every person who'll come in contact with her child. I interviewed seven different pediatricians before I selected one. I had to make sure he could see me before or after office hours. More ways must be found to help working mothers prepare for life with a child. Every time you pioneer, it takes something out of you. No one prepares you for that or says it's OK. Its not easy, but if you have a goal, everything works out within it.

4
SHOULD I RELOCATE?

Ann Reynolds

When I first started working, 14 years ago, I lived in Washington, DC and I had two children, ages 5 and 10. After I was there a year, an opportunity came up for me in another city and I went. Since then, I've relocated four times. I'm a big believer in going where the job is. Every time I moved, it was a step up or one with a better step beyond it. My requirements for relocating were never money related. The important goal for me was the freedom to do the things that were interesting to me. And to learn something new with each move. When I came to work for Kelly, 11 years ago, I not only took a pay cut, but I moved from California back to Detroit. Most of my friends thought I was insane. What I knew was that Kelly was a big company and growing. I would have more steps available to me with them. Sure, there were times when I was unhappy with my decisions. On one move I left Detroit for California and stayed there less than a year. That experience taught me the variety in East Coast and West Coast operations and made me more credible in the temporary-help business. It turned out to be a valuable move even though I resented it at the time. I'm really convinced that nothing you do, if you learn from it, is a waste.

As to the effect of relocation on my children, it was positive. They grew up knowing how to live in lots of different places, how to get around, direct dial long-distance calls, fly on planes, meet new people. My younger daughter, who is now in college, went to 13 schools before she graduated from high school. I never believed in waiting for the school year to end to relocate. When you do that, the kids mope around all summer in a new place without any friends. When you move mid-term, that doesn't happen.

Andrea Velletri

After we were married, my husband did some postdoctoral work in New York so we could be together while I was finishing my doctorate. When he got a job in Pittsburgh, we moved there and I completed my thesis long distance. Since we've been in Pittsburgh, a whole new set of relocating circumstances has arisen, which I think is one of the major issues double-career couples have to face. My husband's on the faculty of the medical school here, and there's a 95 percent chance that he won't get tenure. I, on the other hand, finished my postdoctoral clinical training in psychiatry. I have a great job in the psychoanalytic center as a therapist, and a flourishing private practice. I have roots and a career in this town, and my husband may have to leave this town. We now are faced with the question of how to make the trade-offs between our two careers. I don't know what will happen. We've drawn the line by agreeing that neither of us will do anything we really don't want to do. I won't allow him to take a job he doesn't like, and he won't let me throw my career down the drain. We also won't opt for living apart.

I think that is destructive to a relationship. We both put our relationship first, which sort of defines other choices for us.

5
SHOULD I CHANGE JOBS?

Linda Grant

I was a business writer for *Fortune* and had never had the experience of working for a major metropolitan daily newspaper, which, I decided, would be a valuable next step. I contacted the *Los Angeles Times,* and they were interested immediately, taking all the necessary steps to lure me there. I evaluated the paper, too. The *Los Angeles Times* has a million readers a day and plenty of clout. Taking a job with them filled a gap in my career development. As a business writer, I'm in a growth area in journalism. I average two or three breaking news stories a week. My beats are airlines/ aviation and energy, both of which are enormous businesses in southern California. It's very exciting and certainly was the correct job change for me.

Diana Harrison

For me, changing jobs was a case of deciding what my priorities were. Once I did that, everything else fell into place. It took me a year to think this through. I chose to take five months off, unemployed, so I could pursue a new position. I wrote at least 100 letters and went to 22 interviews. It was a full-scale endeavor. Making a life-career plan depends upon the extent to which you can project into the future. I asked myself where I wanted to be 20 years from now and decided that entrepreneurial work was the place. I came to the conclusion that in setting up any business I would have to know how to sell the product, and that has to do with marketing. There were a number of ways to learn, but I decided to do it under the tutelage of one of the finest marketers in the business. That narrowed the field.

I created a job-quality index which I used to rank each job in relation to several factors such as the importance of opportunity versus life style. I defined life style in terms of location, personal relationships and professional contacts. I made a list, and what came out at the top was the need for professional experience in marketing. Since location was way down on my list, the problem of relocating resolved itself. If the job satisfied all the above, I would move. But I would caution people about being too clinical in their approach. I underestimated the impact of two factors: one, losing my lifelong friends; two, losing track of some good professional contacts. Even so, professionally, it's the best decision I've made.

6
SHOULD I TAKE A JOB THAT REQUIRES TRAVEL?

Ann Reynolds

I travel a great deal and enjoy it. I've never measured the actual time spent but, for example, in the last two weeks I've been in Miami twice, Washington twice and Toronto once. There are lots of one-day trips, too. I try to make travel as much fun for myself as possible by scheduling a trip near the weekend so that if I like the place, I can stay on for a few extra days.

Linda Grant

I traveled a great deal when I was at *Fortune* and found it exhausting. Now I try to keep my travel time restricted to day trips. When I travel overnight, I usually don't go out because I have materials to prepare for the next day's interviews. That means I'm stuck in an uncomfortable hotel room, eating terrible food. It's tiring and demanding, and I don't enjoy working that way. I would definitely turn down any career move that required a lot of travel.

7
SHOULD I BUY OR RENT IN THE AREA WHERE I WORK?

Linda Hurlston

After working for seven and a half years for American Airlines in its Westchester County suburban office (located 30 miles from New

York City) and watching the rents go up and up and up, I examined my financial situation and realized that my landlord was getting the tax break, while I was paying for it. Economically, it made a lot more sense for me to develop an equity base in a home rather than to continue to pay rent. Also, I preferred living in a house to apartment living, so I began to look around the area. It took me awhile to find the right property. I looked from summer until December and didn't move until February of the following year. Part of the problem was that real estate in the area was fairly expensive, and I was holding out not only for a house in my price range, but also for one that would have resale value. Even though many of the agents kept trying to lure me to other areas, I refused to give up on the one in close proximity to my job. Ironically, a year after I bought my house, which by car was only four minutes door-to-door from my office, American Airlines closed their Westchester branch and moved that part of its business to Tulsa, Oklahoma. I chose not to relocate and took a job at Chemical Bank in New York City. Now I commute by train an hour each way, but I still have the house, which was a good investment. It's probably doubled in value.

Jewell Jackson McCabe

I rent an apartment in New York City. My husband and I anticipate buying a summer property; if we do, it will be just a "get away" place. For me, the city is the only place to live if you work there, and, even though I haven't invested in the city by purchasing an apartment or home, I've certainly invested my energies. I feel the vibrance of city life the minute I step out of my door, which is a continuum of what I'm all about as a professional working person. I want to be near my work, and since I'm involved with community affairs, keeping close to the city's inner workings is important to me.

Success comes from momentum, not inertia. That's the motivating echo and inner balance of every one of the working women we interviewed. Movers and shakers in the business world, they still know that ducking is a human, natural response. Dealing effectively with life's toughest questions is a skill that requires practice and caring and time.

JACQUELINE C. WARSAW *is a frequent contributor to* WORKING WOMAN *and the president of her own advertising/sales and promotion company.*
Carole Beller, *president of Frances Denney Cosmetics in New York City; married, with one child*
Linda Grant, *business writer for the* Los Angeles Times; *divorced, no children*
Diana Harrison, *brand management and advertising for Procter and Gamble in Cincinnati, Ohio; single, no children*
Linda Hurlston, *assistant treasurer for Chemical Bank in New York City; married, no children*
Dona MacDonald, *management-development training for MacDonald and Associates in Seattle, Washington; married, no children*
Jewell Jackson McCabe, *manager of government and community affairs at WNET Thirteen, NYC; married, no children*
Ann Reynolds, *associate director of public relations for Kelly Services, Detroit, Michigan; divorced, two grown children*
Andrea Velletri, *PhD, psychotherapist in private practice, Pittsburgh, Pennsylvania; married, no children*

HOW TO QUIT—AND WIN

by Mary Alice Kellogg

Three years ago Liz Scofield, a magazine writer in Philadelphia, decided it was time to take stock. She was 26 and had been writing professionally for three years. A part of her wanted to write the great American novel. Her more practical side wanted to put her creative talent to use in another field. She applied to Wharton School of Business and left her job, intending to devote five months to self-evaluation and finding out if she could write fiction for a living.

Mona Kerr (not her real name) took five months off, too. After five years of working a seven-days-a-week job as manager of a touring opera company in the Southwest, 27-year-old Kerr had reached a point of mental and physical exhaustion. Kerr realized she had gone as far as she wanted to go with that organization. She wanted to explore her next career move and to "make some room in my life for other parts of me."

Thirty-two-year-old Gladys Dobelle also lacked time for herself. A public-relations executive in San Francisco, she was moving to New York with her scientist husband and was determined to take a year off. Although Dobelle and her husband were in radically different fields, both held high-pressure jobs that left them little time in which to relax or share. Dobelle wanted to get to know her husband again. She also wanted to carve out a new career, using her past experience and incorporating the things she hoped to learn about her new city.

Taking the Plunge

Scofield, Kerr and Dobelle took career breaks—"time off" periods in which to assess their personal and professional lives and decide what steps to take next. These three women are not alone. What they did is being done by more and more working women who are willing to risk three months to a year without jobs in order to explore their potential.

In these days of assertiveness, it's suddenly all right to feel discontented. Perhaps you've been in a job for a few years. It's a good job, maybe an exciting one; still, you're beginning to feel restless. Perhaps the job has lost its challenge and the rosy future you'd anticipated looks a bit pale. Perhaps

it's time to move into a new field. Or maybe you're just plain tired, in need of a breather, and you would like to take some time to contemplate your next career step.

Whatever the reason, if you decide on a career break, be alert to the potential pitfalls in leaving a job without having another one in sight. Take such a break only following a thorough, realistic evaluation of your reasons for doing so. The reasons should be sound, having to do with growth and with seeking a new, permanent career direction. Totally frivolous reasons for leaving your present job do not bode well for the constructive use of your career break.

Weighing the Risks

Once you're secure about why you are taking time off, consider the risks. If you don't, you could be in for a big shock when you start looking for a new job.

One risk is not finding the job you want at the time you're ready to go back to work. Others are losing seniority in your company or field and having to take a salary cut. You risk criticism from colleagues, who may consider career breaks unprofessional or self-indulgent, and negative reactions from those who interview you for future jobs. Remember, there aren't many people who wouldn't like to take a year's sabbatical if they could figure out how to do it. The fact that you did it—and now are approaching them for a job—may create some resistance.

Finally, consider your age. Generally speaking, the younger you are, the better. If the bulk of your work life is ahead of you, you can afford to be flexible in your career choices. On the other hand, if you have spent years establishing yourself in a field or career, you should be aware that you may have to start at the bottom in some new career. While it may be worth it to you, it deserves forethought.

If your reasons seem right and the risks worth taking, then you should begin to make some serious plans.

Figuring Your Finances

Money is the first and major consideration. Scofield, Kerr and Dobelle found they spent just as much money during their career breaks as they did when they were working. To plan accurately, you should figure out exactly how much money it costs you to live now—including rent, utilities, food and spending money. As you no longer will be covered by group medical insurance, be sure to set aside money for individual coverage. It is important to have the money you'll need in the bank ahead of time. Remember, you'll have no paychecks coming in during your job break. Make a strict budget and stick to it. Your budget should allow for more time than you think will be necessary to find another job. A realistic budget will tell you precisely how long you can live without panic over impending starvation.

Exhilaration, Then Sleep

Once the financial realities are reckoned with, then what? That's up to you. At first, Dobelle, Scofield and Kerr felt exhilarated by taking fate into their own hands and giving themselves the gift of time. Each woman also faced the temptation to use her time unwisely.

"I slept for the first two months—literally," Kerr said. "I was frazzled." A job that had provided for no leisure time—even on weekends—had taken its toll on her. By the third month, she'd begun doing some of the things she'd always wanted to do but hadn't had time for. She became a passionate reader of career articles and books of all kinds. She finally finished James Joyce's *Ulysses.* She had lunch with friends she hadn't seen in a long time and began to keep a personal journal.

Scofield, who had wanted to write, initially plunged into reading and cooking. "I went through the collected Henry James and even read the Bible," she said. "Then I went through James Beard's *Book of Bread*— twice. Everybody I knew got one of my home-baked loaves." Occasionally, she planned day trips with friends; more often, she slept late.

Dobelle, too, caught up on lost sleep, but what she enjoyed most was being able to decide what she would do each day. If it rained, she stayed indoors reading stacks of magazines and books, or she went to a play, a concert, the ballet or opera. If the weather was good, she explored New York, street by street, with an eye toward creating a new job for herself. She tried to become better acquainted with her husband's family and to get closer to her own.

The 8:15 Panic

Although these activities were important to each of the women, something more important was missing: discipline. "I was on a real self-improvement course," said Scofield. "I did get very smart, but there was no one to discuss ideas with. Every morning at about 8:15 I got a vaguely panicked, what-am-I-going-to-do-today kind of feeling." Although Dobelle wandered the streets of New York, she didn't take notes for future reference. Used to dynamic life and work styles, Kerr found it scary "to see how lazy I could be. I realized that if I didn't set some goals, the time I had taken would just disappear."

Just as all three women had had the presence of mind to realize they needed time off, so they realized they had to stop wasting their time. Kerr began attending monthly meetings of professional performing-arts groups and planned lunches with those who worked in her field. At the same time, she worked harder on her journal, analyzing what she wanted out of a job and what she had to offer an employer, and trying to incorporate the lessons—many of them painful— she had learned during her time alone.

Scofield set a daily schedule, devoting specified hours to each project. She began to write short stories and discovered she preferred working under pressure, in a more organized atmosphere. She learned that she enjoyed working with people more than she liked the solitude necessary for writing fiction.

Dobelle set a schedule, too, organizing card and clip files of potential educational courses. She spent hours contacting night schools, universities and corporations, finding out what they offered, what they needed and how her knowledge of her environment could work to mutual advantage. Her goals became more focused.

Your goal needn't be spectacular, but it should be constructive. If you mean to dabble in poetry, then set a specific time each day for poetry writing. If you were used to keeping to a schedule while working, it's doubly important to schedule yourself now. Set goals for the week, the month, the entire break—and meet them.

Hindsight

In retrospect, Dobelle, Scofield and Kerr agree that their career breaks were valuable. Yet all would do some things differently if given the chance again. Dobelle, who jokes about her career break as "my movie and bonbon year" (exactly what it *wasn't*), said that 12 months was too long a period for her; she'd take a shorter break next time. At the end of her year, Dobelle formed her own public-relations agency, specializing in New York City. She now teaches four sellout college courses on the city, lectures and works as a consultant for corporations that are moving personnel into New York.

Scofield thinks of her five-month break in progressive stages: "First ecstasy, then smugness, then serenity, then vague depression." The depression set in at about the four-month mark. Suddenly, she was eager to return to the mainstream, having written five short stories, all of which she describes now as "terrible." She was accepted at Wharton, received her MBA and went to work as an account executive with a top New York advertising agency.

Kerr, who also took a job after five months, feels she could have used more time off. "If I had planned it wisely, five months

would have been enough," she said, "but I didn't plan at first." Currently, she is vice-president of a national performing-arts organization.

There's no question that taking a break runs counter to the tried-and-true career advice: Don't leave one job until you have another. Kerr, for instance, was concerned enough about her marketability to take a job sooner than she had planned. Dobelle felt she'd fallen a year behind in her profession. Scofield felt that being out of the mainstream for a few months had slightly lessened her job prospects, but that she would be able to recover. Even with their reservations, all three women said they would do it again.

Professional Benefits

Management and career counselors are seeing more people choosing to take time off and say that, if approached correctly, a career break can be a constructive force in a woman's life. Janice LaRouche, a career and assertiveness consultant, believes a career break can be an asset when you're being interviewed by a prospective employer. "Since you're taking a break for good reasons, why not tell an interviewer?" she said. "If you make it clear that you have committed yourself to this line of work after giving it careful thought and evaluating your skills, it can be a plus. I would explain it in positive terms."

When you are faced with the question of a résumé gap, it's important to be frank, to stress that the time was taken to grow, to become solidly committed to the work for which you're now applying. Did you take courses, do projects? These questions undoubtedly will be raised, and the fact that you did work on your own time may impress an interviewer.

Judith Gerberg, a career therapist, said that in these days of job hopping, taking time off is not a bad thing. "You don't even have to have dates on your résumé anymore. There are so many people switching fields and changing companies that taking time off in between is just not unusual," she said. "If you're in a corporation, there's a danger of your losing seniority, but you also might become more valuable to that corporation if you have used your time well."

Gerberg cautions her clients about the stress that comes with having no paycheck and the anxieties you're sure to have about entering a new field. These are natural by-products of a career break, and one way to handle them is to form a support group. Many students in Gerberg's "Creating Your Career in Art" course at New York's Parsons School of Design are considering taking career breaks and planning to switch fields. They use the class not only to learn, but to discuss the pros and cons of taking time off.

You Can Go Back Again

Of course, many break takers do return—refreshed—to their former fields. Some jobs—in secretarial, educational or other skill-related fields, for instance—have universal requirements that facilitate a return to a comparable or superior job. In any field, it is important to keep up with the latest developments, so you'll be on top of your profession when you go back. Whatever profession you decide to enter or reenter, the time to start looking for a job is when you feel the first faint stirrings of ennui. (Perhaps at the beginning of what Scofield called the "serenity" stage, before "vague depression" sets in.)

How long you will want to stay out of a job is up to you, your goals and your pocketbook. It is essential to realize that you will be coming back into the work force—perhaps with a new career, new perspectives or a new view of your former job—and to plan for the day when all your newfound wisdom and energy will be applied. To that end, it's smart to keep up with your old and new interests, to get out of the house or apartment, to meet with professional groups.

If you have used your time constructively, kept up with the field you intended to enter, set goals, taken courses and generally made

the break work for you, then the professional benefits are numerous. Even more important may be the personal growth you gain from the experience. Career-consultant LaRouche sees breaks as important if "you are trying to get something out of your system or are reevaluating long-term career goals. Many people find it difficult to do that while working full time, as both tasks are demanding and energy consuming. For some, taking a career break is possibly a wise thing to do."

Should You or Shouldn't You?

How do you know if you're among the "some" who can benefit from such a leap? LaRouche classifies successful career pausers as those who are confident of their personal worth and value in the job market. They are people who are risk takers and aren't frightened of job interviews.

A career break isn't for everyone. For those who take them, who gather their courage and plan ahead, who risk some short-term profit for some long-term insight, the rewards are many—and, in some cases, unexpected. Kerr, who left her opera-management job partly because her employer could not see the wisdom in giving her some time off, thinks that career breaks can be a plus for your next employer as well as for you. "It's of tremendous benefit to my present employer that I took a break," she said. "I emerged from it more organized, disciplined and focused. I have weekly, monthly and yearly plans of the things I want to accomplish—something I had not had before. It was important to get to know myself, my limits and my demands."

That knowledge is at the heart of a career break. Ultimately, it is what the process of growth—professional and personal—is all about.

MARY ALICE KELLOGG, *a senior editor at* Parade *magazine, took a one-year career break and found it to be the best and worst year of her life. "It was definitely worth it."*

THE 5-YEAR CAREER PLAN: WHAT'S IN IT FOR YOU

Here's how—and why—you should set goals for the future. Marketing expert Carole Beller practices what she teaches

by Jacqueline C. Warsaw

In Carole Beller's office, invisible electrons pulse out neon sign messages you feel instead of see. Action words, such as plan, chart, check, examine, evaluate, are the syntax of her five-year career plan, a business strategy that she insists really has a payout. "I've always been goal-oriented" she said. "I grew up that way, never realizing it's not typical."

Goals are essential to Beller, especially in business. With goals you progress vertically. Without them, you perpetuate the pinball syndrome, coursing through a maze, constantly being pushed and tilted into place by someone else.

A marketing vice-president at Frances Denney cosmetics company, Beller, along with a group of other businesswomen, has lighted a fire under women to plan their own careers. Operating within the cosmetics industry, they began a service program in which women were invited to take seminars, join symposiums, gather information on what jobs are available.

But the how-tos and tips of her career-planning program are not restricted to just one industry. They work everywhere, in every job market, including the home.

Q. *What are the major ingredients of your career-goal program?*

A. It's based on questions such as: Where are you today? Where do you want to be in five years? For example, you might be an assistant in a production company now and want to be head of a production company and earn $40,000 in five years. Well, how do you get there? It may not be a straight line, you know. The plan needs a lot of research. Talking with people in various fields; con-stantly evaluating and examining. It's a methodical format, a system.

Q. *When should you structure your first five-year plan?*

A. Women should know by the age of 25 what they want to achieve.

Q. *Are you saying that without a career plan you can't have a career?*

A. If you don't do something about planning your life, you find yourself—especially in business—moving neither up nor down, but horizontally. You will spend your life in a maze waiting for someone to show you the way out. You know, socially, women have always had five-year plans, with specific ideas for marriage, size of family, type of house in the country. But they just don't relate planning to their careers.

Q. *If women are naturally good organizers and planners, why hasn't that expertise spilled over into pursuing their own goals?*

A. I think women have always been intimidated by personal goals, or they feel that it's too masculine or too selfish to ask, "What is my plan for me as a person? What am I about and where am I going?"

Q. *Isn't it more difficult for the woman managing a home and family to plot a career?*

A. If a woman who is sitting at home with two children says she can't make plans about her life until the children grow up, I say she's on the wrong track. It's called the "wait until" syndrome.

Q. *Do you attribute that to reluctance, laziness or both?*

A. It's really a matter of having an untrained mind. People often don't know how to articulate a plan, especially women. A five-year plan will apply more realistic pressure to the importance of taking the first step.

Q. *In general, don't women tend to wait for direction or for someone else to develop their potential?*

A. Yes, they do. But I don't feel anyone owes you that. You have to do it for yourself. So many women today roam from job to job, career to career, aimlessly wondering what's going to happen to them. Will an envelope arrive in the mail appointing them head of a college or publisher of a magazine? But in their daydream, it never happens at their insistence. We don't take enough charge of our lives or our careers. We have to start selling ourselves, marketing our talents.

Q. *But all effective marketing starts with knowing the product.*

A. Exactly. We should be asking ourselves: Who is this person I am? What are my interests? What do I like? What are my skills? What kinds of people do I prefer? What kind of money am I looking for? Is money the most important thing in my job? Is location? When you have the answers, put them all together and give them priorities.

Q. *Will the answers to that kind of personal probing net you a good career plan?*

A. That's what career planning is all about. After all, priority listing is something women do already with so many things, from selecting an apartment to shopping for clothes. But they can't do that same objective listing for themselves.

Q. *Is that the biggest roadblock? The one that really keeps women from making a game plan for themselves?*

A. In part. I'm not sure women are confident enough, early enough, about handling and balancing all of the pressures society, family and business ask of them.

Q. *But haven't those pressures always been part of a male's checklist?*

A. There's still enormous pressure upon women *because* they are women. Pressures to marry, reproduce, achieve a certain social status.

Q. *Is it primarily peer pressure?*

A. It's also societal pressure. It's parental pressure. We can't just peel away 20 years of growing up in a family where marriage was applauded. No one ever said, "Isn't it wonderful, she didn't get married." Women rarely learn about options in that kind of environment.

Q. *So it's all these psychological tuggings that keep women from solidifying a personal direction? From committing themselves to a career?*

A. Yes. And I think we never stop thinking about them. When I talk with 22- and 23-year-old women, women who should be doing a five-year plan and then updating it as they develop, I find that what's holding them back are all the social stigmas attached to ambition.

Q. *If women really want to carve out a new status profile by responding to challenges, why are they still so bothered by the old stigmas?*

A. American women are still the classic overachievers. We have to overachieve socially, with family and at the job. We haven't learned that it's O.K. to be enthusiastic but it's not essential. Too many women are willing to take the hall closet for an office just to prove they can do it.

Q. *Are women too easily compromised?*

A. Women seem to want a job so badly they're willing to compromise on salary, responsibility, title, advancement. They are so eager to prove themselves at lower levels, they forget about setting higher goals. It's a whole different psychology.

Q. *Can the bottom line of a career program help make it easier for women to make that higher job bid?*

A. Absolutely. We want to structure a program that shows women where the real opportunities are. Right now, every time I get an assistant, she is overtrained educationally or has no professional skill to sell. When that's the case, I send her out for an MBA program. But even an MBA isn't enough. Sure you learn accounting, financial data or international marketing, which may give you a better head and possibly more maturity, but that doesn't make you valuable to a company. Because the question always is, "What can you do for me today?" Not next month or even six months from today. But right now.

Q. *Do you think that women just don't know how to take a stand for the better job? That they don't know how to express ability?*

A. Yes. I'm finding that even with the incredible numbers of women graduating from professional schools, there is still a beat missing. And it's a simple course in how to present themselves.

Q. *You mean presentation, even starting at the résumé level.*

A. I get résumés from Wharton, Stanford and Chicago business-school graduates who tell me all the negatives and none of the business pluses. Here I am trying to evaluate a person, and they're telling me they have no experience. And they think that's wonderful. Well, that's not what people in the business community look for. Business is much more hard-hitting. It asks, what can you do *for me?*

Q. *If you take it one step back from actual entry into the work force, don't you find that women are at least going after more specific schooling and higher degrees such as MBAs?*

A. I think now they are. I'm not sure there would have been a payout if they'd had that interest ten years ago. For example, when I was in graduate school, I was discouraged from going to Harvard Business School so I went to Harvard graduate school. Everyone told me that the pressure on women pioneering business careers was extraordinary. That I'd be educated but, at best, I'd be the token woman in any corporate network. Frankly, I don't think I was mature enough then, socially or emotionally, to have handled that. No one really wants to get into a company as the oddball.

Q. *Without the encouragement of a job-promise afterward, women did things that were socially acceptable.*

A. Yes. I don't think you can put up with sex-role pressure in business in middle- or even senior-management for very long periods of time. I don't think you go on for 30 years being a pioneer without having a distorted personality.

Q. *But there are real payouts now?*

A. Women whom I've seen coming out of business school now are much more energetic and confident that there is a place for them in the world. There are opportunities for them enforced by the Government. Yes, there are real payouts now.

Q. *Let's get back to presenting oneself. To the interview.*

A. Many women are not ready for the kind of male-slanted, hard-hitting interviewing that still takes place in major corporations. They are, by and large, still negative interviews with loaded questions, such as: Do you plan to have children? Why do you think you deserve the job?

Q. *That doesn't leave much room for positive response.*

A. Right. And not enough women are prepared for such a devastating experience. Or understand that it's O.K. to take command of the situation by telling the interviewer that you don't feel the questions are appropriate or productive.

Q. *Don't you think women have to learn to discriminate between strength and aggression as a first step in handling these kinds of situations?*

A. Yes. Lots of women in business today are learning more about assertive managing and aren't trapped into using excess tactics—those clichés such as pounding the table to make a point. But the evolution is slow.

Q. *With more role models for women, the progress should accelerate.*

A. I think so. In my early career, the models you had were all men. If you were a sponge, you took something from one, something from another, but by the time you were finished, you were a patchwork with no idea of who you really were.

Q. *Instant identity doesn't happen, either.*
A. No. And unfortunately, too many women think they're going to wake up one morning and know the answer. Well, there's a struggle you have to go through. Identity isn't automatic. And women will have to learn that. With more difficulty than men because we have so many more diversions and allowances. So many more people who always want to pat us on the head and say, "It's O.K., you don't have to achieve today." With those kinds of excuses, we get detoured very easily.
Q. *It makes it difficult to hang in and not lose sight of goals.*
A. I think women have to start learning how to direct themselves to a focal point. And I think that ties in with what the payout is. What the benefits are. I don't believe anyone works just for the sake of working. You work for money, and money is in some sense a measure of worth. It's a reward, not a negative goal.
Q. *It seems to come down to an ability to balance goals and objectives with rewards and pleasures. How can women balance them better?*
A. When I started in business, I rarely saw a balance. There were women who were super executives and unhappy wives and mothers or vice versa. They were never total people. Today, with so many career development programs, women increasingly are able to handle multiple roles.
Q. *So as the options grow clearer, the "either-or" attitude fades.*
A. Yes.
Q. *Are more women facing the hard-core realities of the business community, like them or not?*
A. I find this missing a lot. And it's a lack that begins with inadequate training. Knowing what the real environment is like can only be helpful. Pressure and politics are all part of the business structure. For example, the political network in a company may be different from its organizational structure.

And that's a part of business many women refuse to face. It's a real handicap. But, if you've mapped a good career plan, you should be able to spot the handicaps and take steps to correct them.
Q. *How does one evaluate a goal-plan properly. And couldn't the entire validity of the plan flop if the evaluation is dishonest?*
A. I think you're always being evaluated in a job. If you're getting the advancement, either in salary or title, or if people are recognizing your talent, evaluation is obvious. I don't think it's so unpredictable.
Q. *There are large signposts?*
A. Yes . . . And even if a person is blind to the signs, a five-year plan gives them something to hold onto. It's like a self-appraisal. You can't really run away from it.
Q. *If the plan indicates a career change, don't you find women are often unwilling to give up the years invested in one area and will opt for the unfulfilling route to avoid a move?*
A. Yes. And it has no bearing on age, background, experience or education. Women are nesters. They get into a job. They want to be loved. They want to know who the people are they see every day. They like familiarity and routine. In a sense, they don't want any abrupt behavior around them.
Q. *When should you start evaluating your plan?*
A. Any plan has both some real guts to it and some hypothetical aspects. You can do the concrete part of a five-year plan only in terms of the first two years. That's because you can't know for certain what your capabilities will be beyond then.

A plan, after all, is like an insurance policy. You should keep all that you do in a folder, so you can plot your progress. Everyone owes it to themselves if they're going to be in business. Although it can be both painful and exhilarating, if you're intelligent enough to be in business and to want to stay in business, you'll want the tools to go further.

Beller's regimen for career training is as precise as an athlete's, because she knows that, in the reality of the business world, you're competing against more than your-self. In her effort to help women define goals, discover potential and develop careers, Carole Beller is as dedicated as a cornerstone.

FIVE-YEAR CAREER PLAN
OBJECTIVE
To outline career interests and personal development goals that can better direct one's energies and talent.

GOAL REVIEWS
Plan should be reexamined several times a year to implement, change or redirect goals.

GOAL REWARDS
Should include any of the following:
- monetary upgrading; money; salary
- added responsibility; more power
- additional company benefits, i.e., perks, stock, cars, bonus
- relocation potential
- executive advancement opportunity
- expansion possibilities
- peer recognition

EVALUATION
Need to evaluate self based on:
- recognition in job
- salary advancement
- peer recognition
- superior encouragement

Need sometimes to:
- have professional appraisal of goals, targets with boss, respected colleague, personnel director
- review weaknesses as opportunity to incorporate specialized training into your schedule
- accept job changes, horizontal or vertical change, and perhaps reapprentice in a new field entirely

PERSONAL GOALS
Important to list desired personal commitments and then use them to plan a series of alternatives. Marriage, divorce, children can become "excuses" for ignoring one's professional growth commitment.

RESEARCH TOOLS
Gather career data:
- personal interviews with successful career models
- read, subscribe and purchase books, magazines in your field of interest
- get to know personnel specialists in your field
- develop contacts in other departments in your company
- attend local professional seminars, luncheons or one-day meetings
- use vacations to take specialized courses that meet your goals

12 CAREER MISTAKES
by Jacqueline C. Warsaw

The time was 1973. The ERA stockpot had been moved to the front burner. Although companies were interested, they were not campaigning to employ women; female entry into boardrooms represented corporate tokenism, not enthusiasm.

Janet Jones-Parker had just turned 26 to become one of the airline industry's youngest operations managers. Ambitious for further vertical hikes in her career but facing up to a lack of them, she left.

Almost simultaneously, Anne Hyde, highly polished in European and US finance, marketing and corporate protocol, was deciding what her next career progression would be, having just resigned from a major American firm.

Their first meeting focused on the same question: How does a woman look for a job? At the time there were three choices: Go to an ordinary employment agency, which had no jobs at the appropriate level for women with substantial tenure; go to a traditional male-oriented executive search firm, which, working primarily on commission, would put the thrust where the money was, and it wasn't on women in 1973; or she could market herself directly to a company.

Certainly the need, if not the climate, for an executive search service for women seemed ripe. Jones and Hyde decided to enter the entrepreneurial arena and incorporated Management Woman Inc. Early resistance was instant. Company executives thought Jones and Hyde were jumping on a bandwagon—that they were a cause, not a business. Now in its fifth year, Management Woman employs five recruiters, three support staff and deals with major corporations nationwide.

Because of their first-hand exposure to executive women and career dynamics, we talked with Jones and Hyde for an inside look at the major mistakes women make in business.

Q. *Where do you find executive-caliber female talent?*
A. Anywhere and everywhere. It's only been four-and-a-half to five years since women have been in the mainstream of business; they need more time to develop a base in certain work areas. There is no substitute for seasoning, unfortunately. When you're looking for a man, you can press a button on the Fortune 500 directory and out will come 500 men in whatever area you are searching. That's not so with women.

Q. *What seem to be the most glaring career blocks that women experience?*
A. Let's start with lack of self-confidence. We'd like to share a story with you. During a top search we were working with a woman—highly qualified, with a track record and in the $70,000-a-year salary bracket. At the end of the day's interviewing, the client said that two things had struck him very forcibly about the woman, and about all the women he had screened: Each one had wondered whether or not she could handle the challenge. Each stated or implied some self-doubt. If he had interviewed men with the same credentials, every one of them would have taken the bit between his teeth and run.

Q. *How did you interpret that reaction?*
A. We said that he was seeing the results of discrimination over a long period of time. Developing confidence is a building process. If you are told constantly that you cannot, you must not, you should not, chances are you will not.

Q. *Are women aware of the need to build confidence platforms?*
A. Yes. When women can see themselves in a new role, usually they will step up to that promotion. The problem is that they haven't been in the big-league arena long enough.

There are not many role models for women in a lot of the senior corporate positions.

Q. *Does any of this relate directly to an inability to take risks?*
A. Women don't take risks. Which is another major career block. When the dice are in their favor, women should roll with them; they don't. It's easy to fantasize about what you would do "if," knowing that the chances of that "if" ever happening are practically nil.

Q. *Is it fear of success or fear of failure that stops women from taking risks?*
A. Failure is so much more comfortable than success. Women are taught how to cope with failure—how to rise above it or live through it. Nobody teaches them how to deal with success. Women need to learn to enjoy power, visibility and money.

Q. *What are some other major mistakes made by women?*
A. The inability to make trade-offs. Life doesn't come in a neat package, you know. There is a reality in evaluating what you can expect and what you can do with what's given to you. Suppose a woman in an administrative assistant's position decides to prepare to be an assistant manager. Looking at the skills the other assistant managers have is her first step. This might mean making an investment in night school, special study programs, whatever. It's a trade-off situation. If you really want to play in an arena, you've got to look at what the other players in that arena already have. Not evaluating the competition within a company is a big mistake women make.

Q. *A hard-edged realism is part of many aspects of a woman's life, yet that same evaluation technique isn't applied to her career. Why?*
A. I think it's because it means making trade-offs. It's the difference between fantasizing success and actually facing up to it. Also, it's much easier to feel you're discriminated against than to look realistically at why you didn't get a promotion.

Q. *Is "facing up" another side of taking control?*
A. Absolutely. This is a big problem for almost everyone. It's a newer problem for women because we haven't had to think that way before.

THE DOZEN *DON'TS* WOMEN DO TO BLOCK BUSINESS CAREERS & (SOMETIMES) PERSONAL GROWTH

1. **Are unwilling to make trade-offs**
2. **Don't evaluate the competition**
3. **Disregard lateral moves**
4. **Don't develop a power base**
5. **Have no political awareness**
6. **Overpersonalize company problems**
7. **Don't take control**
8. **Become overly involved in nitty gritty**
9. **Have excess loyalty**
10. **Display a lack of confidence**
11. **Fear failure (or success)**
12. **Are unwilling to take risks**

Q. *What problems do you see relating to movement within a company structure?*
A. Women often disregard lateral moves. They tend to have come up through a single channel. This is not particularly effective in developing top management. Many companies have realized this and now move men laterally across the business—staff, line, staff, line—to cover marketing, sales, finance, accounting and so forth, touching many bases to broaden experience. Women need this exposure, too, even though it sometimes means making a lateral move status-wise and salary-wise. Whether you're judging a next move internally or externally, judge it on what it's going to prepare you *for*. Always look for the learning curve that goes up. A company executive recently told us never to present to him anybody who could just do the job. Never. He was looking for promotability. That is the corporate return on investment.

Q. *That requires specific career goals and strategies.*

A. Sure it does. But remember that flexibility is key to any career plan. Progression doesn't always follow a straight line.

Q. *Aren't lateral moves often avoided because of their effect on earning power?*

A. Ask yourself what you're worth in a job in which you have less expertise than the job you're in. The realistic answer is that you're worth less to a company. Women should look at the lower salary as an investment in themselves—in their training, in their future. That's perfectly O.K. Change and growth often exact a price.

Q. *Does getting involved in the nitty gritty to the point where they're not aware of corporate politics prevent women from rising up the pyramid?*

A. Not developing a political awareness is a major, major fault with women. Women forget that when they were children, they could easily figure out which parent was good for a nickel for candy. That was one of the most political acts of their early lives.

Q. *Do you find women expressing an exaggerated discomfort with power?*

A. That is another critical mistake. You can have no change without power. Not wishing to be visible is unrealistic. As you move up, you're naturally going to become more visible. The price you pay for promotion is having to leave behind those people who are your peers; you have to be willing to cut some umbilical cords. For instance, if a secretary moving to an administrative position is going to start showing managerial responsibility, she can't continue to associate on a girl-to-girl basis with the other secretaries. A lot of women give up a promotion because they can't deal with this separation. They feel insecure.

Q. *Does that reluctance to move stem from a need to be liked or from the fear that they can't do the new job?*

A. It's a balance of both. From infancy, women are conditioned to play the support role—the nurse versus the doctor. Think about the traditional definition of female: quiet, supportive, subjective—whereas male is equated with aggression, dominance, daring. Which characteristics would you rather have for a top executive in your company?

Q. *Is this distorted feeling women have about gaining control over themselves or others self-destructive?*

A. It's a block at every level. When I asked a $100,000-a-year female executive if she was a success, the question so threw her that it was hours before she whispered back to me, "No." When I asked why, she said because she'd never had to fight for her top position.

Q. *She equated success with clawing one's way to the top?*

A. Yes. She felt guilty because she hadn't had to go that fictional route—her talent had been recognized. If she'd had to force people to acknowledge her credentials, she probably would have felt comfortable with the idea of being "a success."

Q. *As if she'd earned it?*

A. Exactly. What had never occurred to her was that she *had* earned it by using her opportunities. Several days later, after much soul-searching, she was able to say, "Yes, damn it, I am a success and I'm pleased about it." What she finally had done was to take control of her life. And that leads us to talk about another major omission in women's careers.

Q. *You mean knowing the difference between reacting and responding?*

A. Yes. Women tend to be reactive. In a company situation, for example, women should make maximum use of what's internal and not immediately react if things aren't going their way. There are solutions in a big company if you just look around. You can't wait for people to know what you want. They won't know if you don't tell them.

Q. *Usually, there's less business acumen involved in reacting, while responding requires thought, synthesis and evaluation.*

A. That's a major point. Responding is less

emotional, more logical. It is very important both to the business situation and to yourself. When you respond, you take control of a situation; when you react, someone else usually is in control.

Q. *Do you see many examples of reacting during an interview?*

A. All the time, especially when an interviewer asks what we call illegal questions. For instance, suppose someone asks you to define your weaknesses. In an actual situation I know of, a woman answered, "I'm not going to tell you my weaknesses. We haven't come here to discuss those." What she was saying in neon lights was, first, that she had not thought herself through and second, that she was overemotional. She was in a senior managerial position; if she couldn't recognize that she had weaknesses, she was expressing insecurity and a real roadblock about personal growth. Nine times out of ten, all the interviewer wants to see is how the person handles the question.

Q. *Are there any other important interview mistakes women tend to make?*

A. Yes. They don't do their homework before a key interview. They don't bone up on the company, its products or performance or philosophy. If they are prepared, it gives them another notch up on gaining control.

Q. *It's often argued that women are too willing to discuss their inadequacies openly. Does this work against them?*

A. Women tend to beat themselves for anything less than perfection. The perfection-package is sold to them from a very early age. It's tough to be the perfect beauty, perfect body, perfect hostess, etc. So women tend not only to emotionalize their mistakes but also to elongate their suffering. They must learn to cut the pain of failure and get on about the business at hand. They must understand that something isn't a failure until you repeat it, that failure in its broad sense is a learning process. Another tendency among women is to overpersonalize what is going on around them. Corporate life is like a good game of poker. If you show or

speak too much, you expose your hand. Then you become vulnerable. The determined competition knows where to strike.

Q. *What about the problem of excess loyalty?*

A. Women often carry company loyalty to a fault; they don't realize that there is an acceptable cut-off point. Companies are in business to make a profit; in the end, it's performance that matters most, not your personality or loyalty or relationship to a boss. The reality may seem hard, but it's a fact.

Q. *What about career expectations—where is the threshhold for women today?*

A. The woman who has set her expectations too high is as blocked as the woman who has set them too low because she will not understand her apprenticeship period. Early success can often abort future growth in that it bypasses the experience platform we need for dealing with added responsibility. Experience and seasoning are important.

Q. *Are women more motivated by negative fears than positive drives?*

A. Power, money, visibility, manipulation, recognition—all are real motivations of work. They are what success is all about. Only when women realize that it is O.K. to want them will they be motivated by them.

Q. *Why have women avoided management as a viable career?*

A. Management is motivating and listening to people. The higher you go in management, the less you do of the nitty gritty and the more time you spend on the intangibles . . . meetings, conferences. It's the equation of visual accomplishment versus nonvisual accomplishment. Unfortunately, women tend to equate success with how much time they spend at their desk.

Q. *Can women, despite their frequent single-channel experience, make major changes in career direction?*

A. Specializing isn't always restrictive. Every bit of experience counts. Never, never throw away or discount experience, however unrelated it seems to be to a change in direction. It *is* related. It has made you. It has given you the perspective you have.

Q. *How would you like to see women define success?*

A. Success is never static. It is dynamic and flexible, and it's measured in different terms. Goals are never used up. Reach one, make another. There is an equation between career goals and career blocks. Contemplating a presidency can cause a tremor that all too quickly turns into a trauma. As women earn time and gain seasoning, what seems titanic will become scalable. One cannot do less than respect one of Goethe's couplets:

Whatever you can do, or dream you can, begin it.

Boldness has genius, power and magic in it.

QUIZ:
ARE YOUR CAREER IDEAS READY FOR THE 1980s?

by Shirley Sloan Fader

The 1980s are here. It's a new decade with dazzling new career opportunities for women. Are your job attitudes up to date, ready to let you take advantage of your 1980s career chances? Take our career quiz to find out.

True or False?

☐1. Women who go into men-only luncheon and social clubs and try to break down the men-only rules are wasting effort on an unimportant kind of discrimination.

☐2. Some business districts are quite deserted at night, and it's understandable if women aren't offered executive jobs in those areas. Executives often have to put in overtime and a woman supervisor might find herself in an unsafe situation.

☐3. Contrary to what people say, if you are promoted and have men assigned to work for you, they will accept you readily as the boss.

☐4. Women in general aren't more emotional on the job than men are.

☐5. If the job involves a lot of travel, a company shouldn't offer it to a woman with children.

☐6. Educated, ambitious women are socially unattractive to men.

☐7. It's important to use such terms as business people, chairperson and people-made instead of businessman, chairman and man-made.

☐8. You can't change a man's negative attitudes toward careers for women.

☐9. Though women have many human-relations talents that are useful in business, they are not comfortable thinking about money or dealing with fiscal realities.

☐10. Women in general are good at creating new ideas and being leaders.

Answers:

1. *False.* It is important to your job chances that men-only luncheon and social clubs be abolished. If a club will not admit women, it amounts to denying the women the business opportunities, discussions and information they could have acquired there. In addition, because employers know a woman will be unable to represent the company at business meetings in these clubs, they frequently hesitate to offer a woman the job. If a woman does get the job, she is hampered in succeeding at it by being excluded.

2. *False.* The women should be offered the executive positions. When women work

as nonexecutives, such as telephone operators, nurses, night-shift factory assemblers, charwomen and baby sitters, nobody thinks of denying them the positions because of night dangers. They're expected to arrange to get safely to and from work. Why when a woman is about to get a high-level job, should it be assumed that she lacks the intelligence to arrange transportation?

3. *True.* While the media continue to produce anxious discussions about "Will men work for women?", the question already has been answered. Millions of men work for women bosses. And more and more men are acquiring women managers. Just as they would with any boss, the men try to keep their own jobs by working well for their female supervisors. Women are in charge of blue-collar factory and craft workers of all kinds, and in charge of offices, stores, banks, company departments and corporate activities of every conceivable type. The governors of two states, Connecticut and Washington, the mayors of hundreds of municipalities, including Chicago and San Francisco, and the Prime Minister of Great Britain are women. Together they are boss to hundreds of thousands, perhaps millions, of male government employees.

4. *True.* Women in general aren't any more emotional on the job than men are. Studies of men and women repeatedly have indicated that women are better able to cope with stress than are men. Scientists believe this is one of the major reasons women as a group live longer than do men. As for behavior in crises, as one analyst put it, "Women are not considered too emotional to cope with the life and death situations in a hospital or in the home but somehow there is the fear that a profit-and-loss crisis will shatter them."

5. *False.* Women should be allowed to decide whether they want jobs that involve travel. Many married men are unwilling to accept positions requiring travel. But no one considers "protecting" all men from such job offers. Individual men are seen as grown-up people capable of controlling their own lives who should consider and decide job offers for themselves. Women should receive the same treatment.

6. *False.* Styles in women who are attractive to men change from decade to decade. (Remember in *Little Women* how unacceptable Jo is because she refuses to faint and flutter? Today's man would regard a woman who swooned as a kook.)

As men learn first to enjoy and then to depend on the psychological security and the material comforts of a two-paycheck family, their attitudes toward women's careers alter noticeably.

Just as the behavior of the 1920s woman made the swooning, fluttering Victorian female obsolete, and the 1960s women made the 1920s–1950s clinging vine uninteresting, so men's experiences with the new, exciting, ambitious American woman will transform their expectations of what an attractive woman is.

7. *True.* It's important to use such words as business people, chairperson, people-made. Words define, reinforce and to a large extent control the way people see and run their lives. As long as general discussions of work are done in terms of businessmen, man hours, the right man for the job, chairman, we are strengthening the average person's picture of the job world as being "naturally" male with women as interlopers. When we change our language to *include* both sexes, we change the image of who is "natural" in the work world.

8. *False.* During the last few decades, men completely have changed many of their basic ideas about women's careers.

A 1936 Gallup poll asked, "Should a married woman earn money if she has a husband capable of supporting her?" A massive 82 percent of Americans declared no. So strong was this feeling that until World War II a man was ashamed to have his wife work outside the home.

After World War II, men's attitudes toward women and careers changed once again. Married women without children worked with universal approval. Yet, as recently as the late 1960s, if a married woman with children wanted to continue her career, men and society believed she was "sick," "fighting her femininity," "attempting to emasculate her husband." All these ideas about women and careers have disappeared almost totally within the last decade.

9. *False.* As long ago as 1955 (in the midst of the passive female "feminine mystique" age) it was evident that within the privacy of their families women were recognized as being competent with money. The well-known sociological study by Blood and Wolfe on division of labor within the family revealed that when it came to the tough "bottom line" of keeping the family solvent, Americans usually wanted their woman involved—either as the *only* active person or as an equal. In 41 percent of the families, women were always either responsible for paying all the bills or responsible for paying most of the bills. In another 34 percent of the families, wife and husband shared equally in coping with family bills. In short, three out of four families depended on the women to understand and deal successfully with the family's fiscal realities.

A recent nationwide survey of women in executive positions revealed that of the top eight types of management that women are entering, six are fiscal/math occupations: accounting, programs/systems, engineering, marketing, data processing and systems analysis.

10. *True.* In general, women seem to be *more* talented than men when it comes to creating ideas and are equally capable of leadership.

Until recently, the problem has been that although women are born with the abilities, they have been taught not to use them. The Johnson O'Connor Research Foundation, a nonprofit nationwide organization, has tested more than half a million men and women for work aptitudes during the past half century. The research revealed that *more* women than men are high in the kinds of creative thinking and general mental ability that is required in order to succeed as bankers, managers, executives, politicians, lawyers, insurance adjusters, teachers, writers, sales representatives, etc. Altogether the foundation has isolated and tested for 19 aptitudes. One of the abilities the researchers test for is called "ideaphoria," a measure of the rate of flow of ideas. In any group of 1,000 women and 1,000 men, they reported that more of the women than the men will be talented in ideaphoria. Based on inborn aptitudes alone, the researchers concluded that there ought to be more female executives than male.

Other experts have noted women's natural leadership ability. Arthur A. Witkin, PhD, chief psychologist of Personnel Science Center in New York City, which has helped employers select 50,000 employees for hiring or promotion since 1956, said, "There is one major personality factor that separates executive and entrepreneur women from their male counterparts—a factor in which women generally are superior."

Witkin explained that, contrary to the myths, this superior quality in women is "independence, which includes the ability to make a decision without a committee to support it, and also emotional detachment that allows the person to see herself or himself and surroundings objectively, as well as an ability to react to criticism without undue sensitivity." On the average, he continued, "Women rank higher in these areas than males *who are on their employment level* [emphasis added] based on our psychological test results, evaluations during personal interviews and the experience of employees who come to us for career counseling."

THE YOUNG TURKS ARE COMING

by Cherie Burns

Ten years ago, as women laid siege to corporations across the country, they longed for a day when getting into management would be as easy for them as it was for men. In many companies, that day has come. Young women college graduates pour into these newly accessible training programs, ambitious and ready, very ready, to succeed. But managerial women find themselves greeting these eager arrivals with unexpected reserve, even outright antagonism. The "old girls," aided by the women's movement and their own ever-expanding ranks, paved the way for this generation, but they didn't expect these young women to be quite so pushy. Or impatient. Or single-minded. Or ungrateful.

The woman who heads for the business world today has thought about her career for several years before graduation and picked her courses accordingly. She expects to rise quickly. No typing pool or handmaiden assignments for her. She and most of her peers know that there once was a battle for equal rights, but from their vantage point, it has been won. She'll be well paid and advance on schedule or else she'll be moving on.

Kay Shackleton, a 32-year-old assistant vice-president of Chemical Bank in New York, recalls her resentment four years ago when a 22-year-old woman trainee asked, "How can you have been at the bank for four years and only be an assistant manager?" Says Shackleton, "I was angry. I asked her if she realized that four years ago there had been hardly any women bank officers at all."

Shackleton taught school before she switched to banking. She began as a platform assistant, opening new accounts. At the time, 1971, there were no women corporate division lending officers at Chemical Bank. In 1973, Shackleton became the first woman inside the bank to join that division's training program. She earned an MBA in finance at night and presently heads the bank's metropolitan cash management sales group.

"These new graduates fascinate me," says Jane Bittinger, 29, a corporate lending officer at Chemical who also interviews bank recruits. Bittinger's career goals emerged slowly after secretarial and paralegal jobs. In contrast, she finds, "The women I interview now who are fresh out of college are far more serious-minded about becoming bankers. Their goals and plans are clear."

Most college women today consider their job prospects from their junior year onward. Delores Brien, PhD, director of career planning at Bryn Mawr, a prestigious liberal-arts college for women outside Philadelphia, reports, "Women students are more aware and eager to find career-related courses and programs. They are much more interested in planning how to get a job after graduation than ever before. They don't wait until the end of their senior year to come in and talk about it."

For the businesswoman-to-be, Bryn Mawr added an international finance seminar, language study abroad geared to foreign economics and other undergraduate programs. Whereas law was once a favorite choice, Brien finds, "Business is now running neck and neck with law."

Elsewhere, too, business and economics—widely scorned in the late 60s—are top choices. At Dartmouth and Yale, enrollment in economics courses rose more than 30 percent from 1978 to 1979. And the Scientific Manpower Commission reported that 29.1 percent of women graduating from college chose business careers in 1979, a three-fold increase since 1966, and a far cry from 1974, when the US Census Bureau reported education was the most popular major for women.

Several factors have contributed to this increase. "From both sexes I hear, 'You can't get a job if you have such and such a major,' " says Toni Scott, a career counselor at the University of Colorado. She thinks this is a myth, but it's one undergraduates believe. Changing family and social patterns during the past ten years also have helped to mold the current female graduate.

Jacqueline Dickerson, 23, a management trainee at Morgan Stanley & Co. Incorporated, an investment banking firm, attributes her career orientation largely to her upbringing. "My family didn't differentiate between the sexes. I was encouraged to work at summer jobs with learning potential and career orientation," she says.

A 1980 Bryn Mawr graduate in sociology, she can tick off summer intern and study programs during her college years as punctiliously as any résumé would list them. Dickerson's assets, in her opinion, include "involvement in team sports, from which you learn to work and compete with team members." "Mentors," "priorities" and "juggling trade-offs" already are a part of her vocabulary. By the end of her sophomore year she had met with campus recruiters from Stanford and Harvard business schools.

Working women who entered their professions during the 70s often have common experiences that separate them from today's graduates. Like Bittinger and Shackleton of Chemical Bank, they had not yet decided on a career when they graduated from college. Later, in pushing for advancement, they relied on patience, dutifulness, corporate loyalty and perseverance—traits missing, or at least less obvious, among the current crop.

New college graduates and those with one or two years of work experience don't always take kindly to advocates of patience and gradual advancement. "I'd like to get on top as quickly as possible," says 24-year-old Jeanne Wagner, a 1978 graduate of Purdue

University in mechanical engineering. Now a project engineer for Samsonite in Denver, Wagner has set her sights on a management position. She hatched her career plans while working summers at Procter & Gamble, at an Indiana steel mill and at an oil refinery.

Wagner's zealous approach to her career offended her first boss. "She was a very competitive woman and she didn't have a degree," Wagner explains. Their differences, she believes, were widened by the lack of any women's support systems among women in management and technical positions. "I think women should get equal pay for equal work," Wagner declares, "but I wouldn't call myself a feminist. The secretaries are the only staunch women's libbers here."

Women who fought their way up in the feminist 70s find these attitudes abhorrent and ungrateful. A woman banker in her 30s tells of a brash young MBA who recently asked why a women's bank exists in the first place. "She totally pooh-poohs that women ever had less of a chance in business because she can name women in high places today," the senior woman grumbles. "She doesn't realize *she* wouldn't be here now if it weren't for the efforts made on behalf of women ten years ago."

The newcomers see it differently. "A lot of older women aren't friendly to younger women," says Deborah Spillman (not her real name), a Wellesley graduate with 18 months of banking experience. "I'm aggressive and I've been told that I pose a threat to some of the older women here. A lot of people have told me that I'm too impatient and energetic, and to slow down."

Spillman, who believes she landed her job largely because of her aggressive instincts, prefers to take her cues from younger women professionals. "The 28-to-30 age group has befriended me," she says.

The age distinction many women mention is a new sort of success-generated generation gap. Margaret Wheatley, EdD, a senior program director with Good-measure, Inc., a consulting firm in Cambridge, Massachusetts, divides women professionals into three categories: "Women who made it in spite of everything; women who were part of the consciousness-raising era of the past decade; and new, young females."

"Women who have made it in spite of everything, who have been working 20 years, are firmly entrenched in a male world," says Wheatley. "They are often less willing to help other, younger women and resent seeing opportunities they didn't have. They are maybe less generous about sharing their successful moment in history."

"I sit in planes on business trips and talk to gals who have just arrived on the working scene," says Sue Marchand, 53, president of Irvinware, a housewares manufacturing company. "I think they are impressive."

Marchand says she does not feel threatened by these newcomers ("I know where I sit"), but she does note with disapproval: "Some of them see everything as a confrontation. They want too much too quickly and see everything as a challenge." Her philosophy is: "It's better to be an assertive manager than a pushy broad."

"Women who came into business earlier and did it on their own resent those who hang on to the feminist movement," observes Ann Ostergaard, who is a vice-president of human resources and administration for Dollar Savings Bank in Pittsburgh.

But this pattern is not universal. Lucille Larkin, president of Larkin & Company, Inc., a cable television consulting firm, is one of those who made it in spite of everything, but she also is founder and executive director of Women in Cable, a national professional society for women in the cable television industry. Her career began in the 60s, before any women's network. "There were mostly men around when I started. I was welcomed to lunch with male colleagues who were starting out as I was. But when it came to 'business lunches' with senior male staffers, I was not included but my male peers were."

Several years ago, Larkin began to host a wine and cheese party for women at cable industry conventions. As the occasions evolved into Women in Cable, it became clear that the older, more successful professional women who had frequented Larkin's informal get-togethers at the convention shied away from membership in a women's collective. Larkin attributes this reluctance to the fact that these women had "made it" on their own already. "Ten years of the women's movement didn't yet give a women's group respectability in their eyes."

One senior executive who attended her 20th reunion at Marymount College, a woman's college in New York State, last spring, observed, "The seniors really were independent and arrogant. I don't know how I'd like having some of those strong little egos around. It's no wonder some women go bonkers and gnash their teeth over them. I did wonder what my life would have been like if I'd prepared for a career as early as they do."

What's more, while ten years ago or more, professional women felt obliged to choose between a career and a family, or at least postpone family life, new graduates expect to achieve both early in their careers. College counselors and job recruiters report growing expectations among female graduates that they can simultaneously raise children and maintain full-fledged careers. "A few years ago they wanted one or the other, but now they want both," says Alla O'Brien, vice-president for college relations at Wellesley College. One 30-year-old corporate recruiter, single and single-minded about her own professional life, was amazed to find graduating seniors at Denison University in Granville, Ohio, ask how she managed to blend career and child care more than any other question. "*That* was what they were interested in! I was shocked."

New women graduates are considerably more comfortable about revealing their family plans than older career women were. Eileen Scudder, 32, is the first woman partner in the Chicago office of Touche Ross, a major accounting firm. When she graduated from Northern Illinois University in 1970, she remembers, "I wouldn't have mentioned I hoped to have children because I thought nobody would give me a job if they thought I might get pregnant. The college girls I interview for jobs almost all mention it. It's much easier."

"Things are changing fast," according to Felice Schwartz, president of Catalyst, a New York-based national organization that fosters participation of women in corporate and professional life. She is hopeful that current professionals will welcome new women graduates despite differences in backgrounds and philosophies.

Has the work place changed so much? Can today's young women rise in their chosen professions as they expect to, unhampered by prejudice or other sex-linked pitfalls? Counselor Scott expresses special concern for them: "They've been well-insulated against the ugly realities of corporations. Some employers arrive with propaganda about equal opportunities for women, then when they get there, women are still moving up from the typing pool in some areas." Also, while promotion (of sorts) occurs at the end of each semester in the classroom, advancement in the work place can take years, a frustrating reality for students whose mock-business environment in class clips along at an ideal pace.

At Chatham College in Pittsburgh, nearly 70 percent of the graduating seniors participate in an intern program. Jane Cordisco, director of career programs, reports, "At the entry level, most of our graduates feel they are doing well. But the longer they work in a position, the more realistic and skeptical they are about how far women have progressed."

Still, new women graduates are better prepared than their forerunners for professional life. They may have to make compromises, but if their competitive instincts and energy continue unabated, they may shortly be a credit, if not a comfort, to the women whom they follow.

Chapter Nine

Your Job Counselor

ON-THE-JOB ADVICE FROM THE EXPERTS

by Anne P. Hyde and Janet Jones

Q. *I am a vice-president in a consumer products company. Yesterday I received an entirely unsolicited phone call from a management recruiter whom I did not know. He said that he had been given my name by a friend of his as someone who could fill the position for which his client was seeking candidates. I have never actively sought outside help from recruiters, and am not looking for another job at present. Since he would not reveal his source, or even the name of the person through whom he obtained my name, should I respond? Is that form of contact usual?*

A. Executive recruiting, or "headhunting" as it is more often called, is, among other things, a "contact" business, and knowing and hearing of likely candidates and their follow-up is the name of the game. However, a word of caution is needed. There are many recruiters who are on the fringes and who are quite blatantly jumping on the bandwagon. Care should be exercised in checking out the reputation and credibility of an unknown firm or individual before you explore. For instance, ask if the recruiting firm is a member of a recognized independent trade association, such as the AERC (Association of Executive Recruiting Consultants). Question the recruiter as to their company's method of operation, be sure that you know how they handle your credentials. Do they check with the applicant on file *each* time *before* they talk to or submit your résumé to their client company, or do they tell you *after* the fact? If the organization does appear to be a creditable organization, then we would suggest that by all means explore the suggested option. If nothing else, it will give you some basis for comparison and judgment from which you can determine whether or not you are at the appropriate salary level for your experience, function, and responsibility. That knowledge is both useful and essential in reviewing your progress to date.

Q. *More and more corporations are placing*

women on their Boards of Directors. One hears that companies "don't know where to find qualified women." Could you tell me, what are the qualifications necessary in order to be considered? How can I be nominated? I have never sat on any boards and don't know how to go about it.

A. Based upon our experience in assisting companies find women candidates for their boards, corporations are looking for specific expertise from their board members. The "old boy's club" attitude is slowly dying out, because of the radically changing laws and resultant responsibility that board members have now been asked to assume. Chairmen are relying on their Directors for sound business advice, counsel, and direction. Stockholders are becoming more and more educated in such areas as law, consumer affairs, and environmental issues, so that it has become imperative that the Directors bring knowledge and experience with them.

Since you have never sat on a board, we would suggest that a preparatory method would be to explore the nonprofit route. The issues that would be under consideration would be different, but many of the procedures are similar and the demands of the function would become familiar to you.

How do you prepare? First, create your file or dossier with great care and attention to content and presentation. It is interesting to note the difference between the way women and men sought vacant government positions when the Carter Administration sent out the clarion call during the first days of office: women sent in two-page résumés, whereas the men, over the course of time, had carefully compiled a virtual "book" covering every aspect of their careers, their present functions, and future contributions.

Make it known through a low-profile, informal network that you would like to be considered. Develop the ability of communication through speech-making; write and get published, i.e., articles, and so on. These methods lend credibility and build a reputation in the marketplace.

Yes, it is a campaign in the true sense of the word, and to be truly successful, it should be approached in this manner. Credibility, professionalism, and knowledge will all tend to convey that you can make a strong, valuable contribution.

Q. *I am at middle-management level and wish to travel upward as far as I can within the corporate structure. Apart from the obvious need for strong and capable functional skills, a sound track record, and a measurable accomplishment pattern, are there any other ways that I can prepare myself for needed mobility and eventual management elevation?*

A. "Power" and "political savvy" are three words that cause more furor among women at all levels than any others, but realistically, without a sound understanding and use of both, ultimate top management progression may be unlikely. Now that women are living and working in the same corporate arena as men, they will have to learn to play by the same rules and use the same tools, IF and only IF they want the same prizes at the top of the pyramid. Having political savvy and using and enjoying power can be two necessary and constructive ingredients to corporate progression.

Now what does that really mean? Knowing and recognizing the players around you, the power bases, making those power bases work for you, identifying those persons clearly marked out for advancement and those who are not. This pragmatic recognition is not destructive or devious, merely expedient knowledge, and its utilization can bring you to be in the right place at the right time, and will most certainly help you to recognize opportunity when it appears—and sometimes it appears in many different forms.

Women's approach to this aspect of corporate life was very well defined in Michael Korda's recent book, *POWER!* when he wrote, "The main reason why women find it hard to break into the world of power is not so much that men put obstacles in their way, but rather that power is thought of as being essentially male." By training and example, men have always been led to believe that they had a *right* to power and its use, consequently they have assumed it as a natural extension of living. Women involved in the same structure must learn the same lesson.

Q. *Due to the location of my previous company (the Midwest), my salary is much lower than the salaries being paid to managers at my level on the Eastern Seaboard. If I want to relocate to the East, will that fact jeopardize my chances of being considered for a higher level position? I am a CPA with a major accounting firm.*

A. Companies vary greatly in realizing and tackling this particular problem. We recently faced this same situation with two of our candidates.

In Case A, the company chose to examine the candidate's functional responsibilities and responded to their value at the current market price. Result: more than a 50 percent increase over her previous salary. In the second case, the company's grading policy had to be observed because to lower the salary below company guidelines would have been to downgrade the job, preventing the Affirmative Action goals from being met. The company chose to pay the going rate. On the other hand, there are companies that rigidly hold to percentage increases as being the normal *modus operandi* and thereby are unwilling to compromise. We suggest that when you are faced with this situation, you determine what the functional level of the position being offered pays in the marketplace and negotiate from that point of view. Traditionally, women have earned considerably less salary than their male peers, particularly in certain parts of the country and in certain industries, so that adjustments will be obvious and necessary. The best results are obtained on a one-to-one basis involving reality and demand.

Q. *Recently I read that this is the age of the "super bionic woman." Is this true?*

A. Yes, in many instances this is so. The truth is, that in this transition period that we are traveling through, *each* woman represents *all* women, and it is wrongly assumed that if a woman fails, it is ALL women who fail, whereas if a man fails, it is just an individual failure. Each woman is a standard bearer for all women, and this in turn causes great pressures and responsibilities. Even though a married woman pursues a career, she is still expected to be a housekeeper, wife, mother, partner, AND career executive, all at one and the same time.

A recent study covering women worldwide concluded that a large percentage of working women still did upwards of five hours housework daily even though they worked. In the years to come, women will gradually develop supportive networks of other women with whom they can share knowledge and help in tackling and facing many of the current pressures.

In the business world men can share ideas, because there are always other men with whom they can receive input; many times a woman may be the only woman at her level within a company. Such a position is lonely and restrictive and builds its own stress factors. Times will change, but probably more slowly than any of us would like.

Q. *All of my past experience has been in management in the public sector, but now I want to work in a corporation. I believe my skills are transferable to the private sector; however, companies have not responded well to my telephone calls. I was told by a friend not to send a résumé because I can sell myself best in a personal interview. Can you give me some advice and explain some of the negative reactions?*

A. There are built-in biases among certain groups against corporations and vice versa. For example, some nonprofit organization leaders feel that corporations represent personal sacrifice for the almighty dollar (at the expense of loftier goals), and some academicians believe that many excellent theories have been destroyed by less intelligent executives. In turn, many corporation whiz-kids pooh-pooh the thought of doing anything for nothing and place academicians in glass boxes to contemplate the stars.

Note: We say *some* individuals have these beliefs while many are openminded and judge each person on his/her merits, looking at past accomplishments and achievements (that is, proven track-records) as an indication of future potential. In the case of a career change from the public to private sector, you need to find the environment that engenders such a fair and creative method of evaluating candidates or you need to meet the manager who has such an approach. And therein lies the problem—how to locate the right person at the right time.

First, based on the position you now see yourself filling, write a résumé emphasizing the skills you are now selling to the corporation. These could include: Management (of people), Financial (budget responsibility), Administrative (organizing), Creative (developing ideas), Marketing (new business or client development), etc.

In other words, after analyzing the skills required to do a job, writing a résumé should show how your past activities prove you can do new work. Mention specific achievements.

Second, make a list of every person you have met in business or government socially or professionally, who might be able to help you directly or who might know someone who can. Most women find they can put together quite a long list of names once they get bold enough to include even those they have met only briefly.

Finally, establish a time schedule for accomplishing your goal. In most cases, six or nine months is adequate, although a year is not unreasonable at higher levels. Decide which people are most likely to be helpful and contact each one with a letter and résumé (both on expensive printed stationery), following with a phone call in an effort to get a personal meeting.

Remember: We all like to be of assistance when called upon in the right way. (When we were deciding whether or not to start our business, we asked men and women in senior executive positions who did not know us

if we could take 15 minutes of their time to discuss an idea. No one refused.)

Look at changing jobs as you would a research project. As you contact a person and feel follow-up is unnecessary, mark off the name. No doubt you will have been given several leads to add to the end of your list. Remember, you need to find the right person at the right time, and, although the process can be discouraging, every "no" brings you one step closer to a "yes."

Q. *My field is small and people tend to know each other. How can I explore other opportunities, knowing that if my boss finds out I am looking, he'll probably fire me.*

A. In the past, when a male manager found that a female employee was looking for a new job, she was considered "disloyal," whereas a man was considered "career-oriented." In turn, the woman might have been fired while the man might have been offered a promotion. Today this philosophy seems to be changing. We know several women who, upon being offered jobs in a new company, received a higher counter-offer, better title and increased salary from their current employers. In every case, these women stayed where they were. (We wondered: Where were the accolades for the many years they were undertitled, underpaid and under-recognized?)

At any rate, everyone needs to exercise some caution when seeking a new job. Although it's particularly difficult in small circles, there is a strategy that works. Follow the first two steps outlined in the preceding answer. Because your field is small, you may not need a résumé, but preparing one helps define your direction (and, besides, you just might need it). This time list *only* those people most likely to be useful to you—those who know you well, directly or by reputation. Then contact each one informally—"to have a drink, to lunch or to discuss the 'state of the art.'" During this meeting, talk about yourself and your long-term career plans; establish an image of yourself as a progressive professional who considers all her options. Talk about growth and direction will implant the thought in each person's mind that you might be available. On many occasions, the only reason you may not hear of an opportunity is that everyone believes you would never move or that you are too happy where you are.

HOW TO MEET THE HEADHUNTER OF YOUR CHOICE

by Jacqueline A. Thompson

Don't confuse executive search firms with the licensed employment agencies. An executive recruiter—or "headhunter" in common business parlance—is an advocate for its clients, which are generally large, well-known companies. Unlike a personnel agency, which welcomes unemployed applicants off the street, a search firm may not even answer your letter unless, by coincidence, it happens to be working on a search for a person with your precise background, which is highly unlikely. And a recruiter may not speak to you at all if you are noticeably unemployed or openly dissatisfied with your present employer. Most recruiters subscribe to the theory that the prize executive is never out of work.

A search firm does everything with careful attention to detail—from an in-depth analysis of the position to be filled, which may take days of discussion with the client, to exhaustive interviews and reference checks with a pared-down list of every conceivable person in the industry with the right qualifications. All this probing usually takes two to three months, while a difficult search takes six months or more. But for quality results, companies are willing to wait—and pay dearly. Search firms charge clients either 25 to 30 percent of the first year's compensation or for time and expenses, regardless of whether the position is filled. Some firms are on a yearly retainer to keep an eye out for good prospects—even though there may be no specific openings currently.

Personnel agencies, on the other hand, work on a contingency basis. No placement, no fee. No research goes into compiling their list of suitable applicants. The names come straight out of their files. Candidates are put through short interviews, and because time is usually of the essence, the client is not about to engage in lengthy salary negotiations. The offer is extended and the client can take it or leave it. Once you've passed the $25,000-a-year mark, however, recruiters will begin to pursue you.

Can a woman really expect a fair shake from a profession that has traditionally traded exclusively in male executives? Sometimes. Most of the large, established recruiters—like Boyden, Heidrick & Struggles; Spencer Stuart; and Ward Howell—claim that their clients never voice any racial or sexual prejudices. In fact, they insist that companies are clamoring for high-caliber females and blacks. Don't be fooled. Recruiters are experts at reading between client rhetoric. As Ed Lubin of the Edward-Warren Organization put it: "We develop a sixth sense about such matters."

Any company that is really serious about hiring a minority usually retains a handful of smaller recruiting consultants who specialize in that area. The old-line recruitment firms seldom have many women's résumés on file and have little idea where to locate them.

This is largely the fault of women who frequently lack the flair for self-publicity. A recruiter looks for likely candidates in all the obvious places: their own résumé files, which are usually elaborately indexed; professional, trade association and alumni directories; *Who's Who, Standard & Poor's* and other executive and professional businesswomen's registers; university, trade and industrial periodicals, which carry by-lined articles by experts in particular fields; and, very occasionally, the local social register. If you want a recruiter to find you, see that your name and credentials are displayed in as many of these sources.

Recruiters also call upon their vast network of contacts for names. They seek referrals from people employed in the same industry or a related field, their country club associates, and the people they've met at trade shows and conventions. To locate qualified female candidates, they would call the directors of professional women's groups and prominent female executives. This is why it is so important for the ambitious career woman to plug into any existing networks of female professionals.

In a last-ditch attempt to get names, a desperate recruiter might even purchase an appropriate mailing last and send out query letters, place ads in newspapers and trade journals, or conduct a bogus telephone survey. A typical ploy is to call companies in the target industry, claiming to be an economic researcher conducting a joint study for the American Management Association and American Marketing Association regarding, for instance, the changing role of product managers in the _____ field. The end result is an organization chart, replete with names and titles, for the marketing groups in X number of firms—a virtual blueprint for the search.

Janet Jones of Management Woman, Inc., an executive search firm specializing in the recruitment of women, and Richard Clarke of Richard Clarke Associates, who started employment counseling and executive recruitment of blacks and minorities before the civil rights movement, said they cope with clients' doubts and fears every day and claim clients are generally tougher on women and minority candidates and subject them to more rigorous screening than their white, male counterparts—in an attempt to "share the blame." Clarke also has noticed a tendency to hire overqualified blacks and women. "I warn clients it's risky. When they hire a tiger, they'd better have some tiger food around!"

But no matter what race or sex you are, the characteristics that attract the attention of recruiters remain the same: a successful track record and a short list of prestigious employers. Recruiters are extremely impressed if you work for a company reputed to be an executive training ground, such as Proctor & Gamble and IBM, or a leader in its industry, such as Citibank and Bank of America. Furthermore, they expect your superior achievement to be reflected in a salary that at least keeps pace, in thousands of dollars, with your age—and exceeds it by the age of 35—although there are plenty of exceptions depending on where you live, your industry and ingrained patterns of discrimination. Smart recruiters realize that women's salaries, even today, are often lower, since women only began moving ahead in business fairly recently. Because minority talent is in such demand, however, any well-qualified woman should be able to negotiate more than the usual 25 percent increase in salary that ordinarily accompanies a change of employer via headhunter.

If you've got the credentials and made all the indirect moves outlined above to attract a recruiter and your phone still has not rung, try the direct approach. Send for a copy of the domestic edition of the definitive *Directory of Executive Recruiters* (Consultants News, Templeton Road, Fitzwilliam, New Hampshire 03447; $10 prepaid, $11 if billed) and write to those firms specializing in your sex, race, function or industry. James H. Kennedy, publisher of the directory, recommends your initial résumé be accompanied by a straightforward cover letter offering assistance as a source on future searches. The idea is to establish a long-term relationship with the firm while making it clear that you aren't currently looking for a job. If you make a major career change, be sure to send an updated résumé.

"Talented young mangers shouldn't wait for recruiters to find them," according to

James R. Arnold, a recruiter for the Chicago consultant A. T. Kearney. "In their late 20's, they should approach a few reputable firms dealing in their specialty and continue to apprise them of their career moves over the years. Such relationships can pay big dividends someday."

SELECTED LIST OF EXECUTIVE SEARCH FIRMS SPECIALIZING IN WOMEN

BENNET HILL & ASSOCIATES
8905 Lake Avenue
Cleveland, OH 44102
(Other office: Chicago)

CALVIN & CO.
Box 84
Rumson, NJ 07760

RICHARD CLARKE ASSOCIATES
11 East 44 Street, Suite 1807
New York, NY 10017

EQUAL OPPORTUNITY PERSONNEL RESOURCE INSTITUTE
26586 Windsor Avenue
Elkhart, IN 46514

HASKELL ASSOCIATES
230 Park Avenue
New York, NY 10017

LEAR PURVIS WALKER & CO.
1901 Avenue of the Stars
Los Angeles, CA 90067

MANAGEMENT WOMAN, INC.
Galleria, 14th floor
115 East 57 Street
New York, NY 10022

PARSON ASSOCIATES
300 South Wacker Drive
Chicago, IL 60606

R. H. PERRY & ASSOCIATES INC.
2607 31st Street, NW
Washington, DC 20008

SYDNEY REYNOLDS ASSOCIATES
342 Madison Avenue
New York, NY 10017

GEORGE BALL:
WHEN E.F. HUTTON'S PRESIDENT TALKS, PEOPLE LISTEN

by Jacqueline Warsaw and Julia Kagan

From time to time, Working Woman *invites leading executives and researchers in the public and private sectors to share their perceptions of their careers, their fields, the economy and the efforts of women to take a larger part in that economy. George L. Ball is president of*

E.F. Hutton & Company, Inc., one of the nation's major investment banking and brokerage firms, and president of its parent organization, the E.F. Hutton Group.

Ability is very difficult to find in quantity. All companies, particularly those with a service, sales or financial bent, are desperately seeking more smart, aggressive, talented, well-trained people who present themselves well. And they don't care very much whether the person is a male or female. In Wall Street, nobody pays much attention to gender one way or the other.

Wall Street may be unique in that way because it is an industry that lives by its wits. If somebody is good, she or he is going to be rewarded, and no one is going to care about sex or background. That may be more true in Wall Street than in some other industries that are more hierarchical. In our business, title and earnings are not synonymous by any stretch of the imagination. It is possible to make a lot of money—on commissions as a stockbroker, or on salary and bonuses as a corporate public financier or trader—without being a senior member of the corporate struture. Pro rata, about the same number of women as men have gone in a very few short years from training positions paying $8,000, $10,000 or $12,000 a year to making $80,000, $90,000, $100,000 or more— and women have an equal shot at this given two things: equal ability and equal work habits.

I think the whole question of work habits tends to be underemphasized. In one sense, you have to be eccentric. I'm not saying you should do nothing but work and not have other interests—very often other interests can help you in a business sense—but the person who's most apt to do well is the one who works more hours than the others. If you are at a senior level in any organization, you have to give up certain things.

You can't work from nine to five and be a high-level successful executive, corporate or otherwise. The competition isn't working nine to five; other people in your own company, who are, let's say, your internal competition, aren't working from nine to five. Assuming one has to sleep six to eight hours a night and needs another two hours for eating—that cuts you down to about 14 hours. Let's say eight hours are dedicated to work anyhow, so that gives you six to eight discre-

tionary hours a day. Senior executives will allocate the majority of that discretionary time for business. Not always—not even generally—at the expense of their families, by the way. But rather than playing tennis as much as they'd like to.

Whether or not it's possible for a woman to "raise a family" and work those kinds of hours is difficult to say. There are people at Hutton and I've seen others who have done it, but, again, what they're doing is saying, I will trade off a certain amount of money to have a baby sitter when my child comes home rather than my being there and instead I will use that time to work.

Even outside the office, concentration is required. You can't really think about cooking dinner or playing tennis or reading a book. You have to have your mind on tomorrow's meeting, tomorrow's potential deal or how you can restructure a department so it operates more efficiently. That's what I call a hidden time cost for senior management. I think that women who arrive at that level are as aware as men are of a cost; but it isn't really a cost because people do it because they enjoy it. They don't necessarily view it as giving up anything, because they truly are gratified by what they are doing. They aren't doing it for money. They aren't doing it for power. They're doing it for the kicks of it.

The ones at the very top generally are not—and were not—motivated by power or the trappings. There are exceptions, of course but, in most cases, the ones that just want the power in today's society have some sort of flaw that would have kept them from reaching the very top in the first place—a lack of humanistic instinct or compassion, a lack of understanding of others.

In a large company today, you find that the more senior you are the fewer direct orders you give and, to some extent, the more you have to convince other, also very senior executives that a course of action is good. If you're ruthless or self-serving or greedy personally, you're not going to comprehend how others are reacting to you and you won't be able to get them to work with you and follow you.

There are those who say, in fact, that women would have an advantage because they tend to be more understanding, more thoughtful of others—which I think is nonsense. I don't think there's a great deal of difference between businessmen and businesswomen.

I *have* seen women executives who are afraid to show their softer side. On balance, that is not a trait you can use to your benefit for the long haul. It may have been ten years ago when women had to worry about being accepted as professionals or managers.

Today, they don't have to worry about that. At least in my observation, most of the good ones don't. You have to worry about being accepted for yourself, but you don't have to worry about being accepted because of being female. Which is a big advance.

The management attitudes of women senior executives are not noticeably different from those of men. Some, I think, work harder than they would if they were men. Having come through a period in the 1960s when they felt, perhaps correctly, that they had to work harder, the habit pattern is carried forward.

I think that women dealing with the somewhat younger generation of businessmen—those who are under 45 or so—don't have to run faster. But older men, who came up in business before it was common for women to be in executive positions, still think of women as secretaries and women do have to deal with this attitude.

Half of E.F. Hutton's employees are women, but less than half of our officers are, though the number of women officers has been increasing rapidly in recent years. But it's just a question of timing. The great movement of women into the management and executive sides of business is really a phenomenon of the last decade. You don't get to the top in a decade.

As I look around the securities industry, I'm starting to see more women as new account executives, financiers or members of the marketing department. Now, they're advancing to the vice-presidential level at about the same rate as equally talented men, and in another five years certain of them will be good enough to be senior vice-presidents. But it does take time.

I would say that the 80s will probably be the decade for women of ability. These women are going to be moving into top posts in companies of all sorts without anybody thinking very much about it one way or the other. Corporations will not be able to accept mediocrity or average productivity in the 1980s. There is a paucity of people who are very well trained, very well motivated and willing to work very hard. Whether male or female, black or white, people who have those attributes are going to be in tremendous demand.

SHEP POLLACK:
"MANAGEMENT THEORIES ARE UTTER GARBAGE," SAYS THE PRESIDENT OF PHILIP MORRIS USA

by Cornelia Wyatt

Shep Pollack, 51, has been with Philip Morris Incorporated since 1959, and president and chief operating officer of Philip Morris USA since 1978. He has an undergraduate degree in economics from Harvard University and did graduate work in public and international affairs at Princeton University. He worked in the executive office for President Harry Truman and also has worked for the Curtiss-Wright Corp. and Ford Motor Co.

I'm as likely to get cussed out by my subordinates as to get stroked by them. We like mavericks. I'm turned off by people who try to replicate me. At meetings, I'm addicted to turning to juniors and asking, "What do you think?" But formal management theories are utter garbage. They're only an attempt to formalize a fundamental question: How do you identify what you want to do and then how do you do it?

To Be a Good Manager

"Fair" is a word rarely used in discussing management. People have to believe you'll be as fair as possible. Sometimes circumstances prevent you from acting fairly. You won't be believed under those circumstances if you're not perceived as fair when you have the chance to be.

Motivating Employees

We listen to masses of jargon and act as if you required a PhD in psychology to know that people feel better about their work if you treat them well. The only way to buy yourself credibility and the option to tell a staff member you're not satisfied is to give praise when you are.

One word we use here is "excellence." The problem is how to demonstrate it. People who strive for excellence are going to be as productive as they possibly can be at their level, maybe even more so. In our research and development department, we've introduced a system to motivate people to be most productive in the work that they do best. There are two career paths, separate and also equal. One can move up purely along scientific lines or advance up the managerial ladder. The point is not to encourage good scientists to assume managerial roles to earn more or gain respect.

No Formal Award System

If you have succeeded at communications, people being recognized for their achievement will know it; their peers will know it. You recognize them verbally, financially, reinforced by notes, memos. If you don't do this automatically, do it deliberately. But don't make it look deliberate. That's counterproductive. It should appear to be sheer pleasure.

The Worst Thing Employees Can Do

The biggest crime of all is to fail to bring your boss in on a difficulty because you're embarrassed or scared. By the time the boss gets involved, it's not a difficulty anymore but a major problem. Management has to create the climate in which the staff realizes that the organization is best served by their coming forward as difficulties arise. To do so they need a feeling of security. This means employees must have access and quality of access. It's no good if access means you give them 62 seconds wedged in between one appointment and the next. To succeed in this requires working long hours. You read the IN box after office hours. In the office you're available for people.

When Someone Doesn't Work Out

It's more merciful to cut the tie earlier than later. The longer the company waits the more it must accept that it has an obligation to the employee. If you hired the person in the first place and it isn't working out, it's not just the employee's fault. After a few years, if a staff member and you just don't belong together that person knows about it before you bring up the subject. You've done something wrong if you have maintained silence for two years, then drop in on a Friday afternoon with the bad news. It's the hardest thing in the world to speak negatively, but it's the most necessary.

Do You Need an MBA?

You must understand finance, although you don't have to be an expert. It's the language we've found to serve as a common denominator for all aspects of enterprise. I don't like the current emphasis on the MBA degree—it's exclusionary of good talent. After five to ten years, it won't be the MBA that'll make the difference but performance.

How to Impress Your Boss

There are no paperback solutions. If you have a collegial atmosphere your achievement will show. I dislike too much calculated self-advertisement. In this company, that kind of person doesn't come, or doesn't stay.

WOMEN WHO SUCCEEDED

by Helen Paltis Silver

The words job hunting seem to imply that there are jobs out there and all you have to do is find them—which often is the case. But many of the most interesting jobs are created when someone sees a need for a service and convinces a prospective employer that she is the very person to meet that need. Creating your own job may require starting your own business, but not always. You may be able to get what you want within an organization that already exists. The important thing is to know what it is you want to do.

Ina Yalof of Livingston, New Jersey, knew what she was interested in—medical sociology, a new field that combines medicine and the social sciences. The mother of two small children and wife of a department-store executive, Yalof discovered, while working as a hospital volunteer, that "hospitals turned me on," and went back to college when her youngest child entered second grade. Four years later, she learned that jobs in medical sociology were not easy to find in the routine way. It took her nine months to land one.

"How do you convince a hospital administrator who wants to cut costs to hire someone with an innovative idea? I was considered frivolous," Yalof said.

Then, one night at a dinner party, she was seated next to Victor Parsonnet, MD, head of a heart bypass team at Beth Israel Medical Center in Newark, New Jersey.

"When I told Dr. Parsonnet I was a medical sociologist, he stared blankly and said, 'Hunh?' But he listened because he had to," Yalof said. "When I explained that I could do spot medical research for his team doctors, serve as liaison between the family doctors and the surgical group, the doctors and the patients, and the doctors and the family, he was more receptive.

"He invited me to come to watch his team in action, and I was captivated. More than anything, I wanted to work with them. But interviews led to nothing. There was no money and they saw no crying need.

"At that point, while I still had Dr. Parsonnet's interest, I offered to serve as a volunteer. He relented, and I worked six weeks without pay to show how useful I could be."

It worked so well that Yalof was soon being paid on a part-time basis. She still works part time, but her hours are longer and her job responsibilities have broadened considerably in the four years she's been at Beth Israel.

During the long hours of a heart bypass operation, she confers with the referring doctor, the waiting family and other concerned doctors. A closed-circuit TV in her office shows the operating room so that she can stay up to the minute on progress. She also has written special patient pamphlets and formed pacemaker patient clubs. Her $16,000 salary will rise if she becomes a full-time staff member. Meanwhile, her part-time schedule has made it easier to fit her work hours into her family life. Her absences are longer now but the family is reassured by her refrain that she is "never more than a beeper away, if I'm needed."

Susan Dietz returned to her job as an executive secretary at the MacMillan Publishing Company in New York with career development the last thing on her mind. The death of her young husband had left her at 33 with a 6-year-old son. "The job gave me a chance to pull the pieces together," she said of those first years, "as well as being my primary income source." She moved from MacMillan to work with radio talk-show host Barry Farber, who was then running for mayor of New York. From Farber's campaign, she went to Revlon, where she rose to the job of assistant to its temperamental founder, the late Charles Revson.

The difficult Revson interlude paid off in the end. Dietz decided to write a book about the turmoil at Revlon. Her novel, *Valency Girl*, coauthored by Robin Moore, was published by Ballantine Books in 1976, launching her on a new career as a writer.

At this time, Dietz's experiences as a young widow convinced her that a column about the single life would be a good idea for a newspaper syndicate. She dubbed it "Single File," and placed ads in publications around the world asking singles to write her about their problems. From their responses came her ideas.

"Single File" sold slowly at first, and Dietz took office jobs to support herself and her son. She was published in a Manhattan neighborhood newspaper and interviewed on a local TV show. Then one day she offered the column to the *Chicago Tribune-Daily News* syndicate. Though the top man didn't like it, the assistants did. A year later, when one of those assistants was named head of the *Los Angeles Times* syndicate, he remembered her column and bought it.

That was in 1975. Today, "Single File" is published in 50 newspapers and Dietz continues to call editors in an effort to increase its distribution. Its success has brought Dietz a seminar series on single living for the New School for Social Research in New York, many magazine articles, a week-long series on the New York single in the *New York Post*, a "Today Show" interview and a weekly radio program. Her book on the singles subject has been published by Rawson, Wade. "Now," Dietz said, "after years of pegging away, it's all coming together."

Bebe Antell's career also grew out of tragedy, but in a different way. When she left her job as infants' and children's wear buyer for Gimbels department stores 25 years ago to have a baby, she planned to return quickly. Her son suffered brain injury at birth, and her focus changed.

Working to make sure that her son would grow up to be as independent as possible, Antell met parents of other handicapped children. In 1965 she founded—and later headed—the New Jersey Association for Children with Learning Disabilities. She initiated a Saturday play group for these children and took a master's degree in behavioral science to give her the educational background she needed to counsel their parents.

In May 1978 Antell started *Perceptions*, an easy-to-read nonprofit newsletter for parents of learning-disabled children to keep them up to date on the latest research findings and to review toys, games and books. First issue in hand, Antell made the rounds of local corporations and obtained grants from the Prudential Insurance Company of America, CIBA, Warner-Lambert, Bristol-Myers, the Beneficial Management Corporation and American Telephone and Telegraph. She also received a $3,000 grant from the Foundation for Children with Learning Disabilities, a nonprofit organization. Today, the newsletter has a circulation of 4,000 and corporate subsidies of $7,000. Her son, who has learned to read and write, holds a job in a nearby town, where he lives alone with minimal supervision.

One of the fringe benefits of surviving a drastic career change is the confidence it instills. The woman who does it once has less fear for her future. She knows she will be able to do it again.

Helen Hoffman, a lawyer in Palm Beach, Florida, is making the third major career switch of her life. The assistant dean of Rutgers Law School in New Jersey until 1978, she is now an adjunct professor in labor relations at Florida International University School of Business in Miami. In addition, she teaches at the University of Miami's School of Business.

A graduate of Columbia Law School in New York, Hoffman found it easy to go from legal work to volunteer jobs when her two children were growing up and the family moved from Washington, DC, to New Jersey. "It was restful being home with the children," she recalled. "In my volunteer work, I learned about the community we lived in and made friends. I met the people who later helped me get back into law."

Conversations with young law students and lawyer friends gave Hoffman the idea of setting up a job-placement service for law-school graduates at Rutgers School of Law in Newark, New Jersey. "There was no such job and no funds," she said. "I had to convince a lot of people that this kind of service would be of great material benefit to the school. When I finally got a commitment, it was on the outer fringes of administrative officialdom, with the odd title of assistant to the assistant dean." In time, Hoffman became assistant dean in charge of placement, a member of numerous state bar committees and a teacher of labor law at the Rutgers Graduate School of Public Administration. Her salary now is $30,000 a year.

Two years ago, Hoffman's husband, also an attorney, was offered a chance to head a Palm Beach law office. For nearly two years, Hoffman kept her post and traveled to Florida on weekends. But commuting became too fatiguing, and she decided to move to Florida. Last summer Hoffman was named to the masters panel to hear cases concerning Florida public employees and to the American Arbitration Association Panel of Labor Arbitration. She is now fully qualified as a Florida labor arbitrator and already has heard several cases.

Dena Skalka found that federally mandated affirmative-action requirements were her ticket out of a routine job as a salary administrator for Bell Laboratories in New Jersey.

"I made no secret of the fact that women were flocking to me with their problems. There were ten levels of management; women never had risen above the second. Federal contracts were demanding affirmative action. The company was seeking sensible solutions and I had some," said Skalka, who is a statistician. "Within a year, the company named me affirmative-action officer. My salary was upped to $29,000, tripling my entry wages.

"It was an exciting eight and a half years," Skalka recalled. "I helped change the company climate. I ran special sessions for middle management. I pointed out that women could travel on business trips. I found women right in their ranks who could be brought up to fifth-level management. It was a simple matter of reevaluating the job and the job title.

"And as for seeking out women with scientific talent, I made the rounds of top colleges, looking for top women students. I actually rewrote the handbook so as not to exclude women." She also founded a scholarship program for women, which provided each winner with a summer job at Bell and a Bell Laboratory scientist as her mentor until she graduated from college.

In 1978, Skalka had to quit because her husband became ill and was advised to move to a warmer climate. She is doing volunteer work in Florida and hopes to become a corporation consultant, based on her affirmative-action experience.

ONE JOB, TWO CAREERS

by Sharon Grady

Talk to almost any working woman and you'll hear the same lament: "I love my career, but I wish it left me more time for . . . my family, my hobbies, work in the community" [pick one]. It seems the feeling is that it has to be one or the other. You can have a personal life *or* a career, but you can't possibly manage both.

Talk to Assistant Professor Patricia Dean and you'll hear a different story. Dean shares a full-time teaching contract with her husband, William, at Gustavus Adolphus College in St. Peter, Minnesota. They divide a single position; she teaches one course in the Women's Studies Department and he teaches two in the Religion Department. Their salaries are prorated to reflect the difference in their teaching loads and credentials (he has his doctorate; she's working on her dissertation). Their combined annual income of about $20,000 is comparable to the salary of one full-time professor at Gustavus Adolphus.

The Deans say their arrangement allows them to "focus on both sides of our lives—the domestic and the professional." They first began job-sharing in 1971 to accommodate their child-care needs. At that time, William took care of their preschool children while Patricia taught her morning class; she stayed home in the afternoon while he taught his courses. As their children grew, they devoted their former babysitting time to research and special projects, work they might not have been able to do with a full teaching load.

Something More Than Part-Time Work

The Deans are unusual, not because they are working part time—for decades part-time workers have constituted a significant proportion of the labor force—but rather, because they are *job sharers*. By definition, a *part-timer* is an independent worker who puts in fewer than 40 hours a week on a particular job for which he or she has sole responsibility. A job sharer takes on part of the responsibility for a full-time position, while another worker shares the burden. Job sharers divide the work and arrange their schedules to provide full-time coverage on the job.

New Ways to Work, a San Francisco-based advocacy group for nontraditional work patterns, further differentiates job-sharing: Job-sharing, it says, "implies a career orientation, a labor-force attachment and a potential for upward mobility, which, historically, has not been associated with part-time work."

What's in It for Employees?

Interest in job-sharing has been on the rise since the mid-1970s. Work-force analysts point to social and economic changes as the dynamics behind this growing trend away from the traditional 40-hour workweek.

On the social side, many employees are attempting to put their work and family responsibilities on a more equal footing. Male and female workers are demanding fewer hours at work and more free time to devote to their children.

Family responsibilities aside, employees frequently complain that work alone does not provide fulfillment. For those who want to devote more time to some aspect of their personal and social lives—whether it be education, community work or hobbies—job-sharing offers an attractive alternative.

Economic changes over the past decade, such as the record increase in the size of the work force—precipitated by the influx of women and minorities—have far outstripped the number of new job opportunities. As a result, many men and women who would prefer to work full time are having to settle for part-time or job-shared positions.

Why Employers Like It

While employees usually are the first to express an interest in job-sharing, employers, too, are finding that it often suits their needs. In addition to the Deans, Gustavus Adolphus employs four other job-sharing couples. Robert Karsten, dean at the college, is enthusiastic about this new work style: "We support it. We recruit for it. We see it as a way of getting the talents of two for the price of one."

Bill Connolly, a recruitment and staffing manager at TRW Vidar, an electronics firm in California, also is sold on job-sharing. He supervises Nancy Creamer and Cris Piasecki, who share a $20,000-a-year job as personnel representative, a recruitment position that requires a great deal of travel and contact work outside the firm.

"It's a super arrangement," according to Connolly. "It is every bit as good as, if not better, than having one full-time worker. Having two job sharers means I benefit from two points of view on every problem. Between them I get more than 40 hours' worth of work a week."

Such reactions are not unusual. Proponents are quick to point out that increased productivity often is a bonus of job-sharing. Fewer hours mean a more concentrated effort, more job satisfaction and a lower rate of absenteeism and turnover than is true of full-time workers.

Employers also have found that job-sharing eases a number of scheduling problems. Double coverage can be arranged for times of peak activity, and personal necessities, such as doctors' appointments, can be scheduled for nonworking hours. If a job sharer is out sick, his or her partner usually can cover.

Finally, job-sharing provides a certain continuity in job performance: If one member of a team leaves, the remaining member can pick up the former partner's slack while a new person is being trained.

Problems and Pitfalls

A successful job-sharing program requires sound planning and good communication between the job sharers and their supervisor. Too often, according to Gail Rosenburg, president of the National Council for Alternative Work Patterns, employers embark upon an ill-conceived program, then blame its failure on the nontraditional schedule, rather than on their own lack of planning.

Connolly of TRW Vidar agrees. "When Cris and Nancy first began job-sharing, Nancy worked in the morning and Cris in the afternoon. I'm a morning person, so naturally I was more in touch with what Nancy was doing than I was with Cris's work. As a result, when evaluation time rolled around, Cris got shortchanged. But she spoke up, we discussed it, and I learned a lot." Creamer and Piasecki now split the workweek, each working with Connolly in the mornings.

Another common mistake in working out a job-sharing program is the failure to recognize each worker as an individual with strengths and weaknesses of her own.

When It Works Best

Perhaps most important of all to a successful job-sharing program is selecting the right people. Not everyone is suited to that kind of arrangement, nor to each other. Ideally, job sharers communicate well, think somewhat alike, trust each other's work and are well organized.

New Ways to Work made an extensive study of job-sharing that pointed to the following requirements for success: The arrangement must be voluntary; have parity with full-time positions in terms of benefits, salaries and job rights; have the support of the supervisor; have clearly understood expectations; be well organized; draw on strong communications skills; and be cooperative.

New Ways to Work identified positions most likely to benefit from job-sharing as being characterized by one or more of the following:

• requiring a broad range of skills
• alternative periods of intense activity with slack periods
• requiring creativity
• including monotonous duties
• being high-pressured enough to produce employee burnout
• requiring more than eight-hour-a-day coverage.

On the Downside

Despite the many attractions of a well-planned job-sharing program and the growing number of job-sharing enthusiasts, the concept still meets with considerable resistance—from employers and employees alike. Objections most often voiced by employees are reflected in a statement made by George J. Poulin, general vice-president of the International Association of Machinists and Aerospace Workers in Washington, DC: "I still feel that most part-time and job-sharing positions are involuntary and offer second-class employment because of limited income (both straight-time and overtime opportunities), reduced fringe benefits and career opportunities."

Employee resistance to job-sharing largely is financial. In today's economy it's not easy to exist on a partial income, and those who *do* job share often have additional income sources.

Nancy Sides and Pam Jacoby experimented with job-sharing the position of office manager at the Reston Publishing Company in Reston, Virginia. As Jacoby points out, in real terms they were making more than their paychecks indicated since they had no child-care costs: "Nancy worked from 8:30 AM to 12:30," she explains, "and I worked from 1:00 PM to 5:00. I took care of my children and hers in the morning, then drove to work and met Nancy at 12:30. I handed the children over to her in the parking lot, and she took them home for the afternoon."

Despite the savings in child-care expenses, Jacoby concedes that job-sharing would not have been possible for her without her husband's income. "I couldn't make it on my salary alone," she says.

For Patricia and William Dean, job-sharing means getting by on less money. Even though inflation has eroded the buying power of their $20,000 salary, the Deans say they still wouldn't consider a return to full-time work. "My husband and I have constructed a simple life style," Patricia explains, "and we are greatly disturbed by what we consider inflated living standards."

The Question of Benefits

Partial benefits, as well as partial salaries, are a source of concern to many prospective job sharers. Benefits are expensive, and most employers are reluctant to give job sharers the same benefits they provide for their full-time workers.

Some firms offer no benefits whatsoever to job sharers. Most prefer to prorate benefits, giving a job sharer who works 20 hours a week, for example, one-half the sick leave, vacation time, health insurance, a full-time employee would get.

An alternative method of benefit allocation, called the "market basket," awards the job sharers one full set of benefits, to be divided between them as they see fit. Thus, if one member is covered by a spouse's medical insurance, he or she might opt for full life insurance and let the job-sharing partner take all medical benefits.

The allocation of benefits varies widely from one job-sharing situation to another. At Reston, Jacoby and Sides received full benefits.

At Gutavus Adolphus, Patricia and William Dean each receive full vacation time, full life insurance coverage and full travel expenses. The medical plan covers the entire family, and William Dean is eligible for standard retirement benefits payable on their combined annual salary.

Piasecki and Creamer started at TRW Vidar with no benefits at all. Soon they got prorated sick leave and vacation time. Now, with the support of their supervisor, they are pushing for one set of full benefits.

Can You Get Ahead?

Advancement can be another sensitive issue when job sharers and employers sit down at the bargaining table. How can an employer promote one but not the other and still keep the team intact? Many employees, fearing that managers will make team preservation a higher priority than promotion of its members, view job-sharing as inhibiting to career advancement. In fact, the opposite may be true.

Jacoby and Sides have found that job-sharing the office manager's position did not handicap their careers. While job-sharing at the Reston Publishing Company, Sides handled the financial aspects of the job while Jacoby took charge of personnel matters. Both women enjoyed their work and decided to return to full-time schedules once their children were older. By that time the firm had grown enough to accommodate each woman's activities within a full-time position. When Sides and Jacoby assumed their new full-time jobs, each received a promotion—Sides was promoted to financial coordinator, Jacoby to personnel director.

Unfortunately, not all firms are as flexible as Reston. Many employees who, like Sides and Jacoby, would like to job share for a while, then return to full-time work later on, are discouraged by strict personnel policies that require so much time in one position before becoming eligible for another. In such situations, job sharers working half-time would need to work twice as long as their full-time counterparts before promotions.

Employer Resistance

Every conceivable objection to job-sharing raised by an *employee* can be turned on its head to fit an *employer*. For every employee who feels that work should reap full pay, full benefits and full opportunity for advancement, there is an employer who feels that salary, benefits and advancement opportunities should only be offered for a full 40-hour week.

Employers are particularly concerned that two people will be more costly than one in training and supervisory time. Not so, according to the National Council for Alternative Work Patterns: "Training two people initially may take more supervisory time," the organization concedes, "but, in the long run, the time involved will be reduced. Two people will absorb material faster (than one) and reinforce each other with the new information. Because of their high productivity and low turnover rate, job sharers will more than repay the investment the employer makes in training."

Another employer objection stems from the fear of higher benefits costs, though job-sharing enthusiasts point out that a market basket, or prorated, approach to benefits makes a job-sharing team hardly more expensive than a single full-time worker. A job sharer would be more expensive than a single employee only when the salary shared exceeds $29,500.

Since an employer's Social Security tax is computed as a flat percentage of a maximum salary of $29,500 for a single position (effective January 1, 1981), the company pays more for two people in one job when their combined salary exceeds that maximum.

By encouraging employers to use job sharers only in positions that pay under $29,500, the Social Security tax system perpetuates the traditional bias as to the types of positions well suited to job-sharing: "In the private sector when employers think 'job-sharing,' most of them still think 'nonprofessional,' " says Judy Hodges, who shares the presidency of Job Sharers, a Virginia affiliate of New Ways to Work.

The final and perhaps most fundamental reason for management resistance to job-sharing is the newness of the concept. In June of 1979 Project JOIN, a job-sharing program of the State of Wisconsin, published a survey of 70 private employers in the Madison area, arriving at the following conclusions: "Although a good percentage of permanent part-time positions exist [in the surveyed firms], few are paired at the professional or paraprofessional level. . . . The problem is not additional costs, since all benefits are prorated. Rather, the difficulty in creating more high-level part-time positions appears to be a result of inflexible personnel policies."

Seeing Is Believing

Proponents hope that as more research is done and more information made available on the advantages of job-sharing, employer resistance will lessen.

Connolly, for one, believes that as managers try job-sharing, they'll find that "the pluses outweigh the minuses. If you have an opportunity to use job sharers," he says, "do it. You'll find that the best thing about job-sharing is that it works!"

Job-Sharing, European-Style

Work-sharing is widespread in Belgium, France, Italy, Great Britain, Norway and Austria and it is preferred as an alternative to employee layoffs, according to the October 1980 World of Work Report. In practice in Germany since 1927, work-sharing has helped to lessen the impact of recession by benefiting both employers and employees. It helps workers by allowing them to maintain full health and retirement benefits and it helps companies by maintaining workers' job interests and skills.

In Sweden, workers between 60 and 65, who are approaching retirement age, may choose to share their job with another worker, thus easing the transition from full-time labor to retirement. More than 25 percent of eligible employees have enrolled in the plan. Sweden's National Social Insurance Board estimates that this plan reduces total working hours by 50 percent while reducing income for job sharers only 13.8 percent.

Back in the States

Since 1978, California employers have had the option of using work-sharing as an alternative to layoffs; their employees receive partial unemployment insurance benefits for time lost in work reductions. So far, California is the only state to offer such an option under its employment-insurance program, according to World of Work Report. For example, if a worker were eligible to receive $100 in weekly benefits on full layoff, she or he would receive $20 for each day lost on a work-sharing program.

Participation in the program is voluntary, but if employees are covered by a collective bargaining agreement, the union must agree to the job-sharing plan.

On the other side of the continent, New York City hopes to implement work-sharing programs to increase productivity and make the city a more attractive employer. Mayor Ed Koch has asked that city commissioners submit reports on how they could relax work schedules—job-sharing will be an important option.

Victor Gotbaum, leader of the city's largest labor union, says that he has not yet seen the details of the plan but that he endorses the concept. He points out that flexibility in city workers' hours also would ease rush-hour traffic on mass-transit systems and highways.

FOR MORE INFORMATION
Contact New Ways to Work, a national clearinghouse on job-sharing, at 149 Ninth Street, San Francisco, CA 94103.

PLUGGING INTO THE OLD GIRL NETWORK
by Patricia Brooks

"What about Anderson, the manager? I hear he's tough on women," the younger of the two women lunching together asks.

"He's tough on everybody," the other answers, "but one thing about him, he respects honesty. Just level with him and you'll do fine. What you should watch out for when you get to Pittsburgh is. . ."

This is not idle luncheon conversation. The two women, professionals in a large corporation, are practicing their version of an age-old male business prerogative—the Old Boy Network. They are exchanging information that will make it possible for the younger, less experienced woman to function more effectively when transferred to a new location.

That's one of the things the Old Boy Network is all about. With generations of input behind it, it is the most efficiently organized non-organization around. It operates among top- and middle-management men—Old Boys—in a variety of ways.

As a **job referral service**: "By the way, George, if you hear of a bright young marketing man, the bank's looking for such a fellow to take charge of our business development group."

Talent scout: ". . . met this go-getter the other night, name of Talbot. Sales V.P. for United Carbon. Good man to keep in mind when we need someone in . . ."

Information circuit for business Big Deals: "I hear Amalgamated Biscuit is reorganizing—might not be a bad time to consider a merger or buy-out."

Career counseling: "Frankly, John, I'd try to make a lateral move into sales. No one at T & M ever makes it to the top without a couple of good solid years of sales experience behind him."

Social Advisory service: "I want you to meet Jeb Baxter on the Hunt Club board. Good person to know if you're thinking of joining."

Services exchange center for lawyers, bankers, brokers, doctors, real-estate or insurance agents, et al.: "Ted Hughes was sure you'd know a good man to handle a small trust fund I'm setting up."

Lifestyle guidance: "If you're looking for permanence, I'd buy in Greenwich. It's a more stable community than those Jersey towns you mentioned. And you know, the chairman of the board lives there, which wouldn't hurt your chances a bit."

The word "network" may connote something highly structured and formal. Yet in reality it is simply a constellation of exchanges and a collectivizing of one's contacts. It's a way to keep current, spot trends, and stay on top of your job.

Men learn the "network" system early in life in the bonding of team sports. "It doesn't matter to a boy," a sociologist commented, "whether the other eight players on his baseball team are his friends so long as they want to play ball and are reasonably good at it."

Such bonding—or developing "kinship" through grouping together for a specific purpose—is not part of our early female conditioning. Until recently women in business rarely thought about the need of such bonding. This was partly because there were so few jobs available to women in the upper levels of management that we had to compete against one another to get them, and were forced to be rivals rather than colleagues.

The door-opening of equal opportunity legislation and the consciousness-raising of the women's movement have made more career-committed women aware that we *can* and *must* help one another, that we are more effective together than alone.

Women are also learning to strategize and plan their careers—and that's where networks enter the scene. As one young woman executive who has moved rather quickly up the ladder of a major multinational firm puts it: "I used to think it wasn't 'nice', that it was 'using' people, to make friends with someone because of his or her job or because of their possible usefulness to me later, but I've learned to do it in order to develop my contacts, enlarge my options, build my networks." She has also learned to be tough-minded about her career; to consider clubs in terms of professional development, not as social gatherings; and to appreciate business associates for their job-related abilities, without feeling they have to become her best friends.

Basically, it's not a case of "using" people for your own ends. It's exchange for *mutual* benefit, the trading of information, ideas, and favors. One successful Washington management consultant, who helps other women form networks to help themselves, calls it brokering. "A. had a TV talk show and was always looking for interesting guests.

So when I'd meet a qualified person, I'd say, 'Call A. if you'd like to be on the show.' Then I realized it was better if I called A. myself and told her about B. or C. That way I was in a position of having done both A. and B. or C. a favor. A successful network involves doing favors for one another."

The basic element of an Old Girl Network, however, is information exchange, because job development or advancement is often dependent on knowing what's happening *before* it happens. Inside information is crucial. Bureau of Labor Statistics figures show that almost half (48 percent) of all jobs come through personal contacts.

"Much of the information exchanged in a network is trivia," Joan Thuebel told me, "but it's helpful trivia." As AT&T's personnel manager of equal opportunity activities, she has observed that it's the trivia that can trip a woman up in a new job. "She received the promotion because she can handle the major aspects of the job, but she has to learn to deal with the nuances or politics of the office." In this way a network can not only help you find a new job, it can help you make a success of it.

In my own work as a freelance writer, I have often gotten job clues through an informal Old Girl Network: a friend mentions that her company is buying a new magazine; a colleague tells me her editor is leaving to start her own publication; another remarks that advertising on a particular publication is up, so that there might be more editorial space alloted, and thus a need for more outside writers.

In a more formal way I learned the importance of a network a few years ago, before the word had currency. I joined a group of suburban women writers who met once a month to read and discuss each other's work and talk over work-related problems. Many of us had young children, and we swapped solutions for scheduling working and mothering time. We also shared information about markets for our work. One supplied me with the name of her literary agent to handle my pieces. I shared the names of editors I had found sympathetic to new writers.

At the time we didn't think of our monthly meetings as anything so formal as a club or network, but that's what it was. We were both exchanging valuable career-oriented information and bolstering and encouraging one another in what is essentially a lonely profession.

An Old Girl Network has multiple dimensions. According to Brenda Broz Eddy, a Georgetown University professor and management specialist, "There are six 'support' needs we all have that an OGN provides: Intimacy, sharing, self-worth, assistance, guidance, and challenge."

Support—that's the key word, and the key function of any Old Girl Network. It's a support system. And because there are still all too few role models for women in business, we need all the support we can get.

Washington's Old Girl Network in Action

Ellen Frost, the Treasury Department's $29,000 Deputy Director in the Office of Trade Policy and Negotiations, had originally planned to teach at the university level once she completed her own studies. She majored in political science and international relations at Radcliffe and studied the politics and foreign policy of Communist China in graduate school at Harvard. However, by the time she finished her degree, Ellen decided to abandon the academic life in favor of a more active career with the government in Washington. Through references and good tips from her Cambridge contacts, she found a job almost immediately as legislative assistant to California Senator Alan Cranston, advising him in areas of foreign policy. After three years in Senator Cranston's office, Ellen felt she should get experience in the executive branch of the government rather than continue on the "Hill." She also wanted to specialize more deeply in economic issues. Through Washington's "Old Girl Network" she landed a job with the Treasury that served just right.

Ellen explains, "Sarah Jackson, a woman I know who now works on the staff of the Joint Economic Committee in Congress, left a job with the Treasury Department to take a new position on the Hill. Sarah remained on good terms with the people she used to work with in the Treasury, and with one man in particular. When she learned I was looking for a new job, she volunteered to talk to her friend about me. He interviewed me, and then, since he was not in a hiring position himself, referred me to a second man who was. I would never even have known whom to talk to if I had approached the Treasury cold. And even if I had, it would have been extremely difficult to get to see the man who hired me. It was through Sarah's help and influence that I was able to get my foot in the door."

Ellen describes Washington's Old Girl Network as a group of well-placed professional women who keep an eye out for each other and for bright newcomers. "Just hearing about a good job," she says, "and talking to the right person about it are giant steps toward getting it. Our "network" is not organized or structured in any way, and there aren't really that many of us. We're just women who know, or know of, each other, and who try to help out when we see someone good. And we don't stick exclusively to women. We pass along men too, if we feel they're right for the job. Actually, we go to great pains *not* to be exclusive and restrictive like the Old Boy Network was or is. We naturally make friends with both sexes at work, and we try to help everybody. But we do have a tilt towards women.

Old Girl Networks That Already Exist

Financial Women's Association, New York (200 members)

Feminist Economic Network Association, Detroit

National Association of Women Deans, Administrators, and Counterparts Counselors, nationwide

(Affirmative Action directors in 25 major U.S. corporations)
Women's Forum (150 members)
Women's Bar Associations, nationwide
Alliance for Women (150 women employees at AT&T)
Advocates for Women, San Francisco
Women in Wisconsin Apprenticeship (for women in skilled trades)
Advertising Women of New York
Women's Media Group
Associations of Women Business Owners
Women in Business in Washington
Women's Political Caucus
National Association of Commissions for Women
Wider Opportunities for Women, Washington, D.C.
Working on Working, Washington D.C. (30 to 40 women looking for jobs pool information once a week)

1. If you are a professional, join not only your professional society open to both men and women, but the women's society as well, if there is one. If there isn't a women's society, poll some women members of the existing society to see if they are interested in starting one. You may want to start the ball rolling informally by going out to lunch with one or two of the women.
2. After informing management (so as to allay any fears they may have about your intentions) of your desire to talk to other women about women's business development, seek out career-oriented women in your organization. One way might be to put up a notice asking who would like to meet to discuss a subject of wide interest to working women, such as "Improving Our Management Skills" or "Overcoming Emotional Handicaps on the Job."
3. If you are in a mostly male field, seek out the few women who are in it. Call them and suggest you get together for lunch, as you think you might share common interests and problems.
4. Become a joiner. Alumnae groups, women's groups, civic and community groups, all can provide you with an opportunity to meet women with similar career interests. Attend as many meetings as possible, be as visible as you can, become recognized and known.
5. Keep apprised of the women who are making a name for themselves in your field (by subscribing to trade publications and reading the business section of your newspaper). Call them for advice or to ask them to lunch. Don't be timid. Most people are flattered to be approached by a colleague with similar interests.
6. Talk to everyone you possibly can, in your organization, from mailroom clerks to top management. Small talk and pleasantries can sometimes turn you on to opportunities to enlarge your network.
7. Keep track of the women you work with, even after you leave a particular organization. The administrative assistant you got along with so well yesterday may be a vice-president today.

PATRICIA BROOKS *is a freelance writer who reports frequently on affirmative action for corporate publications.*

THE STATE OF THE UNIONS—FOR WOMEN
by Sue Hubbell

Some years ago, I held a middle-level management job in an organization that employed mostly women. Salaries were low, job classifications nonexistent, promotions and raises capricious. Frustrated by our powerlessness and inability to bring about change, some of us aging liberals with knee-jerk good feelings toward the labor movement began to talk about organizing a union; but the staff as a whole was timid and not willing to take such a drastic step. Unable to see an interesting future for myself there, I quit my job and changed careers.

A short time after I left, the clerical staff, many of whom were my friends, withdrew from the employee group and formed a local of the Service Employees International Union, AFL-CIO. In negotiating the first contract, management stood firm on a poor offer and the clerical workers went on strike. The strike was a long one, but expensive only to the strikers. Business went on as usual. Management hired student workers at low pay to do some of the work and supervisors put in extra hours. Eventually, the union settled on a contract that virtually was what management had offered in the first place. Unions don't like to admit losing strikes, but if any strike ever was lost, that one was. My friends had won the right to representation, but little more.

I was left wondering whether I had helped or hurt my friends by laying the groundwork for union organization. In the long run, considering the management with which they must deal, the clerical workers are somewhat better off having representation than not, but it is clear that we expected too much from unionizing. The union has not solved many of their problems, nor has it addressed even their most basic one—that of being workers in a female-employment ghetto.

Union Frustration

Over the years, I've talked with many working women in a variety of fields—manufacturing, production, clerical, professional. Many of these women had work-related problems. Some of them belonged to unions. When I asked how effective their unions had been in helping to solve their problems, almost without exception the women union members told me their unions had been no help. Often the women never even thought of taking their work problems to their union representative. Union leadership, to them, seemed remote and uninvolved, their own membership perfunctory.

In fact, the American labor movement never has been vitally concerned about women workers, and few women have had positions of real power in its hierarchies. Lane Kirkland, new president of the AFL-CIO, has announced that he is going to see to it that women have more policy-making jobs in the federation. He intends to appoint a woman to the AFL-CIO Executive Council and said that he will interest himself more with women's issues than did his predecessor, the late George Meany. He hardly could interest himself less.

No women ever has been seated on the AFL-CIO Executive Council in its 23-year history. Although women make up 27 percent of union membership, they hold only 5 percent of union policy-making jobs. The Coalition of Labor Union Women (CLUW) was founded in 1974 to promote women's issues and interests within the AFL/CIO, but soon found itself in the unfortunate position of fighting the male-dominated AFL-CIO leadership rather than working with that leadership on issues that would benefit all workers. CLUW has made some modest gains but largely has failed in increasing the power of women within the labor movement and has failed, miserably, in one of its stated goals: to organize the millions of unorganized women throughout the United States. Sally Field's award-winning performance in the film *Norma Rae* aside, employees of the J.P. Stevens Company still lack a contract, and many other factories throughout the South, employing great numbers of women, have no union at all. In addition, despite the rhetoric, unions have been unenthusiastic about organizing clerical workers, most of them women.

Unions Need Women

It is not surprising that Kirkland has begun to try to please working women. Today, traditional labor unions need women more than women need unions. Unions are in deep trouble.

- Union membership has fallen to less than 20 percent of the labor force. In 1975, 20.6 percent of the total labor force were union members as compared to 19.7 percent in 1978; during the same time, the economy has added eight million jobs.
- Unions continue to lose more elections than they win. Even when won, successful decertification campaigns sometimes follow.
- Unions today lack the power to win contracts for their members that keep pace with inflation. Although it is true that unorganized workers' wages slipped even more, last year workers averaged only 8.8 percent in wage increases while inflation was more than 13.3 percent.
- Today, 91.5 percent of the employed adult population works for someone else. More of us are "workers" than ever before and yet sympathy for unions is low. Mistakenly or not, unions are viewed as crime-riddled, corrupt organizations. Inconvenience caused by strikes, particularly those in the public services, is more often blamed on visible "greedy" striking workers than on greedy, recalcitrant managers and owners.
- Unions and union leadership have grown old in the service of industrial and production workers. Today, work is changing. Electronics and robot production lines are eliminating jobs and, with them, union dues. Typically, union activists and leaders are over 45, and, according to reports, unions are finding it hard to recruit younger people, of either sex, to leadership jobs.

What the Record Shows

All of this is not to say that unions have not, in the past, achieved their goals of preserving jobs and rewarding those who held them, usually white males. Trade unionism, in this country, with a couple of exceptions, scorned a class approach and built instead upon the old guild tradition of preserving crafts, skills and jobs. In doing this, women fared poorly. Although as early as 1850 women accounted for nearly a quarter of the industrial work force, their membership in unions usually was barred, never sought. Their presence in the work force was regarded, at best, as an anomaly, at worst, as a threat to wages and jobs of men. As an added fillip, women's wages were *so* low that it did not pay for unions to organize them.

It would be too much to say that unions have caused the problems that women have had in the work place. Union policies have been a simple reflection of social attitudes. Nevertheless, those policies have tended to freeze those attitudes and institutionalize them. Organized labor often has relegated the woman union member to second-class membership, refused her admission to apprenticeship and job-upgrading programs and has kept her, through classification schemes, in low-paying, low-skill jobs. Seniority, not competence, has been the requirement not only for job advancement but for union advancement. The union seniority system has hurt women who have had to take breaks in their careers.

Organizing Alternatives

Since 1970, employee associations have grown faster than unions and have recruited more women members. Some of these, such as the National Association of Working Women (NAWW), which advocates the organization of clerical workers in "appropriate ways," occasionally serve as halfway houses to unionism. The NAWW helped women in its Boston affiliate, 9 to 5, organize as Local 925 of SEIU, AFL-CIO (See "Getting Organized," Working Woman, March 1979). But other employee associations, such as the American Association of University Professors, the National Education Association and the American Nurses

Association, have won the right to bargain and represent their members outside of the labor-union structure.

The women's movement, the consumer movement and government concern with social welfare all have sparked actions that broadly benefit women workers. For example, the US Labor Department filed 85 actions against New York sweatships, charging violations of the Fair Standards Act.

The Equal Pay Act, although still narrowly interpreted, and Title VII of the Civil Rights Act are powerful tools for women. Suits under these acts have been brought by the International Union of Electrical Workers and the AFL-CIO and by other groups outside of unions. Nine nurses in Denver, with funds provided by the American Nurses Association, filed suit under the Equal Pay Act in an attempt to establish the principle of equal pay for comparable work.

What Does This Mean for Women?

Despite their declining economic and political power, unions will be around for some time to come, serving as they do as a counterweight to management power. When that counterweight is needed, women will join unions. Join and change them. But unions, by their very nature, are an essentially conservative force in a world where work is rapidly changing, and, we should not expect too much from them.

Employee associations are becoming an increasingly popular alternative. They are free from the enormous burden of more than 150 years of organizational traditions that unions carry and so appear to be more flex-ible and responsive to change. We should form and join them. We need to work for a broader interpretation of the Equal Pay Act and the ratification of the Equal Rights Amendment. Class-action suits, consumer pressure, lobbying and political action can help. We need to push for technical training and innovative thinking rather than apprenticeships in dead-end jobs.

Finally, we women are changing work itself by our presence in the work force and will continue to do so more rapidly as our numbers increase. We nearly always have been on the side of progressive work changes. It was women, after all, who really won the battle for the ten-hour day (an enlightened improvement over the 14-hour day!). Today, as we enter the work force in greater numbers, we are bringing such changes as flextime and job sharing, improved day care for our children, maternity *and* paternity leaves, family sick-time allowances, equal pay for comparable work—all changes that humanize work and benefit workers of both sexes.

It is gratifying to see women moving into new fields and into positions of real, not token, power; and I cherish the belief that as women consolidate their power and grow accustomed to its use, they will exercise it in a more compassionate, fairer, less capricious way. The rage that unions have tapped for strength and membership grew from antagonism between employer and employee. That antagonism, perhaps, never can be taken away fully because it comes from disparate views of work, but if women can bring to management, as I believe they can, more understanding and more sensitivity, surely some of that antagonism can be eased.

Part Four

Changes

Chapter Ten

Changing Careers

HOW TO MAKE THE MID-STREAM SWITCH

by Sylvia Rabiner

Glinda was a stockbroker; now she runs a restaurant. Maggie switched from writing books to running for Congress, and Abigail dropped the literary life to enter law school with plans, not to become merely a lawyer, but a Supreme Court Justice! These female torpedoes, capable of blasting out of old careers into new ones without so much as a quiver of misgivings, appeared in a *New York Times* column written by Lois Gould some months ago. Its main thrust (not meant, I grant you, to be taken entirely seriously) was that Gould's friends could do anything they put their minds to, and so (it was implied) could you and I.

A second article that appeared several weeks later in the same newspaper described the seemingly effortless career changes of "a select group of women in their 30s." Among these were Carol Rinzler (who went from writing/editing to law), Rosemary Masters (law to social work) and Carol Reich (interior design to child psychology).

By coincidence, I was trying to switch careers myself right then, an experience much like driving down an unfamiliar road in the rain while running out of gas. Was I defective: genetically doomed to do everything the hard way? Or had *The Times,* in focusing on an elite group, presented an unrealistic picture? The women described were either at the top of their professions or married to men who had admittedly bankrolled their efforts. Surely there were others making changes without these advantages: single women or wives whose mates couldn't foot the bills while they returned to school for retraining. And what about those most burdened of all—divorced working mothers? How were they doing it? In order to find out, I decided to talk with some women who had made the difficult transition from one career to another—unassisted.

Buyer to Sales Representative

If a social worker decided to become a mar-

197

keting executive, you would rightfully assume she'd have some difficulty convincing a potential employer that her skills and experience were transferable, whereas changing from retailing to sales is no problem. After all, business is business, or so many of us suppose.

But for Linda Gonnelli, the transition from buyer to sales representative involved a job-search that lasted two years. During that time, she answered countless newspaper ads (usually getting no response), filled out innumerable employment agency applications (which were filed and forgotten) and had interviews that led nowhere. In a thick looseleaf notebook, Gonnelli has kept a meticulous record of that experience. On each page are careful notations of résumés sent and phone calls made. A less determined person might have given up, but Gonnelli, an animated young woman of 30, did not. Gonnelli started at Bloomingdale's, a New York department store, right after college and worked her way up to branch department manager. The job was exciting but demanding. "I worked every other Saturday—nights and holidays." After seven years, she left for a better position at Ohrbach's, another department store, but shortly after her arrival, the store's management changed and, unfortunately, so did the nature of her job. "I wasn't allowed to do what I had been hired for," she explained. This frustration, in addition to the excessive demands retailing made on her time, brought her to a decision: not simply to quit her job, but to change fields altogether.

Gonnelli's game plan was to live on savings for about six months while looking for work in the areas of marketing, advertising and sales. To get some tips, she sought professional help but didn't find the consultants especially helpful. "I didn't know how to make them work for me," she admitted. Consequently time was lost in fruitless visits to employment agencies and personnel departments. When her savings began to run

out, Gonnelli took temporary jobs that gave her the opportunity to investigate different companies and talk with people in departments where she thought she might fit in. This direct contact brought results. While filling a temporary position in the Xerox showroom, she left her résumé with the director of personnel. The result? Her present job—a good one, which makes her grateful for her tenacity. She advises those considering a new career to take action. "Seek out avenues to the fields you're interested in by calling people for advice. Even if you haven't totally analyzed the situation and made a definite choice, if you're badly frustrated at your job, don't hesitate to quit."

Elementary School Teacher to Insurance Saleswoman

Myrna Rabkin made the improbable leap from an elementary school classroom to a Manhattan office with a sweeping view. Seized by the powerful conviction that she could sell insurance (and do it well), she virtually bombarded her way into a new and successful career.

Unlike others of her generation, Rabkin, 32, didn't become a teacher because it was a suitable occupation for a woman. It had long been her goal. "I was so thrilled to be accepted, to have a class to myself." This feeling persisted for over five years, and it was not dissatisfaction with her job, but the dissolution of her marriage, that precipitated the change. "It was a rude awakening. I never thought my marriage would end. It changed my whole life." Shocked and unable to accept the divorce, she tried to regain her husband's affection by leaving the profession he had never admired. She returned to school to learn educational film production, but halfway through the first semester she realized her plans were impractical. On all levels of Government funds for education, including those for visual aids, were being sharply cut back. She reconsidered: "I felt insecure. I was depleting my savings. I had to think of a way to make money but I didn't know how. My greatest asset was me."

By chance, a close friend suggested that Rabkin meet a salesman to discuss buying some life insurance. She wasn't interested, but her friend insisted. The meeting was a revelation. "Could women do this?" she asked herself. "I decided they could and that I was going to buy insurance for myself from myself. And I wanted to sell to other women."

It was a turning point. The next day, Rabkin called the insurance company to request an interview. Learning she was a teacher, they suggested she sell encyclopedias. "I told them I didn't believe in encyclopedias but I believed in life insurance." Undaunted, Rabkin called again the next day—and the day after that. "I pushed, which was exactly what they wanted. Perseverance is needed in sales." Finally she was granted an interview and offered a job.

The awards on her office wall attest to the fact that Rabkin is a top-notch saleswoman. In her first year, she earned more money than she'd ever had before and reveled in the excitement of the work. Looking back, she said, "I'm convinced that if you have a strong need to do something, it's eventually going to materialize. The hardships are easy to bear when you have a goal. I came with a desire to succeed in this business, to prove that a woman could. I wanted to break down barriers—and I have."

Teacher to Psychologist

Changing careers doesn't always involve a dramatic metamorphosis. According to Dale Hiestand, PhD, professor of business at Columbia University and author of *Changing Careers After 35* (Columbia University Press) many women make a "45-degree turn" by moving into new but related fields, often returning to school to do so.

"If someone had told me six years ago that I'd be working on my doctorate, I would have laughed at them," Frederica Balzano said

quietly, looking back on what has been one of the most difficult, but perhaps most productive, periods in her life. Balzano, a tall, striking woman of 36, has heroically juggled a full-time job, graduate school and family responsibilities in her move from education to psychology.

Her teaching career began in 1962 in a Bedford-Stuyvesant elementary school. She taught for over five years with only brief time out in 1963 for the birth of her daughter, Tracy. "Around the fifth year I was getting restless. I didn't know what I wanted to do but I suspected that I wanted out of the classroom."

Opportunity came in the offer of a job as an educational consultant for Headstart. Balzano worked closely with the program's psychologist and became interested in her techniques. "She was testing kids and working one to one with them and their families. I wanted to do something similar." The wish didn't lead to immediate action because Balzano was coping with the break-up of her marriage: An event that left her with the primary care and sole financial responsibility for her daughter. To get through this crisis, she started therapy. "I talked to my therapist about wanting to work with kids, but the idea of going back to school was so foreign. I thought I wasn't smart enough." She procrastinated. Finally with trepidation, she applied to New York University and was accepted.

Balzano attended night classes, keeping her full-time job to pay expenses. Her education, thus far, has cost about $10,000. It has cost much in time and energy as well. "I don't know how I did it. I worked and carried a full school load because I had so many credits to earn. When I wasn't studying, I needed time for Tracy. I just kept going—like a robot." The grueling schedule took its toll. Balzano developed a spastic colon from the pressure, and her social life—well, it was last priority.

At present, things look brighter. Balzano

started work on her dissertation and in September, she began a job in her new field as a psychologist in a private school. Has the struggle been worth it? "There were times I felt overwhelmed," she said. "Times I wished someone were there to pick up the pieces, times I've said, 'I can't do this.' Then I got up, went to work, went to school, took care of my daughter and listened to people's problems. It's been a difficult, difficult thing but if I had to do it all over again, I would. And in exactly the same way."

Social Worker to Lawyer

Paula Galowitz, 30, went to work for a city agency after she graduated from college. After two years, she decided to go to social work school, financing her full-time studies with a student grant and financial help from her husband. Upon completing her master's, she got a job with the Bureau of Child Welfare, where her work frequently took her to court. From her observations there, she decided social work could be combined with law. "I was a child of the Sixties," she explained. "I believed in the self-help concept—that people should have more control over their lives. I knew the way to get change was through the legal system."

She had doubts about going to law school. "I thought I was too old. It was a major change and since I'd been divorced, there was no one around to support me." Despite her uncertainty, she went ahead, took the entrance examination and passed, left her job and returned to school full time.

As she suspected, the adjustment wasn't easy. "Law school is taking notes and memorizing. I didn't particularly like being a student." Not only was school occasionally tedious, it took most of Galowitz' free time. "I couldn't do many things I had enjoyed doing. Even when I was out having a good time, I felt I had to go home and study. At times, I was jealous of everyone who wasn't in school." And it was expensive. Galowitz

estimates the cost at almost $6,000 (in loans she's still paying off).

During her third year, she began writing to legal-aid agencies and landed her present job before she had even taken the Bar, a tough, two-day examination she passed last July. Now a lawyer for the civil division of Legal Aid, she said, "I do all kinds of work—housing, consumer, welfare, matrimonial and family law. It's varied, which I love, although it's often demanding and draining—but that's the choice I've made. In his poem, 'The Road Not Taken,' Robert Frost speaks about making choices. I didn't want to go through the rest of my life saying, 'If only I had done it.' "

Given the risks, emotional stress and investment of time and money, how many women are pulling free from familiar moorings to steam into uncharted waters? According to Sylvia Porter, syndicated columnist, "record numbers of Americans are changing jobs midstream, and in the closing years of the 20th century, there will be five to seven occupational changes in a typical lifetime."

Who are today's career changers? They can be divided into two groups: Those who have to change (because their skills are no longer in demand) and those who want to (for any number of reasons). People in the first category (where I found myself) are often flung out of work with little warning and must feverishly attempt to reorganize their lives before their unemployment insurance runs out. Those who choose to change have less pressure.

Are there any discernible change patterns? What fields, if any in particular, are women leaving and which ones are they entering? Sara Thornhill, director of career advancement at Barbara Holt Associates, said that most of the women she advises about new alternatives are between the ages of 23 and 35 and work in traditional female areas: education, social services or the secretarial field. As a rule, they've held their present jobs for over five years and feel dissatisfied. They want to work in management or administration. Ruth Shapiro of Ruth Shapiro Associates claimed a number of career changers are leaving the female "ghetto" for jobs in engineering, banking, accounting and the sciences. A number are returning to graduate school to earn MBAs.

What are a career changer's most pressing problems? Lack of confidence, fear of age discrimination and anxiety about acceptance in the new field are the primary difficulties that Shapiro helps her clients to deal with. Lee Hammer, director of Mainstream Associates, said that many of her clients don't know how to transfer their abilities to the market place. Thornhill concurs. "Numbers of women have difficulty identifying their skills well enough to market them." Given these stumbling blocks, what are the chances of making a successful transition? Shapiro supplies what is probably the most realistic answer: "So much depends upon the women—her motivation, willingness to research her new career thoroughly, persistence and ability to market herself."

The impulse to change careers may be attributed to a number of factors: an emphasis in the media on work as a source of gratification, an optimistic belief that equal opportunity legislation will make hitherto male-dominated fields accessible to women and the availability of a widespread support system that has grown from the Women's Movement. Furthermore, the generation of women now most actively seeking new fields of work has undergone a deep, internal change. No longer able to count upon the security once offered by marriage, they've given up their dependence. If they must work for most of their adult lives, as men do, they want more than just a job.

Today women with heightened aspirations are, indeed, refusing to remain in low-paying, low-prestige jobs. But the media does women no favors by focusing only on those at the top. Glamorous women who switch careers as easily as they change lipstick do not represent the majority. The woman who sets out on the road of change thinking it well-paved and easy to traverse may unexpectedly find herself knee-deep in brambles. Career changing isn't easy, but that doesn't deter those who now have the brass ring from trying to grasp hold of the gold.

TIPSHEET

If you are considering a career change, you'll find self-help books and organizations in proliferating numbers. Often the library is your most useful, least expensive source of information, but if you do seek professional guidance, shop around. I visited a number of consultants whose fees range from $100 to $1,500 for similar services. Most offer a basic program that includes self-evaluation (which may or may not involve a battery of tests to determine skills and interests), research of the job market, résumé and letter-writing as well as interviewing techniques. Ethical counselors will offer assistance and encouragement but won't promise to get you a job. Some agencies run a placement service, others merely give informal job leads. Don't be afraid to ask. You're entitled to know what you'll receive for your money.

After attending a number of workshops, I concluded that the most widely accepted present method is based on Richard Nelson Bolles's popular book *What Color Is Your Parachute?* (Ten Speed Press), which one counselor dubbed the job-hunter's bible. Bolles's advice is this: Decide exactly what you want to do, where you want to do it (through your own considerable research and personal survey), then approach the one individual in each organization who has the power to hire you. The object is to bypass all intermediaries. At a session given by The Sales Executive Club of New York that I attended, the instructor, Tom Gallagher, gave us the same message: "The most effective way of getting a job is to pick up a phone, find out who can hire you and go in and talk to that person." Advice, simply stated, is not always so simple to follow. During the discussion period, members of our group asked Gallagher questions ranging from "How can I call up a stranger?" to "What do I do if his secretary fends me off." Most of us have qualms about asking busy people to give us any of their time, but if you're willing to try it, you may be happily surprised to find that people, even busy, important ones, are flattered by a request for advice. After all, it attests to their expertise.

While this particular premise seems to have widespread acceptance, methods of résumé writing, presentation of cover letters or ways to dress for interviews, among other things, may vary widely. A friend reported that, in consulting three experts, she'd been shown three different ways to write her résumé. She evaluated them, selected the best then discarded the others. "No one can give you better advice than yourself," Cicero wrote. His words remain true: You'll not only advise but depend upon and encourage yourself in the difficult task you've undertaken.

ESCAPE FROM THE SCHOOLHOUSE

by Dedra Hauser

Today, significant numbers of educators are looking at alternative careers, and it's not only teachers who are interested. Women in all aspects of education are seeking a way out. They are dissatisfied with the general lack of upward mobility in the profession, and they fear that the shrinking school-age population eventually will eliminate even their job security. Many educators also feel that the status they once enjoyed is being eroded by changing values of our society. They want a share of the money and prestige they associate with jobs in business. At a Counseling Women seminar on Career Alternatives to Teaching, one high-school teacher put it this way: "It's not a job anymore; it's a slap in the face. We're not respected by the kids, the parents, the administration or the society at large."

Translating their desire for moves into action is tough for many teachers. Sarah Hodge, cofounder and president of Churchill Executive Resources, Inc., an international recruitment service, has found that teachers she encounters often go to one of two extremes. "Either they have unreasonably high expectations or they are totally discouraged." Hodge claimed that educators can be trained for a great many jobs in business, if they are willing to learn and are able to take an initial salary cut.

Both career counselors and former teachers urge women to explore career alternatives by talking to people in a wide variety of jobs. Find out what other people do and what steps they took to get where they are. "The only way to get started is to expose yourself to new ideas, to talk to women who have made changes or are in the process of doing so," advised one former teacher.

Getting out of teaching *can* be done. It *is* being done more and more often. Here, four women tell how they graduated from educational jobs and went on to pursue challenging new careers.

Day-Care Teacher To Stockbroker

After separating from her husband, Sandra Murphy soon discovered that "he wasn't big on support payments." Since the $10,000 salary she made as a day-care-center teacher was inadequate to support herself and her two young children, she knew it was time to take action and resolved to find work that would make her financially independent.

Her first move was to attend Bermon's Career Alternatives to Teaching. Murphy walked away from the seminar feeling depressed. Convinced that she was incapable of taking the recommended job-search steps, she saw herself as permanently trapped in teaching. Her first job interview served to undermine her confidence still further. That interview, with an executive at IBM, had been arranged by a friend of Murphy's father. She remembers making "all the classic blunders. I knew next to nothing about the company, and offered no concrete reasons as to why they should hire me over thousands of other people who were better qualified." The meeting ended with the executive telling Murphy to stick with teaching and go back to her husband. "When I walked out the door, I felt utterly worthless."

It was a year before Murphy could muster the courage to go on to other interviews. In the interim she read about business and attended several seminars, where she listened attentively as businesswomen talked about their jobs. Gradually, she revised her childhood expectations that had included work as simply a sideline to marriage and child rearing.

To her second round of interviews, Murphy brought renewed self-confidence. "I felt I had at least as much to offer as most of the people I met. If I could just sell myself, I thought I could learn to do most jobs." She convinced a skeptical employer to give her an entry-level job selling a mutual fund on a commission-only basis. After a few remunerative months, sales slacked off and she was back into the job market.

A neighbor who worked for the Merrill Lynch Pierce Fenner & Smith brokerage firm arranged an interview for her there. "The interviewer asked me how much I wanted to earn in two years, and I said $50,000." Thinking big paid off for Murphy. "He identified me as being 'hungry,' and he said that with so much motivation I would do well." After two meetings, Murphy was offered a job that would train her to sell securities.

She remembers that cramming for the broker's exam during her first few months at Merrill Lynch was nervewracking. "It was like translating Greek, and I was terrified that I had oversold myself." So terrified in fact, that she once fainted on the train en route to a class. But she regained her cool in time for the exam—and passed it. Today she works as an account executive in a Merrill Lynch office ten minutes from her home.

Murphy finds many of the same satisfactions in her present job that she had found in teaching, except that now she sees tangible results from her efforts. "One of the big frustrations in working in antipoverty programs and in the educational system is finding out how little you can accomplish." In her new profession, although she works long hours, her schedule is flexible enough to accommodate her child-care needs.

Her advice to dissatisfied teachers is this: "Find out what interests you and go after it. Don't put limits on what you think you want, and don't label anything unattainable. When I first started looking, I thought I had about as much chance of becoming President of the United States as I did of being a broker."

Vocational Counselor to Radio Executive

Rae-Carole Fischer decided to leave her job as vocational counselor at a New York public school because "the kids were graduating and I wasn't." She loved the work but felt it had become too easy, and the salary (paid by the New York State Department of Labor) was too low.

After spending eight years in education, Fischer was intimidated by the business community and insecure about her qualifications to enter it. "A background in education is a terrible handicap," she said. "But the biggest handicap of all is us: We don't represent ourselves as having any skill."

Attending seminars gave Fischer the impetus and the tools to start looking seriously for a new career. "Since all of my friends were teachers, I had to make new contacts." After deciding to go into sales, she immersed herself in books, courses and magazines about advertising and sales. She was offered a sales job that was supposed to open up soon, and for a year she waited. "I was scared anyway, so I didn't mind when my starting date kept being pushed ahead." The job never materialized. Fischer warns teachers not to wait to be handed a job on a silver platter.

An article she'd read about women in radio prompted Fischer to explore opportunities in the field. Boldly she telephoned Karen Anderson, local station manager at WCBS–FM, who had been profiled in the story. Anderson turned out to be extremely supportive, providing Fischer with contacts and arranging several interviews for her.

For the next three months, Fischer waged a massive campaign. She listened to 12 major radio stations and, upon being interviewed, provided her own comparative research on the station programming. She prepared a list of five professional strengths she wanted to emphasize, making sure to relate them to the job she was applying for. Although she had worked part time in sales, most employers expressed concern about her lack of experience. "I told them I had spent eight years selling a product no one wants to buy—kids with limited skills."

On January 19, 1979, a year and a half after she had begun her job search, Fischer went to work as an account executive for WNBC radio. She already earns more than she did as a vocational counselor and is delighted with her job and with the company. Although she works twice as many hours now, Fischer said she can't imagine going back to teaching. Of educators who cling to their long vacations, she asks the question: "Can you live your life for a vacation? Wouldn't it be better to live for a job you really enjoy?"

Meeting her today, it is hard to believe that Fischer was ever intimidated by the business community. Her advice to those who want to move out of teaching is: 1. Make the most of the many skills you have; they are useful in business. "Teachers are administrators. They have the ability to plan, to design programs, to deal with all levels of the community, to work independently. Never say, 'I'm just a teacher.' " 2. Enroll in a career-counseling group. 3. Use every possible contact you can establish. "It's a difficult path, and you need support along the way. I wouldn't be where I am now without the help of other women."

Elementary-School Teacher To Banker

Virginia Pfeifer chose a path that is popular among dissatisfied teachers—more education. Armed with an MBA she earned while still teaching, the former elementary-school teacher soon found that without work experience her degree was poor ammunition. "It was the old Catch-22," she said. "You can't get a job without experience; you can't get experience without a job." Pfeifer advises teachers to put the horse before the cart and get some work experience first, and then decide whether or not they need advanced degrees.

Her search for a marketing job was long and at times discouraging. "Finally, I developed some persistence and began to view being rejected for a job as a learning experience." Although she pushed her MBA with employers, it was a businesswoman's advice that made the difference. Skills—the skills Pfeifer had developed as a public-school teacher in New York City—were what to emphasize, the businesswoman said, and she helped Pfeifer to articulate and package them. "I had sent out piles of letters that were totally nonproductive, because I didn't identify my skills. At the suggestion of this woman, I pointed out such things as my ability to plan and to interact with all kinds of people."

When she heard through a friend of a job opening at Manufacturers Hanover Trust Company, Pfeifer immediately phoned the woman doing the hiring. The position had been filled. "If this had happened when I was first looking for a job, I would have said thank you and hung up," Pfeifer said. "But I asked if she would meet me to chat about other opportunities."

The woman sent Pfeifer's résumé to the marketing department, and Pfeifer found out about a job opening when she made a follow-up call. She accepted a salary cut for a job as a researcher, which involved, among other things, writing reports about bank services for the sales and product-knowledge department of the marketing division.

Although the MBA didn't help her to get the job, Pfeifer feels that it did enable her to command a higher salary. "I had expected to take a temporary cut in my income," she said, "and since I have only myself to support, it's no great hardship." One small step backward has put her on a forward-moving career track. "You have to set your priorities. I wanted a job in which I could advance on the basis of my performance."

From Teacher to School Psychologist to Corporate Trainer

Career counseling introduced Lucille Granfort to the concept of "networking." "The best move I made was talking to people," she said. At parties, school meetings, anywhere she came into contact with people, Granfort spoke with them about their careers and discussed her own professional goals. When she became interested in career planning, she made it her business to meet people in that profession. (Corporate trainers teach specific skills or general management concepts to employees at all levels.) Granfort also joined the professional association of trainers, the American Society for Training and Development.

Granfort had already made one career switch. After leaving teaching to raise four children, she went back to school for a master's degree in psychology and then got a job as a school psychologist. She developed the job from part time to full time and incorporated administrative duties, Granfort made another move. "I was in a situation I loved,

but felt there was no room for personal growth."

With the help of a recruitment executive she met through a friend, Granfort identified the skills she could apply to business. She familiarized herself with business language in order to articulate her skills most effectively. "When teachers create a lesson plan, they are doing 'needs analysis' and designing a program to meet those needs. The same process takes place in corporations."

Although she answered newspaper advertisements, the most interesting opportunities came through her network. Two job offers materialized from career-counseling groups, and one led into her present position as a training representative at Consolidated Edison Power Company, where she is conducting a pilot planning program.

It was less than a year between the time when Granfort first flirted with the idea of changing jobs (September 1977), and the time when she began working for Con Ed (July 1978). The only mistake she thinks she made was in "not exploring more options. In my career-planning program at Con Ed, I encourage people to explore areas that interest them."

For information on counseling organizations in your area, write: Ms. Gurley Turner, Director of Information Services, Catalyst, 14 East 60 Street, New York, NY 10022.

Counseling Women has prepared a fact sheet on post-teaching alternatives. Send a self-addressed envelope with 35 cents postage to Counseling Women, 14 East 60 Street, Room 704, New York, NY 10022.

IS THE RIGHT JOB WORTH IT?

by Kay McConathy

The Decision

When I graduated from a small, Texas liberal-arts college in 1966 I had the obvious

job choices of a decade ago—social work, secretarial jobs, teaching or homemaking. I became a teacher.

At the time, I had my doubts, but what other choices were there for a woman with a BA in history and a minor in English? Seven years later, the frustrations of teaching had caught up with me, and after a complicated job search I managed to make the career switch I wanted from teaching to broadcasting. But the transition was not an easy one.

I started out teaching in ghetto schools—for three years in a large west-side Chicago high school and then an even larger, predominately black and Puerto Rican high school in Manhattan.

Those years brought some shocks to this white, Scotch-Irish Protestant from Oklahoma. Before then, I had been sheltered from flagrant racism, anti-Semitism, urban restlessness and the desperation of poverty. Militancy was growing among black students and teachers, and there was an increasingly open resentment of white liberalism in the Chicago schools.

It seemed that remediation and instruction in the basics were to be the sum of my teaching, graduate school or not. The New York City school where I taught during the year after I got my master's degree put an end to my illusions about the rewards of teaching. The demands of being a disciplinarian overwhelmed all of my attempts to educate.

I left New York. The teaching experience that followed—three years of teaching for the Department of Defense outside the United States— was almost pleasant after Chicago and Manhattan. It was meaningful on a personal level—but finally it only increased my sense of professional alienation. Education, it seemed, was continually taking a back seat to a carload of other American priorities.

Teaching overseas caused me to stick it out in the classroom longer than I might have. But I resented the holding-action function I seemed to be serving. And above all, my professional ego and ambition could not accept the premise that my annual salary increase was not based on merit, but on perseverance.

The Dream

So, when I left Okinawa in the spring of 1974, full of anticipation for a new future, San Francisco was to be the focus of all my energy and ambition. By this time I had made some definite decisions about a new career and way of life. I wanted to live in a city. I had tried the East Coast—why not now the West Coast? I wanted to break into broadcasting—on the production side—and work my way into being a reporter and eventually a talk-show host. But—and this is a big but—I did very little research about the training needed, job availability in the region and pay scales.

A military broadcast-operations man in Okinawa had told me it would be tough. But I had been infected by the American dream of "You can be whatever you want."

The Search

I came to the Bay Area in September of 1974 with a small savings, less than $800, and the name of a cousin's friend, with whom I stayed for a couple of weeks while I looked for an apartment. My car, fully paid for, had been shipped from overseas and gave me the mobility to search first for an inexpensive apartment and then for a job. Luckily, I found a large one-bedroom apartment for $150 a month.

My first blow was being turned down for unemployment compensation because I had quit work overseas "without good cause." I had to earn $450 or more in bona fide employment to reopen my claim. To keep myself afloat, I worked for a temporary-office service from early October through mid-November.

In the meantime, I filled out applications for job listings in reporting and public relations with the Employment Development Department in Berkeley, Oakland and San Francisco. I received a code number from the Dictionary of Occupational Training. I took a test to demonstrate my aptitude for handling data, people and things. I also applied for my California teaching certificate so that I could do substitute work. But even if I had wanted to teach full time, finding a job was next to impossible because of the glut of unemployed teachers in the area.

The counselors with the Employment Development Department told me that everyone wanted to get into broadcasting. Nevertheless, I made a list of television and radio stations in the Bay Area and sent letters of introduction to personnel directors, trying to get my "foot in the door." In many cases I received form letters indicating that my résumé and letter would be kept for one year in an "active" cross-reference file and that I would be contacted when there was an opening that seemed to match my qualifications. I became accustomed to that particular brushoff, but often I followed up with phone calls anyway, trying to elicit information.

The Crunch

After my temporary office assignment had been completed, I scoured the classified ads for part-time secretarial work to enable me to continue my job search. Temp work was not a reliable source of income. I listened to the radio and watched television, trying to pick up leads through public-service programs and announcements for job seekers.

I learned to stop mentioning my master's degree to lessen the burden of being "overqualified." I avoided mentioning my age—30 at the time. I simply was a "teacher out of work" in need of some kind of job.

During this time, my real career-job search expanded into a variety of work related to journalism, public relations and advertising, where I thought my background could be put to use. I applied for executive-trainee programs with two big department stores, a sales position with an environmental media company—selling outdoor advertisements on waste receptacles—a part-time position as a girl Friday for the *San Francisco Examiner*, etc.

I went to some broadcasting stations and filled out applications at the door and, if possible, with employees, who were helpful

with tips. I always tried to acquire information about other places and people to contact. I kept a notebook with notations on dates, people, places and follow-ups. I made many follow-up phone calls and sent many thank-you letters. I was conducting the classical radial job search—not leaving a stone unturned.

At the end of November, I got a temporary, Christmas-season job typing envelopes for credit-card applications in a large department store. I remember feeling claustrophobic while sitting at a typewriter in a large room filled with other typists. I began to ask myself questions about my job search—would I find myself doomed to this— typing, punching in and out, observing male management in glassed-in offices at the edges of the room? After this seasonal job ended, I reapplied for unemployment, which I started receiving in January 1975—$90 a week.

Those unemployment checks gave me a reprieve. I could relax a little.

I checked out a couple of women's groups but found that their nonprofit status gave them very little reason to develop placement expertise. I also went to employment agencies, where there wasn't much interest shown in my career aspirations—the preponderance of jobs for females was in dead-end clerical positions. To the employment agencies I was a salable commodity with a price tag.

Off and on throughout January and February, I did substitute work for a private elementary school in Oakland. The disciplinarian approach I had to take even there brought back my feelings of dissatisfaction with teaching.

The Turning Point

In the spring of 1975 I interviewed for jobs as information officer at a junior college; production specialist for an educational station in San Jose; coordinator of utilization services with a public-education station in San Francisco; public-relations director of the San Francisco Bay Girl Scout Council; public-information assistant for the University of San Francisco; elementary utilization coordinator for the Catholic Educational Television service in the Archdiocese of San Francisco; and so on. At each turn, there was someone more qualified.

In March I did some volunteer work answering phones for a non-profit community-oriented Berkeley radio station, KPFA. This work led to my doing some writing for a women's program and helping with its on-air presentation. I hoped this was an opportunity that might lead to a job inside the world of broadcasting. But the station and its staff were just scraping by and couldn't offer me a living wage.

The experience at KPFA exposed me to a part of the women's movement—displaced homemakers, older women without husbands who were trying to reenter the job market without job skills or with skills from years of volunteer work but no paid experience. I sympathized with the problems they encountered because these were my problems, too.

At the same time I became a member of a group of unemployed professionals, Experience Unlimited, sponsored by the Oakland Employment Development Department. This gave me a base of group support, higher expectations, tips on résumé writing and interviewing techniques. I talked openly with the group about my frustration in facing a committed job search and career change. I met many other people who had come to dead ends in their careers.

I received an emotional boost from becoming a leader of this group, presiding over meetings, helping others with their job searches. I became skilled in the use of euphemism, translating my teaching skills into such terms as communicator, administrator, supervisor, communications media expert, researcher, lecturer.

I became a professional rather than an amateur job searcher. I recalled past achievements that might have a bearing on my job search. I probed my marketable skills, talents, likes and dislikes. I read Rich-

ard Bolles's primer for the job seeker, *What Color Is Your Parachute?*

I also was facing the lines at the unemployment office—an unpleasant experience in which the bureaucracy determines your worth. I saw honest and dishonest people, individuals in dire straits, many out of work not by choice. Upon receiving my voucher to pick up my "cash," I often felt victimized and guilty, even though I was conscientiously trying to find a job. There always was the fact that the person on the other side of the counter called the shots, had the advantage because he or she *had* a job.

In July, I was turned down for an extension of my unemployment compensation because I had refused a position as a complaint adjustor at the department store where I had worked during Christmastime. At this point I was without funds and in a state of despair.

After I finally *did* receive a job offer, I demanded an appeals hearing on the decision to withdraw my unemployment compensation, which took place after I was employed. I was informed that because I had once accepted work with the store, it was unacceptable to turn down work there at a few more cents an hour. I was angry. I wondered if a male in a similar situation would have been advised to accept a position clearly out of line with his vocational potential.

As I look back now, I can see also that the economy's problems in 1974 were hostile to any career change.

Getting There

Through working on publicity projects for Experience Unlimited I made contacts at several radio and TV stations that were required by the FCC to air public-service announcements. A local TV station showed a slide of me as "Job Seeker of the Day": "With her background in media writing and production and audiovisual equipment," the voiceover said, "this former teacher would like to enter the broadcasting field. She did a great deal of this kind of work for her school system and thinks she would be good in either public affairs or broadcast journalism."

The volunteer publicity work led to an interview on a radio program. The moderator of the show took an interest in me and sent me two internal secretarial job listings with San Francisco radio stations. Although I did not land either job, one interviewing employer recommended me for a sales secretarial position with a local TV station—which I began in August 1975.

With the secretarial job in a field I wanted, I seemed at last to have my green light, my cosmic stamp of approval. I still had financial and ego problems to contend with as I worked my way up to a more responsible position. This job paid $145 a week, almost $4,000 a year less than my last salary as a teacher. But I had kept the faith, and my determination finally had pulled me through.

I have only now begun to recover financially from the decision to change careers. This is my fourth year in the Bay Area. My sense of confidence is healthier. I have established a network of contacts.

My decision to move into broadcast sales rather than into production, my original "creative" goal, has not been a disappointment. Production, it turned out, requires more of an investment in terms of years of preparation with less opportunity for advancement for women and probably less money.

After what I'd gone through while unemployed, I did not want to wait again—without certainty about money and the possibility of real professional achievement. And after I'd had a glimpse behind the scenes in my job as a sales secretary at a San Francisco television station, the romance and glamour of "show biz" faded for me.

My ambitions, my communications skills and my desire for professional status I decided would be better served on the business side of broadcasting, where there was greater incentive. Also, the understanding of what real financial independence is had become clear to me and one of my most important goals.

But my career building is not over. I feel, after changing careers and positioning myself on another path, I'm now on the threshold of realizing my creative and business potential, potential that is leading me to new goals and achievement. The biggest hurdle has been cleared.

I've had to change jobs five times in four years to gain promotions and raises: sales secretary, media assistant at the San Francisco branch of McCann Erickson, Inc., an advertising agency, assistant buyer, media buyer and account executive. Ahead lie sales commissions and possible management responsibility.

Sales seems to be the area where a woman can obtain earning power comparable to a man. In other areas of advertising, the discrepancy in salary levels still seems to exist. The rewards of my hard work and incentive are no longer locked into an annual salary. As an account executive at a San Francisco radio station, I now have a $12,000 base salary with commissions on any sales I make above $5,000 each month.

I am sure that there are easier ways to go about changing careers, but I implemented my decision in my own style and tempo. My story is not one of a series of lucky breaks. I worked to make it happen.

Has it been worth it? My answer is a definite yes. I took a risk, and it's beginning to pay off.

Chapter Eleven

Your Own Business

HOW TO BECOME AN ENTREPRENEUR

by Fran Weinstein

Why are more and more women today starting their own businesses? Why does *anyone* start a business?

To make money, for one thing. And to provide themselves with a more solvent alternative to joining or returning to the work force via the corporate ladder. Certainly, taking the entrepreneurial route is a high-risk venture, but that's where the dollars are.

According to a survey on women-owned businesses compiled by the US Bureau of Census in 1972, 402,025, or 4.6 percent, of the nation's firms are owned and operated by women. Most of these firms, which gross $8.1 billion in receipts, are sole proprietorships, concentrated in the retail trade and selected service industries.

Although these statistics represent modest gains, 1978 purports to be a better year. As part of a nationwide campaign, the US Small Business Administration has pledged

$100 million for guaranteed loans to encourage women to own businesses. Women's organizations and agencies across the country are being Federally and privately funded to expand and develop already existing programs.

Sufficient funding, though the most basic element, is not necessarily the most essential. Financial planning and control are— but traditionally women have been locked out of these areas. According to Beatrice Fitzpatrick, director of the American Women's Economic Development Corporation (a pilot program in New York that runs group sessions and gives technical and management assistance), "There is a scientific approach to running a business. Many women are not as concerned with the money as they are with the rules and resources for operating their businesses. They have to make use of the entrepreneurial skills they've always had—running a household, for instance—and apply them to their own advantage."

An increasing number of resource centers around the country are being set up to help women identify and learn to deal with problems unique to their businesses. Often top individuals in various fields—management, accounting, law, insurance—speak to groups at these centers and offer advice and encouragement. "Most entrepreneurship is a lonely business," Fitzgerald said. But these programs lend support as well as concrete education. If you want to start your own business, first decide whether your idea, product or service is realistic; whether there is a need for it (or whether you can create one); and whether the business will take advantage of your strongest attributes. Then secure venture capital, or start-up money.

Ken Burns, account officer at Citibank, advises the new business owner to seek out partners. "Most entrepreneurs want to hold on to everything themselves and don't want to give up a piece of the action. People starting out are reluctant to bring in partners, and that's where most loan proposals die."

Unless you are fortunate enough to have all the necessary funds on hand, you will need some sort of financial assistance. Commercial loans are given to established businesses only, and if you do not have a track record, you'll have to seek a personal loan.

Banks lend in two ways: against secured—dollar-for-dollar—financial statements that show the firm is a viable entity and can generate sufficient net income to satisfy the loan; and against liquid collateral (stocks, bonds, savings accounts, etc.). Real estate liens (creditor's right to collect debits out of property) are not acceptable.

Another vehicle for financial assistance is the Small Business Administration. Before seeking SBA loans, first you must have applied for a bank loan and been rejected. If you are refused, ask your banker to get you in touch with SBA. SBA assistance requires that the applicant be of good character and show sufficient motivation and capability to operate the business successfully; that the loan proposal is of sound value or sufficiently secured to assure payment; that the financial prospects of the firm are good, and that applicants possess a reasonable amount of capital to withstand possible losses, particularly in the early stages. If the SBA approves your loan request, it will guarantee up to 90 percent or $350,000 (whichever is less).

If you are teeming with self-confidence and are sure your idea can revolutionize a particular industry (or you've exhausted all other resources), you can go directly to a Small Business Investment Company. The Small Business Act of 1958 established privately owned and operated companies that will inject capital with lower interest rates and less stringent collateral requirements than bank loans. These are very selective institutions, sophisticated in procedure, and they naturally want to share in the profits if the business fares well; they finance by purchasing common stock or making straight loans. Usually they tend to invest in manufacturing and service industries (especially new products) because these have a high growth potential. They also provide management as well as financial assistance, which in many cases is of equal value.

Remember: One of the greatest obstacles for women in securing financial aid is low credibility in a male-dominated lending situation. Although the application process is fairly cut-and-dry, societal attitudes about women and money along with overt and covert sexual discrimination persist. Don't become intimidated. Not only are you in the right place, this is most definitely the right time for you to forge ahead.

To make a loan presentation:

1. Prepare an in-depth description of the type of business you want to set up.

2. List all prior experience and management skills.
3. Draw up an estimate of the amount of capital you have at your disposal, your assets and liabilities, and how much you will need.
4. Indicate how much you expect to earn during the first year.
5. Itemize collateral available for security and indicate the market value for each.

For further information about becoming an entrepreneur contact:

US Small Business Administration
1441 L Street NW
Washington, DC 20416 (202) 653-4000
American Women's Economic Development Corporation
250 Broadway
New York, NY 10007
Contact: Jean Reid (212) 566-8270
National Association of Women Business Owners
200 P Street NW, Suite 511
Washington, DC 20036 (202) 338-8966
Women Entrepreneurs
PO Box 26738
San Francisco, CA 94126
Contact: Sue Easton (415) 474-3000

New York Association of Women Business Owners/Enterprising Women
525 West End Avenue
New York, NY 10024
Contact: Ava Stern (212) 787-6780

Courses—for action!

CALIFORNIA
"The Entrepreneurial Woman"
Women's Program/UCLA
Los Angeles, CA 90024 (213) 825-3301
COLORADO
"How to Manage Your Own Business"
Colorado Economic Development Association
Denver, CO 80204 (303) 537-3919
ILLINOIS
"Women Going Into Business"
"Building Self-Employment"
YWCA 37 South Wabash
Chicago, IL 60603 (312) 372-6600

Best book bets:

A Woman's Guide to Starting a Business, by Genie Chipps, and Claudia Jessup, Holt, Rinehart and Winston, $7.95 (Paperback, $2.95).
Small Business Ideas for Women and How to Get Started, by Terri Hilton, Pilot Books, $2.00.

WHAT THE GOVERNMENT CAN DO TO SUPPORT YOU

by Patricia M. Cloherty

Getting into business must be a substantive undertaking, not predominantly an emotional one. It requires realistic thinking, strategizing and risk-taking over a period of time, which adds up to being open to success or failure.

At year-end 1976, women-owned and operated businesses represented some 5 per-

cent of the nation's total. As an indicator of recent activity, take the Small Business Administration's loan portfolio. SBA is an independent agency established by the Federal Government in 1953 for the purpose of giving financial and technical assistance to small businesses to subsist among the larger corporations. Of approximately $2 billion placed in direct and guaranteed loans for the first three-quarters of this fiscal year, loans to businesses owned and operated by women represented 14.3 percent of total loans (units, not dollars). This was up in excess of 3 percent from the same period in the previous fiscal year and was approximately double the third-quarter totals for fiscal year 1975, the first full year in which statistics on women's businesses were collected.

Take figures from professional schools. Women are enrolling in increasing numbers in higher educational institutions and in business schools. In 1966, only six women in 100 attending a college or university planned a career in business, engineering, law or medicine. That number is now up to 17 in 100, which, while still low, is an improvement.

There is evidence, then, of forward movement. If it is not at "deliberate speed," it is also not entirely at a glacial pace. Most encouraging is the evidence that young women are—of their own choice—preparing themselves to a greater extent than did many of us.

The reasons this preparation is taking place are equally evident. On the practical side, more and more women have become independent heads of households, and many other family units have found they cannot manage on the income of only one adult working outside the home. Basic need is one reason.

There is also a more profound dynamic at work, reflected in many women's stated desire both to express themselves in a business framework and, in so doing, to control their environment. In short, women want to be independent, taking their own lumps, but accomplishing—identifiably—their own gains. Looked at slightly differently, women as a group, with some outstanding exceptions, are latecomers to entrepreneurial drive—some women who have been through the rigors of owning a business might call it insanity—which has been fundamental to the build-up of our economy.

If women's participation in the total labor force now exceeds 50 percent, why is the representation of women among business owners/operators not greater? Why is it not increasing more rapidly? And what are the problems and prospects?

Stories abound of the difficulties and obstacles women face, because they are women, in entering the business arena. Male commercial bankers, investment bankers, SBA personnel, salesmen, suppliers, customers, colleagues' secretaries—and sometimes colleagues themselves—often demean women, consciously or unconsciously. This has many manifestations, and we all have our war stories.

This "treatment" issue can eat you alive. I think it should not. It is not the heart of the matter; control of resource *is*.

Not being taken seriously is a problem and a humiliating one, and having always to prove yourself is exhausting. But rather than berate the outside world, I would like to ask where it is that we women may unwittingly create some of our own obstacles.

First, on motivation, women can make a mistake in thinking that running a business is an answer to their negative impulse away from another unsatisfying pursuit. Frankly, business itself involves too much repetition and worry to satisfy that emotional need, by itself.

Second, many women have a diffuse ideological sense that the profit motive, and business generally, is suspect, if not outright bad. This view should be re-examined critically if one is to operate a surviving business entity.

Finally, we women create problems for ourselves when we fail to acknowledge, and then to acquire, the substantive tools that go into managing people and capital in the happy combination that makes for a successful company.

It is easy to think that small businesses, in which many of us get our start on the ownership trail, do not require such know-how, nor too much advance planning.

I wish to disabuse us all of that notion; it

simply isn't true. What is true for the small business owner is that she has less capital to work with, no capital cushion to allow her any serious mistakes and no staff to analyze strategic business options. In a small enterprise, everyone tends to be line—that is, everyone works many hours simply getting the product and/or service delivered, as opposed to having the benefit of staff analysts figuring out what you have, can do and should do.

Entering small business today, in fact, is largely a matter of electing to swim upstream. It is harder and more expensive to raise capital from traditional sources for a variety of reasons having to do with changes in the capital market structures. This is true no matter what sex you are. It is also more expensive to hire people and to buy fuel. It is difficult and expensive to comply with requirements of regulatory agencies, which, while they protect on the one hand, create burdens for small enterprises.

In short, the entrepreneurial option, just at the time that women are taking it, is exceedingly difficult in the US generally.

This adds up to an immense challenge for women seeking to get into business ownership at this time. It is not impossible—and I am the last person to dissuade anyone from trying. You see, I view small business ownership as one of few useful and value-producing activities that one can engage in, having benefits beyond personal gain. At the same time, there is a distinct premium on clear thinking—understanding fundamentals and preparedness for change—if one elects to move forward.

To assist women in this environment, last August the SBA undertook a major Women's Business Ownership Campaign. The goals of this campaign are to increase significantly the number of women entrepreneurs who own successful and profitable firms. By actively promoting women's business ownership, SBA is attempting to give women expanded opportunities in a time when entrepreneurial activity has become increasingly difficult.

The campaign has three major components: Management Assistance, Financial Assistance and Procurement Assistance. These elements will increase the utilization of existing resources and provide a well-rounded program for women.

Management Assistance

For starters, a series of 110 seminars is planned throughout the country to give women the opportunity of improving their basic business skills. Management assistance programs already in effect will also be utilized.

The SCORE/ACE program, a voluntary counseling program, is designed to give interested current and prospective business owners the opportunity to talk with retired and active business executives about business problems and pitfalls. The Call Contract Program provides management and technical assistance to economically and socially disadvantaged small businesses from professional consulting firms under contract with SBA.

Through the Small Business Institute (SBI) Program, senior and graduate students of the nation's leading schools of business provide volunteer on-site management counseling to small business owners. In addition, SBA-sponsored University Business Development Centers across the country provide counseling, training, research and development and technical assistance to small firms.

Financial Assistance

The second and most crucial part of the campaign is financial assistance. For the first quarter of the 1979 fiscal year, SBA has targeted $100 million for guaranteed business loans to women. Between October 1, 1976 and June 30, 1977, 14.3 percent of our business loan approvals went to women, an increase of 3.3 percent over last year.

Procurement Assistance

The Office of Procurement Assistance is now instituting a comprehensive and systematic search to locate and add to our source files the names of eligible, women-owned small businesses seeking government contracts.

Federal procurement specialists with SBA counsel and advise business owners on the mechanics of obtaining government contracting—this includes preparing bids for prime contracts and subcontracts, directing bidders to government agencies that use the products or services they supply and placing their names on bidders' lists.

For the first time, we will station an SBA counselor outside of our own offices. Specifically, at the First Women's Bank in New York City. She will be available to counsel women on how to seek credit, make financial projections, develop a business plan and select personnel.

We have designated a representative for women in business in each of the ten regional SBA offices and in the 63 district offices. This individual will be responsible for coordinating SBA efforts to assist businesswomen in the field. A women's bank rela-

tions officer will also be designated for each region. This individual will be primarily responsible for familiarizing the banking community with the problems and needs of women desiring entry into business. The banks will be encouraged to grant more SBA guaranteed loans to women and to realize the potential of many women business owners.

In time, we expect to increase the number of women loan officers, and supervisory loan officers and managers throughout our field offices and increase our employees' understanding of the problems and business situations women encounter. By utilizing these resources, we expect to show a marked improvement in all levels of Agency operation. We are determined that this program will succeed, and it will.

PATRICIA M. CLOHERTY *now holds the highest appointment ever given to a woman at the SBA.*

Adapted from a speech delivered during the New York Association of Business Owners' "Women In Business Week," September, 1977.

DO YOU HAVE WHAT IT TAKES TO BE AN ENTREPRENEUR?

by Mary Byrnes

Your *own* business. It's the American Dream. Every year, hundreds of thousands of hopeful entrepreneurs set out to make it come true. Most of them, reported the Small Business Administration, fail within their first year. A handful of those who take the risk succeed—spectacularly. The rest enjoy that special blend of profit and personal gratification that only the self-employed know.

What separates the few winners from the many losers? Planning, experience, talent, timing, connections, financial backing, luck—and a cluster of characteristics called

the entrepreneurial personality. Whether you're buying a fast-food franchise, opening a boutique or setting up an accounting firm, this special style and attitude *counts*. It's such a vital ingredient, in fact, that the Small Business Administration, along with a number of consulting firms, has developed a profile of entrepreneurial traits. Before you set up shop—even before you see your lawyer, your accountant or your bank officer—measure your attitudes and attributes against this ideal. It's a gauge that will show you how successful—and how satisfied—you'd be if you were your own boss.

FIND OUT IF YOU ARE AN ENTREPRENEURIAL WOMAN

True or False?

☐ 1. Financial security is extremely important to me.

☐ 2. I take longer than most people to make decisions.

☐ 3. One of the reasons I want my own business is to have more free time for myself.

☐ 4. My family's attitudes about my business plans are relatively unimportant to me.

☐ 5. I would characterize myself as impatient.

☐ 6. I enjoy working with other people.

☐ 7. My energy level is well above average.

☐ 8. I often find new and better ways of doing things.

☐ 9. I am well organized.

☐ 10. I dislike having to take other people's advice.

Answers

Most successful entrepreneurs would respond like this:

1. *False.* If financial security is vital to your emotional well-being, if you feel queasy when your stocks take a dip or when your bank balance drops sharply, you may not be happy or successful on your own. Entrepreneurs are, above all, risk takers—and the most successful usually are the most daring. Even well-established businesses pass through shaky periods, and the "boss" has to be willing and able to endure them.

2. *False.* Entrepreneurs are quick and confident decision-makers. The head of a small business doesn't have the corporate luxury of multiple meetings, conferences and consultations—nor does she have anyone to share the blame with if a decision turns out to be wrong. If you like management by committee, you may not enjoy being the solo decision-maker.

3. *False.* Successful entrepreneurs learn early in their careers that being the boss is a more-than-full-time occupation. And they usually wouldn't have it any other way. In its early phases, running your own business re-

quires more time than a job would require. Of course, you're free to set your own hours, but your workday and work week will be longer. Unless you're planning to establish a strictly part-time enterprise, don't expect three-day weekends and half-days off.

4. *False.* Support and cooperation from your family are vital when you're running your own business—much more so than when you're working for someone else. It's hard to give an enterprise the intense commitment and long hours it requires when you're up against opposition on the home front.

5. *False.* Patience and perseverance are absolutely essential to the entrepreneur. If you tend to explode when you're frustrated or to drop a project tht exasperates you, think twice about going into business for yourself. When you're on your own, you can't walk away from annoyances—without walking away from your livelihood. And remember, those start-up years—especially the first year—will have problems that rile even the most tranquil businesswoman.

6. *True.* If dealing with co-workers bothers you, don't think you can escape by setting up your own business. Entrepreneurs generally enjoy meeting and working with others. And they have lots of opportunity to indulge this preference. Even in a one-woman operation, you'll be in contact with a variety of people—customers or clients, suppliers, sales representatives, government agents. You'll have to relate to them in different ways—which can be a lot harder than just getting along with the "team" at the office.

7. *True.* Successful entrepreneurs usually are *dynamos*. They have to be. Their extraordinary energy is probably one thing that drew them out of the corporate world and into self-employment. If you never seem to wind down, if you're always looking for more to do on your present job, you probably have the kind of energy that could make you a successful business owner.

8. *True.* If you're the one in the company

who always seems to look for *and* find a better, faster, less-expensive way of doing something, then you have a talent that could help you succeed in your own business. Entrepreneurs, invariably, are original thinkers. Whether you're running a catering business from your own kitchen or working as a consultant to the Fortune 500, you have to have a knack for finding fresh approaches.

9. *True.* Be honest with yourself. Do you handle your present job in an organized way? Do you make and follow a plan for each project? Are your personal records, your checkbook, your bills in order? Are you a list maker? Do you keep a daily schedule? If you go into business for yourself, you'll have to do all these things. Even if you can afford a bookkeeper and a secretary, you'll still have to be the main organizing force. If you've already developed organizational skills, you have one valuable quality for success on your own.

10. *False.* Although she is self-confident and decisive, although she trusts her instincts, a successful entrepreneur knows that she has limits. She turns to specialists for special problems—her lawyer, her accountant, her insurance broker, consultants from such groups as the Small Business Administration, the Chamber of Commerce, the Corps of Retired Executives, business and trade organizations in the community. She knows how to balance their counsel with her own sense of what her business needs.

HOW TO ATTRACT MONEY

A Properly Prepared Business Plan Often Makes the Difference in Convincing Investors to Give the Capital You Need to Start Your Business

by Ellen Klugman

Arthur H. Kuriloff, lecturer on entrepreneurship at the Graduate School of Management at the University of California at Los Angeles (UCLA), is fond of children's stories. Excerpts from *Alice in Wonderland* find their way into his classes on small business development:

Alice: Would you tell me, please, which way I ought to go from here?
Cheshire cat: That depends on where you want to get to.
Alice: I don't much care where. . . .
Cheshire cat: Oh, you're sure to do that, if you only walk long enough.

Like Alice, the entrepreneur who lacks the guidance and direction of a definitive plan is sure to get "somewhere," said Kuriloff, "but it may not be a too-happy somewhere: folding up your venture; at best, selling it at a loss; or at worst, declaring bankruptcy."

The need for a business plan is emphasized by the dramatic number of small-business failures—up 25 percent for a record 3,106 from January through May 1980. Insufficient planning is one of the main reasons for such high rates of attrition.

Lenders and investors seek assurance that the business in which they are putting their capital is based on substantial experience, realistic appraisal of markets, competition and costs. The showcase for this information is a business plan or prospectus. Getting your loan or investment money often hinges on having the right plan. Kuriloff estimated that because the vast majority of plans are so poorly constructed, only three out of a hundred submitted to venture capitalists receive any scrutiny.

A well-constructed business plan documents your firsthand knowledge of the proposed business, an understanding of your market and competition, an analysis of financing costs and expected sales and profits, and a synopsis of your management skills and organizational game plan.

It's good business sense to send prospective funding sources a several-page letter summarizing the contents of the plan and to follow up with a phone call three to five days later. Then, if the source shows interest, send the entire plan.

"What potential investors want to see is not a treatise," cautioned Bruce Rossiter, president of the Golden Pacific Capital Corporation, a Los Angeles investment banking firm. Rossiter suggested that a plan be no less than 20 to 25 pages and no longer than 40 to 50 pages, *including* exhibits. The exact length and format will vary according to the nature and complexity of your enterprise.

Know Your Business

Lenders are not interested in having you learn on their money. If you are proposing an enterprise in a specialized area, such as computer software manufacturing, you should have worked several years in the field. If your general business experience and skills are strong and if expertise is not as essential to the business's success, you still may be able to gain the confidence of investors. Find out who the most successful people in your prospective field are—meet them if you haven't—and "pick their brains," as one female entrepreneur phrased it. To reassure lenders, submit the name of a successful specialist in that business who has consented to act as your resource.

You must demonstrate a thorough knowledge of your service or product in the first segment of the plan. This includes summaries of past and projected test data and results, and outlines of blueprints, or prototypes.

If you are offering a product, not a service, technical prerequisites of production, methods of quality control, design, durability, standardization and product safety should be addressed in this section. A discussion of plant locations and layout studies also may be appropriate.

To Market, To Market

There are a number of areas you will be expected to examine in the second part of your prospectus, such as: What are your market opportunities and risks? Who would be willing to purchase your product and why? Be specific about the uniqueness of your item—packaging, pricing, design. What is the existing market for similar products? What distribution and marketing techniques would you employ and why? What type of defensive campaign could you launch against competition price-cuts and other marketing strategies?

In addition, this second segment of your outline should define your main competition and the demographics of your market—age, income level, etc. If your business is cyclical, include your strategy to carry profit and sales through the slow seasons. Finally, outline the nature of your promotional campaign (direct-mail solicitation, newspaper/radio advertising).

Money Makes The World Go 'Round

The three financial documents basic to any prospectus are **the income statement** (profit and loss, or earnings statement); **the balance sheet** (a dollars-and-cents description of your business, listing all your assets and liabilities, as well as equity); and a **cash-flow statement** (a forecast of the cash a business expects to receive and disburse during a given period of time). These "pro formas," as they are known in financial lingo, should be computed monthly for the period of one year and on an annual basis for the next two to three years. An ongoing business concern would provide past statements so that investors can gauge the company's track record not only against similar enterprises but also against its own history. The fact that such companies *have* a history should make monthly and yearly financial predictions easier than that of a start-up company.

How can you project sales and income when you haven't yet begun your business? "I'll admit it's pretty pie in the sky," noted Rossiter. "But the other half in making these projections is that the entrepreneur is stating a commitment that she or he is going to try to do at *least* as well as the figures set out. The business plan is a game plan. We all know it's going to wind up a bit different."

Organizing the financial statements (known as "financials") is a step-by-step process. You can begin by researching each of the elements listed on a standard income form. (Most accounting or bookkeeping guides include income-form samples.) Draw on your past business experience for knowledge of sales patterns and costs, general industry statistics and any research you've conducted to arrive at an approximation for each category.

In addition, would-be investors seek several other financial indicators. The **break-even chart** forecasts the volume of service or product you must sell within a given time period before you realize any profit. **Ratio analysis** pits items from your balance sheet or operating income statement against one another to determine your company's fiscal fitness. Dun & Bradstreet's *Key Business Ratios* (check your library's business section) contains financial figures, sales, expenses, capital needs and profit percentages of several sizes of concerns and shows the low-, medium- and high-ratio perform-

ance of larger ($100,000 net worth and up) "small" companies in selected types of business.

After establishing the financial feasibility of your project, you must state how much of the financing costs you are willing to support. Investors want you to put your money where your mouth is. "You're expected to capitalize until it hurts," remarked Steven Brandt, senior lecturer in management at the Stanford University Graduate School of Management in Stanford, California.

What share of the business are you willing to give to investors in exchange for financial support? What share do you expect to retain? You should include certified statements of your net worth and several credit references as exhibits in this section.

People Power

"In the final analysis, investments generally are made in people, not in companies and concepts," claimed UCLA's Kuriloff. Past work experiences, family or professional relationships, special projects and skills should be related to your ability to make the proposed enterprise successful. You should explain briefly organizational structure, describe positions and include résumés of key personnel.

"I had to sell my banker on my business idea," remembered Ethel Craig, president of Country Classics, Inc., in Penn Grove, California. "By being organized, positive, having accurate statistical projections and showing a willingness to commit my own financial resources to the business, I got the money I needed."

Craig emphasized the importance of character and supplementary references to support your loan or investment application. She included in her plan copies of media publicity of her modest one-woman operation. Since receiving the start-up loan to manufacture redwood crafts kits sold through the invitational Tupperware-type party system, Country Classics, Inc., has grown from a garage operation to a 5,000-square-foot warehouse operation in only three years.

"Don't get discouraged if you don't get capital the first time," Craig said. You can gain valuable insights from rejections and use them in future attempts.

Time and Costs

Expect to spend at least six months of hard work on your business plan. What are the alternatives to the do-it-yourself approach? "As far as I'm concerned, there are no alternatives," Craig stated. "You have to do it yourself." Giving birth to her business plan, rather than adopting it from someone else's, helped Craig to internalize the plan's financials and other statistics. Those months of preparations gave her more confidence and helped her to convey that to her banker.

For the less adventurous, a local certified public accountant or a management consultant, listed in the Yellow Pages or recommended by a university business-school professor, can prepare or double-check your business plan. If you are setting up something more complicated than a single proprietorship, you should consult a local business attorney.

Words of Wisdom

"Be concise and be up front," advised Kuriloff. A table of contents should show the plan's organization. An executive summary should follow the contents, briefly addressing the how, when, where, why and how-much aspects of your proposed enterprise. Your conclusions and summary should recap your business goals and your profit and financing timetables; note projected schedule for a starting date; and restate financing percentage terms. Supporting documents, such as market data, production schedules, organizational charts and your financial sheets, should be included in the plan's appendix.

Writing a business plan is a difficult task.

Used as a vehicle to attract money and as a guidepost to your business's growth, a well-developed plan is a much more direct route "to there from here" than Alice's.

Reader Resources

Where to Find Business Information, by David Brownstone and Gorton Carruth, J. Wiley & Sons, 1979, $34.95. Describes over 5,000 public and private sources of business information, US and worldwide.

Financial Statements of Small Businesses, by S.B. Costales, Columbia Graphs, 18 Ventura Drive, Danielson, CT 06329, 1970, $7.50. Simplified study of analyzing financial conditions of a small enterprise.

The McGraw Hill Dictionary of Modern Economics, Douglas Greenwald and Associates, eds., 1973, $32.50. A lexicon to often confusing financial terms and concepts.

How to Start Your Own Business . . . and Succeed, by Arthur H. Kuriloff and John M. Hemphill Jr., revised edition, 1980, $16.95. A chapter-by-chapter approach to all stages of business planning for the layman. Includes worksheets and an appendix with sample business-plan outlines and applications.

Guide to Venture Capital Sources, by Stanley Rubel, Capital Publishing Corporation, Massachusetts, 1980, $49.50. A three-volume set of financial encyclopedias for the entrepreneur, including a directory of all venture capital firms, their officers, whom to contact and their investment interests and limits.

Start-up Manual #317: How to Develop a Successful Business Plan, $16.95, available through Research Department, American Entrepreneur's Association, 2311 Pontius Avenue, Los Angeles, CA 90064.

Small Business Administration Publications. You can get price and title lists from regional offices.

Note: Check prices before ordering. Many of these resources are available at public libraries.

THE NEXT STEP: EXPANDING A SMALL COMPANY

by Betsy Myers

Even in today's tight money market, some small businesses are ready to grow. But expanding a business is a complicated financial, managerial and psychological step. Raising growth capital, supervising physical expansion or relocation, increasing staff, learning new planning techniques and implementing new systems are just some of the considerations in shepherding your business from a one-woman operation into a larger company.

"The greatest barrier to expansion we've found in our experience with small businesses," says Gene Sheiniuk, vice-president of Gottfried Consultants, a management-consulting firm in Los Angeles, "is inside the owner's head. Changing the principal's mental set and attitude is a complicated task." Loré Caulfield, president-owner of Loré Lingerie, a million-dollar manufacturer of silk lingerie, agrees. "More than any other factor, I was the one that inhibited my company's growth. I was unsure of the company's potential for success, so I didn't plan for it."

Learning to Let Go

Indeed, the skills that make the entrepreneur's venture initially successful are not necessarily those she needs to run a larger business. Generally, the entrepreneur knows her company inside out and does most of the work herself—from assembling the product to selling, packing and shipping it to balancing the books at night. But once the company starts riding a growth curve, once large new orders start pouring in or a current client requires new products and services, the small-business owner may find she's in over her head. That's when she's called upon to make some changes in her

perceptions and business style. "I held onto the nitty-gritty aspects too long," says Caulfield. "I loved being out in the factory. That's the fun part. I felt I was being punished by having to sit in the office, even though I needed to be there."

The largest hurdle, Sheiniuk says, is learning to "let go," learning to delegate responsibility and decision-making authority to others. "In the beginning the business owner gave orders directly to employees," says Sheiniuk, "now, she must make room for a middle level of management if the business is to grow." Stewart Isbell, vice-president of the First Women's Bank in Santa Monica, California, underscores that point. "It's the human element; we like to be surrounded by things we are used to. What you have to look at is your cost per minute; the cost of doing it yourself."

Along with the recruiting and training of qualified personnel must come the willingness to let them make mistakes they can learn from. It may be as simple as allowing an office manager to take over routine administrative chores or as complicated as turning over a large part of the business to a new creative staff. Caulfield hired a vice-president of sales, bringing her number of employees to 40. "I liked running the business out of my head and hip pocket," she says, "but gradually I learned that businesses run on systems, not on people."

The business owner's territorial instincts are even sharper when it comes to capital investors. In the search for capital, the entrepreneur may shun creative avenues for financing (partners, mergers, venture capitalists, acquisitions, shareholders) for fear of giving up her ownership control. Again, it's a matter of letting go—trading off a portion of control for a piece of the larger action. Not wanting partners, Caulfield fought hard to retain sole ownership, waiting for years until her business grew large enough for her to secure bank financing for expansion.

Thinking Big

The business owner must learn to do things professionally and to seek and use outside professional advice. A CPA (instead of the neighborhood bookkeeper), specialty lawyers, sophisticated business equipment and computer consultants are needed as soon as the business grows beyond the expertise of those who helped start it. In an expanding business, the owner is faced with many new demands—providing fringe benefits for newly acquired, middle-level employees, for example, drawing up new contracts for suppliers and customers and introducing computerized billing and inventory-control systems. "Even though I was warned," Caulfield says of her $48,000 investment in a computer, "it set us back eight months to make the changeover." She concedes that computerization has dramatically improved her accounting, production, order-filling and inventory-control systems. Further, you will need to upgrade your offices in order to provide an amicable work environment. This project will require hiring experts in construction and decorating. "Entrepreneurs often are afraid of these costs," says Isbell. "It's a problem of education."

Planning for Growth

Another significant element is the often overlooked area of planning. "Growth is insidious," points out Sheiniuk. "One day you find you need twice as many accounting clerks or secretaries as you did yesterday. In order to avoid a crisis, you have to anticipate growth problems and deal with them before they appear. Small-business owners tend to wait until they're pushed to the wall before taking action. Under pressure, they often misjudge what is needed and have to start over." The tendency to close one's eyes may stem from a reluctance to let the business grow, a lack of financial or managerial expertise, a fear of added costs or limited vision.

As Isbell says, "Owners tell you that future sales cannot be projected. These are the same individuals who haven't done their homework or figured out where their business fits into the marketplace."

Part of the planning process involves evaluating your current status regularly and projecting your future sales and expenses—on paper. According to Isbell, up-to-the-minute statistics on *everything* in the business—from telephones to employee salaries—are a must. Small-business owners keep track of these costs instinctively, but they often can't articulate their systems to others. "Every quarter—and certainly twice a year—sit down and track inventory, sales trends and other factors that indicate how well the business is being managed," Sheiniuk advises. For instance, how many times do orders have to be turned down? For what reasons? What's the inventory size and turnover rate? Does the product satisfy customer needs? These fiscal and operating performance statistics identify key needs and profitability ratios. By carefully monitoring your vital statistics on an on-going basis, you know when growth and personnel are needed. With the aid of her computer, Caulfield prints out monthly financial statements. "I've learned how to analyze a financial statement, ask questions and get more information. I know how much is coming in each month, my needs for the short and long term and when schedules need to be changed."

Next, you should write out two,- three- and five-year pro-forma projections of anticipated sales, expenses and profits based on assumptions, such as growth at the rate of 6 percent (or 8 percent—your internal growth rate less inflation) a year. "Ask yourself," says Isbell, " 'where are the sales coming from? How are they to be financed and collected?' " "For the first time," Caulfield reports, "we have a yearly plan for 1981, and some long-range plans, as well." Taking the long view can alert the business owner to potential problems and opportunities. "It's a discipline, but learn to do it," advises Sheiniuk. "Check your projections regularly against reality and keep updating your plan. That way you'll be bringing scientific management to your business instead of raw intuition." The same principles apply to a business that sells services. "Hiring, delegating, planning, budgeting, marketing and managing also are 'musts' in the service industry," says Sheiniuk. "But that doesn't mean that the graphic designer or management consultant has to do it all herself. She still can contribute to the creative side of the business because she has others handling a lot of the responsibility for managerial chores."

Overexpansion is Tempting

Once the business owner has overcome the psychological hurdles, growth surges and she may feel indomitable. Overexpansion is a tempting lure, but before expanding, either geographically or into other areas (e.g., from manufacturer to distributor), "Make sure you have acquired a knowledgeable, functioning management team," Sheiniuk counsels. "Even if you know the business, success in one area doesn't guarantee success in others." "Always surround yourself with the best people," Caulfield warns. "Get a good staff. In the beginning I settled for fourth- or fifth-rate people because I had nothing to judge them against. I came to expect a lower level of competence. I went through 18 secretaries until I found a crackerjack one, and I pay her well. Now *she* has a secretary!"

Moving On

Finally, employers must offer a sense of the business's stability and growth potential—the livelihood of their employees depends on it. That means providing a competent replacement for yourself should you be unable, for any reason, to carry on. In essence, the business owner's ultimate goal is to work herself out of a job, knowing that the business should, and will, be able to flourish without her. Caulfield, a believer in serial careers, already is making plans for a return to academia and an English professorship, well assured that her business will be in good hands.

The growth from entrepreneur to company head, from doer to mover-and-shaker, is only a shift in job roles. "But it's a psychological can of worms," says Caulfield. "The transition is tremendous. I notice a difference in the way my employees react to me now. Women have a great need to be loved by their employees and co-workers, and that's a pitfall. I've learned that it's enough if they respect you." Isbell agrees, "A successful manager has to be able to tell people the coffee break is over. If you can't handle your authority, bring in an office manager."

By the successful transition from hands-on doer to administrator/supervisor, the entrepreneur has made the difficult step into the big time. "Successful business owners are happy, optimistic people," observes Isbell, "but they do their homework. They are not impulsive; they make well-thought-out decisions. Analytically inclined, they reason out financial and personnel problems and get along well with employees, suppliers and clients." Freed from the burden of the daily routines, the manager-owner gets things done through people. "Learn to train and motivate people," adds Sheiniuk. "Learn to work smarter, not harder."

BEAT THE ODDS:
THE TEN FATAL MISTAKES

by Denise Marcil and Richard Greene

More than half of all new businesses fail within the first five years of operation. "Figures from Dun & Bradstreet suggest that in over 90 percent of the cases, failure is due to the owners' lack of management ability," said Pat Burr, formerly of the Small Business Administration, now a business owner.

Getting the proper business training is the best way to reduce the odds of failing. One group that trains women business owners is the American Woman's Economic Development Corporation (AWED), a nonprofit, federally funded organization in New York. According to AWED, new entrepreneurs typically make the same mistakes:

1.

Not knowing what it will be like to be an entrepreneur. "I had read that you have to work harder than you ever had before," said Dorothy McInerney, owner of Serendipity, a wicker and giftware store in Drums, Pennsylvania. "It's true. When I opened, I wanted to do everything and I was exhausted every night."

Starting your own business takes courage, self-discipline, motivation and time, especially when you don't have the capital to hire people. A new venture requires more than working nine to five; often it means working six or seven days a week. For a year, possibly for much longer, you will have time for little else.

"You can't run a business in your spare time," said Beatrice Fitzpatrick, AWED's chief executive officer.

2.

Inadequate market study of product or service. Before you start a business, you should know whether there is a market for what you intend to sell, how best to reach that market and what your competition will be.

McInerney didn't perform a proper market survey before she opened her wicker shop. "I checked out department stores and gift shops in the area. None had what I wanted to carry." Luckily, there was a market for what she offered. But since she hadn't studied her market thoroughly, she found out too late that it was bigger than she'd expected: "Within ten months there were two other shops copying mine."

Lois Dale of Dale Carpet Center in New York took a wiser approach. She traveled around the country examining various businesses before deciding on the carpet-cleaning industry. She learned that steam cleaning for carpets and upholstery had been available on the East Coast for only two years. By offering on-location steam cleaning, she was able to provide a service unavailable from her competition. Continuing her market research, she was able to branch into carpet sales and installation.

3.

Inability to put together a business plan and to make profit projections. A business plan is at least a one-year projection of marketing and financial goals. "The idea is to *write* a description of your business," explained Mildred Finger, AWED's director of management training. "Define your market and make your operation as specific as possible."

Your marketing plan should describe your customer, pricing, distribution, advertising, publicity and employees. Your financial plan should explain your break-even point, your costs and overhead, cashflow projections and how much money you'll need to borrow.

Karon Cullen and Barbara Taylor of Cullen and Taylor, Ltd., a sales-promotion firm for the international travel and leisure industry based in New York, developed one- and five-year plans that "crystallized our goals," said Cullen. Their plans include having ten major accounts on retainer and five special promotions, such as one they've developed with *National Geographic* magazine.

4.

Lack of business experience. Most business owners open up shop knowing their product or service, but not how to run a business. Fitzpatrick advised, "Learn on someone else's time and money."

Marion Maienthau, an art consultant whose company, Marion/Art, specializes in providing art for corporations, originally worked for an art publisher. "I dealt with artists, organized showroom openings and worked with interior designers," she explained. "I had tremendous exposure to the art world and many contacts and business relationships that have made art available to me now."

Pat Cush, owner of Pat Cush and Associates, Inc., a firm that produces audio-visual and print programs for corporations and educational systems, had over 16 years' experience in educational publishing, sound filmstrips and multimedia packaging. "I knew what I was doing in the media area," she said, "but I didn't know the specifics of being an entrepreneur—financing, management."

5.

Insufficient capital and poor decision-making in expenditure of funds. Before opening your doors, you must determine how much money you'll need. If you're manufacturing a product, you need to know what it will cost you to produce it and how high you must price it to make a profit. Ask yourself such questions as: What are the things I'll need to spend capital on initially? What can be put off? When should I lease rather than buy

equipment? When should I increase my staff?

Raising the money you'll need often is difficult. Banks generally do not lend money to new firms—they want to see a track record before they'll underwrite a loan. Most new entrepreneurs start with savings and help from friends or family.

Judith Kalina, owner of Fable Soft Sculpture in Shenorock, New York, followed a typical pattern: "I worked at home to save overhead. I used my own savings, and my husband had a full-time job when I started. I also had money coming in from books I had written on crafts."

Even when business flourishes, you'll need a long period of success before you can expect outside aid. Although Kalina's sales nearly quadrupled in her first year, she had to put up collateral to secure a loan.

6.

Failure to work for a profit. According to AWED, women often are afraid to charge enough for their goods or services. They may not keep accurate records of income and expenses, so their product isn't priced to make money.

Sandra Merriman, an interior designer in New York, said she lost money during her first two years in business. She no longer offers free consultations to potential clients: "I keep time sheets on everything I do."

When Alice Rowan started Carriage House Coffee and Teas in New York, she was afraid to pass on price increases to her customers. "I found myself refraining from raising my own prices when wholesale prices would go up," she said. "I've since gained the confidence."

7.

Inability to manage time. Proper time management means allocating your time to suit your goals. This includes making a daily list of priorities, such as phone calls, letters and follow-up correspondence.

Art-consultant Maienthau deliberated

whether to spend an hour delivering a painting to a client herself or to pay a messenger to do it. She decided it would be more profitable to devote the hour to making phone calls that could generate income.

Maienthau also found that using galleries as a source for art was more efficient than dealing with individual artists. Although she pays the galleries a higher commission, she can collect ten to 12 graphics in one stop.

8.

Lack of professional relationships. As an entrepreneur, you'll need to establish strong working relationships with accountants, bankers and lawyers. An accountant can prepare financial records, including balance sheets and profit-and-loss statements. Other services include telling you how you're doing in relation to other businesses in your industry and developing accounting systems.

You should get to know your local bank branch manager—it's helpful when you apply for a loan.

You'll need a good lawyer who understands your business. An attorney will help you to avoid costly mistakes in matters such as contracts, leases and incorporation. The best way to find any one of these professionals is to talk with friends and business associates. To give yourself a support system—for your emotional well-being as well as your career—look into professional societies and women's business organizations.

9.

Failure to acquire new business. Typically, when entrepreneurs start out, they have some connections and often some business. When these sources are used up, they must hustle for more clients.

"You have to have the desire to be successful so that you don't give up," emphasized Geraldine Gibney, president of Gerri G., Inc., a Staten Island, New York, personnel agency. "If you believe in yourself and your product, you can generate enthusiasm in others. If you fail to hustle, your business probably will fail."

Audio-visual producer Cush agreed. She feels that in a brand new business, you can spend up to 75 percent of your time hustling. Then, as the work comes in, you must adjust your time, spending more of it to complete obligations. Later on you can pay others to handle the work while you're out selling.

10.

Failure to pick the right location. You must be physically located to best tap your market. Sometimes you can work out of your house, as art-consultant Maienthau does. But in a retail operation, being one block away from the right location can kill you.

Gibney's employment agency is situated near the Staten Island ferry, an active location. "In the temporary-employment business, you must be visible and convenient," she explained, "because the candidates for these positions are impulse people."

Will doing all this planning ensure success? So far, AWED has trained more than 390 women entrepreneurs—and only three have failed. With proper planning and professional advice, you can open your doors with confidence.

FOR MORE INFORMATION

The Guide to the US Department of Commerce for Women Business Owners is available for $2.75 from the Superintendent of Documents, US Government Printing Office, Washington, DC 20402. Ask for *The Guide,* stock #003-000-00556-9.

For a free copy of the revised edition of the pamphlet *Women and the US Small Business Administration,* which describes the kinds of financial management and contracting assistance available at SBA offices throughout the country, write: Office of Women in Business, SBA, 1441 L Street NW, Washington, DC 20416.

Part Five

The Total You

Chapter Twelve

Heart and Home

WHEN YOUR WORK AND YOUR MAN COLLIDE

by Nena and George O'Neill

Last night Mark lost his temper because she had overdone the steak. This morning he blew up because she burned the muffins. His rage was so disproportionate to the offense, Erica was tempted to say, "Why the hell don't you do the muffins yourself?" except that the irrationality of his behavior itself frightened her. He had rattled her so much in fact that when she finally rushed off to work, she left her commutation book behind.

Mark had been keeping up a flow of complaints for the past few months. His fault-finding, on the pettiest level, was tireless. There was never any time to talk, he said, when she worked late. Yet when she was home on time and wanted to talk over vacation plans or her sister Jane's problems, he hid behind the newspaper or a book. He grumbled about cat hairs on the couch, and said her lipstick was too pale, her shoes too high heeled, her hair too short. Two nights ago, he gleefully recounted to friends her latest goof on the new job, the touch of malice in his laughter unmistakable.

What was really troubling Erica's husband was her job. Not an uncommon situation, and guaranteed to be painful and persistent. Jealousy just does not evaporate. Jealousy is a torturous emotion, a passionate and agonizing response to the threat of loss. It is a fear that the person we possess or love is being taken away from us and that we are powerless to prevent it.

Envy too can enter the picture, although it is less intense than jealousy. When you feel envy you want something someone else has, while jealousy is the fear of losing something you already have. The midlife period for a man can be especially trying when his wife has moved into a new career after years at home. When Louis R. talked about his wife Moira, he shook his head at the irony of it all and at his own helplessness. "It was bad enough when she went back to school, but now that she has this new appointment, it's worse. Here she is starting out fresh and enthusiastic when I've accomplished all I can in the company. While I'm routinely shoveling around papers, Moira's racing around looking more vibrant and more attractive. She has a whole new world to conquer, and I feel like a set of files packed away on a shelf. Sure I'm envious."

A man coping with jealousy over his wife's job may be relatively new, but many women have always felt jealous of their husband's work. However, since men have always been expected to work and earn a living, few women could justify these feelings. When husbands worked long and late at the office, spent days on end in overtime or extensive time in travel, many wives did feel a sense of abandonment, rejection or betrayal, but most often they suffered in silence, bottling up their resentment, hiding their jealousy, or diverting it into complaints.

Jealousy can destroy a relationship unless it is recognized and dealt with. Barbara G.'s promotion to the head of public relations at her cosmetic firm made enormous demands on her time. A new publicity campaign and clients to get acquainted with kept her overtime in the office and on the phone during evenings at home. Her husband, Tom, who always finished at his insurance desk at five P.M., began to show his resentment in snide comments or hostile silence. Barbara, in turn, became angry because she found the breakfast dishes still in the sink even though he had been home for hours. They stopped exchanging their customary welcome home kisses, and their arguments increased in both intensity and frequency. When she was free on weekends he managed to be busy with insurance reports. She felt her husband didn't understand the pressures she was under, and he grew increasingly resentful of the glamour of her job. By the time Barbara felt in control of her job and had settled down to more normal hours, they were strangers living in separate inimical camps. If, early on, they had expressed their real

feelings, they might have been able to manage their problem better.

But men are not accustomed to expressing their feelings, least of all about job jealousy. If a man is sophisticated, heaven forbid he should resent his wife's working or question the touted benefits of having an emerging woman around. If he is less sophisticated and more tradition bound, he will feel freer to complain about the lack of wifely services he thinks he deserves. In either case, the real issue of jealousy is rarely discussed. Instead, his resentment goes underground to seethe and percolate through all aspects of the relationship. Job jealousy is every bit as tenacious and dangerous as sexual jealousy. Adjusting to it means a fundamental change in restructuring your life together.

Your husband or lover may have encouraged you to work, he may be justly proud of you and happy for the income, but what he feels most deeply may be hidden not only from you but from himself. He may feel threatened by your contacts with others. He really believes that an interesting and involved wife or girlfriend is better than a dull drone, but he isn't quite prepared for the discovery that she thereby becomes more interesting to others too.

Besides, his jealousy and sense of loss may be justified. Achievement is a demanding taskmaster. You may have become so involved in your work that you have ignored him, and he feels left out. Bolstered by the rewards of long deserved recognition, you may be feeling your oats and a sense of rivalry may develop. How are you behaving toward him now that you feel so good about yourself? Are you, perhaps quite unconsciously, expressing an attitude that says, "See what I can do?" Competition, ever present in any relationship, can lead you into putting him down without being entirely conscious of it.

Since unremitting jealousy signifies insecurity, the real question, however, is not what can you do to alleviate his jealousy, but why is your man's self-esteem at such low ebb? Your job may not be the main factor. Other concerns may be eroding his self-esteem—such as a recent failure, problems on his job, or worry over his age or health, his future, or his other relationships. If a man's self-esteem depends heavily on having a traditional wife around to shore up his ego, then he will be in crisis when you step out of that role.

He may feel that you are withdrawing your love, demonstrating that jealousy is only the top of the iceberg of unresolved problems from childhood. Insecurities about love or self-worth may stem from legacies our parents left us. He may be expecting you to make up for everything he missed at home. You may be expecting the same from him. He expects you to be his mother; you expect him to be forever the father, patting you on the head for your accomplishments, always there to back you up. And neither of you may have yet moved into an adult partnership.

Once you and, more importantly, your man realize the need to tackle these underlying roots of jealousy, you *can* do something about the loss of power that jealousy represents. The noted psychoanalyst Dr. Rollo May has described jealousy as "a demanding possessiveness, which arises in direct proportion to one's sense of powerlessness." And powerlessness if bottled up, will blow up. Some feelings of jealousy are natural in any love relationship. Only if we felt indifference could we get rid of all our feelings of possessiveness. The negative and destructive aspects of this corrosive emotion can be controlled by the following measures. (Only when they can't be controlled do you know the problem needs professional help.)

Talk about it. Tell him how you feel and encourage him to do the same. Leave room for anger but deal with it constructively by putting your feelings in "I" messages, such as "I feel angry because . . . , I am angry when I. . . ." Express your own guilt about not doing all that has been expected of you, if that is what you feel.

Don't be negative and accusatory. Instead of saying, "You're always complaining and nagging at me," make a positive statement like "Hey, I'd really like a compliment once in a while," and you might gently remind him that he for his part can change "You never have any time for me anymore," into "I wish we could share more time together."

Bringing things out into the open will make it easier for him to explore why he is jealous and what he can do to stop feeling jealous. At this point, it is not what *you* can do to stop it, but what *he* can do about it. Powerlessness diminishes when we take action. As Dr. May suggests, "The easing of jealousy requires that one cease continually asking what the other person is doing. . . . It requires turning one's attention to one's self and asking: Why is my self-esteem so low?"

This may bring up his discouragements about his job, his hunger for new interests and goals, or a need to feel more involved in your life. It may open up whole new insights into how you have looked at your roles in marriage. Certainly it will mean self-examination. As one man said, "I had to ask myself, if I really love her, why should I resent her enjoyment and the sense of accomplishment she is experiencing? Why should I feel I have to be the *only* important thing in her life? Most important, but all important, no. For the first time in my life, I had to do some digging into myself." Is his esteem based on his own individuality, his own achievement, or is it based on a masculine ego trip? Does he depend too much on you to fulfill his needs? Some dependency is normal in any intimate relationship, but too much means we are using the other person as a crutch.

Make room for ambivalence in your relationship. Give each other space for down periods, accepting them as a part of any working relationship; realize that our emotions are often contradictory and shaded, rarely pure and simple. Don't give in to hopelessness. Jealousy is not the end of the world. Low self-esteem doesn't have to last forever. Something can be done about both.

Don't give in to placating him, either. This is not the time to say, "Yes, dear, I'll come straight home from work every night," or to cancel a dinner or other work-related meeting because he is not invited and feels left out. This is not the time to underplay your job, fake incompetence, or coddle him. It is not necessary to sacrifice your newly won gains. It *is* a time to reconsider his needs and yours in establishing a new balance in your relationship. You may, indeed, have neglected him and your relationship and need to reconsider your priorities. But change in this area should mean adding something, not subtracting what you already have.

Hold fast to a restructuring of your life together that gives each of you space to grow in your individual spheres and to share this growth with each other. To do this, women need more of what Dr. May calls "nutrient power, in which we assert ourselves for the sake of the person we love." Women must assert their own rights and needs with gentleness but firmness. It can be done with full consideration for their husbands' needs, but not a capitulation to old patterns. By asserting yourself and an equality of needs in your relationship, you help him to grow. To love a man in a way that enables him to grow requires a feeling of inner worth. You cannot give this feeling of inner worth to your partner, you can only help him to gain it for himself.

Involve him in your work. Ask his advice, draw him into your situation. If he feels he is participating, the element of threat will be reduced. Talk about your job. Make it concrete in detail. Express your feelings, concerns, anxieties, and sense of competency gained. Jealousy is aggravated by imagination. He may fantasize about the glamour of your job until you detail the routine. If both of you know more about each other's work, you can share these separate spheres with greater empathy for each other.

Encourage his interests, whether it is his work, a hobby, or a dream. Dreams serve important functions in our lives and provide bridges to the future. He may need to learn to be alone or to fill his spare time now that you are working. If his only interest is his career, suggest that he expand a little and find new ones.

Introduce him to people on your job. The Lothario he imagines hidden in the office may become a lamb out in the open. Describe the people you work with or have lunch with. If he knows something about them, he is less likely to fantasize.

Set aside time for yourselves: This is time for the two of you alone, no friends, no children. It should provide enjoyment in your relationship, a reinforcing of the love and interests you share.

Little gestures—a touch on the arm, a kiss on the cheek, or a squeeze on the shoulder—let him know you're with him emotionally. All of us need these reaffirmations, the touch that tells us no matter what our differences or disagreements, we are still together and that the pain that sometimes causes us to suffer is an unavoidable part of growing, whatever our age.

A Marriage That Made It . . .

When the telephone rings at the big stone front, split-level in suburban Philadelphia and a caller asks for Dr. Feldman, the standard reply is, "Which one?" Husky, gray-maned John Feldman is a physician specializing in allergies. His breathless wife, Janice, is a psychologist and has her hand in more pies than Sara Lee. She counsels private patients, teaches, and as a consultant to several government and religious agencies, has lately been spending an increasing amount of time flying around the country while John is more and more at home alone reading by the bed lamp.

Next March, the Feldmans will celebrate their thirtieth anniversary, and if their good health holds, there's every indication they'll keep toasting each other into old age. How is it they manage to stay happily married in a situation where the wife's demanding career would drive most husbands straight to the divorce courts?

The answer seems to lie in Janice's sense of priorities. She makes it abundantly clear that no matter how busy she is, her family is of primary concern.

For instance, there has never been any question where the Feldman cousins, aunts, and uncles would go for holiday or family dinners, graduation, or engagement parties. When their eldest son returned not long ago from studying in Israel, without batting one of her green-shadowed eyes, Janice organized four separate open houses so he could greet family and friends. And she and John regularly take a two- to three-week summer vacation.

"You see," John explains, "Janice has always worked. During the first years of our marriage when I was in school or, later, an intern making $100 a month, she actually supported us. After our boys were born, she continued to work part time because she wanted to. She'd have gone insane at home looking at four boys and four walls."

The part-time arrangement worked smoothly until 1963 when Janice decided she wanted to change careers from city planning to psychology. The fastest and most convenient route led to a college where she'd frequently have to attend classes during dinner. It was agreed she'd prepare the meals before she left and John would come home to eat with the boys. Some of her other duties were assumed by a cleaning lady and a baby sitter.

If the boys needed shoes and she had to study, John never minded taking them shopping. In fact, when anybody asked how he felt about his wife going to graduate school, he had a ready answer, "It's the best insurance policy I can leave her. If anything should happen to me, she'll always be able to support herself."

But lately as Janice's career has burgeoned beyond either of their expectations,

John admits to an uneasiness he has never felt before. He explains, "When Janice had to travel part of the week or once a month, it wasn't any problem. But she's expanding so rapidly that when she comes back, she's loaded with messages and appointments, and it's like she *isn't* home even when she *is* home. We just don't have the leisure any more to do things spontaneously. If one of the kids unexpectedly drops in from out of town, Janice inevitably has a counseling session she booked six months ago and can't change. Sometimes I feel like she has to squeeze us in."

Janice is well aware of what's happening. Last month one of her sons placed a cupcake with a candle in front of her dinner plate. That has always been the family symbol for a birthday celebration. "They were telling me humorously," Janice understood, "that my being at home had become a special event. I read them loud and clear," she says, "and it's an awful conflict. At one level, I'm riding this great ego trip. I feel valued and I'm making money and I am successful. But at another level, I feel really badly because of the trouble I am creating at home.

"I feel," Janice says, "like I am heading for an impending disaster. I keep saying I'll cut back. The first year I said it, some of the family believed me. The second year I said it, I got, 'Where have we heard that before?' This year they said, 'Show me.' "

Janice sees this as the best and worst time in her life. Occasionally, she has the sense to do something about it. One Saturday, last fall, she turned to John after a particularly horrendous week and said, "What are you doing today?" When he replied, "Nothing special," she stuck her work in the drawer and they went off to the country for a long lunch and an afternoon of antiquing.

Though John keeps quite busy—he's active in Boy Scouts—his is the more flexible schedule. He rarely objects to fitting his plans to Janice's or running interference for her when she needs it. He's the one who answers their home phone, screens her calls, and takes messages if he thinks she ought to rest. He's the one who worries when she goes out of town that she will forget to leave a number where she can be reached, or get lost because of her poor sense of direction. And Janice is the one who knows she's lucky.

"I married the right person for me. I started dating John when I was sixteen. I must have known that I needed somebody who'd be intelligent, share my values, and take care of things. John has always been supportive and nurturing. Some awful person recently circulated ugly harmful rumors that I was having an affair. Utterly ridiculous. John gives me exactly what I need."

And what does he get in return? A wife who is bright, alive, exciting, who loves him and their children in a very traditional way. "I never questioned where I stood with Janice," John says. "Every important family occasion we've shared together. It's like the story of the asthmatic patient who comes to my office complaining bitterly his nose is stuffy yet forgetting he's been so well he hasn't wheezed or needed medicine in weeks. As a physician I consider him a successful case. These problems Janice and I are presently having with her hectic schedule are annoying, even irritating. But in terms of our total life together, they aren't very major. I know she has a strong commitment to our marraige. No matter where she is, a part of her is always here."

. . . and One That Didn't.

Hank Dolan opens the door to a stylish blue and white apartment with hanging plants in the windows, an oriental carpet on the floor, and fresh flowers on the dining room table. The smell of a cake in the oven sweetens the air. Hank, a design engineer in his mid fifties who owns his own firm, introduces his second wife, Mary, and over a Scotch and soda, talks about why his first wife's immersion in her work destroyed their marriage.

"We were married twenty years and ex-

tremely happy for at least fifteen of them. Elaine, my former wife, was working when I met her as head of the English Department at a high school. And she continued until after her first miscarriage. She had problem pregnancies and had to be in bed most of the nine months. In ten years she had six miscarraiges to come up with four children, children we both wanted.

"I guess she first returned to teaching Sunday School when our youngest was two or three. The church had always been very much part of our lives. Then she began tutoring after school, and I had no objections to that either. I never wanted her to feel bound to her apron strings. She was too bright and too energetic. But that wasn't enough. She started substituting in the public schools. That led to a position of permanent subbing, filling in for a teacher on maternity or sick leave. And in the midst of this, she took up tennis.

"Everybody takes up hobbies, but Elaine did things with a vengeance. She would play at seven in the morning and a couple of nights a week. She got the kids involved. I even played for a while, though I never really liked it. I prefer golf.

"Then with the tennis, the teaching, the tutoring, the Sunday School, the big house and the four kids, she decides she's still not happy. She doesn't like permanent subbing because it is not her field. Since there was no market for English teachers, she'll become a math teacher. She'd minored in math in college. So in addition to everything else, she had to study and be tutored at home to get her Teacher Certification in math. And she passed, too. Her day dawned before 6 A.M. and ended after 2 A.M. Through all this, she's an excellent mother, but somebody had to suffer. Guess who?

"It was one of those gradual things. I realized four or five months had gone by and we hadn't been out together. If I wanted to go to a movie on Saturday night, I took my daughter. We stopped playing bridge. We'd had lots and lots of friends and they fell by the wayside, because she'd always made our social plans and she was too busy to keep up the contacts. Her studying or her lesson preparation was so time-consuming that we'd be invited to a party and she'd tell me to go alone. She was too busy with her work.

"Elaine had always been an interested and interesting person, but when she got embroiled in all this, I no longer had somebody at home to talk to. I missed that. I felt she had to shove it in my face that she was a person with important work too. Around this time, I had some financial problems—I had gotten involved in a deal that turned sour—and I asked her to help with our expenses. She told me her money was her own. She earned it. I never saw a penny of it.

"I tried to talk to her. 'Elaine,' I said, 'this is crazy. You're either super keyed up or super tired. I have to make an appointment to see you and when I do, you allot me two minutes and tell me you have laundry, or the kids' homework, or papers to mark. You've got a timetable for everything; I don't fit in it.' She'd say, 'Just let me pass this exam; just let me get through this term.' But nothing changed. I felt like I was standing under a coal chute. I knew what was coming, but I couldn't get out of the way.

"Okay, I understood she needed outside stimulation. I tried to accept that her home and her husband weren't fulfilling her. But it wounded my ego, I can tell you. A man has limits. She complained I didn't assume enough responsibility around the house. But my attitude was I work like a bastard all day, and I'm not coming home to more work. I did my share with the kids. I coached their basketball teams, drove them to piano lessons in the evenings, things like that. But I'd be damned if I was going to help with dishes or the laundry.

"Finally, we went to a marriage counselor. He told her she'd have to make time available for me if we were to survive. We tried going out together more often, but by this point, our communication had boiled down to a vindictive battle. One night I moved out of our bedroom into the study and made up my mind we'd just lead separate lives under one roof so our kids could have a father on the premises. A few days later, my partner reads me from the notices in the newspaper that my wife has filed for divorce.

"I know she never expected it to go through. Mutual friends told me she thought I'd come crawling back, that I was so weak I'd never be able to cope. Well, I called her bluff.

"Elaine had this big fat inferiority complex. She had to prove to the world how able she was. A man can only tolerate for so long a woman who's total energies go into her own thing. Well, she's got her work now. The kids have grown and pretty much look after themselves. She doesn't have me or a house to take care of.

"Certainly, I'm better off. I have a new wife who puts our life before anything else. She'd be bored at home so she has a sales job, and that's fine with me. I don't even mind the Sundays she has to work during Christmas season because I know what's important to her. And I know if I need her to go somewhere with me, she will leave work early. It's such a pleasure now for me to invite people to my home. I never did much of that before. Elaine always acted like it was a chore to be with my clients. Mary is an asset to my business.

"Even more, Mary is my friend first and my wife second. I may not have anything earthshaking to tell her when I come home—where I ate lunch or a funny incident at the office—but she's there to listen. When Elaine went back to work I felt deprived of a companion and a caretaker. Now I have found both again, and I am happy."

GEORGE AND NENA O'NEILL *are an anthropologist team who have been researching modern marriage since 1967. They are the authors of* Open Marriage *and* Shifting Gears.

WHEN YOU'RE MORE SUCCESSFUL THAN HE IS

by Jane Ruppersburg

Tony, a talented free-lance writer whose current job had ended suddenly, hung up the phone on Susan, the woman he lived with, shouting: "I can't stand it! I can't stand it!" What he couldn't stand was the devastating blow to his ego when Susan proudly announced that her first novel had been accepted for publication.

In those few moments, their roles had reversed. Always the breadwinner in the past, Tony was deeply depressed over not being able to support Susan and make alimony payments to his former wife. Susan, on the other hand, had never made enough from writing assignments even to get by. Now with a $15,000 book contract and royalties, she could support them both.

Instead of being proud of Susan, sharing her excitement or at least being relieved that he no longer had to worry about unpaid bills, Tony was shattered. Her good fortune was too much for him to live with and, after a few weeks, he moved out of their apartment. A short time later, Tony had enough writing assignments to live comfortably for the rest of the year, but his break with Susan seemed irreparable.

"I can't help it," he said. "I'm attracted to intelligent women, but I don't want a woman who's going to be the breadwinner, who's going to be the star. I can't handle that. I probably should date a nice file clerk, but I never fall in love with anyone like that."

For Susan, Tony's behavior was a double blow—he'd robbed her of any pleasure in her long-awaited success, *and* he'd destroyed a relationship she had thought they both valued.

A Double-Edged Problem

It would be nice to think that Tony's reaction was unusual, caused by his own peculiar immaturity, but as more women go to work and become successful, marriage counselors and similar professionals find such problems on the increase. In too many cases, society still expects the man to be the more successful of the two, to take home the bigger paycheck, to have more status. Until a few years ago, he almost always did. Today that situation is changing—but stereotypes are slow to die.

Some couples can make the new financial and emotional switch successfully; others are pulled apart. Aaron Weiss, PhD, a New York psychologist, said that this is a double-edged problem, one that affects both sexes but for different reasons. "What we are facing are the effects of social conditioning" said Weiss. "The man may suffer the more obvious psychological feelings of emasculation, but the woman, who has been taught that the man should support her, may be threatened as well."

Early-Warning Signals

To head off the problem, it is important to recognize some early-warning signals and take steps to deal with the tensions that set them off:

- **Competitive resentment:** He may complain about the time and attention she devotes to her job. She may begin to show impatience at his failure to keep up: After all, *she* has made it—why can't *he* go out and do the same?
- **Increasing criticism:** Rather than complaining about her work directly, he may single out more vulnerable aspects of her performance, harping on sketchy housekeeping, hurried meals and so on. She may disparage attitudes and opinions of his that previously she had seemed to accept.
- **Withdrawal:** She finds him unwilling to listen when she mentions new interests

and problems connected with her job, or he finds her preoccupied. One or both partners may turn off sexually.

Money Troubles

Several of these symptoms plagued Michele and Peter's ten-year marriage before they finally split up—a month after she was promoted to a $30,000 position. Peter had received a promotion just weeks before, but his pay was much less than hers.

"We had gotten married at 17," said Michele. "We went through school together, settled down in Lake Worth, Florida, and started out at the bottom. Peter wrote obituaries; I worked as a receptionist, a secretary, all those types of jobs. He became reporter and I worked as a researcher. Then, at about the same time, we both got promotions—Peter to night editor of his local newspaper and I to editor of a larger publication. For the first time, we had all this money. Suddenly I could buy just about anything I wanted.

"Our attitudes began changing. I had tried to be the perfect wife, sometimes spending hours preparing a weekend meal. Then, suddenly, my time seemed more valuable. I would throw a meal together and say, 'Well, it's food.' "

Michele remembered that they had never argued over money until after her promotion, when Peter began accusing her of being too materialistic and she accused him of not being success oriented. "We've both changed," she said. "Peter now heads a team of investigative reporters, but he has become more introspective. I'm more outgoing. I'm taking dancing lessons; I'm traveling. I'm much happier being independent, and I don't think Peter has any regrets, either. He and I share our 7-year-old son, Erik—Peter has him three days a week, and I have him four. Peter and his girl friend are taking a trip to Europe next month. I think he's happy now, and that's what really counts, isn't it?' "

Taking Time To Communicate

The best way to cope with tensions over a woman's success is to communicate, Weiss said. "Talk it through. *Don't* ignore it. Sit down together and evaluate the situation. Both of you should bring your fears into the open. The woman should say to the man, 'OK, I'm making more money than you are. How will this affect our lives? I will be busier; I may have less time for housekeeping.' Get him involved. Give him a chance to say, "I think your new job is terrific, but it could cause problems with the children." Discuss whether you can afford domestic help and how it will change your financial situation—whether you should have a joint bank account or separate ones. Examine the whole relationship, the intellectual, emotional and practical aspects."

Three Couples Who Made It

Some couples have fewer problems coping with the woman's greater financial and professional success. Good communication is the "how" and the happiness of both partners is the "why" their relationships work the way they do.

Carol and Steve live in Brooklyn, New York, and have been married for three years. Carol teaches third grade at an annual salary of $8,500 and is studying for her master's degree. She wants to have a family someday.

Steve, a former liberal-arts major, is trying to build a career in drama. He writes screenplays and auditions for stage parts—he also experiences a lot of rejection. To help Carol support them, he waits on tables in an Italian restaurant for about $2,000 a year.

At this point, Carol feels very supportive of Steve: "People tell me, 'I don't believe what you're doing; you're remarkable.' I don't think I'm making a big sacrifice, and I'd do it again."

Carol is not worried about finances. "Maybe I should be, but no matter how much money you have, it doesn't bring you happiness if you aren't doing what you want to do."

Steve is producing and acting in an off-Broadway comedy. "He asks my opinion, gets me to act as a critic out in the audience," Carol said. "He's trying everything he can think of. He just sent a play off to the West Coast, he's written proposals for ABC-TV, and they've even called him in. Steve has come close. If someday he decides he can't take the rejection, then it will be his decision. Sure, he could always get a regular nine-to-five job, but he wouldn't be happy, and probably neither would I."

Talking and Sharing

Conrad and Mel, who live in New York City, had been married for six years before Conrad decided he hated being a mechanical engineer in a large corporation. "I held on for another two years," recalled Conrad, "so that we could save money. Then I quit my job and started a full-time degree program in clinical psychology. I'm in my second year, and I have two years to go."

His wife, Mel, brings in more than $20,000 a year as an administrative associate of a grant-making foundation. She described her husband's career switch as a "team decision."

"We decided that since Conrad was not happy, he should go back to school. He's interested in politics, psychology, a variety of things. I always thought he would teach.

"We give each other a lot of support," said Mel. "We talk things out and share. I make a fairly good salary, so I tend not to worry about money. If my job fell through tomorrow, we still would figure out a way. The important thing is to do what makes you happy."

Even with the help of a supportive wife, Conrad has difficult moments. "My family has always believed that the man should bring in the income, and sometimes when I'll want to buy my mother something, she'll say, 'Don't; you know it's Mel's money.'

"Sometimes I look at our bank balance and say, 'Oh, my God, I should be out there working.' Then Mel reminds me that if I were still at my old job, we'd be spending our money on a psychiatrist and a divorce lawyer. She's right. I was so miserable, so depressed; it would have torn our marriage apart."

Trust and Admiration

Thomas Lasswell, PhD, a board member of the American Association of Marriage and Family Counselors and professor of sociology at the University of Southern California, is particularly familiar with the successful-woman syndrome. His wife, Marcia, is, by his own admission, "considerably more successful" than he.

"We have been married for 29 years, and suddenly, about five years ago, I realized that Marcia was the star," he said. "She's a college professor, a fine psychotherapist, a good writer—she's appeared on television and radio. She has more general stature than I, and last year she made several times more money than I did.

"You know, I don't mind a bit. Years ago, when she wasn't earning anything, we spent my money; today we have a financial pool and spend our money. I have never been threatened by Marcia. I'm proud of her—I'm glad to be identified with her."

Cushioning the Blow

Can you and your man achieve the same kinds of comfort with your job success that these three couples have managed? The answer has a lot to do with your individual personalities and levels of maturity, but you can take several steps to ease the adjustment.

- Be prepared. Try to work out a joint approach to the problem before it arises. Tony and Susan might have had a better chance to save their relationship if, while Susan was still working on her novel, they had talked about how they would handle the situation if she hit it big.

- Minimize the social pressures. Other people's comments—positive or negative—can aggravate a man's feelings of guilt and inadequacy. The disparity in your incomes isn't everybody's business. If outsiders don't know how much money you make, they can't needle your husband about it.

- Third, recognize the need for tact, understanding and patience.

What the Experts Advise

"As a counselor," said Lasswell, "I advise couples to learn to appreciate each other's talents. There will always be people who are more able, more talented in various areas than we are and we can't fall apart everytime we meet one. It doesn't mean that we are without talent. I point out to couples that the name of the game in this life is change. Nothing stays the same. Positions may reverse farther down the road. Obviously, at this stage, the woman has to be understanding, try to boost the man's ego."

Weiss offers similar advice: "You will have to reassure him subtly. Try and make him a partner in your success. Ask his opinion. He may be a better speech writer or negotiator than you are—consult him. Let him know that societal strictures are not important, that there are more valuable contributions to a relationship than dollars."

Whatever your feelings, it's essential to be honest about them. Weiss cautions against using gimmicks such as the *Total Woman* approach. "They might work if the woman wanted to give up her independence, but a successful woman is unlikely to want to do that. It would be demeaning and dishonest"

Finally, if necessary, seek counseling. According to Weiss. "If your partner refuses to discuss your promotion, if he insists he isn't threatened by it but obviously is, this can indicate a deeper, suppressed problem within the relationship. If communication breaks down, intercession by a third party may be necessary."

Among the experts we consulted, the prevailing thought seemed to be this: If a relationship is relatively equal, if a successful degree of intimacy has been achieved and if there exist genuine feelings of good will between the partners, then who makes how much when will not be a cause of serious or sustained conflict. On the other hand, a relationship too shaky to survive the woman's success probably would have crumbled in the face of some other life change anyway.

That's not to say that even the strongest partnerships are immune to outside pressures or occasional feelings of jealousy or resentment. The difference is in attitude. Is each partner concerned enough about the other's sense of well-being to communicate, compromise and go the extra miles necessary to resolve differences? After all, the point of work is to achieve; the point of love is to share. Learing to do both is the mark of a successful human being.

DOES HE LOVE YOU FOR YOUR MONEY?

by Sheila Eby

Their feelings for each other had remained strong for two years. So sure were they of their love that the lawyer and the magazine editor decided to announce their engagement on Christmas Eve.

Just weeks later, their affair began to take

some oddly contemporary turns. The young woman's contraceptive, an IUD, somehow developed a life of its own. Traveling up her reproductive tract, it left her so ill that she was forced to leave her magazine job until all injury healed. And during those weeks, her boyfriend began seeing a woman of his own profession. Older than the magazine editor, she earned $12,000 more a year.

Suddenly, all marriage plans were dropped. Not because the prospective bridegroom loved his would-be fiancée any less, he said. No, indeed, he called and sought her company often. (Moreover, he soon got the second woman out of the picture.) Yet something about the female attorney had made a permanent impression on him, and the bewildered bride-to-be soon realized that money was part of it. "I still love you," he told his girl friend. But he addded the reservation, "Let's not get married until you're $30,000 a year."

A Passion for Wealth

While young couples often marry in flights of blind exuberance, older brides and grooms have tended to eye their futures more practically and planned their finances carefully. According to marriage counselors, they have the right idea. But as the trend toward later marriages meets up with double-digit inflation rate, money has become a particularly absorbing concern. Especially among the ambitious, a pressing question nags: Can a couple lead the good life, with all its material aspects, despite soaring prices and interest rates?

A whole spectrum of tax, real-estate and business deals purport to help. Yet none can promise so much assistance as one altogether new phenomenon: the high-salaried professional woman. By perhaps doubling the family income, she can finance cars, boats, summer homes and vacations in distant capitals. With money that might as well be coming from heaven, she brings prosperity home.

The fact that a man needn't labor for this opulence rarely seems to pose a moral problem for him. "The new elite," wrote Christopher Lasch in *The Culture of Narcissism,* "identifies itself not with the work ethic, and the responsibilities of wealth, but with an ethic of leisure, hedonism and self-fulfillment."

"I've set my sights high," said one 34-year-old male lawyer. "I plan to drive a Mercedes, travel for a few months each summer in Europe and maintain a town house as well as a country home." Then he went on to say that he could no longer expect to earn $150,000 a year, as he had once hoped. "And I don't come from a wealthy family," he continued, adding with astonishing bluntness, "so I have to marry a woman who earns a great deal of money."

It is undeniable that women today are eager to prove their mettle in the work place. And it is only natural that the men they love should tap and take pleasure in their earnings. But as the first corps of female doctors, lawyers and accountants emerges, the group of men standing in review sometimes looks downright mercenary.

Of course, heiresses frequently have been wooed for their fortunes. But now attention is being focused on a broader class—professional women who may be valued for personal qualities, such as warmth, sweetness and sexiness, but perhaps are valued most of all for their earning power.

Men may defend themselves by pointing out that many women select husbands partly on the basis of income. "When poverty comes in the door," mothers warn daughters, "love goes out the window," although, traditionally, mothers also have imparted ways to handle fiscal problems gracefully. Until recently, how but through marriage could a money-minded woman improve her lot in life? How could she care for her children? Most of the jobs available to her paid virtually nothing.

Now that at least some women can earn

good money, they can pay less attention to their suitors' paychecks. "What do I care about the salaries of men I go out with?" asked a department-store executive dryly (she bore all the trappings of an American Princess), "I'm going to make plenty of money on my own."

No Housewives Need Apply

With her blue-chip education and sparkling credit rating, this woman and others like her are just the ticket for today's eligible professional. These are women who promise to defy the intellectual and financial dependence traditionally associated with their sex.

Meanwhile, women who shun the work place achieve the dubious distinction of curiosities. Men are suspicious of them. "How could anyone be happy just cooking my meals and washing my clothes?" asked a successful young writer, who feared he might find such a woman boring, intellectually inferior and a poor manager of his finances. "I'm afraid I'd react to a traditional woman in a traditional way." The matter was addressed more simply by another man, who had watched his own mother (and other homemakers) retreat into profound sadness through alcohol and tranquilizers. "The women who don't work," he said, "are no bargain."

These are men who grew up in the 1950s, the decade of the family. In what was billed as the best of all possible worlds, fathers pushed pencils while mothers pushed vacuum cleaners. The rebellion of their daughters against these living arrangements is clear: Witness the women's movement. But in a quieter way, their sons have reacted against the same way of life.

"Following their fathers' route to happiness is seen by many younger men as a fate marginally better than early suicide," wrote Gail Sheehy in an *Esquire* article based on a survey of nearly 2,000 of the magazine's male readers. Intellectually, at least, they reject the corporate grind, with its long hours and feigned devotion to superiors. "Yet," Sheehy pointed out, "prosperity is taken for granted by these young men." In fact, money is the key item in their vision of happiness. The new dream entails plenty of leisure, growth and personal expression, Sheehy reported. How do women fit in? "The central importance of the women's movement may yet turn out to be private subsidies for men," she wrote.

Interviewing men across the country for *Dominus: A Woman Looks at Men's Lives* (1978), writer Natalie Gitelson found much the same situation. "Many unmarried men announced with apparent sincerity that they hoped to give up their single status 'someday,' but very few, whether sooner or later, dreamed of marrying a girl like Dad's. She was not only outmoded, what was worse, she was costly. Owing in part to the high-priced economy and in part to the new sociosexual environment, the most attractive of wives was she who required no upkeep; whose middle name was, so to speak, Self-reliance."

Equal but Separate

When these young men finally do find the well-salaried women of their dreams, the marriages are planned as meticulously as a corporate merger, with private bank accounts, separate investment portfolios and real-estate leases carefully worded to protect each partner from the other's future avarice.

Even in their most intimate dealings, couples shield themselves with the language of the corporation: they "negotiate" and devise "contracts." Both husband and wife may see themselves as members of an emerging Super Class, which eventually will eradicate the vulnerability of the female sex. What had soured their parents' lives won't intrude here. Freedom to earn money is equated with a much broader type of liberation.

It is undeniable that a high dual-career income offers greater leeway. But it also means that the wife's salary is no longer a fringe benefit, no longer pin money high-earning women confront problems their mothers didn't have to face. Suppose she's offered a new position with a raise in pay but decides that she simply does not want the job? Suppose she'd like to move to a less lucrative field or start her own business? Suppose she gets fired?

Men with ambitious wives always have wrestled with these issues, and one might hope that having two incomes would give each partner more freedom to take risks. But for the woman whose husband sees her as half of his ticket to the good life, a choice may not exist.

One young executive broke her engagement after a dispute about home financing. Said her fiancé, a lawyer, "We'll each pay half." Replied she, "But you're seven years older than I am and earn almost twice my salary."

"I'll make you a loan," he offered, "with just enough interest to compensate for inflation. Pretty soon, your earnings will soar."

She mused for a moment. "What happens if I decide to have a child?"

The man reported that he'd just read a pertinent article in the *Wall Street Journal.* Corporations, it stated, were now required to rehire women following maternity leaves. "And while you're taking advantage of maternity leave," he added, "they have to pay you."

This was more benevolence than the young woman was accustomed to receiving from the business world. "How long do these leaves last?" she queried.

"Oh, as long as a month," he replied.

"Gosh," she answered, with all the ingenuousness she could muster, "I'm very capable and I can do a lot of things. But it's unreasonable to think that I can raise a child that quickly."

"It was the last straw," she told a friend later, "proof positive that he wasn't interested in nurturing a family. He just wanted to protect himself from whatever demands a wife and kids might bring." Unfortunately, many men share his views.

"Who can blame him?" one man remarked, speaking of a friend's refusal to let his 30-year-old wife have a child. "It's like taking an $18,000 cut in pay."

Similar difficulties may arise when women consider making career changes. A cosmetics-firm executive decided to return to magazine publishing, although the change would mean a substantial cut in pay. She was willing to make sacrifices—to forgo long annual vacations, for example. But her spouse considered such niceties essential and fought ferociously to keep her in the job she found tedious. Her final decision to take the magazine job nearly broke up the marriage.

A woman who loses her job may find her position at home undermined, too. "I hated knowing I was carrying someone," asserted an advertising man who earned plenty of money. "It was a psychological thing. Her financial dependence turned me off."

But what happens when a woman's earning power outshines her husband's? A well-paid young accountant once assured his ambitious bride—then a fledgling assistant in an advertising agency—that he'd be delighted if she ever earned more than he. "After all," he smiled, "it would just make my share of the rent that much smaller." It was easy to say when he pulled in twice her salary. But six years later, after his wife had scrambled through a succession of ever-more-impressive positions—and had signed a book contract, to boot—he seemed less than sanguine about her success, despite the increased income it brought to the household.

To be sure, all high-salaried couples are not inevitably bound for these difficulties. But as anthropologist Lionel Tiger recently noted [*Working Woman,* March 1979], a woman's job has become part of her "courtship apparatus." A discerning woman should ascertain whether that apparatus might someday become the means by which her marriage is pried apart.

"Does she love you for your money?"

mothers have always asked their sons. As female salaries rise, the warning becomes pertinent for daughters too.

RELOCATING YOUR HUSBAND: WITHOUT DISLOCATING HIS EGO, HIS CAREER, OR YOUR MARRIAGE

by Jane Dedman

The Pioneers: "It's Us Against the World."

On the chessboard of corporate politics, the winning strategy can be summarized in four words: "Have ambition, will travel." Until recently, women played the relocation game strictly as portable wives. But it's no longer unusual for a district manager to tell his company that he won't transfer from Boston to Atlanta unless his wife can also find a job in the new city. Now there's a newer problem. The hot district manager being transferred is likely to be a woman, and in small but growing numbers, husbands are being asked to move along with their relocating wives. Men are transferring their jobs, enduring long commutes or separations, or even changing careers—all the painful things that corporate wives have had to do to help relocate husbands.

Joe McManemin had left his engineering job to get a college degree in business when his wife was asked to move from Maryland to New Jersey for the Bell Telephone Company.

Karen McManemin works in the accounting department. She is one of a number of women who have been recruited from the various subsidiary Bell companies to work several years at AT&T headquarters, then

return to their original company—although not necessarily to their original location.

"When the job was offered to me it was a big decision—not exactly traumatic, but one of the major decisions you make in your lifetime," Karen McManemin says. "It had to be made overnight, so we stayed up until two in the morning and hashed it out.

"Joe was in school, and he felt that since he wasn't working, and it was best for my career, we would just do what we had to do. He didn't have any real ties in Maryland except for his family, and it would have to be my decision, depending on whether I wanted to take the job or not.

"So we stayed up and talked it out and decided to say yes, we'd go ahead and do it."

The McManemins, with their two daughters who are four and twelve, moved on New Year's Eve, 1975. "It was kind of a mess after Christmas and everything," she says. "One thing that made it rougher was that a few days later I had to leave for Atlanta for a week. Fortunately Joe had three weeks between semesters and he was home.

"I took Janet (the twelve-year-old) to school in the morning before I left and got her registered. My four-year-old was at home with Joe and he checked around and interviewed babysitters. I was really concerned about finding someone as great as the sitter I had in Maryland. It worked out though. Most things fall into place eventually."

Her concern about finding a babysitter is echoed by other women. Babysitters and housekeepers provide the logistical support often essential to working women with families, and re-establishing this support in a new location is an important matter.

Karen McManemin is also like other relocated women in her de-emphasis of the problems of the physical move—adjustment to her new job was her overriding concern. "I had a different kind of assignment and I was the only woman in this particular department. The men were a little bit leery, and I had to learn how to fit in. The actual move wasn't so bad. As a matter of fact, it put me on a more equal footing with the men. It gave me something to talk about with them—it was a lead into conversation."

As for her family's adjustment, she thinks it has brought them closer together. "It's like it was us against the world. That sounds pretty dramatic, and I don't mean it that way, but you feel you moved as a group and you look to each other.

"Seeing my husband in a different environment makes me appreciate what he did, leaving the area where he'd lived all his life. I'm more sympathetic and understanding.

"Now he really likes it up here," she adds. "He's a very secure person; he has many hobbies and things to do. And studying in school, he's wrapped in his own world."

The adjustment was easy for her younger child, but was hard for her twelve-year-old daughter. "She is in sixth grade and moving was rough for her. At first, she missed her friends, but now she has new ones and doesn't want to go back to Maryland.

"We do have to move back, but I wouldn't like to move again until Janet finishes school. I moved a lot as a child and it's very hard. Especially when you are a teenager, there are a lot of problems and you don't want to add more."

As for the move itself, Karen McManemin

feels almost a sense of obligation. "These are pioneer days for women in business," she says. "I think that women can't expect to have everything given to them without giving something in return. The women who move and do things like that make it easier for other women. They shouldn't think of themselves as martyrs, since men move, and they are expected to do so, and I don't think women should be treated differently. They have to make decisions."

The Resisters:
"We're Unwilling to be Pawns."

While willingness to relocate is one measure of career commitment and company loyalty, it generally involves a promotion and a pay raise, and being selected to go makes it tempting to go. A different set of motives comes into play when it's the company itself that relocates. Then employees at every level must choose to go with the company or go job-hunting, and for many, the tradeoffs are tradeoffs of risks, not advantages.

According to a recent report in *Fortune* magazine, almost 15 percent of the top 500 corporations in the past five years and others are soon to go. Some corporations have trekked from the Northeast to the Sunbelt, from New York to Phoenix, Atlanta, Houston, and Denver.

A year ago, Time-Life Books, a division of Time Inc., stunned its employees with an announcement that it would move out of New York. Until now, all of the company's divisions (including *Time* magazine) have been headquartered at the Time-Life Building in Manhattan's Rockefeller Plaza.

After the announcement, a number of sites were considered for the new headquarters, including New Hampshire, Connecticut, and New Jersey. Since then Alexandria, Virginia, a city adjacent to Washington, D.C., has been selected for the division's new home.

The move was viewed with cynicism and resentment by many staffers, despite an all-out effort by Time Inc. to marshall forces and cheer up the troops with counselors, surveys, real estate appraisers, memos, trips to Washington, buffet lunches, buffet dinners, and drinks. Lots of drinks. Rumor has it that the cheery representatives of Homerica/Home Inc., the company hired to sell old homes and find new ones ("Transplanting torn-up roots is our business") for Books' employees, found them a particularly hardbitten and mordant group, unresponsive to the usual assurances.

There was in fact a strong current of resistance among the 370 employees of Books, many of whom are women and many of whom are married. We talked to a number of those women; they enjoy their work, and by publishing standards, they are well paid for it. Nevertheless they resisted, and less than half were expected to go. Susan Kauffman was one of the resisters.

Susan Kauffman (not her real name) has spent ten years on the editorial staff of Books. Now almost forty, she earns about $20,000 a year—an income that helps support her elderly infirm parents and her three-year-old daughter, and would act as a cushion if her husband's job with the New York State Drug Abuse Control Commission were cut back as has seemed likely in the past.

She says that she and her husband were "intrigued" when the move was first announced. "Our roots are in New England and we would have moved to southern New Hampshire gladly. And southern Connecticut and New Jersey would have been attractive because I could have commuted from our present house. However, nothing screams at us 'Come to Washington.'

"We live in a big old 1916 house that's situated on two lots in a town just north of New York City. It's roomy, wonderful, convenient—I adore it and don't want to leave."

She and her husband visited the Washington area to look at houses and to see Books' new offices in Alexandria. The offices are located in a quaint old section of the city and are housed in a charming new building. The house hunting wasn't as successful.

"I hated northern Virginia. It's all tract houses and shopping centers, even in the $50–$75,000 range. Depressing. There wasn't any sense of being in one place or one community. The atmosphere bugged us: rootless and indefinable. You can't find anything solid that you can put your hand on."

The Kauffmans have strong ties to their present community. He is a a part-time Episcopal minister in addition to his job with the state drug abuse commission.

"Working for the state bureaucracy isn't the most loyalty-inducing job in the world-and for a while his job was uncertain anyway because of cutbacks in staff," Susan Kauffman says. "Leaving the parish would be the real wrench, not leaving his job.

"I think he would want to go if I really wanted to go. We have friends and some family down there, and we would form new ties through the church."

Both she and her husband were up and down about leaving. "One week it's 'No! Absolutely not!' The next it's 'Well, maybe we should get away from New York.' My husband's moods aren't necessarily synchronized with mine—they depend partly on his job, and sometimes he wants to go just because he has a chronic need for change."

Asked what would make her say yes to Washington for sure, she laughs and says, "Well, if they dropped a bomb on New York City. . . .

"I'm not so sure I want to work for Time Inc. the rest of my life anyway," she continues. "Loyalty to the company is falling away because of the strike (the Newspaper Guild struck all the Time Inc. publications in June 1976) and because of the move itself. At first people felt that they were pawns in the move, whether they wanted to be or not; now they are unwilling to be pawns."

If she decides not to go, her accumulated vacation time plus her severance pay will give her almost a year at the same salary. "I think I'd like to take the year off and fix up the house, or if I can't stand the slower pace, to work part-time. I've thought about working on children's books or in crafts, and maybe it's a good time to switch into that.

"I hate job hunting, but maybe it won't be so hard," she muses. "I've kind of forgotten what it's like out there in the real world."

The Rolling Stones:
"We're Very Drifty People."

Susan Kauffman's sense of roots in her community and even, with reservations, in Time Inc., contrasts sharply with the extraordinary freedom and nomadic existence of Claudia and David Widckham. Only ten years younger than the Kauffmans, they seem to be of another generation, a product of the restless sixties. Their restlessness might seem feckless were it not for her flourishing career as a radio advertising saleswoman and his success as a landscape architect.

Claudia Wickham's career has generated three of their four major moves in the past seven years. "We've moved from Lansing, Michigan, to Seattle, to San Francisco and around the Bay area, back to Bloomfield Hills, Michigan, where we are now," she says. "I knew I'd be moving before I married. I love it and so does David. We consider ourselves very drifty people.

"We love new environments, new experiences, and the contact with people from different parts of the country. We both make friends very easily and we are fortunate that we can transfer our jobs without much difficulty."

She adds, "Moving is a hassle no matter where you go, but we've enjoyed it—and our cat too, who has schlepped around with us for seven years."

The Wickhams have chosen to be wanderers. "When we were first married we decided that we'd like to live on the West Coast. We made a deal—we both wrote letters all over and agreed we'd go with whoever got the first job. I got a job in Seattle so we up and went there. The various moves on the Coast represented promotions for me, but the move back to Michigan was made because of deaths in the family and because my husband's mother was very sick."

David Wickham has never needed more than a month to establish his landscaping business in a new location and apparently is not at all threatened by his wife's dynamic career or resentful that she usually determines the moves. Claudia Wickham says, "You really have to establish who's going with whom at the very beginning when you trek around. You have to establish who has the most earning power, who has the easiest time finding a job, and all those things, or you will find one moving to New York and the other to Chicago, and the marriage headed for the rocks."

She goes on to say, "We find it very easy to discuss these things—not everyone can do that. You need an open relationship from the first. Four years into the marriage you can't say, 'Well now I want an open relationship because I want to travel with my company.' "

The Wickhams have no children and plan to have none. "We've discussed it and we know they are not in our future. We are very independent and like to pick up on a Friday night and go camping. Children wouldn't work out in that kind of lifestyle. And it would be difficult to move, too."

David Wickham chuckles, "We look forward to moving again, even though my job is stable for a while—at least for six months. We spend a lot of time looking over maps and thinking, 'Hey, wouldn't it be fun to live there?' And in six months, who knows?"

The only place he doesn't want to move is New York City. Since Claudia Wickham's career inevitably will lead there she says, "I'm working on him."

The Confident Veteran:
"Make Me an Offer I Can't Refuse."

Anne Hyde, director of Management Woman, an executive recruiting firm that places women in top jobs, says that the easiest husbands to relocate are those in real estate or sales (where travel is part of the job), or who work as consultants. As for women, the management level requiring relocation peaks when they are twenty-eight to thirty years old, and not surprisingly, younger couples find it less difficult to move than older ones. Anne Hyde adds that in three years of relocating women she has never seen a couple split up over the question.

"If they've both got careers, one of them has to make a tradeoff," she says. "A woman has to sit down with her husband and talk realistically. One reality is that if a woman is going to be competitive and play in the same ballgame, she must play by the same rules. That means she must be willing to relocate."

When a husband is supportive, it is actually easier for a married woman to relocate than a single one. She has one built-in friend in the new place.

Susan Bassin and her husband, who works for a large bank, are now in New York after having completed a stint in Belgium for their respective corporations.

Susan has a Harvard M.B.A. and works in corporate strategic planning for International Telephone and Telegraph. ITT has a corporate reputation for developing the best and the brightest new talent, and executive recruiters eye ITT's staff greedily, so she has sizable negotiating power and numerous career options.

"My transfer to Belgium was self-initiated," she says. "My husband and I thought that working in an international setting would be appropriate to our careers at some point. When his company asked him to take a post in Belgium, I began exploring opportunities for me to transfer to ITT's European headquarters in Brussels."

She remained in Brussels almost three years. Her husband was asked to return to the States after the first year, but she felt that she had not had enough time to do anything significant. "I was just beginning to understand what was going on and I wasn't

ready to request a transfer back," she says. "My husband agreed to return to the U.S. to work on a project for six months while I stayed on in Europe alone. His company let him return to Belgium when the project was completed."

When Sue Bassin decided that her experience in Europe had been meaningful and she had completed a significant number of projects, she requested a transfer back to New York. "After an appropriate position was identified for me, my husband began negotiations with his company. Within four months we were both back in New York."

When approached by executive recruiters for other companies, she feels she doesn't have to prove her willingness to relocate.

"I've paid my dues in a way. I've been able to move and to work 6,000 miles away from my husband. And I know what I can do, so in a new job I'd be taking a bigger risk than the company that wants to hire me. For me to relocate, the job has to mean more than a 20 percent increase in salary. It has to mean increased responsibilities plus opportunities for my future.

"So I tell them 'Make me an offer I can't refuse.' "

Whether they refuse or not, most women, and their families, deal rationally and realistically with the relocation decision. Tradeoffs are analyzed, balances struck, and problems are solved with the husband's support. There is satisfaction in the promotion and the raise, but within the family, women seem to have no particular relish in the role of prime mover.

And yet, as promotions involving relocation are offered more often, as the compliment of *not* being passed over loses its novelty, women will face difficult choices. They have the benefit of two decades of hindsight, having seen young male managers shunted from place to place, sometimes with devastating effects on their families.

As women comprise an increasingly significant part of management, they will have an increasingly significant influence on corporate policy and will help to decide whether relocations are in the best interests of both employee and employer. When offered a transfer, they will have to decide whether upward mobility is worth the upheaval, the transience, the rootlessness, the suburban gypsy existence. They will have to define their values carefully and each woman will have to decide for herself if the patterns of the organization man are acceptable to her as an organization woman.

THE GIVE-AND-TAKE OF A 2-PAYCHECK MARRIAGE
Her Salary Isn't a Second Income, It's "Half of the Family Income." Sherry and Jonathan Woocher Split Expenses, Decision Making, Child Care and Chores

by Sally Platkin Koslow

Like a lot of women, Sherry Woocher, 32, never set out to be the kind of earner whose salary, almost dollar for dollar, matches her husband's. Nor did Jonathan Woocher, PhD, 33, expect that to help make his wife's career commitment possible he would become—as he and Sherry chose to term it—a "primary" parent, as adept at car pooling as at cooking a tuna-noodle casserole. For both, these roles evolved gradually, taking shape as they and their relationship matured.

Sherry, associate director of promotion at radio station WGBH, a national broadcasting public station in Boston, earns $17,500 a year, a figure only $500 lower than Jonathan's salary as an assistant professor at Brandeis University in Waltham, Massachusetts.

Although the Woochers have salaries that match neatly, they've never considered their money "his" or "hers." Nor do they think of Sherry's salary as a "second" income. "Once two people are on career tracks, it's not a question of one salary being secondary," Jonathan said. "It's one-half of the family income."

The Woochers' financial decision-making is as equal as their incomes. "Almost everything we earn goes into the basics," Jonathan explained. But it is their agreement on what, exactly, is basic (a cleaning service, for instance) that keeps this tightly budgeted couple financially afloat and in emotional harmony.

Their History

The Woochers' mutual trust has been earned over the course of what seems—by current standards—like a long time. They married when Sherry was a Vassar College junior in her home town of Poughkeepsie, New York, Jon a senior at Yale University. When he embarked on a doctorate program in religion at Temple University in Philadelphia, she followed him, earning her bachelor's degree from Vassar and taking additional courses at Bryn Mawr College. "One of us then had to work," Sherry said, "so in the organization of time I took a low-level job as an archivist, which is like a librarian but even duller."

When their daughter, Meredith, was born in 1970, Sherry became a full-time mother, a role she continued for four years in Northfield, Minnesota, where Jon was teaching at Carleton College, a small, prestigious liberal-arts school. In 1976, after free-lancing as an editor and publisher's reader, Sherry took a series of editorial and administrative jobs that—interrupted by the birth of a son, Benjamin—prepared her to become, in 1978, the promotion director and editor of a monthly program guide for the local public radio station. She earned $13,000 a year.

At about this time, Jon decided to get a job on the East Coast, and he and Sherry weighed offers from a Manhattan institution and from Brandeis. When they decided on the latter, Sherry made a five-day visit to the Boston area. Her goals: to find a job and a house. Seven job interviews and numerous real-estate appointments later, she had accomplished both missions. They moved last summer.

Their Move: a Capital—and Costly—Investment

The Woochers' move certainly was not cheap. In Northfield, they had owned a roomy house with sprawling land, and they wanted the same when they moved. They got it, but for $72,500, which was about $30,000 more than they received for their former house. What's more, Minnesota property taxes are approximately a third of Massachusetts taxes, and their current mortgage rate is much higher than the 8 percent they paid in 1972.

Commuting to both their jobs not only "changed our life style," but brought increased expense. Their three-bedroom, red-brick ranch house is located in a 20-year-old section of Framingham, about 30 miles west of Boston. Every weekday morning Jon drives their 1971 Volvo 25 minutes to Brandeis. Sherry's commute to the city, in their newer Chevrolet, takes about 35 minutes. Compared to Northfield's five-minute commutes, gas is now a significant expense.

Other expenses—a big-city working wardrobe for Sherry, for example—also have eroded the seeming gain of their new, higher salaries. "We didn't make any killing to come here," Jon said, "especially when we consider that I gave up a tenured position. But our decision to move was a capital investment, made with long-range, rather than immediate, opportunities in mind." Both hope that their jobs will lead to more interesting and/or lucrative work.

A $60-a-month after-school program, associated with Framingham's public schools, influenced the Woochers' choice of that community.

One of their next hurdles was locating suitable child-care accommodations for 2-year-old Ben. What they selected was steep ($286 a month, since they're at the high end of a sliding scale) but, they felt, excellent: a cooperative center on the Brandeis campus.

Ben's day care "is the reason I could accept my job, which is physically and mentally demanding," Sherry said. The center is located a short walk from Jon's office, and he delivers Ben there around 9:00 AM each weekday and collects him by 4:30 PM. On the way home, before picking up Merry, Jon completes the family's marketing.

Sherry and Jon eat meat about twice a week, the children one time more. Jon, because he can bend his schedule to get home earlier, does much of the cooking. He brings his lunch to work. Except when she has a business lunch (for example, taking out John Irving, author of *The World According to Garp,* in order to book him for a show called "Anthology"), Sherry eats in the station cafeteria or at her desk in order to shorten her workday by about half an hour.

All the Woochers, even little Ben, put in long days. Jon cuts his campus time short to facilitate his carpool run, then extends his workday at night at home. Sherry gets to her office at 9:15 and leaves around 6:30. Their schedule has almost no slack and one potentially costly component of their life has had to go: entertainment.

Were they not constantly tired, Sherry admitted, they might feel frustrated at not being able to afford to go to many of Boston's restaurants and cultural events. "As soon as we can keep our heads above water in terms of energy," she said, they will resume home entertaining—a big yearly party and a few simple dinners with another couple or two. For the moment, though, beyond spending time with Merry and Ben, the Woochers' principal recreation—and splurge—is watching cable television and its accompanying Home Box Office. An additional luxury for Sherry, a "notorious subscriber," is reading newspapers and women's and professional magazines.

To help make ends meet and advance his career, Jon does outside lecturing and seminar leading in his specialty—Jewish communal service—and consulting. Some months, he earns $500; other months, about $100. The trade-off for this extra cash is travel—an additional strain on Sherry, who then must add Jon's daily car pooling, shopping and cooking to her day. "There are times I've had to say that for the money a particular job may bring, it's not worth it," she said. "I'd rather have Jon at home than an extra $400."

MONTHLY INCOME

Sherry Woocher's salary	$1,458
Jonathan Woocher's salary	1,500
Jonathan Woocher's supplementary income	300

Total monthly income	**$3,258**

MONTHLY OUTGO

Federal tax	$375
State tax	120
FICA/Social Security	180
Jonathan's pension	75
Jonathan's supplementary life insurance	3
Health insurance	56
Mortgage	517
Property tax	146
Utilities	150
Auto insurance and excise tax	78
Ben's day care	286
Merry's extended day program	60
Synagogue dues, Hebrew school tuition and building fund	60
Telephone	50
Home insurance	48
Transportation and auto maintenance	150
Food	300
Medical expenses	30
Books/periodicals	20
Recreation	40
Clothing	50
Professional expenses	20
Household cleaning and furnishings	150
Charitable contributions	100
Personal loan repayment	50
Gifts and savings	100
Miscellaneous	44

Total monthly expenses	**$3,258**

Nuts and Bolts

"We find it easiest to have two joint checking accounts," explained Jon. "This way we don't have to worry about both of us writing a check at the same time and overdrawing. We deposit in both accounts, depending on which we want to jack up." The mortgage payment is automatically deducted from one. Sherry handles all school forms; Jon balances the checkbooks, reads bank statements, completes their taxes. They don't work within a formal budget, but they keep close tabs on their income and outgo.

The Woochers' only significant investment is their home, which was financed with equity from their previous residence, a $4,000 loan from a brother (they have repaid $2,500), a gift of $1,000 from each set of parents and a mortgage. Each child has a savings account, set up by grandparents, "with enough in it to pay for about a month's college tuition."

The Woochers have a full deck of credit cards, but they try to pay each bill on receipt, rather than to see 18 percent interest balloon their debt. "We try to get a month's free use of the credit-card company's money," Jon said. Quite a few of the credit cards are in Sherry's name. "I feel strongly about establishing my own credit line," she said, "particularly since a friend who was earning a substantial salary divorced and couldn't get credit because she had no record of her own."

Sherry and Jon joined a group health-insurance plan through Brandeis, where they've also taken out supplementary life insurance for Jon at a low rate. They're talking about buying more insurance for Sherry. Each has term life insurance as an employee benefit.

Family Support

The Woochers dual-earned income allows for comfort and a certain degree of grace—they have a Calder poster over their fireplace, a redwood deck, a well-equipped kitchen and ten-speed bicycles, and they pay $40 a month for a professional cleaning service. Yet they have little cash to spare. "We know few people who do," Jon said, "especially with children."

Two things allow the Woochers to be cheerful about what other couples might regard as a financial bind: First, they like their jobs and their professional futures look promising. Second, psychologically and financially, each of their sets of parents offers dependable, no-strings-attached support. Said Sherry, "Almost all the steps we've taken have filtered through our families," who also have provided plane tickets back and forth from Minnesota, long-term loans with low interest rates and occasional help with major purchases.

"I'm not embarrassed to admit that in many ways we're able to sustain our style of living because of the family relationships we have," said Jon. His father is a dentist, hers is a physicist with IBM. Their parents, Sherry explained, believe it's better to help out children during a parent's lifetime than the alternative.

Chapter Thirteen

The Working Mother

SHOULD I HAVE A BABY?

by Terri Schultz

The hardest decision most women must make is when to have children. As a 28-year-old married woman said, "My mother keeps asking Bill and me when we are going to start having kids. I tell her we're working on it. That embarrasses her, and she drops the subject." She smiled and went on. "What I don't tell her is that we're working on the *decision.* We may decide never to have kids."

Until recently, women who chose to remain childless were viewed as selfish, immature or incomplete. Yet, despite some lingering social stigmas, more and more women are postponing children until their 30s, and many are saying no, thank you, to motherhood at any age.

"For the first time, women are asking themselves not only whether to have children, but *why.* While many women choose to be parents, others are choosing to remain child free. Both are positive life styles; both have their advantages," said Carole Baker, executive director of the National Alliance

for Optional Parenthood. "Women now have more responsibility, more choices, and one of those choices is when—and whether—to become a mother." Baker feels that most women cannot rear children and plunge full speed ahead with careers at the same time.

"A woman who has a high level of energy and ability may be able to do everything. But most of us aren't superwomen, which means that if you say yes to motherhood, you're saying no to other things, just as if you say yes to becoming a lawyer, you're saying no to becoming a doctor. You devalue motherhood and parenting if you believe you can bring children into your life without making some very important changes," Baker said.

According to NAOP, television shows such as "The Brady Bunch" and "Father Knows Best," advertisements that use children to sell products and promote motherhood, religious tradition, educational systems and even the tax structure all perpetuate the myth that people can be completely fulfilled only through parenthood. "Pronatalism glorifies parenthood. It's left over from our frontier days, when children were an economic asset, and fewer children survived to adulthood. But you can love kids and still not want to become a parent," said Baker.

Baker herself is a 41-year-old mother of two teenage sons, and for 12 years she worked as a homemaker. She left her job as a social worker at the age of 23, when she was pregnant with her first child. "Motherhood was not a conflict for me because it was a role I had been conditioned for. I never thought about *not* having children. But motherhood can be more of a conflict for women today; they have more roles to choose from.

"This is the International Year of the Child, and we're hearing more about the rights of children," Baker added. "For me, the basic right is to have a parent who is willing to make a commitment to the child and to understand what that commitment means in terms of time, energy, financial resources and love."

Several years ago, columnist Ann Landers asked her readers how many parents would have children if they could do it over again. Out of 10,000 responses, 7,000 parents said they would, in retrospect, prefer to be childless. In a separate survey conducted by *McCall's* magazine, 15 percent of the respondents said that they would choose against parenthood if they could do it over. "These are not scientific surveys," Baker pointed out. "But what you have are thousands of women who are sorry that they became mothers, and their children may be the victims of their regrets. Things have changed. Today we're saying it's OK not to have children if you don't want to."

Baker suggested that when considering parenthood, women ask themselves some questions about the following areas:

Work: "We all know women who've tried to work full time and raise children," Baker said. "Some women can handle it. But for others, it can turn into a catastrophe because they are torn between their responsibilities to their children and to their careers, which can result in a lot of guilt. I think this idea of 'quality time'—that the quality, not the quantity, of time you spend with your child is important—is just a rationalization. Your children have a right to see you day to day, in all kinds of situations. If you plan to have other people raise your children, you should take another look at why you're having children."

Personal relationships: "The myth is that a child will save your marriage. In fact, nothing will break up a shaky marriage faster than kids. It's destructive to have a child if it is a concession or a compromise; the reluctant person may end up resenting the trade-offs. You and your partner should have a solid, loving relationship before bringing kids into it."

Feelings about children: "You may love cuddly babies, but how do you feel about toddlers and teenagers? If you're not sure, it's a good idea to spend time alone with children—nieces and nephews, friends' children, or to do some volunteer work or foster care. A lot of women say they don't want to miss the experience of childbirth, but once the birth experience is over, you have a commitment for at least 18 years."

Self-growth: "First, a woman has to decide what she wants; she has to clarify her values and goals and then decide how a child would contribute to or detract from reaching those goals. Will having children help you fulfill your needs and meet your goals? Will not having children?"

Even with all this sensible advice, many women wonder: How will I know whether I like it until I've tried it? Some who hesitate are pleasantly surprised. One woman who had her first child when she was 34, cuddled her 18-month-old son and recalled, "While I was in the hospital after giving birth, I had the feeling that this was a much nicer thing than I had ever expected and that people had somehow misled me. Everything I had read warned me that having a child was the end of your life. Now it chills me to think I never might have had this child."

"If a woman is ambivalent about having children, I would rather see her analyze her feelings about kids than see her just go ahead and have them without thinking about it—and maybe spending the rest of her life regretting it," Baker concluded.

"WOULD I BE HAPPY AS A PARENT?"

Nobody can answer that question for sure. But we can be sure that many people have become parents without really thinking about it. And we can be sure that people are more likely to be happy as parents if they know in advance that it won't be easy. Remember, it is *your* life that will be affected.

Here are some of the reasons why people decide to have children. Rate each reason according to its importance to *you*; see the scale below. A reason that hardly influences you at all rates 1, while a very important reason rates 8.

This is not a scientific test. There is no score that tells you whether or not you should have children. It is an exercise to help you think about your reasons for becoming a parent or not becoming one.

1	2	3	4	5	6	7	8
Unimportant					Important		

Reasons for having children:
- So I won't have to cope with people wondering why I didn't have children _____
- To experience the sheer entertainment that children can provide _____
- To nurture in someone characteristics that I believe are important _____
- To have someone to stand by me when I'm old _____
- To make my partner happy _____
- To be needed _____
- To have a feeling of accomplishment _____
- To carry on the family business _____
- To have the satisfaction of giving myself to someone else _____
- To add interest to my home life _____
- Because my life wouldn't be complete without a child _____

Reasons for remaining child free:
- My partner and I will have a more satisfactory relationship without children _____
- I want to concentrate on my own growth and development _____
- My partner wants to remain child free _____
- I want to be free from the responsibility of child rearing _____
- I want to travel freely _____
- My partner and I want to continue to enjoy our leisure time _____
- My partner and I want to put our full energies into our careers _____
- I want to be able to use my income for things I want to do _____
- I want to do my part to control population growth _____
- I'd prefer to use my talents in other ways _____
- My partner and I want to maintain our privacy _____

Take a look at the reasons you rated with high numbers. Are there more high-numbered reasons for remaining child free or for having children?

Perhaps the reasons you marked as important will show you something about how you really feel about having children or about not having them. Everyone has reasons pulling both ways. When you know what your reasons are, you'll have a better chance of making the right choice.

Research shows that having a child will not *necessarily* make you happier or make your marriage more satisfying. Like other decisions in life, having a child has both joys and sorrows, rewards and costs. It will be right for some people and wrong for others; for many, it will be in-between. Whatever you decide, make sure it is *your* choice.

Often, decisions are easier to make if you talk about them with someone else. You may want to talk to:

- a school guidance counselor
- a parent *and* a child-free adult
- a close friend whom you can confide in easily
- a counselor at a family-planning clinic
- and, most important, your partner.

FOR MORE INFORMATION

The NAOP offers a number of leaflets, including *Am I Parent Material?* and *Children, Why Not?* Write to: National Alliance for Optional Parenthood, 2010 Massachusetts Avenue NW, Washington, DC 20036.

TERRY SCHULTZ *teaches journalism at New York University. Her most recent book is* Women Can Wait: The Pleasures of Motherhood after 30, *published by Doubleday/Dolphin.*

TIME & THE WORKING MOTHER

by Nancy Hechinger

There are 16 million working mothers' stories in America. This is just one of them.

Each working mother has her own special problems: One is a city-dweller with two teen-agers, another lives in the country with six kids, another is career-oriented with an infant . . . and so on. For all this diversity, there is one thing they have in common. They don't have enough time.

I am a single, working mother. That is to say, I am a mother, a businesswoman and a single woman. One day as I was looking in the mirror at these three women, I noticed that we looked awful: Certainly we were not the superwoman others thought we were.

I knew I wasn't doing any of my jobs as well as I could but I didn't see what I could do to improve. My three roles, as I saw them, were practically mutually exclusive. To be a good mother and housekeeper, I would have to spend more time with my child, playing, nurturing—spending eight hours a day in an office squelches that. To advance my career, I would have to be able to work all hours, compete in time and energy with everyone around me—the time I must spend with my child eliminates that possibility. A single woman has the luxury of some time to herself before going out to dance until dawn. She doesn't send interesting swains home to their own beds before daylight either. But who can stay out late when they have to get up at 7:00 AM—even on weekends?

What's a mother to do? Who can I talk to? In some way I am isolated from each group to which I belong: Isolated from mothers who get to know each other in the park or at school, isolated from co-workers who get together after work for a drink, isolated from singles who pop off for a ski weekend without having to deal with baby-sitters, or guilt.

Then one day something happened that helped me toward a solution. A doctor kept me waiting three hours for an appointment, then took a man ahead of me "because he's a businessman and can't wait." Instead of fuming or walking out, I told the doctor that my time was just as valuable as the businessman's. I had taken time off from my work and from my child, and he could expect a bill from me for the time I'd spent waiting at my hourly rate. He deducted the amount from my bill—right then and there.

Later, I realized two important things. One: No one automatically considers a woman's time valuable unless you tell them it is and demand respect for it. Two: As a mother, you are entitled to put a market value on the time with your child. Like a bolt from the blue, it suddenly occurred to me: Time is the key. It had been managing me. Now I would manage it. I put a meter on every minute of my life and made several discoveries that have cut chores to a minimum.

1. Appointments

When making any kind of appointment, ask what the average waiting time is. If it's too long, either ask for a reference to another doctor, dentist or whoever, or ask for a time of day when you won't have to wait. Demand to be called if there will be more than a 15-minute delay. Indicate that you'll charge for wasted time.

Any appointment you have regularly, schedule regularly. Example: When you pay for your haircut, make your next hair appointment at the same time. Better yet, set up a standing appointment.

2. Clothes Shopping

I am not crazy about shopping and I don't have time for it. All the same, I need to look put together at work and I like clothes. The answer: Go into a store(s) you like. Talk to the manager or saleswoman about the kind of clothes you like and are looking for. Give her your telephone number at work and ask her to phone you when something appropriate comes in. Set up an appointment for a half hour of trying on pre-selected clothes. As for children's clothes, I buy for my son by mail order.

3. Packages

Have all packages mailed to your office so you don't have to go to the Post Office to pick them up.

4. Your Child's Behavior

All working mothers have to deal with baby-sitters and schools and must rely on them for information about your children's development. You must forcefully ask your child's teacher for a full conduct report. Since you don't get to see that much of his/her interaction with other children, you need the teacher's assistance. (I had to find out from a good friend that Alex was, for a while, the class biter; the teacher didn't want to worry me!) Try, also, to persuade school authorities not to hold meetings and events in the middle of the day when working parents can't attend.

5. Home Maintenance Chores

This is an area that can eat your time alive, but you can save hours of it simply by going to every service store you use and saying to the owner or manager: "I am a working mother and I want to be your customer. What time-saving services can you offer me?" Or suggest a few, to wit:

A. Supermarket: I leave a shopping list at the market on my way to my son's school in the morning. The food is delivered to my home at 6:30 PM. In many stores you can charge your order. If not, you can call midday to find out the amount and drop a check off on your way home. By shopping this way, you save money, too—there's no impulse buying.

B. Cleaners: Make an arrangement with the owner whereby you don't have to wait in line. Mornings are always busy. Take your clothes in with instructions pinned to them, drop them on the counter and you're off. She/he will write up the ticket later. My cleaner delivers. I can pay him at my door, or charge it.

C. Specialty Stores: There's a wonderful fruit and vegetable man on my street who is usually closed before I get home. He asked me once why I only came in on weekends. I told him. Now I call him from my office, and he delivers to my door—like the milkman of yesteryear—and I pay him in the morning.

D. Repair Shops: A broken toaster will stay broken forever because repair shops are only open nine to five. Two solutions: Find a repair shop near your office, or tell your neighborhood repair-shop owner your situation, and ask what accommodation he can make. The appliance handyman near me said if I'd call him when I have something to be fixed, he'd wait till I got there.

E. Drugstore: Whenever you need something, order it ahead of time by phone, so that it will be packaged and waiting for you.

Of course, if you have a full-time housekeeper, she/he will probably handle some of these chores for you. I found that when I did have one, it took me almost as long to instruct her as it now takes to do the chores myself.

The three key elements in making services shops serve you are:

Deliveries—Always ask about them. I have found that every shop in my neighborhood will deliver. Supermarkets charge for the service, others don't.

Check-writing or charge privileges—Use whenever possible so you can shop in absentia. (Note: Never bounce a check to a neighborhood store or you will endanger the relationship. It's better to tell the owner you'll pay next week.)

Gratuities—Don't forget your friends at Christmas. Remember, their services save

you time and money every day; give them a generous tip once a year.

These suggestions apply primarily to urban areas where most working mothers live. I happen to live in "cold, heartless" New York, where people supposedly don't care about each other and yet I've succeeded in getting service businesses to serve me.

6. Housekeeping

Nobody ever died from dirt and clutter. That's the first lesson. Your house is where you live, it shouldn't be another burden.

The second lesson is that housekeeping is the responsibility of everyone who lives there, no matter what age. Alex, three-and-a-half, is my partner; he vacuums, waters plants, makes his own bed and admonishes me to make mine if I try to leave the house without doing so.

If you don't want to look at the inevitable toys, papers, books, whatnots that get scattered around, get a large basket and dump things into it. Once a week, you and your kid(s) put everything back where it belongs.

7. Meals

The first law of Working-Mothers'-At-Home-Activities should be: Never take longer to prepare something than you'll take to do it. In other words, don't spend an hour cooking a meal that will be left half-eaten in 15 minutes. Alex has a big lunch at school and so we spend our time together at night, for the most part, outside of the kitchen. When I get home from work, we have "cocktails"—cheese and juice/wine. He tells me about his day and I tell him about mine. Then if it's a nice day, we go to the park and take along some carrots, green peppers, cold chicken, whatever. If the weather's inclement, we play with toys, games, etc., and eat our snack at home.

Time should be figured on a cost-benefit basis. Prepared foods are not always more expensive. For example, there is a good (pure, no additive) take-out Bar-B-Q chicken place near me. A cooked chicken costs me between 50 cents and a dollar more than an uncooked one, saves time and something on my gas bill. It all adds up to a bargain.

Once a week, Alex and I do make a big meal. But, it's for the fun of it, not of necessity. Children like to cook and clean. Washing dishes, especially, should be encouraged. A self-reliant, competent child is well on the way to being a happy child.

8. Time for Your Child

Since you have only a few hours to play with your child, you must abandon the idea that early evening is for winding down. It won't work anyway. The kid is eager to see you, to touch you. The main hurdle is realizing that you can't sit down and relax until your parenting time is over. Go to the park, a museum, a playground, the firehouse—make an adventure. Once, as we were walking to the park, we jumped on a double-decker bus instead and rode it to the end of the line. Big deal? It seemed like a treat.

Another trick: Create a Playtime Litany to make the time you have together seem longer, "Remember the time we . . ." Talk about it over and over, like a bedtime story . . . one adventure is usually good for several weeks.

9. Time for Yourself

A nasty trick I have, which won't work forever, is setting the digital clock in my kitchen (the only one Alex can read) ahead 20 minutes. By doing so, I can appear to make concessions and still enforce an 8:00 PM bedtime. I'm a firm believer in bedtimes. It's important to have time to yourself—to relax, eat dinner, go out, watch TV or work. Often I work because I am pursuing a career that is more than a nine-to-five kind of job.

10. Time for Your Work

Some of your most productive work can be done at night when you can concentrate uninterrupted by office phones, co-workers, meetings, etc. You tell your boss at the outset that although you must leave at five to be with your child, you will do work that doesn't involve other people at home at night. If you are in the kind of organization in which people make a show of how much they're doing, conspicuously hand the secretary a report or letters to type first thing in the morning.

These are some solutions that have worked for me. But I still have lots of questions: How do you deal with guilt—all varieties? How can you compete with a man who's at work at 8:00 AM and leaves at 7:00 PM because he's got an efficient life-support system (a wife) at home? If you're single, when do you have time to develop a serious relationship with a man? Before bathtime? Between meetings? The list is endless. I am only one single, working mother. Many others share my problems—maybe they have different solutions. I'm all ears.

One last question—does everyone, but me, remember to have their kids brush regularly?

NANCY HECHINGER *is a film producer with Zacks & Perrier, a multi-media production company. As a single, working mother with a 3½-year-old son, Hechinger said, "I may look fairly disorganized but, in fact, I've worked out my priorities and have become very organized out of necessity."*

HOW TO MAKE YOUR KIDS MORE SELF-RELIANT

by Carol Saline

We were in the yard when the telephone rang; I, working fertilizer into the rose bushes, and my then four-year-old daughter, digging in her sand box. Since my hands were coated with mud, I told her to run in the house and answer the phone. She didn't budge, involved as much in her play as I was in my gardening. I started to get angry. "Sharon, go answer that phone," I repeated. And she, looking thoroughly annoyed, said, "This is supposed to be a free country. Why do I always have to do what you tell me?"

By now the ringing had stopped. And though I read her my standard because-you-are-the-child-and-I-am-the-mother lecture, I was secretly delighted. I knew I had a daughter who was already on her way to self-reliance.

Nine years have passed since that little incident and I now spend most of my time in an office instead of the garden, but I find a greater need than ever to develop in my children the germs of the self-reliance I saw that morning. Like all working mothers—especially those living in suburbia, where bus lines are as scarce as leashed dogs—I get fed up with 4:45 P.M. "emergency" phone calls to my office asking me to pick up colored pens and/or graph paper on my way home; or with returning from an evening meeting to notice nobody's remembered to take out the cans for the trash pickup; or with being told at dinner that it's hairwashing night and we're out of shampoo.

It occurs to me that although self-reliant kids are an asset to any family, they are almost a necessity for working women, women whose time is at a premium and whose guilt about how much they ought to do for their children is a question rarely faced by hot-dog day and Little League mommies. For advice on where I ought to be heading, I asked psychologist Matti Gershenfeld to stop by my office. She's been through it all, raising four sons while earning her doctorate and establishing a dynamic career as a consultant, a speaker, and a private therapist.

Dr. Gershenfeld bounced in the next morning between a breakfast meeting and a class at Temple University where she's been part of the psychology faculty for ten years. She admired a wall-hanging I'd brought back from a trip to Mexico, smoothed her Buster-Brown-style frosted hair, complained she'd like to lose ten pounds as she poured a sugar substitute in her coffee, took out a sheet of notes typed the previous midnight, and said, "Let's talk."

She agreed that working women need more self-reliant kids—the guilt trip is a lot rockier for women who split themselves between home and office. We all worry that our kids will somehow suffer from our absence and not turn out as well as they might have with more attention. (Though, Dr. Gershenfeld assured me, statistics don't support this fear.) One of the means she used with her own boys to avoid this projected failure was to train them to develop a strong sense of responsibility and the knowledge that they could handle many things without leaning on her.

Time is another obvious consideration. We've all suffered intermittently from the rigors of dual personhood. Between her job, and the hours housework can consume, a working mother needs a system of sharing or she'll be too tired to do anything well.

But it goes even deeper. If a woman understands the value of self-reliance in her children, it can become, like pension plans and hospital insurance, one of the added fringe benefits of a job. In a rapidly changing world where people more and more must make decisions based on new information rather than established norms, Dr. Gershenfeld believes we cheat our children if we don't teach them to think for themselves. So many of us well-meaning moms act as benevolent dictators all through childhood, calling the shots and cushioning the blows. Then we set our kids loose in the adult world without the skills to cope when we're not whispering advice.

Whether or not a woman encourages self-reliance seems to be related to why she's working in the first place. If she'd really prefer that her husband support her but works because the family needs the extra income, she's likely to be unconsciously angry and to feel used. "This kind of woman plays the martyr," says Dr. Gershenfeld. "She doesn't divide the jobs, doesn't ask for help, and complains she's overworked and underappreciated."

In similar shoes is the woman who works against her husband's wishes. When she voices a desire for a career, he retorts, "Who's going to do the housework and take care of the kids?" She assures him that she can handle everything and sets out to kill herself proving it. She takes on her new role with the job added, as if it were still her old role without the job. Nothing changes. Though she moans that the kids are selfish and lazy and nobody wants to help poor mom out, she actually fosters their continued dependency just to show how marvelously she manages.

Self-reliance seems to flourish among couples whose husbands support their wives' work. In this situation, the family may actually sit down as a unit and examine how to share the load. Whichever way the chores are divided, the father sets a model for the kids to assume added responsibility. And the mother, instead of being the same old mom with a career on top of her original duties, sets an example for a different way of life.

Another factor in the degree of self-reliance is the sex of the children in a given family. "Children in single sex housholds," says Dr. Gershenfeld, "become more independent. When there are sisters and brothers, the activities are routinely split along sex role lines." But when there are only boys in the family, a working mother will train them to help with the dusting, cooking, and ironing. In the same vein, a father of two girls will need assistance hanging the storm windows, raking the leaves, and washing the car, and he'll turn to his daughters. When girls take on boys' business and vice-versa, their self-reliance blossoms.

But developing self-reliance isn't a question of who clears the dishes or shovels the snow. It's a conscious shifting of impetus from some outside authority—parent, teacher, boss—to an internal signal that flashes "this is my responsibility." The seeds of self-reliance are sown in the crib, and many mothers unwittingly bolster dependency in early infancy by confusing coddling with maternal concern.

We know from numerous studies that babies who aren't stroked, fondled, and talked to grow up with emotional handicaps. They feel abandoned and fight that aloneness all their lives by clinging to others. Never blessed with the security nurtured by regular doses of TLC, they lack the foundation for self-reliance. But here's where the issue gets tricky. There's a thin but important line between enough attention and too much. How a mother straddles that line determines the self-reliance her child acquires. Many mothers are unconsciously so wrapped up in doing for their helpless infants, that they can't kick the habit as the baby matures.

Take a simple act like buttoning. Dr. Gershenfeld explains that when a toddler asks for help buttoning a shirt, the instinct of a mother is to button it herself and send him off to play; a different approach would create greater independence. The mother ought to say, "Maybe you can button it yourself. Let me see you try." The child answers, "I can't." The mother says, "You try and I'll watch." She lets the youngster fumble a bit, then says, "Okay, now move the button a little higher or lower." This kind of interaction occurs all day, and the problem is that it's usually easier for the mother to do it herself than to take the time to help the child master the task.

Feeding is a similar situation. "When a mother feeds a baby," Dr. Gershenfeld says, "what she does *not* want is for the baby to experiment and get the food all over his hair, the highchair, and the floor because she's the one who gets stuck cleaning it all up. She prefers that the baby sit there passively and be fed to avoid the mess. The same thing goes for climbing around and getting dirty. The cleaner the baby stays, the less laundry."

She continues, "The kids who are urged to be clean and quiet—that is, passive and dependent—the ones who sit dutifully in their playpens until mother says, 'It's time for our naps," have learned very early to take their cues from others. They don't gain a sense of what tasks they can or can't accomplish and don't evolve the self-confidence that precedes self-reliance." What's worse, little girls are far more likely to fall into this dependency trap than boys. Studies as recent as 1974 conclude that female children aren't given enough parental encouragement toward independence.

We see it all the time. "Boys," Dr. Gershenfeld points out, "get praised for jumping out of the crib, crawling all over the furniture, building blocks and knocking them down, while little girls get strokes for being pretty and docile and for not making waves."

Dr. Gershenfeld believes mothers, and working mothers in particular, ought to recognize and break up these patterns. "Accept the fact that to be adventurous is good. To climb is good. To question is good. To be clean and obedient is *not* good. Whenever you see a kid who has worn a dress or overalls all day without a wrinkle in them, see that as bad. See that as passive dependency and say, 'I'm not going to play into it.'"

It's still possible to introduce self-reliance into a household even if you've missed the boat in early childhood. A good place to begin is establishing your child's obligations to other people. A mother shouldn't call a grandparent and put the child on the phone to say hello or buy a birthday card for a favorite aunt and have the child sign it. Instead a mother might discuss with her child the importance of telephoning grandma once a week because it means a lot to her. Then the responsibility becomes the child's. He has to initiate the call and deal with grandma's disappointment when he forgets. In the same way, kids can be driven to the store to select birthday cards and gifts themselves. "One of the worst things parents do to create dependency," Dr. Gershenfeld says, "is tell their kids what to do every minute they breathe, remind them of their obligations, and run interference for them when they fail. To become self-reliant, a child must learn to

deal personally with people he's hurt and take responsibility for his mistakes."

A second area for teaching self-reliance is household duties. If you've just returned to work or are already working but want to alter existing family patterns, you can begin with a straightforward family confab about what working means. Tell your kids that everybody in the house has a function. Kids go to school. Dad is a businessman. Mom is a key punch operator. You each have independent lives, but you also have a life together and that life involves shared responsibilities. There are jobs to be done and you *all* have to do them.

"One means of dividing those jobs," says Dr. Gershenfeld, "is to make a list of literally every chore in the house and let the family—kids first, then mom and dad—choose who wants what. You might use a point system since clearing the table is not as difficult as washing the windows. The important issue is not to assign jobs, because assigning becomes an authority play and giving orders is what you want to avoid. After all, self-reliance means 'I can depend on me; I can gather my own information and filter it to make independent decisions.'"

Just as adults don't like to be told to the nth degree what to do, neither do children. And both make mistakes. That's why jobs must be negotiable and subject to periodic review. Sally may have opted for cooking twice a week as one of her chores and then discovered she hates it. She should be allowed to switch. Or David may ask his sister to walk the dog on the days he has football practice but he, in turn, must perform some work of hers.

What you are aiming for is personal responsibility and you won't succeed if you rely on a system of rewards and punishments that shifts the burden of getting a job done from the child onto a monitoring parent. "A parent can't be a conscience for a child," says Dr. Gershenfeld. "This isn't what self-reliance is about. Nobody punishes mother if she doesn't do the laundry and the family is without clean underwear.

She washes because she knows she has to. That's all there is to it."

It works like this: Let's say John has elected to set the table after school every day. Mom comes home from work and the table is covered with schoolbooks instead of placemats. Does she call John in from play, scold him, or take away his TV? No, says Dr. Gershenfeld. She makes dinner and when everybody is ready to sit down, she puts it on the table. The family will obviously be angry because there's nothing to eat with. John will feel lousy and the negative feedback about shirking his duty should be enough to pull him into line.

As children grow older their responsibilities should increase and extend beyond the home. "A kid has to learn," Dr. Gershenfeld explains, "how to handle other people and make decisions in dealing with the world around him." While you dash into the supermarket, send your child to the bakery with a fixed amount of money. Let her figure out how to spend $1.50 when the clerk says a dozen rolls are 60¢ and donuts are 15¢ each or how to substitute when the cherry pie you requested is sold out.

Developing self-reliant children puts some special burdens on parents. You may have to swallow certain things you don't like, such as the way they spend their own incomes. "Because," says Dr. Gershenfeld, "if you want a self-reliant child you must let him make decisions about the money he earns. You can, of course, set limits. No drugs. No alcohol. Nothing against the law. But within those limits, if he works to buy a car that you

don't want him to have or she squanders $20 from baby-sitting on a foolish rock concert, you may voice disapproval but little else."

And you will find it's easier to raise a passive child who follows orders than a questioning youngster. Self-reliant kids are testers. They push to see how far they can go. Bedtime is a typical case. You've set a firm bedtime for school nights, but your child always has some convincing argument for why he should stay up later; There's a TV special; he hasn't finished his homework; none of his friends go to bed this early. "At some point," Dr. Gershenfeld advises, "the buck must stop. You must shut off his arguments with a simple 'because I said so.' One of the ways parents destroy themselves is by wanting to be well-liked liberals."

Fired by Dr. Gershenfeld's suggestions, I held a family conference at dinner and talked about the meaning of personal responsibility, and the necessity to share jobs around the house and to not depend on me as family errand-runner. The following Sunday I was awakened by the tinkle of a little bell and the announcement by my son that breakfast was waiting in the kitchen. It wasn't even Mother's Day! Now if I can only get them to remember to call my mother-in-law, I'm home free.

CAROL SALINE *is associate editor of Philadelphia Magazine. She has contributed to a number of magazines, including McCall's and Reader's Digest. She has been singled out by both the Philadelphia chapter of Women in Communication and The National Press Club for awards in the field of journalism.*

HOW LONG A MATERNITY LEAVE CAN YOUR CAREER AFFORD?

by Mary Schnack

¶**Peggy O'Neill** *had been a clothes buyer at a San Francisco specialty store for eight yeas when she and her husband decided to start a family. After careful consideration, she decided to take one year's leave from her company, Joseph Magnin.* ¶**Laura Johnston** *is a systems engineer*

IBM. Although IBM has no official maternity-leave policy, Johnston knows co-workers who
taken off six months or more. She decided to return to work as soon as possible after
' her daughter. ¶Norma Dubois, owner of The Kids' Clothing Company in San Rafael,
nia, was a buyer for a major retail store when she had her baby, in March 1978. She was
to return after six months of leave but, because she did not want a different type of
.on, had to wait four more months for a buying job to open up.

nore and more women view their work as eers, maternity leave—the chance to v at home, with or without pay, without ʒing one's job—has become an issue ʒross the country. While fewer women are nclined to take five to ten years off to raise a family, many do want to spend some time t home with their newborn before returning to the job. Recognizing the value of their women employees, companies are becoming flexible, often extending the old policy of six weeks' leave.

It is important to keep in mind that maternity leave often amounts to personal leave—that is, leave at one's own expense. A company may hold a woman's job and pay disability benefits for several weeks or even months, but, by law, it is required to do so only for the time a doctor declares a woman is unable to work. (See box.) Once she is medically able to work, further maternity leave—paid or unpaid—is at the discretion of her employer, as is the promise of holding her job or an equivalent position when she returns.

A recent report by The Conference Board, a nonprofit business-research organization, shows that 97 percent of the 309 companies surveyed provide maternity leave. The most common allowance is six months. Less than one-fourth of these companies offer less than six months, and 79 percent provide for extensions based on continued disability with a doctor's certification.

Economic Considerations

The state of the economy is one reason maternity leaves have become increasingly popular. Many women no longer can quit their jobs expecting to find another in a year. Los Angeles County, which employs about 65,000 people, offers three months to a year

of maternity leave, depending on the department and certification by the woman's doctor of the time needed. "Professional women have always returned after taking leaves," said Carol Zolin, personnel analyst for Los Angeles County, "but clerical staff usually didn't come back. That seems to be changing now with the need for two incomes."

Keeping a Career Intact

Even women with the economic luxury of being able to quit for several years are taking maternity leave instead, because of their careers.

Dubois left her job as a high-volume, or top-level, buyer and returned as a low-volume buyer. But the first position that opened up for a high-volume buyer was hers. "It took a while; but I don't think there was any career sacrifice. I was able to move up when the opportunity came along. And the initial shift to lower-volume buying was perfect because the job wasn't as highly pressured and there wasn't as much traveling involved. I was able to ease back in."

A low-volume buyer usually is paid less than one buying at high volume, and Dubois said she had to fight to maintain her previous salary when she returned at the lower job level. She stressed that before women go on leave, they should be aware of their rights as determined by company policy and state law. After their return they should make sure the company holds to them. But she said she didn't have to convince the management that she would be willing to travel again. "That's part of the job and, just by returning, you make it clear you're still ambitious."

Even in a field where changes can occur quickly, women may discount possible damage to their careers by taking time off.

Mattie Park, now with the Lockheed Corporation, was a computer programmer at the System Development Corporation (SDC), a computer software company, when she took four and a half months off after having her son. She doesn't feel she missed out on developments. "The concepts behind programming computers stay the same, and once you know these, it's easy to learn a new language if you have to."

As a computer systems engineer at IBM, Johnston's projects usually entail overseeing the installation of new computer systems for a customer. "Many times an installation takes so long that a woman could work on the same project after her return."

Among computer technicians, the decision to take a leave is made easier by the labor market: The demand for programmers and engineers far exceeds the supply. The situation in nursing is much the same.

Pilots and flight attendants accrue seniority while they are on leave. But, unlike most women, they have no choice about when to go; they must stop flying the moment they learn they are pregnant. At Western Airlines, pilots and attendants are allowed 90 days without pay after the birth of their children. Time taken beyond that is classified as personal leave and does not count toward seniority. Very few women request more than 90 days. When a flight attendant returns, she actually is in a better position than when she left, since seniority usually determines her pick of flights.

The Corporate View

Many companies contend that extended pregnancy leaves and the need to reposition women in similar jobs do not cause major problems. A spokesperson for IBM said the company has experienced virtually no difficulty for the women or company and that a leave rarely has interrupted a woman's career. Libby Evans, vice-president of employee relations at one of the nation's largest banks, Security Pacific in Los Angeles, said, "It's to our advantage to retain women and attrract others by giving them the time they need to have a baby and organize their life style." (The bank allows three months' new-child-care leave for women and men and provides disability pay during a woman's disability period. Only one or two men have taken advantage of the policy, which has been in effect since the early 1970s.)

On the other hand, Toby Rothschild, executive director of the Legal Aid Foundation of Long Beach, California, which offers six months' maternity leave, said that an employee's extended leave will affect the office. "Either we're an attorney short for six months or we hire a temporary," he said, "who probably will not have the same level of expertise. The temporary will have to learn the system of the local courts and that takes time." Johnston of IBM said she noticed the problems her pregnancy was causing at her office as soon as she announced it. Although she was gone only six weeks, "The projects and accounts had to be given over to others, and it did cause some confusion for the company."

Although the companies interviewed said it is rare for a woman to take an extended pregnancy leave and not return, this happens. Cheryl Kosta, a physical therapist at the Veteran's Hospital in San Diego, California, at the time of her leave, took the full three months she was allowed but quit work three weeks after she returned. "I missed my son and didn't feel anyone else could give him the care I could. We could manage financially, too."

Kosta is not home full time, though. Because her occupation is highly marketable, it is easy for her to work part time. She hopes to have another child and, when the children are old enough for preschool, to begin a private practice. "At a hospital, there isn't much upward mobility anyway. This is a bigger step for my career," said Kosta.

Potential Drawbacks

No matter how liberal the company policy, there may be some risks in taking an extended leave. Joseph Magnin's benefits manager, Donna Tewart, said it would not be fair to an employee replacing a woman on leave to give the returning woman her former position; this could mean demoting an employee who did well for six or more months. An extended leave should not affect a woman's upward mobility, though, Tewart added, since "promotions are based on performance and taking time out for a family does not change the woman's performance."

An extended leave could affect advancement, believes Prior of SDC. "If a promotion comes up, and you are not around, you're less likely to be considered."

Also important in figuring the overall effect is the size of the company. "We're large enough now that although the woman may not get the same position, we'll put her in a similar job but on a different project than the one she was working on when she left," said Prior.

On the other hand, when a woman's career depends on building up a clientele—if she is a stockbroker, for example—it is difficult to take maternity leave without suffering a setback. When a broker goes on a maternity leave, she must refer clients to another broker, taking the chance they may not want to switch back when she returns.

Making It Work

Sociologist Jane Prather, a professor at California State University, Northridge, and a specialist in the changing roles of women and their impact on the work force, said women should make clear before they leave what they want upon their return. "Watch your wording. Make a clear statement: 'I want my job back,' not 'what if?' Don't give them ideas about not giving you your job back. But don't sound threatening. Stress before you leave what it is you want, but don't negotiate.

"Once you've left, keep in contact with the office," Prather advised. "Call in and check new developments each week, and offer to do some work at home. Write up a report in your leisure time. And keep up on business-related reading. Above all, make sure people back in the office know about your efforts.

"Once a woman returns to her job, she should voice her displeasure at any changes that are to her disadvantage," Prather said. "Level with your supervisor, saying you hope the change is temporary. Deal with it!"

Prather said no studies have been done on the effects a short-term or pregnancy leave can have on a woman's career. She suggested, though, that one possible effect could be ostracism upon the woman's return. "The rule may be that you can take a leave, but to many it means you are following a different career pattern. This is particularly true if you're in a highly competitive organization since these still tend to be male oriented. To take time off is not playing by the rules. So it is important that you keep in contact with the network while you're out."

THE LAW ABOUT PREGNANCY LEAVE

The amount of time given a woman for maternity leave varies from company to company, but, for the most part, she will receive pay only during the time a doctor certifies that she is disabled.

In 1978, Congress passed a law forbidding the government and private companies to discriminate in their disability payments, insurance or benefit programs on the basis of pregnancy, childbirth or related medical conditions.

Any disability benefits granted a woman's co-workers must also be granted to her. A company's insurance policy makes no distinction between pregnancy and other types of disability. (Abortion constitutes a disability only if continuation of the pregnancy would have endangered the woman's life. Illness resulting from any abortion entitles a woman to disability pay.)

The law sets no maximum or minimum time for pregnancy disability. Most companies, though, allow for a maximum of 15 to 26 weeks, with the majority of workers with an uncomplicated pregnancy missing a total of six weeks of work because of certified disability. Limits vary from state to state. For example, in California, where the average paid disability leave is ten weeks, the maximum time allowed for payments for any disability is nine months. Prior to the 1978 law, California's maximum-payment period for pregnancy disability was six weeks.

According to the Civil Rights Act of 1964, an employer must pay a worker returning from disability what she was receiving when she left. This applies to all workers on disability. Unaffected, too, is seniority ranking. Once a woman decides to take an extended leave beyond the time when she is disabled medically, the law no longer protects her job or her salary. Companies are increasingly lenient about allowing a woman on an extended leave to return to a similar, if not the same, job at the same salary; in some cases, there is no loss of seniority, but it's worth checking into before-hand.

CHOOSING THE RIGHT DAY CARE

by Irene Pickhardt

As the number of women in the work force continues to increase, more children are cared for in nurseries, day-care centers or day-care homes. In 1979, over six million preschool children were in need of care because their mothers worked outside the home. Working parents often worry about their child's adjustment to day care and feel helpless when their child isn't happy.

Parents *can* help their children adjust to day care. Here are some pointers from psychologists and day-care specialists.

- **Say good-bye when you leave your child at the day-care center or with a sitter.** Martin E.P. Seligman, PhD, in his book *Helplessness: On Depression, Development and Death* (W.H. Freeman, $5.95), says that parents may "sneak off" without saying good-bye in an effort to keep their child from crying. Children whose parents depart without letting them know are then never sure when they are going to be left and may become anxious and clinging.
- **Remind your child that you will return for her.** Give a specific time, if possible. Sally Provence, MD, director of the model day-care center at Yale University, reported that one of the major fears of children at the Yale day-care center was that their parents wouldn't be back to get them. This fear was especially strong when the child had behaved in a naughty way for she then seemed to feel that she didn't deserve to be taken home again. Even if you are angry with your child's behvior, reassure her of your love and remind her that you will be back to get her.
- **Provide your child with a link between your home and the day-care center.** According to James Boynton, MD, a child and adolescent psychiatrist who consults with Head Start programs, a favorite toy, a blanket or a doll can make a child feel secure.
- **Make sure that your child has one special caretaker who is responsible for his welfare.** This does two things: It prevents a child from getting lost "between the cracks," and it gives your child a special person to go to when feeling sad or tired. At the Yale center, most children had a caretaker they knew especially well. This person became the major link between home and the center, providing parents with someone to tell when "Johnny had a fight with his brother this morning and still is upset about it. He may need a little extra attention today."
- **Be patient with your child's greeting and good-bye rituals.** Provence noticed that children and babies often developed elaborate rituals to help themselves make the transition between home and center.

These might include peekaboo, running and hiding, or hugging parents over and over again. The strain of leaving one world and entering another was often eased by the patience (within reason) of the parent.

- **Make up a "blues bag."** There's nothing worse than being away from home when you're feeling down. One day-care-center owner suggested that a shopping bag full of small treats, left in the hands of a sensitive caretaker, can ease the troubled spirit. The contents should depend on the age and interest of your child, but here are some suggestions: a box of raisins, a favorite book (read to her as she sits on the lap of a favorite person, of course), a chance to call Mommy or Daddy on the telephone, silly pictures that she and Daddy drew last week, an inexpensive new toy, even a tape recording of Mommy singing a favorite song.

- **Talk about separation in positive terms.** Be careful never to tease or threaten your child by saying that you are going to leave her if she is bad. John Bowlby, a British psychologist who has published a book on separation in infants and young children (*Attachment and Loss*, two volumes, Basic Books, $4.95 each in paperback), believes that some children think their parents have left them in a center because they are "bad."

- **Watch for signs of day-care jitters.** According to Boynton, children of all ages, especially young ones, may get anxious when they are away from their parents. The sooner a parent responds to signals that the child isn't thriving, the easier it will be to avoid serious problems. Here are signals to watch for:

  Does your child frequently protest when left at the center (crying, clinging, refusing to get dressed in the morning)? Does your child look unhappy (seem somber, have a furrowed brow, appear older and more serious in demeanor)? Does your child seem more agitated, tearful or anxious (cry more easily, not be comforted quickly,

cling to you for no apparent reason)? Has your child reverted to babyish types of behavior (thumb sucking, wetting)? Has your child become less active, less interested in the world (wants to spend more time in bed, plays less)? Has your child begun to do self-damaging things (head banging, many more "accidents")?

If you notice these signals and think they might be linked to a day-care experience, here are some things to do to remedy them:

- **Plan a ten- to 15-minute solid "connect" time with your child each morning before going to the center.** When a child feels solidly connected with her parents, she is more ready to take the initiative to move off and explore the world.

- **Try bringing your child 15 minutes early each day.** Stay with your child while she adjusts to the center. Provence and her staff reported that sometimes this brief adjustment time, with her parents nearby, was all a child needed in order to feel secure.

- **Work with the day-care staff to come up with a plan for finding out what is bothering your child and remedying it.** The skill and knowledge of the staff members at your day-care center make them valuable partners in any plans you make. At the Yale center, the parents were regularly invited in to "put their heads together" with the staff.

- **Don't be shy about making inquiries or about asking for things for your child.** "As a professional," said Boynton, "I am not easily intimidated, but as a parent I am. My son started looking unhappy when we enrolled him at a nursery. I called the owner and said I wanted to visit. She told me it was against policy for parents to visit, and it was weeks later before I finally *announced* that I was coming in to observe. I wish I had acted sooner."

- **Check on your child's diet while at the center.** Large doses of sugars, starches or salt may affect a youngster's mood. Boynton suggested that parents regularly inquire about the snacks their children receive.

- **Drop in at the center at odd hours to watch portions of your child's day.** Too much time spent in a crib, a bed or a chair can be difficult for young children. Wendy Drezek, PhD, formerly a day-care consultant and now a preschool teacher, researched how children spent their time at day-care centers. She said that parents often visit during morning times, when activities usually are better planned. In her 155 hours of observation, she noticed that late morning and late afternoon times were far less organized.

- **Try to give your child more control over her time at the day-care center.** Seligman explained that one of the problems children have in nurseries and day-care centers is that they frequently feel helpless because, many times, the sequence of activities proceeds according to the clock and not according to the needs of the individual child. This feeling of helplessness can cause a child to become lethargic and, at times, depressed. One mother gave her 3-year-old more control when she purchased a small beanbag chair for her daughter and explained to the nursery staff: "This is Amy's quiet-time chair. Would you store it above her locker and give it to her when she lets you know that she'd like a quiet time?" At first, Amy wanted her chair every 15 minutes, but soon, when she realized that she could have it any time she wanted to rest, she asked for it only when she felt she needed it.

- **Ask the day-care staff to give your child extra "mothering."** Leticia Gaitan, who cares for babies and young children in her home, believes her practice of hugging and holding the children greatly helps their adjustment to her center, particularly when they are sad.

- **Help your child make a special friend at the center.** Bowlby, in his study of babies'

adjustment to separation, found that children who were with a brother or sister showed less anxiety when separated from their parents. If you can't enroll a sibling at the same center, try to help your child develop a close relationship with another child. This might involve inviting that child over to spend time at your home or to join you on family outings.

- **Try to cut back on the number of hours your child spends at the center.** Provence, in her book, *The Challenge of Daycare* (Yale University Press, $15), said that a full day of separation is difficult for many children under 3 years old and that children often become anxious as the day wears on. If parents must work full time, perhaps grandparents or close friends would be willing to stay with the child for part of the day.

- **Make sure that the caretaking style of the center matches the needs of your child.** Drezek, in researching day-care centers, found that different *types* of children were described as thriving in different types of centers. For example, some children appreciate a great deal of structure, while others prefer to putter on their own. One child might enjoy being around a lot of other children, while another child prefers a smaller group. A child who was happiest in a quiet environment might not do well in a relatively noisy center—no matter how good the center is.

- **Consider enrolling your child in a different center.** The search for adequate day care can be discouraging for parents. A study of 431 centers, published in *Windows on Daycare* (by Mary Dublin Keyserling, published by the National Council for Jewish Women, $2.50), found that only a minority of the centers provided average or above average care. The quality of a center often was not related to the fees charged. Some of the best day-care centers charged the least; some of the worst charged the most. Bearing this in mind, a parent needs to choose a center carefully.

You can find a good center. Here is a checklist to help with the search:

- **Does the center have a low staff turnover?** Once a child begins to depend on a caretaker, it can be difficult if that person leaves.
- **Does the center welcome parents' questions, concerns and visits?** Since your child may spend eight or more hours a day there, you need a place that encourages active dialogue with parents.
- **Have you visited the center for at least two hours?** Spend part of that time talking with child-care workers and the owner. Spend at least half of the time observing the normal operation of the center.
- **Is the center safe?** Make sure that plug covers are on all electrical outlets and that the play equipment is in good shape and free from sharp or jagged edges.
- **Does the center encourage exploration and learning?** Avoid a center where the television is on for most of the day or where children are confined to chairs for many hours.
- **Do the adults seem to like the children?** Do staff members encourage children's questions? Do they play with the children at times? (Avoid a center where you hear the adults saying bad boy or you're naughty to a child.)
- **Are there opportunities for children to get away from the crowd?** Some centers divide the space so that there are quiet areas where children can go to be alone. Others create hideaway nooks—piles of pillows, large cardboard boxes to sit in, a bathtub lined with cushions.
- **Is there a variety of environments?** At the minimum there should be one indoor play area and one outdoor area.

You may have to change centers a few times before you finally settle on one. One mother tried four centers in the period of a year until she found the right place for her 21-month-old son. She knew that the changes were costly both to her and to her child, but now she goes to her job each morning with peace of mind, knowing that her child is happy.

For More Information

A Parent's Guide to Day Care (OHDS, publication no. 80-30254), published by the Department of Health and Human Services, is a comprehensive guide to appraising and selecting day-care services. You can obtain a free copy by writing: LSDS, Department 76, Washington, DC 20401.

Choosing Child Care, by Stevanne Auerbach and Linda Freedman (Parents and Child Care Resources; $3); a guide to child care. Write: *Choosing Child Care*, Parents and Child Care Resources, 812 Howard Street, San Francisco, CA 94103.

Chapter Fourteen

Mind and Body

HOW TO GET TO WORK ON TIME

by Myron Brenton

Benjamin Franklin said that people who get up late wind up rushing all day. Does that sound like you? If so, you have plenty of company. Professor Samuel DeWald of Pennsylvania State University, who conducts time management seminars, says that invariably about 60 percent of the men and women who attend his seminars report having been late to work more than they would like during the preceding year. Some people are so compulsive about being late to work that even the threat of being fired doesn't get them to move faster in the morning. But even if you consider yourself a hopeless case, take heart. Experts have come up with pointers that should not only get you to work on time, but maybe even transform you into an early bird.

Pinpoint the Source of Your Lateness

Is it a problem of not being able to crawl out of bed? Do you like to linger at the breakfast table? Are you constantly caught in traffic jams? Do you grapple with so many morning chores that you can never catch up? Those morning chores especially snag many married women. Psychotherapist Anna Waller-Zemon points out that even in our supposedly emancipated times, working women probably have many more housekeeping and family responsibilities than working men. Realistically, therefore, you probably have lots to do before heading for work. And you also have more ready-made excuses for procrastinating. At any rate, try to locate just what it is that keeps making you late for work.

Look for a "Hidden Motive"

People who habitually arrive late at their jobs do so because they don't know how to manage their time, because of an underlying emotional problem, or because of both factors combined. Psychotherapist Oscar Rabinowitz has counseled a number of habitually tardy working women whose late-

270

ness could be traced to unconscious motivations.

Elaine had a crush on her boss and regularly came to work half an hour late so he would notice her. Alice came late because her boss was always so kind and reassuring when she apologized for her lateness—it made her feel she was valued and liked. And Helen was late because she literally dreaded going to work—she disliked her job that much.

It takes a great deal of unflinching self-searching to uncover hidden motives for lateness (you might even want to get some professional help to do it), but if emotional conflicts are keeping you from getting to work on time, and you want to change that pattern of lateness, it's essential to unearth and understand these conflicts.

If You Can't Get Up in the Morning, "Cheat"

Trick yourself into leaving the seductive comfort of your bed. Some people rely on clock-radios with "snooze buttons"—the alarm goes on at regular intervals. Others pull up the shades just before going to sleep; the glare of the morning sun forces them awake. Some resort to extremes. Trudy, for instance, invested in three very loud alarm clocks. She has set each twenty minutes apart, placed the first clock by her bed, the second in the hallway outside, the third near the front door. Each morning when she finally switches off her third alarm clock—set to the correct wake-up time—she's awake enough from having had to turn off the other two not to stagger back to bed and fall asleep again.

You might consider using one of the wake-up services that are available in a number of cities (some will call you twice—to make sure you're up—for the same moderate fee). But place the phone where you have to get out of bed to reach it.

Finally, go light on alcohol and heavy foods just before bedtime. Alcohol may produce a morning headache; heavy foods make it hard to fall asleep. Both force your body to work overtime digesting them, so you wake up tired.

Analyze Your Morning Activities

"Most people don't understand the nature of time at all," says DeWald. "Some think they have an unlimited number of hours available to them—or behave in a way that assumes they're going to get more time than they really have."

Does that sound familiar? Do you cram an impossible number of tasks into that thin hour between 7:30 and 8:30 in the morning? DeWald suggests making a time chart that will show you exactly what you are doing— some of which you probably should leave to another time. List all of the morning's activities as you go about performing them; time each one to see how long it really takes. Chances are, a number take longer than you thought. If, all together, they take more time than you have available between the moment you wake up and the time you should be leaving the house, you can adjust for the discrepancy by getting up that much earlier. Or, if that seems like a horrendous alternative, DeWald has some other suggestions. "Eliminate something, do it another time, give it to somebody else to do, or do it smarter."

Use Strategems for Saving Time

For example, do as much as you can the night before. Prior to going to bed, set the table for breakfast, make the orange juice, lay out your clothes and, if you have young children, their outfits. (Getting a late-evening weather report will help you decide what to wear.) Check your refrigerator; make sure you don't have to run to the supermarket in the morning because you're out of eggs or milk.

Search Out Ways You Might Be Doing Some Morning Dawdling

Do you really need that extra cigarette? That second cup of coffee? If you do, why? (Hidden motives again, perhaps?)

Enlist the Cooperation of Others

Ask friends not to call you in the morning. If your family treats you as the morning work-horse, try to distribute the workload more equitably. Avoid doing the same thing twice—for instance, if you have a family, don't make two breakfasts, one for the kids and the other for yourself and your husband.

Refrain from getting into arguments or heavy discussions over the breakfast table. Postpone emotional issues to a more appropriate time.

Allow Some Leeway

Don't make your schedule so tight that every minute is accounted for. You never know when something unexpected—like a button that needs sewing or a huge traffic jam—will slow you up. As DeWald puts it, "Just assume every morning that something will go wrong." He counsels building an extra ten or fifteen minutes "emergency time" into your schedule.

Be Good to Yourself

Use "behavior modification" techniques to help you. Ms. Waller-Zemon advises not making impossible demands on yourself—for example, promising yourself you'll never be late to work again. "Make a contract with yourself to try your new get-to-work-on-time plans only for a short period," she says. "Something manageable, like a week. Then renew that contract with yourself for the next week, and so on. It makes your goal more attainable. As week after week goes by, and you see that you're being successful, the easier it will be to get to work on time. Being punctual becomes its own reward."

Meanwhile, reward yourself in other ways. Waller-Zemon tells of one woman who decided to give herself a treat for each full week she made it to work on time. One week she ate a sumptuous lunch, the second she bought herself a shirt she liked, the third she got theater tickets for herself and her boyfriend.

Get to Work Early

What a revolutionary idea! Yet, Dr. Rabinowitz points out, some people find it easier to get to work early than on time. Consider the joys of arriving thirty minutes or so before everybody else gets there: it's quiet and peaceful; you can read the paper or catch up on your correspondence; you have the time for that extra cup of coffee; you've beaten the rush-hour traffic.

One other thing. If you get to work early, you'll know for certain that you'll be there on time.

FATIGUE AND YOUR EMOTIONS

by Greta Walker

You wake up in the morning, after eight hours of sleep, and it's an effort to drag yourself out of bed. You listlessly go through your workday, sit heavy-eyed through dinner with friends, and later doze off in front of the TV. "I don't understand it," you tell people, "I get plenty of sleep, the doctor says I'm perfectly healthy, yet I'm always tired. I guess I'm one of those people who needs extra rest."

It's true you're tired, but extra rest may not be the answer. According to New York psychotherapist Patricia Catalina, "Fatigue can be a symptom of something that is going on in your life, something you find too difficult and painful to confront. You may be in a job you hate, an unsatisfactory relationship, a situation that lowers your self-esteem, but you don't want to come to grips with it. By becoming tired, you literally close your eyes to the problem."

Freelance TV producer Mary L. is aware that when she is in an uncomfortable situation, such as a meeting where she feels she's not getting adequate recognition, her reaction is to get tired.

"Recently I was in an agent's office," she recalls, "and in the midst of our talk concerning work possibilities for me, the phone rang. The agent began to speak to the caller at great length about a big deal he was negotiating for someone else. He seemed to have forgotten I was there. Suddenly all I wanted to do was curl up on the carpet and go to sleep, to obliterate the whole scene. When I left the office I was so exhausted I could barely make it to the bus stop. At home I collapsed on the bed. Five minutes later a friend called to discuss a mutual business venture. I was immediately filled with energy, alive and excited. Gone was the enervated creature of a moment before."

What Mary doesn't realize is that she needn't have become that "enervated creature." She was tired because she thought her only choice was to allow herself to be demeaned by the agent's rude behavior, as if she had to sit there until dismissed. Actually, she could have left; she could have interrupted him for a minute to suggest they make another appointment when he had more time; she could have told him that she had made this time available for him and she expected him to keep the half-hour free for her. In other words, she could have acted, which would have elevated her self-esteem and energized her. Instead she perceived herself as helpless, which lowered her self-esteem and exhausted her.

But of course action can bring unpleasant consequences. The agent could have been annoyed, might not want to represent her. Yet better to take that chance—the agent didn't seem to be doing that much for her anyhow, and if she had spoken up he may have had more respect for her—than to reduce oneself to a humiliated, exhausted lump.

"Action, not sleep, is the best antidote for emotional fatigue," says Patricia Catalina. "Although we fear the consequences of action, most often we are pleasantly surprised by the results. A client of mine, who loved her job and was highly creative in it, lost all interest when a new boss came on the scene. Her new employer seemed to value her less than his predecessor and greeted her efforts with a minimum of enthusiasm and interest.

"My client's solution was to sleep twelve hours a night, to come in late to work, and to go through her work chores somewhat like a sleepwalker. When we discussed her job situation, she complained that she was too tired to do anything about it. She was using her fatigue to conceal her fear of taking action. If she complained at work would she be fired? If nothing was done to alleviate her unhappiness would she have to quit? Where would she get another job? Since her self-esteem had been shattered by the indifference of the new boss, she was sure only the worst could happen. Finally, encouraged by her therapy sessions, she forced herself to ask for a transfer to another department. To her amazement the request was granted. Gone were her problems at work. Gone was her fatigue."

Tiredness can also be a clue to a flagging relationship. "I was yawning over our candle-lit dinners and dozing off before we could make love," reveals Irene S. "I just assumed I was overworked and not getting enough sleep. Slowly I came to realize that early in our relationship we would stay up until three in the morning making love, and I would be buoyant the next day on four hours sleep. I also recalled our lively conversations that went on for hours. Now it seemed all I wanted to do was sleep away the time we spent together. Then I began to think about our relationship, and it became quite clear it had run its course."

There is also the other side of the coin—when the man breaks up the relationship and the woman wants it to continue. Many women report becoming extremely depressed and exhausted for months, and even as long as a year.

"I managed to go to work, and that was all," remembers Lillian G. "Then I'd come home and crawl into bed. On weekends I'd sit in front of the television set or sleep. Going to the market was such an effort that I'd be wiped out and have to take a nap. After about eight months of behaving like the walking dead, I figured I'd better do something or I'd end up sleeping my life away. A friend suggested I try a yoga class, so I enrolled. I went every other day, and I began to meditate each morning for twenty minutes before going to work. After the first yoga class, I came home and went to bed, but after two weeks I could feel the new energy. Within a month I began to live again."

In addition to yoga, New York psychotherapist Judith Antrobus advocates any kind of physical exercise as an aid to coming out of a depression that causes fatigue. "Just getting the adrenaline going and unlocking your muscles is helpful," she says. "The more you sit around the house and the more you sleep, the worse you will feel. Any movement you do to break the pattern is a plus. You can start with the simplest kinds of exercises such as bending, stretching, or jogging in place—even if you can only do them for a few minutes at first.

Of course," Dr. Antrobus continues, "ultimately you have to examine what is going on in your life. You can't solve problems mechanically. I realize that's not too easy to do when you're severely depressed, but when you come out of the depression, you should ask yourself what caused you to be so fatigued. What could you have done to prevent the extreme reaction? Usually in cases such as Lillian G's, the woman feels that her self-esteem comes from the man. When he leaves her, it's as though he has taken her identity with him and left her an exhausted shell. Once you realize no one can do that, you'll be less likely to cling desperately to a faltering relationship and less liable to be so devastated when it finally breaks up."

While some women fight to drag themselves out of fatigue, others work from morning to night to become tired. These are generally women who can't allow themselves relaxation unless they are falling down with exhaustion. They constantly complain of overwork, of hardly being able to keep their eyes open at the end of the day, yet too often the endless tasks they perform are of their own making, not of necessity.

"This kind of woman," explains Patricia Catalina, "gets her self-esteem from being the most overworked person around. She feels if others see that she's limp with fatigue from her countless chores, they will value her more. Often she is disappointed, and complains, 'I knock myself out for everyone and nobody appreciates it.' The reason all her frenzy and exhaustion aren't appreciated is that most people sense that the activity is superfluous, engaged in to heighten the image of the door, not really to help others.

"In these cases," counsels Ms. Catalina, "it's a good idea to give in to the need for rest before exhaustion sets in, but you must explore why you are compelled to keep active. Why do periods of quiet and relaxation make you anxious? Why do you think people will be impressed with your eternal bustle? What do you think you gain by getting so tired? Why can't you allow others to do things for you before you become helpless from fatigue? Try to pare down your work to the real necessities—make the change gradually so you slowly become accustomed to a different pace. Substitute some quiet time for yourself, or some simple pleasurable activities. You'll find that when you're rested and alert you'll be able to get much more satisfaction out of your activities than when you were overworked and tired."

Just thinking about too many burdens is another source of fatigue—the apartment needs painting, your parents are coming to town next week and you have to think of ways to entertain them, bills must be paid and you're short of funds, mountains of papers sit on your desk at work waiting for your attention. It's all too much to contemplate, so you become weary and your eyes start to close.

Sleeping, of course, won't make the problems go away. Just the reverse. As you sleep, time passes and chores pile up, causing you to be even wearier and more behind when you awaken. On the other hand, you can't tackle everything at once—it's impossible. Having overly high expectations of yourself is a sure way to exhaustion. What you can do is cut tasks down to manageable size. Make a list of the things that must be done, then consider only one item at a time, in the order of their importance.

For example, there's no sense painting the apartment if your parents are coming next week. That can be tackled after they leave, when you're not feeling so pressured. If your parents are the kind who would put you down for not having pristine walls, you may have to cope with a little anxiety, but

that's preferable to fatigue.

Perhaps paying bills has the highest priority on your list. Think about how you can pay a portion of each bill, where you might borrow money, which bills can be deferred until next month. Concentrate on that problem until it's resolved, then check it off and move on to the next.

The point is, when you handle each chore separately it's not nearly so tiring as trying to manage everything at once, or even thinking of everything at once. If you respect your limits and pace yourself realistically you'll acquire extra energy and in the long run accomplish much more.

"Sometimes it's difficult, and even painful, to come to terms with the reasons for our fatigue," concludes Patricia Catalina, "but it's better to experience the difficulty and pain than to sleep our precious time away. Life can be exciting and challenging. We owe it to ourselves to face it with our eyes open."

CHECKING UP ON YOUR CHECKUP

by Edythe Cudlipp

A complete annual physical examination can and should be one of the most significant parts of your medical care. It might even be called a life-assurance policy. Not only is it the best preventive medicine you can buy, but it also provides your physician with a yardstick of your present health, by which he can measure your health in the future.

One of the most important points to keep in mind regarding preventive medical care is that both you and your physician have responsibilities. Your physician is responsible to you for performing and interpreting the examination. You are responsible to him for helping provide the information necessary for him to decide what special or further

tests you may need beyond routine tests and for him to make his evaluation. And you are responsible to yourself to make sure you understand what he is doing and why.

Choosing the Physician

"Choosing the right physician is especially important for women," according to Dr. Benjamin Natovitz of Executive Health Examiners, a clinic that specializes in diagnostic examinations. "Most women tend to depend on their gynecologists for health care, whether or not they have children. Since this specialist knows the most intimate part of their bodies and their lives, they may feel that he knows the rest of their bodies just as intimately. As a result, they're unfair to their gynecologists, and they're cheating themselves."

The fact is that a gynecologist is concerned with a woman's reproductive system, and there's more to a checkup than a Pap smear. For a checkup, you should go to an internist (or physician in family practice) who is trained in the general functioning of the body which includes the gynecological.

If you don't have an internist, ask your friends or the people you work with about theirs. And remember, there's more to it than finding out whether the internist is "nice." Find out what hospitals he or she is affiliated with. A good physician will be associated with good hospitals, and this is important should you ever need hospitalization. (You can check with the local county or city medical society.) Find out if the internist is a diplomate. It means he has passed national boards to qualify him to practice his specialty.

Another important factor that friends can tell you about is what the physician considers a complete checkup to be. An internist in private practice points out that some women want to be spared what they consider the indignity of certain examinations, such as a simple digital examination of the rectal canal, and avoid physicians who perform them. Actually, they should be avoiding physicians who don't perform them. Since rectal cancer is most easily detected in its earliest stages by this examination, no checkup is complete without it.

Because most internists are men, you want one with whom you're comfortable, one you feel you can talk to, one who doesn't take the "macho" or "Big Daddy" attitude that it's not necessary for you to know about your body since you probably wouldn't understand anyway. In this respect, you have to trust your instincts. Keep in mind that going to a physician one time doesn't tie you to him for life. If you're uncomfortable, if you have to wait for a long time without an apology, if you're rushed through the examina-

tion, if you're treated like a child or your questions go unanswered, find another internist.

Preparing for Your Checkup

Your physician needs a good, complete medical history. Sometimes you'll be asked to fill out a printed form. Other times, the physician may discuss your history with you. Either way, your answers should be as complete as possible. A physician isn't clairvoyant. He must rely to some extent on what you may be able to tell him, especially when it concerns illnesses in your family or your own past and your present health picture. And since you don't have ESP either, question him if you don't understand what he wants. It's your prerogative as a medical consumer.

A good medical history includes such questions as whether any blood relative ever had diabetes, kidney disease, heart disease, nervous sytem disease, or stroke. These diseases, among others, have a relationship to family or heredity. If a parent or grandparent has had any of them, the physician will want to check thoroughly to see whether you have any latent or early symptoms that may not show up in a routine checkup. If a blood relative has had cancer, moreover, the type is important since some types seem to be more genetic than others.

What detailed information about yourself you give the physician will help, too. He will ask about past illnesses and operations and will want to know about any complaints you may presently have or changes in your body you may recently have noticed. For example, have your urinary habits changed—which can be an early symptom of diabetes or kidney disease? Are you thirsty more frequently? Have you had dizzy spells or frequent headaches? Do you have stomach or intestinal pains and do they occur at specific times, such as before or after eating or after specific foods? Does other food, like milk, help? Have you had a noticeable weight gain or loss? What about your menstrual cycle?

Your physician must also know about any medication or drugs you may be taking. These may not only be related to your complaints or symptoms but are also necessary for him to know about in case he has to prescribe other medication, since certain medicines and drugs taken in combination can be harmful. Medication means all prescription drugs, including birth control pills, tranquilizers, and sleeping pills, as well as medicines to control illnesses, like insulin for diabetes. A complete drug profile also includes whether you drink alcohol and how much, whether you smoke marijuana, and of course whether you use hard drugs. Knowing how many cigarettes you smoke is important, too.

Dr. Natovitz adds, "Tell your physician about over-the-counter remedies, as well. If you take aspirin regularly, tell him. Tell him what kind and how many vitamins you take, because some vitamins like A and D can be toxic if taken in large quantities. Tell him what other kinds of remedies you use, such as breatholators, some of which have been found to be dangerous if abused."

A good idea may be to jot down all the above information (and your questions) in advance of your appointment. In the anxiety of the actual examination, anyone can forget something. What if your physician doesn't ask for all this information? He probably will, but if he doesn't, you bring it up.

One last point: Holding back information, such as excessive drinking, drug use, or smoking marijuana is cheating yourself. A physician's duty is to pass judgment on your health, not on you.

The Physical Examination

Women should have exactly the same physical examination as men, with the exception of the gynecological checkup," says Dr. Natovitz. "For example, the female hormone estrogen is thought to protect women in their childbearing years from heart disease and stroke, since women of that age have lower rates than men. However, with women working more than ever before and moving into positions of responsibility, they are up against the same stresses as men—stresses that can cause heart disease and stroke. The checkup, then, has less to do with sex than age."

If you're thirty-five or forty, your physician may want a few extra tests. So, if the tests are new to you, ask about them, but don't worry that something may necessarily be wrong. He is most likely simply following sound medical practice.

You'll be weighed by the physician or his nurse or technician. One or the other will check your blood pressure, using a stethoscope and a sphygmomanometer, the familiar cuff that's placed on your upper arm, expanded, and then released gradually. Although a "normal" reading is considered to be 120/80, these figures may vary depending on several factors, including weight and age. Excitement or stress, even the stress of the physical may also heighten your reading artificially. Hence, your physician may double-check and retake your blood pressure when you're more relaxed. If you have any questions, especially in the event that anyone in your family has or had high blood pressure, be sure to ask your physician. If you want to know what your blood pressure is and he doesn't tell you, ask him, and if you don't understand the numbers, make him explain them.

The physician will check your eyes, ears, and mouth. If you're over thirty-five or forty, he may check for glaucoma if he has the equipment. Glaucoma is a major cause of blindness that usually first becomes evident after forty. While there is no known cure, it can be successfully treated and arrested— and the earlier the better. So, if he doesn't check for it, ask him why not, and if he doesn't have the equipment, get a glaucoma test elsewhere.

When you're undressed and on the examination table, your physician will listen with his stethoscope to your heart to detect any murmur or abnormality. He may want an electrocardiogram (EKG), especially if you have a family history of heart disease. If you're over thirty-five or forty, an EKG may be performed routinely.

Again using the stethoscope, he'll listen to your lungs, asking you to inhale and exhale so he can hear how clear they are. He may take a chest X-ray. Your neck will be checked for any enlargement of the thyroid gland, and your abdomen area for any swelling in the liver, spleen, or other organs. The physician will make a digital examination of your rectum to check for cancer. Especially if you're over thirty-five, he may examine your lower intestinal tract for polyps—a kind of benign tumor that can be easily surgically removed—with a sigmoidoscope, a tubular instrument similar to the speculum used in the pelvic examination. And naturally, a pelvic examination will be made and a Pap smear taken, and your breasts examined lying down and sitting up.

These tests form the basis of the physical part of your physical examination. While they're being performed, ask questions about them and about what your physician is looking for, if you want to know. It's your right.

The other tests don't require your presence—although they do require urine and blood samples. From the blood sample, as many as twelve factors in the blood can be checked. These include enzymes, various minerals, and substances like cholesterol and triglycerides, fatty particles that have been proven to have a relationship to heart disease and stroke. The results will tell how such organs as the liver, kidneys, spleen, and others are functioning.

The Consultation

Once you're dressed, your physician will go over the results of your examination with you—insofar as possible. Although the final results of the blood and urine analyses may take a few days, he can tell you what he's found that may reassure you about your specific complaints and general health. This is your last chance to ask him any questions you have, so ask! Don't leave until you're satisfied with his answers.

One further point: An annual checkup doesn't mean that you won't develop a disease in the next week, month, or year. It does mean an attempt was made to detect diseases in the earliest possible stages, even before you have symptoms. High blood pressure, for example, has been called a "silent disease" because it often doesn't have any symptoms, although it can result in stroke or heart or kidney malfunction. Yet, it's easily detected; and, as in the case of so many diseases, the earlier it's detected, the more efficiently and easily it can be controlled. That's why your annual checkup can often be the best value you can get for your health dollar.

Speaking of dollars, what should an annual checkup cost? A lot depends on where you live. Medical fees vary from locality to locality. Other factors include whether X-rays are taken or an EKG or other special tests performed. Laboratory costs also play a part in determining your bill.

Being an intelligent medical consumer, then, means giving your physician all the information he needs to decide what tests you should have. It also means knowing what to expect and insisting you get it. There may be reasons why your physician may not perform every test mentioned. If you're under his care for treatment of a specific condition, for instance, he may have performed some of the tests recently enough so that he feels it isn't necessary to repeat them all again. Still, in this as in other matters concerning your checkup, it's your right to ask what he's doing—or not doing—and why.

Checkup Check List

The following examinations and tests should be part of your annual checkup:
Height and weight
Blood pressure reading

Examination of eyes, ears, mouth, and throat
Neck examination for thyroid gland
Breast examination
(lying down and sitting up)
Pelvic examination and Pap smear
Rectal examination
Examination of abdomen for

enlargement or sensitivity in organs and lower abdomen
Heart, with stethoscope (and EKG, perhaps)
Lungs, with stethoscope (and X-ray, perhaps)
Urinalysis
Blood tests

GETTING OUT FROM UNDER STRESS

by Julia Kagan

The Stress Syndrome

In 1973, a young *Washington Post* reporter named Sally Quinn was hired to co-anchor the CBS Morning News. After a strenuous publicity tour, Ms. Quinn, a successful journalist with no previous television experience, made her debut on the air with a severe cold and a 102-degree fever. By the time she left the job some four months later, she had developed insomnia, an ulcer, and a full-blown case of acne. She was a textbook case of what can happen to a person under too much stress.

If you're lucky, you won't have to live through an experience like that. But, to one degree or another, you do have to live with stress and cope with what it can do to your health and your sanity. Strangely enough, the things that create stress don't even have to be unpleasant. You may not be surprised if you develop a headache when your boss is in a bad mood, but what about the nervous stomach you got the day you were promoted? Anything that has a strong effect on you—mentally or physically—can cause a stress response, even falling in love. It is when your body overreacts to the situation or has to deal with too many stressful events in a short time that you can get into trouble.

Everyone is familiar with some of the ways this happens. The young executive with

ulcers who is chomping antacid tablets on his way to the top is a cliché by now. But he could just as easily be *she*. Thirty years ago, men with ulcers outnumbered women twenty to one. Today, the ratio is two to one.

And if you think your estrogen protects you against stress-induced heart trouble or high cholesterol, you're wrong. American women do get fewer heart attacks than men, but this "immunity" is limited to white American women. Black American women are even more likely than black men to develop coronary heart disease, and white women in many other countries develop it at the same rate as their men.

According to Drs. Meyer Friedman and Ray H. Rosenman, it is your personality, not how much cholesterol you consume, that determines whether you'll have a heart attack. They divide people into two groups: Type A—hard-driving, rushed, competitive, pressured human beings—and Type B, the complete opposite. Type A, both male and female, are the most likely coronary victims. Type A people also have higher levels of cholesterol in their blood than Type B. (Cholesterol levels seem to rise when a person is under stress.) In fact, the Type A women they tested had even more blood cholesterol than the Type A men. The reason women suffer fewer heart attacks than men (our death rate from heart diesase is less than and declining faster than men's) is simply that fewer women are Type A. But, according to Friedman and Rosenman, if we adopt men's high-pressure lifestyles along with their jobs, we risk getting their diseases.

Ulcers and heart attacks are only two of the ailments caused or worsened by stress. A complete list would run for pages. Many of them take years to develop; some show at the drop of a hat—or the thought of a job interview. Among the major ones are:

High blood pressure, atherosclerosis, angina pectoris, palpitations, stroke, insomnia, spastic colon, constipation, diarrhea, migraine headaches, tension headaches, backaches, hay fever, asthma, arthritis, facial pain, colds, cold sores, teeth grinding, clenched jaws, hair loss (excluding loss due to pregnancy or ordinary male baldness), skin problems, anorexia nervosa (refusal to eat that results in dangerous loss of weight).

Also, for women: irregular menstruation, cramps, vaginal infections, difficulty having sexual relations, inability to get pregnant when there is no physical cause, certain problems during pregnancy.

Plus a host of mental distresses: anxiety, depression, panic, phobias of all kinds. And harmful behaviors such as alcoholism, drug addiction, smoking, and compulsive eating.

Stress is thought to make us more susceptible to infections, which explains how we can live surrounded by legions of harmful viruses and bacteria and only sometimes get sick. Some researchers even think stress may influence the development of cancer.

The Stress Mechanism

When the brain senses a sudden or severe stress, it sounds the red alert, releasing a flood of adrenalines and other body chemicals and mustering defenses all over your body. You breathe faster, your heart pounds, your blood pressure goes up, all your senses become more acute, your muscles tense for action. You may get cold hands and feet and sweaty palms. Your hair "stands on end" and you feel anxious, ready to spring. This is the alarm reaction, the first stage of your body's adaptation to stress. It is a survival mechanism from the earliest times in our evolution, designed to enable us to fight or flee danger, a useful reaction to a saber-toothed tiger—or a mugger. The problem is that it is excessive for most of the threats modern humans are likely to encounter. When your supervisor reminds you of a deadline, you can't punch him (or her) in the nose or run away. Yet you may be filled with the same "red alert" hormones.

(Your body also fights stress in more specific ways. It may cause the skin to inflame around a bee sting so the poison won't spread, or send white blood cells to the site of an infection.)

If stress continues, your body can usually adapt to it. But we have limited resources for adaptation, so the process leaves us more vulnerable to other stresses that might occur at the same time. That's why you may get the flu while your body is busy reacting to the threat of a work deadline. Or why your kids got on your nerves more than usual when your husband was laid off. Usually your body wins the battle and returns to normal. But if it has to deal with too much stress over a long period of time—or if, for some reason, it habitually overreacts to relatively minor irritations—you can get a stress disorder.

Everyone has a weak spot—a target organ for stress, as doctors call it. That's where you get zapped when your body has had too much stress. If your target organ is the stomach, you may be nauseated easily or develop an ulcer. If it's the blood vessels, you may have high blood pressure or migraine headaches. Most of us don't have major stress diseases, but we all have target organs. To find yours, take a look at where you hurt when you feel pressured.

Your weak spot depends on a complex interaction between the kind of body you inherited from your parents and the way your personality was conditioned. Your family may be prone to ulcers, but the way you react to life is what gives you one. You may even have unconsciously learned your reaction to stress. Perhaps as a child your family paid more attention to you when you had a headache; you may have carried this attention-getting habit with you into adult life. Your target organ can also change with time: the child who threw up on Mondays to avoid going to school (stomach) may grow into an acne-ridden adolescent (skin) and end up as an adult with palpitations (heart).

How much stress you can take also varies from person to person. Obviously, how healthy you are is one factor. Here are some others:

Too many changes in your life, major or minor, can more than double your chances of getting a stress-related disorder in the next two years.

Boring, unchallenging work—or a job you hate—can be just as dangerous or more dangerous to your health than lots of pressure, long hours, and heavy responsibilities.

Three things have been shown to make a stressful event worse: not being able to predict it, the frustration of not being able to do anything about it, and feeling ambivalent about it.

The Stress Strategies

If you have a serious stress disorder, you're probably under a doctor's care. And if you think you have some of the symptoms, don't dismiss them out of hand as "all in your mind." "Don't assume that changes in your menstrual periods, for example, are due to psychological causes," cautions Dr. John Astrachan, assistant clinical professor of psychiatry and obstetrics-gynecology at The New York Hospital-Cornell Medical Center. They may not be, and if there is a medical problem, it should be treated medically.

However, traditional medical treatment can only do so much. For example, curing an ulcer may not end your ulcer problem. According to Dr. S. Philip Bralow, clinical professor of medicine at the University of South Florida College of Medicine, though peptic ulcers heal rapidly, 40 percent of all ulcer patients get new ulcers within two years and 80 percent within four. If your stress symptoms are crippling, you may want to try psychotherapy. There are two approaches to choose between: 1) Traditional psychologists and psychiatrists believe that stress disorders are often manifestations of deep emotional conflicts and that dealing with the conflicts can help improve the physical symptoms. 2) Behavioral therapists go after the symptoms themselves. They use a variety of methods to help people recognize and change the ways they deal with stress—keeping a daily journal to find out which experiences bring on the symptoms, mental and physical relaxation exercises to short-circuit the body's tendency to go into red alert too often, and biofeedback to train patients to revise body processes over which they usually have no conscious control. By having their body's functions monitored with a biofeedback machine, people have learned in some cases to lower their blood pressure, reduce the muscle tension that creates chronic headaches or backaches, control uneven heartbeats, and raise the temperature in their hands (which diverts blood away from the forehead and helps reduce migraine headaches).

But if your main problem is deciding what to do besides punching the boss—or throttling the kids—here are some things to try before you reach for a cigarette. Or a tranquilizer. Or a double Scotch. They are simplified versions of some of the techniques therapists use to treat stress. You can do most of them right at your desk. (If some look a bit peculiar, you can always retreat to the couch in the washroom.)

Remember how your mother used to tell you to count to ten and take a deep breath before you picked a fight with someone? This is a Yoga breathing exercise based on counting that can actually help you relax. Close your eyes and sit up straight. As you inhale—slowly, deeply—count silently to two. Hold the air in on "Three." Then let the air seep out, "four, five." Hold again, "six, seven." Continue breathing and counting for ten minutes. Open your eyes.

This one will unknot tense muscles. It was adapted from the relaxation exercises of Dr. Edmund Jacobson. Sitting comfortably in a chair with your eyes closed, clench your right fist as hard as you can. Then relax it. Let your whole arm go limp. Feel the difference? Do it again. Then repeat with your left arm. Next, with your arms hanging relaxed at your sides, raise your eyebrows, crinkle your forehead and tense the muscles of your scalp. Relax. Tense. Relax. Do the same with your eyes and nose, then your jaw and neck, your shoulders, your chest and stomach, the muscles of your buttocks, then your thighs, your calves, your ankles, and your toes. When you finish with each part, it will be heavy, calm, totally relaxed. Sit quietly for a few minutes. Open your eyes.

Here's a mental relaxation exercise, a simplified version of a German technique called autogenic therapy. Again, sit comfortably in a chair. Close your eyes and focus your attention on your right arm. Say to yourself, "My right arm feels heavy, warm." Feel the warmth spreading up your arm, but don't push for the feeling. Let it come to you. Then concentrate on your left arm, shoulders, stomach, legs, and feet. Say the same words to yourself about each region of your body. Feel the warmth and the heaviness travel down your body, ironing out the tension, leaving you deliciously relaxed, heavy and sleepy, as if you were sitting under a warm spring sun. And say to yourself, "My body is calm. My mind is calm. I am totally calm." After ten minutes or so, take several deep breaths. As you breathe, say to yourself, "I am filled with energy. Each breath is filling me with life." Open your eyes. Stand up. Stretch.

This is a simple form of meditation. True believers do it cross-legged on the floor (or twisted into the lotus position, if they're really limber), but you can do it just as easily in a chair. Sit straight (but not rigid) with your hands resting comfortably in your lap, one inside the other. Feel yourself breathe—in, out, in, out—slowly, regularly. Concentrate on your breathing. Each time you breathe out, say a one-syllable word or sound—"rest," "soft," "baa" (or "om," if you want to go Sanskrit). Repeat the word over and over for ten minutes or so, twenty if you have the time. Then slowly open your eyes. (Regular meditation—practitioners do it twice a day—has been found to help lower high blood pressure. In experiments at Harvard Medical School, experienced meditators showed lower rates of oxygen consumption and lower levels of lactate (a substance thought to produce anxiety) in their blood while they were meditating.)

Here's one for insomnia. You can't do it in the office (unless your job is testing mattresses for a mattress company), but it may help you get to sleep so you'll be more alert tomorrow morning. First, get up. Tossing and turning will not put you to sleep. Smooth the sheets, plump the pillow, and climb back under the covers. Lie on your back, arms rseting comfortably at your sides. Problem after problem has been flooding into your mind, keeping you awake. What you need is a vacation. Take one, miles away from everything.

Example: You're barefoot in a cool, green glade. Spread a satin-covered down comforter on the grass and lie down. Feel the softness on your skin. There's nothing in the world but the earth, the grass, the faint scent of mimosa from a nearby tree. The sky is so blue, and so far, far away. A puff of milkweed floats by. Blow on it gently. Watch it rise into the sky, higher and higher. Concentrate on it, a glimmer of white disappearing into the infinite blue. . . .

If worries about a particular situation are making your life a misery, analyze it. It will give you a feeling of control which may help you live with the problem, to say nothing of solving it. Write the name of the problem at the top of a blank piece of paper. Underneath it, list all the reasons it is a threat to you. Study each reason—is the danger a real one or are you just unduly worried? Cross out all the unrealistic dangers. On another sheet of paper, list all the real dangers. Underneath each one, write a specific action you can take to deal with the danger. One by one, carry out each specific action. If there is nothing you can do, write "There is noth-

ing I can do about this problem. Therefore, I will not let it make me miserable." Save this piece of paper.

Use these techniques every time you feel yourself getting tense—in the office, at home, in the dentist's waiting room. Try to find the one that works best for you. And remember, you can always go home and kick the cat. . . .

THE SECRET STRENGTHS OF WOMEN
Elizabeth Janeway Talks About the Powers of the Weak

Interview by Uta West

Brooklyn-born Elizabeth Janeway, the distinguished novelist, journalist, critic and lecturer, is no stranger to the nine-to-five world. She had to interrupt her studies to take a job in a bargain-basement store when her family lost its money during the Depression. Eventually, she returned to Barnard College in New York City, graduating in 1935, the year she won *Story* magazine's intercollegiate contest. Three years later, she married economist Eliot Janeway, then a correspondent for the *New York Times.* They have two sons.

When Janeway's first novel, *The Walsh Girls,* a psychological study of two New England sisters, appeared in 1943, one critic compared her to Jane Austen, adding that Janeway was more aware of "the larger theme of world tragedy." Another reviewer declared: ". . . no man who wishes to make even a fumble at understanding the other sex can afford to miss this novel." The author's concern with women and the world at large was developed further in five subsequent novels. In addition, Janeway wrote books for children and edited works on literature.

With the publication, in 1971, of *Man's*

World, Woman's Place, Janeway crystallized her philosophy into nonfiction, providing a historical and sociological framework for the growing women's movement. A study in social mythology, the book explains how myths affect the structure of our society. Janeway argues that myths are grounded in wishful thinking and cannot be changed by disproving facts, only by changing emotions—a process that takes time and patience. In 1974, *Between Myth and Morning: Women Awakening* brought the earlier book up to date, with the emphasis on contemporary women's practical problems involving careers, family, child rearing, sex and aging.

Janeway has been praised by critics for her "absolute sociological pitch," as well as for her incisiveness, clarity, wit and goodwill—qualities evident in her most recent study, *The Powers of the Weak,* published by Alfred A. Knopf. In this book, Janeway extends her discussion beyond the woman question to universal and timeless concerns with the nature of power. Drawing on history, psychology and economics, Janeway gives us the "underview" of power, from the vantage point of the governed majority rather than of the ruling elite. In the book, as in the following interview, the author continues to use the experience of women as a basic reference point.

● **How is women's experience a guide to "the Country of the Weak?"** All kinds of people make up the governed majority, but women are the most numerous, have been there longest and are the most central. The division of the world into two sexes is at the very bottom of people's consciousness. When the powerful want to say to another group, "You're different," "You're not *normal,*" they look for physiological differences that hark back to the assignment of inferior attributes to women. If there are no obvious differences—skin color, slanted eyes—they make them up, giving Jews yellow stars, branding slaves, making the lower orders wear special clothes.

● **How do the powerful keep the weak— women, for example— "in their place"?** The most important question in the world is not what's good or bad, or what's right or wrong, but what's *important.* If you don't think you're important, you're not going to stand up for yourself. The right to define what is important is a power often used, without recognizing it as such, by the establishment, as well as by revolutionary movements dominated by men. "Why do you bring up these 'unimportant' female goals when we're trying for the working-class revolution you're a part of?" Well, how much a part of it *am* I? What's in it for me? These are very basic questions.

● **Lord Acton's dictum that power tends to corrupt and absolute power corrupts absolutely has caused many people, especially women, to think of power as a dirty word. Is it?** We should begin by realizing that power is neither an attribute nor a possession of the powerful, but *a process of negotiation and bargaining among human beings.* Power relationships exist between people who have some kind of goal in common. You want the country you live in to be governed reasonably well.

You hope the business you're connected with makes enough money to pay good wages and return good dividends to stockholders.

Both sides of the power equation have something to contribute and both sides can mess things up. There are plenty of ways to intervene in the political process, whether you're top cat or underdog. What the weak don't realize is that the powerful *need* the consent and cooperation of the governed, not only to validate their rule but to allow them to use their power efficiently.

● **How can the weak use their power to hold their own against the strong?** The first power of the weak is that of disbelief. We withdraw our consent, either overtly or, if that's too dangerous, covertly. There's nothing passive about passive resistance. Blacks who were "lazy and shiftless" actually were practicing disguised disobedience. We need to assess our relative importance in the world, to step back from a role we've been playing and look at it objectively. We need to ask not only, "What's in it for me?" but also, "What do I contribute? What value should be placed on what I do?

Years ago, I resigned as a mother. I said, "I don't care if Jim eats another green pea as long as he lives." My family still remembers and talks about it. Of course, personal relationships are different from business.

● **Yes. In business, you can always be replaced. Which leads me to my next point. Women who have begun to make it in the work world may feel that since they're just getting a foothold, it would be wise for them to maintain a low profile.** I can understand the feeling, but it doesn't work that way. Take the House of Representatives. They're only on the ladder of political power, but they dissent, they argue, they discuss. Liz Holtzman [Democratic representative from Brooklyn, New York] told me how they had set up a women's caucus in the House and not everyone had come to the meetings. A few women weren't sold on the idea. Now they *all* come. Because things get done.

- **But women in business are told it's a man's game and they must play by the rules. They fear that making waves may cause them to lose what they've gained. Are they mistaken?** I think they are. Let's ask ourselves if everybody plays by the rules and if the rules are realistic. The idea that you'd better be a good little girl because you've been allowed in the door is meant to keep women quiet. What can you do about that? First, don't try to change things all by yourself. Find people who share your goals. Power is working together.

I know a woman who works as an ombudswoman in a major university. When she first got there, she thought she'd be lucky to last two years. She's been there seven years now, helping women at all levels, from cleaning personnel to full professors. She arranges regular lunches, open to all women, for the exchange of basic information. I said, "Don't you get a lot of gossip?" She said, "No, we *kill* a lot of gossip. We can dissipate crazy rumors."

During a recent trip to the Midwest, I met with women executives who had started to have regular biweekly lunches. They'd been doing it only for about six weeks, and they'd learned so much already. I noticed several male executives there pricking up their ears with great interest.

- **Are women wrong to want to make it just on their own merits?** If you try to work alone, you're going to be co-opted. You're going to become a token. If you think that working with other women is going to mark you as a woman and, therefore, an inferior, remember that you're marked anyway. It's not how you see yourself but how they see you. You'll never get rid of the stigma of being female by acting like one of the boys. For example, the

proper dress for women in business is the briefcase and business suit, but with a *skirt,* not trousers. It says: Be like us, but not really.

- **Could you talk about the crucial difference, in terms of power, between being a token and being part of a minority?** Tokens are brought in for show. No one expects them to do or know much, and just to make sure, the regular ongoing processes are kept from them as much as possible. Tokens are thought of as "other," not quite human; you can't predict what they're going to do, since they aren't "normal." But as the number of tokens increases, you begin to get more of a political situation.

A professor at the Cornell School of Engineering figured that in a class of 40, five or six women ceased to be tokens and became a minority. They could be differentiated from each other. They began to be seen as human beings.

In union there is strength. You still may not be welcomed. But you can ask questions—embarrassing ones as well as helpful ones—and if you think things should be run differently, you can call attention to the fact and maybe pick up allies that way. This is true not just for women. The powerful don't like troublemakers, but if there are ten determined troublemakers out of 70, the management is going to have to start thinking about the problem.

- **Couldn't making the "female" life style as normal as the "male" benefit men also? I am thinking of women with careers who want to take time off to have children.** Certainly. I can think of two examples, one from history. The first limit on hours of work in New York State was a ten-hour day for women. The unions fought for it, though they didn't really want women in the unions. And when they got it, the men came tumbling after.

In Sweden, instead of maternal leave they give *parental* leave, which can be taken by the mother or father.

- **Women now want a slice of the pie and**

are more likely to unite for specific economic goals rather than for political ones. Is this practical? I don't think so. You may say, "All I want is equal wages, I don't care about politics." But you're not going to *get* equal wages unless you begin to go past this immediate goal. You can't cut economics off from political action of one kind or another. You can't cut it off from a profound psychological evaluation of what you're worth and what you deserve.

• **In the women's movement, there has been a split between the radicals, who urged us not to cooperate with the male establishment, and the moderates, who wanted to work within the system. What is your opinion?** I don't think it matters whether you work within the system or outside it, as long as you know what you're working for and you don't do it alone. In my book, I give the example of Czarist Russia, where the secret police infiltrated the radical movement. This has been done by the CIA, and during the 1960s, the FBI got into the student movement. These groups thought they were working outside the system, but they were being used by it.

The best way is to say, "This is what we want—we hope we don't have to go after it outside the political process, but we will if we have to." The feminists before World War I, having been promised things that weren't delivered, threw bricks through plate-glass windows on London's Bond Street. They got attention, as did the feminists here who chained themselves to the White House fence.

• **Are you suggesting that women may have to go outside regular political channels to get what they want? And, is nonviolent action the way?** It's what we know how to do best, but let me suggest this: All politics is nonviolent action. It's when the system falls down that we begin to get involved with what is generally thought of as nonviolent action. The prob-

lem with women doing that is that it's thought to be characteristic of how we operate. It can work perfectly well, but at times we may have to do other things to get noticed. As I've said of terrorism, it's drama. All politics is drama.

• **Can how-to books and self-help courses help women gain power?** It's very useful to learn the rules and know what is supposed to be proper behavior, as long as we don't blindly believe the rules. Assertiveness training, like transactional work, should be learned by *everybody*, preferably in their teens. The powerful absorb all this stuff in prep school. These are basic, useful tools, but take all this knowledge with a grain of salt, keep your disbelief, and be especially wary of "charismatic leaders."

• **You describe the current view of the world as deeply negative and pessimistic. Why is this so, and what can we do about it?** The "waiting for Apocalypse" mood is due to the fact that the system isn't working. The social myths that underlie our world views don't fit reality anymore. The ruling elite put the myths in place— maybe not consciously—and now they're stuck with it. They feel that since they're the only ones qualified to make decisions, if *they* can't make it work, nobody can. We need to draw on women's experience, black experience.

• **A final question. How do we invent a more hopeful future? What advice, warning or predictions would you offer to today's women?** For the first time, I think history is on our side. We can control whether or not we have children, *when* we have children. Muscle power is no longer important. You don't have to tote that barge and lift that bale. You get a forklift truck. Technology, medicine and other factors are minimizing the importance of the physical differences between the sexes.

To invent the future, we have to observe what's going on and not be taken in by the old shibboleths. We want to ask questions—an old talent of women—for our own good now, not just for others. We want to continue to perfect our communication skills, for which we are famous. We want to continue to take personal relationships seriously—for which we also are famous. Ours is the great evolutionary potential of people whose talents have not been used. It's not going to be easy. And we can't do it alone. But I'm very hopeful.

EMOTIONAL PASSAGES OF WOMEN

by Patricia Bosworth

Maggie Scarf is a 48-year-old journalist who has written prize-winning articles on the behavioral sciences for the New York Times *and* Psychology Today. *Several years ago, while she was researching an article on the subject of women and suicide, she came upon some startling statistics. They indicated that far more women than men suffer from depression. "Forty-two million people in this country have depressive symptoms," says Scarf, "and two-thirds of them are women. The figures just didn't make sense to me. I had to find out why."*

Scarf decided to investigate. With the help of a Nieman Fellowship at Harvard University, an appointment to the Stanford University Center for the Study of Behavioral Sciences (she was the first woman journalist to be appointed there) and an Alicia Patterson Foundation grant, Scarf completed the book Unfinished Business: Pressure Points in the Lives of Women *in 1979 (published by Doubleday & Co.). By that time she had interviewed more than 150 women in treatment at leading psychiatric clinics around the country and had talked to scores of experts in the field.*

The result is fascinating series of portraits that explores the pivotal kinds of female experience—the psychological and emotional pressure points of women's lives from the teens through the 60s. The book shows how failure to resolve these pressure points can result in emotional "excess baggage" that weighs a woman down, often causing depression. The book has been widely praised.

Scarf lives in New Haven, Connecticut, with her husband, a professor of economics at Yale.

Unfinished Business is so dramatic in its use of case histories that it reads like an emotionally charged novel. How did you discover the women you wrote about?

The more I interviewed women who were in treatment for depression, the more the archetypical episodes in their lives unfolded—there was a 25-year-old woman who desperately wanted a bigger commitment from her man; a 30-year-old mother with two children whose husband had just abandoned her; a 40-year-old woman who still acted like a child. Each of the case histories in the book exemplifies a set of problems that I was seeing over and over again. As I progressed in my research, I found that a woman's depression very often had to do with what "stage" she had reached in her life—that is, although there were certain overarching depressive themes and issues among all women, the issues and difficulties of different life decades tended to fall into distinct psychological baskets. [See "Six Stages."] So I decided to examine the stages—six decades of a woman's life, with representative case studies for each decade.

How do you define depression?

Depression is a very complex phenomenon, both psychologically and biologically. But the mood itself, which we all know, is of a loss of pleasure in life. If you can imagine somebody you really care about saying terrible things about you, and then further imagine walking around with that person inside your head talking about you all day long—well, that's what depression is like.

What are the warning signs?

Sleep patterns change. That's one of the key things—snapping awake in the middle of the night or wanting to sleep all day long. If a marked change goes on too long you should definitely see a doctor. Watch out for loss of energy, loss of appetite. Food may taste like cardboard. Impotence. Frigidity. Feeling helpless; feeling inferior. Most of all, there is a general loss of enjoyment in life. [See "Signs of Depression."]

What should a woman do if she realizes she's depressed?

Go to a doctor. And if he or she diagnoses your symptoms as depression, make sure you get the proper treatment—you should probably go to a specialist; GPs do not necessarily know how to treat depression.

Do you believe that tranquilizers are effective in treating depression?

No. Tranquilizers, such as Miltown, Librium and Valium, which are the three most often prescribed, depress the central nervous system. Such antidepressants as Elavil and Tofranil, however, are excellent when properly administered. The important thing to remember is to go to a doctor who is knowledgeable about diagnosing and treating depression.

Why do so many more women than men suffer from depression?

I think it's because emotional attachments tend to be much more important to women than to men, and hence women tend to take much bigger emotional risks in relationships. When a marriage or an affair crumbles, even if it's been a bad one, the loss can be so terrifying to a woman that her sense of identity is threatened and she becomes depressed. Women have a powerful fear of being alone. Emotional attachments are essential to women.

What do men get depressed about?

Men tend to become depressed when they aren't "making it" in a worldly sense. Generally, men are most concerned about whether or not they are in control—whether or not they are in power-making situations. With women, depression generally arises out of a much more personal emotional situation. Women care much more than men do about being lovable, being worthwhile, being cared for; and when women think that they are failing in these, they often get depressed.

In *Unfinished Business*, you wrote that the urge women feel to connect emotionally may be a biological trait.

I believe so. Nurturing is very female. There is excellent evidence that, during the course of evolution, not only human beings but other social primates developed certain kinds of behavior that insured survival of their offspring. You know, primates—monkeys, apes and man—all have very vulnerable newborn infants, and the human infant is absolutely the most helpless and vulnerable creature in nature. The problem of newborn survival may have been solved by this thing called love—an intense bond that forms between the mother and the child; it tends to keep them close to each other. If you watch chimpanzees in the wild, you see that the mother cuddles the offspring and carries it with her; and when the offspring becomes able to walk, they may stay very close to each other. Having mother close by has life-and-death importance for the offspring. And so a bond—an emotional attachment—springs up between them that insures survival. Hence, there is a bias for women to invest themselves very heavily in the love bond. There is a lot of evidence to support this.

Do you think that it's harder for women to form emotional attachments today?

Yes. The idea in our culture now is to be free and independent. Dependence has become a dirty word, and dependence *does* very often conflict with a woman's need to develop an identity of her own. But the difficulty of sustaining emotional attachments is one of the reasons for the rising rate of depression among women.

Is there any one group of women who get depressed more often than other women do?

Young mothers whose husbands have left them seem to go through the deepest depression. Such a young women feels overwhelmed—and with good reason. She has retreated probably—she may be angry but can't release anger—and she hurts.

In your book, you speak of 30 as a crucial age for a woman. Why?

More women tend to be depressed in their 30s, because that's the time of life when marriages tend to break up and when women begin to look back at what they did and didn't do in their 20s and before. They may think, "I've been had! I thought I was going to live happily ever after!"

But women can change. Much of our depression comes from not confronting our "unfinished business"—the unsolved problems and conflicts from our childhood and our old relationships. These things cause disruptions in the regulation of our self-esteem. If we refuse to deal with them they will continue to repress and depress us; and the longer we go on depending on others to make up our minds for us—the longer we go on behaving like little girls instead of like women—the more difficult the process is.

Speaking in general, are working women less susceptible to depression than homemakers and nonworking mothers?

Surprisingly, no. I've met extremely suc-

cessful women—women who have important positions, earn big salaries, live in lovely places, seem to have everything—who suddenly have stopped and looked at their lives and said, "I'm not feeling good about this. I want those other things."

Meaning the more traditional things—a husband and children?

Yes. But then, if you *are* married and a mother and you have a job—well, that can be another bind.

Just to take one example, your magazine, WORKING WOMAN, ran an article about a woman reporter who had been pregnant and, when she returned to work part time, found that her women coworkers were antagonistic to her. She said they'd been totally supportive of her until the baby was born, but then they thought she was asking for special privileges by working part time.

What does a woman's gender identity, which can get pretty complicated when she is "liberated" and working, have to do with depression? In the book, you have the example of Terri, the brilliant second-year med student at Harvard, who fell into a deep depression after a male doctor—one of her colleagues—told her that the reason she didn't understand the problems of a female patient they both were treating was that she, Terri, wasn't feminine enough.

Terri was depressed for months by that remark. You see, Terri wasn't fitting into that male doctor's stereotyped notion of what womanly is, and his stereotype made her question her sexual identity. After that, she took her hair out of the sensible bun she had been wearing and began to wear uncomfortable high-heeled shoes around the hospital.

Do women suffer loneliness more often than men?

We all fear loneliness. But I think that this fear is a special one for women—very little in their own lives or in the history of the human race prepares them for being alone.

And yet, every woman has been or will be alone at some point in her life. And when a woman is alone she must face the terrifying questions of who she is and what she is.

There is a lifelong struggle for women to give shape and meaning to their lives. The question for women is not only, what do I want? but also, what will I be and do?

How does a woman eventually learn to be someone?

By getting sound psychiatric treatment— good advice to which she responded positively. One woman had plenty going for her. She was attractive, pleasant; she was fluent in French, but she was unaware that she could do anything with this gift. Today she is teaching French.

You say that you've never been depressed much.

No, I haven't been where those women in my book have been. If I had, perhaps I couldn't have done the interviewing or the writing of *Unfinished Business.* Have you every noticed that people who get seriously depressed can't stand to be with other people who get seriously depressed? They're afraid of contagion. They get pulled down.

Once a friend of mine was very depressed and I gave her a lot of emotional support. Then, suddenly my mother-in-law died. My husband and I drove to Atlantic City, where she lived; she was a bit of a recluse. I started to go through her things and, oh, it really got me down. We came home, and then I realized what people meant by the loss of strength and the terrible fatigue that comes with depression. I crawled into bed and I lay mourning my mother-in-law's unhappy life—I could see it had been unhappy from all the pills she'd been taking. And then my friend telephoned, and I cried out, "Oh, I'm feeling so depressed. My mother-in-law just died, and I've been going through her possessions, and it's so sad." My friend was off the phone in two seconds flat.

You say in your book that women friends usually are very helpful to one another.

Why?

Women experience one another. Women comfort one another. Women learn about themselves and grow through intimate friendships. We're good at that. We invest in one another. The only time friendships between women can be altered are in competitive situations—in job situations where women in power positions become wary of each other.

My husband and I talk about this a lot. He sometimes says he can't let so and so know his secrets because they're in a competitive position at the university. Women who are powerless have a wonderful capacity to be open and listening in a friendship because they have nothing to lose.

Men don't usually get involved in telling one another how they really feel about their private lives. If they want to confide in somebody they confide in a woman, perhaps, because they perceive that a woman can't use the information against them.

How can women come to terms with their depression?

You have to try to pin it down—confront it— which is hard. Everybody likes evasion. At the end of my book there is a list of questions a reader can ask herself—such as, are you blue or down in the dumps and have you been that way for at least two weeks? If so, you should seek consultation. Another thing: It's amazing how helpful it is to see your thoughts on paper. If you write down what is bugging you, it tends to be easier to combat—the roots of depression, that is. [See "Critical Periods."]

We've said that it's harder to form lasting attachments today. But is it easier for women to cope with and reveal their emotions in general?

Certainly women are more sophisticated today. They have more insight into themselves, I think. But their lives are incredibly complex and full of pressure. Women have always had to deal with an unending barrage of contradictory signals coming from the outside world and telling them what to do. Now, thanks to the women's movement, the sexual revolution and the Pill, we are aware of our options. To a certain extent, we have been liberated, so we are taking more risks; but we risk more depression. We are now told we can do it all, have it all; and when we end up not having it all or not doing it all well, we feel guilty—and depressed.

As far as I'm concerned, the central problem in women's lives will continue to be how to reconcile the need for independence with the equally strong need to form loving attachments to other human beings.

Are you saying that it will be an endless struggle?

Life has always been a struggle—a gorgeous struggle.

SIGNS OF DEPRESSION

1. Are you bothered by feeling sad, blue, hopeless, down in the dumps?
2. Have your eating habits changed recently? Have you lost your appetite? Or have you been stuffing yourself *without* increased appetite?
3. Have you had trouble falling asleep and staying asleep? Or have you been sleeping unusually much or long?
4. Are you feeling fatigued, tired, run down—without your usual energy?
5. Are you less interested in sex, and do you find sex less pleasurable?
6. Are you having trouble thinking, concentrating or making decisions?
7. Have you been unable to sit still? Or, on the contrary, are you feeling unusually slowed down, as if it's too much trouble to move about and there's nothing much worth doing anyhow?
8. Have you been preoccupied by thoughts of taking your own life—or by wishing that you were dead?
9. Are you more prone to anger, more irritable, more easily annoyed and more resentful than is usual for you?
10. Are you feeling discouraged and pessimistic about most things?
11. Are you feeling guilty, worthless, down on yourself?
12. Have you been brooding about unpleasant things from the past?
13. Have you been feeling inadequate and self-critical—as though you've recently realized that you're much less attractive or competent than you thought you were?
14. Are you crying more than usual?
15. Do you feel desperately in need of help or reassurance from somebody?
16. Have you been suffering from physical complaints lately—gastrointestinal problems (constipation), severe headache or backache—for which no medical cause or explanation can be found?
17. Does your mouth feel dry a good deal of the time, or have you got a persistent bad taste in your mouth?

If you answered yes to the first question and then answered yes to two or more of the subsequent questions, you ought to consider the possibility that you are depressed, and that it might be advisable for you to seek some form of assistance, or at the very least, a consultation with a doctor.*

THE SIX STAGES OF A WOMAN'S LIFE

The depressions that women experience in the various decades of their lives *do* reflect underlying issues and concerns of *that decade of life:* What a depression is about has everything to do with where a woman *is* in terms of life stage. This list may help you to identify some of the things that you, your friends and children are likely to be depressed about:

- In *adolescence,* for example, depressive concerns usually have to do with the wrench of separation from one's parents and with a changing body-image—in other words, with the frightening journey of transformation from child into sexual woman.
- In the years of *the 20s,* focal preoccupations tend to have to do with the search for intimacy and

*©*Unfinished Business,* Maggie Scarf, Doubleday, 1980.

commitment: A woman worries about the career costs that may be incurred if she puts "loving" tasks ahead of work tasks, or the costs that may accrue from putting things the other way around!

- Issues of *the 30s* frequently have to do with the mistakes that already have been made in life and the payment that has been exacted—and the "I've been cheated" sense that the fantasies and dreams of girlhood have not been and might never *be* satisfied.
- At *midlife*, major preoccupations are with the loss of certain identity-conferring roles or ways of being—roles that, in many instances have been perceived as a person's sole source of personal meaning or interpersonal power. It may be that a fading of attractiveness is experienced as an overwhelming assault on identity and the ability to attract attention; or it may be that depressive symptoms emerge from the departure of a child, perhaps the youngest child, who takes with her the nurturant mothering role that has formed a woman's reason for being.

As the wheels of the decade turn, so do a person's needs, desires and tasks. Seen over the period of a lifetime, a depressive disorder is an inability to cope, at some juncture, with the ongoing changes that each of us must confront. Knowing what they are can be the first step toward making peace with them.

CRITICAL PERIODS OF A WOMAN'S LIFE

This exercise is a good way to find out what "unfinished business" you carry with you in your life—what problems and conflicts have gone unsolved. Write down your answers or speak them into a tape recorder. Break your life into periods, staring at as early an age as possible.

1. Group years that seem to go together.
2. Give these years a title.
3. What are the most significant things that occurred?
4. What were the most important episodes you recall in this period? What was important about them? What issue were you working on?
5. What made that period end?
6. How did you feel during that period? in general? about yourself? about others around you?
7. What did you want most during that period? How much do you feel you achieved of what you wanted?*

*© *Unfinished Business,* Maggie Scarf, Doubleday, 1980

Chapter Fifteen

Managing Yourself

MANAGING YOUR SPACE

Shape up your Work Area and Streamline Your Work Life. An Expert Tells How

by Priscilla Adams

"Organization," said Stephanie Winston, "is like a car. It gets you where you want to go." Winston has made it her business to organize anything. "If it's in the English language and not so technical as to be unintelligible, I'll organize it."

It's a skill she believes we all have. "Anybody who can cross a five-way intersection without getting killed is organized," Winston said. But some make it across better than others. For those left floundering, Winston—originator, owner and president of The Organizing Principle—will lend a hand. Consultant to large corporations and individuals in distress, Winston cast an organizing eye on a problem we suspect many of our readers share: How to hack through the paper jungles that our desks—whether at home or the office—all too easily become.

Sorting Out: Winston immediately sets one's mind at ease by stating categorically: "There are only three things you can do with

a piece of paper: 1) throw it out; 2) take action on it (e.g., answer it, see someone about it, make a decision about it); or 3) file it." She suggested having three corresponding baskets: one for waste, one "to do" and one "to file." As each piece of paper comes in, put it in one of these three places. At the end of the day, every paper will be in its proper place. "It's the paper lying about at random that spells danger," Winston warned.

"It's best to have a regular time of day to do your paper work," she continued. "Take your to-do basket and start at the top working steadily down, doing whatever needs to be done with each piece of paper in turn. The next eay, start at the bottom and work up. Alternate each day. That way you'll eventually get to every paper in the basket."

Filing: Once a week, go through the to-file basket and relegate those papers to folders with appropriate headings. "The main problem here usually is with the file headings."

293

Winston explained. "Don't overparticular-
ize. Find a single word to capture the general informational concept and mark the
folder with it."

Choosing the word is what Winston calls
a "significant act" because your ability to re-
trieve information depends on being able to
identify these single alphabetized words. If
months from now, when you're looking for a
folder, the word has gone right out of your
head, you're in trouble. As an example, Winston cited a client who filed some information under the heading, "new lists." Of
course, by the time he needed the information, the lists were no longer new, and he
had no idea where it was filed.

Typed labels attached to folder tabs work
better than handwritten headings. Winston
prefers lettersized files to legal size, and
files called "one-third cut," on which the
tabs are staggered, are easiest to use.

If you're confronted with masses of papers, Winston recommends a "tickler file"—
in particular, the Globe-Weis Every Day
Logger, which has $8\frac{1}{2}'' \times 11''$ pockets, num-
bered one to 31, corresponding to the days
of the month. Estimate the day on which you
expect some action to be taken on your piece
of paper—i.e., a response from Mr. Jones,
an anticipated order or phone call, a deadline—insert the paper in the Logger for that
day and, when the time comes, you'll have
the information right in front of you and can
follow up as required.

If the quantity of your paperwork is less
formidable, a simple calendar should suffice. Everyone *must* have an appointment
calendar," Winston said, "a big, clear calendar with squares large enough to write in.
Only one person should be the keeper of the
calendar." You can also use the calendar in
the same way as the Logger, as a reminder
of what to do when.

Another *must* for the desk area is a file
cabinet; since cabinets come in attractive
finishes, you needn't worry about some ugly
gunmetal-gray steel structure disfiguring
your living-room. A two-drawer standing file

cabinet with suspension drawers will fit
neatly under a Parsons table or can go into
a closet, as long as it's accessible. (Suspension drawers are slightly more expensive
but essential, Winston said; the non-suspen-
sion kind don't pull out all the way, leaving
an unreachable space at the back.)

Clippings: An article or recipe caught
your eye. You meant to save it. Now you can't
remember what magazine you saw it in.
"Don't wait," Winston advised. "Read the index page first. Flip immediately to the article you want, read it and tear it out then and
there. Take whatever action is needed or, if
it's something you want to save, file it under
the general subject heading."

Bills: "People almost invariably overcom-
plicate paying bills," Winston remarked. Her
method is simple. Whenever a "money paper" comes in, just throw it in some designated place (a basket, a bowl or an empty
drawer). You don't even need to open it.
Once a month, sit down with your bills and
your checkbook. First, reconcile your bank
statement. Then pay the bills, writing the
date and amount paid (some people include
the check number) on the stubs of the bills.
Put the stubs and your cancelled checks together in one envelope. Winston recommends a note-sized expanding folder, one
marked for each month (e.g., "September
Bills"). Winston's tips:

- Revolving credit accounts: Throw these
  bills into the bin with the others and don't
  worry about the bothersome due dates.
  You'll be charged a small penalty if you
  miss the actual day. But as long as you pay
  within one month, your credit rating won't
  be affected. (This is true of all bills. It's
  only when you're two months late that
  trouble begins.)
- Charge accounts: If you engage in *very*
  lively transactions with stores, involving
  numerous returns and exchanges, it might
  be a good idea to keep a separate folder for
  each store to make sure you're getting all
  the credits you're entitled to. Otherwise,

charge-account bills can be treated as the rest and kept in the same monthly folder.

Equipment, Supplies: Any home office, even if it's consigned to a corner of the kitchen, should have its own phone extension within reach. Decide on a central place for messages (magnets on the refrigerator work well) and discard them as soon as they've been acted upon.

Bulletin boards are not good reminders, which is what most people use them for. "The tendency is to tack something up on the board and forget it," Winston said. "People look at a bulletin board and their eyes glaze." But when used in conjunction with a calendar, they're useful. If you come across a sale announcement in the newspaper, for instance, make a note of the date on your calendar and attach the clipping to your bulletin board.

Chronic Chaos: The person whose desk is an absolute mess, whose papers are strewn hopelessly but who says, "I know exactly where everything is," may be telling the truth. "I'd leave that person alone," Winston said.

What explains such chaos? Winston's interpretation of chronic disorganization is that the person—no matter what her age or intelligence— is still saying no to an authoritarian parent. "No, I won't clean up my room." "No, you can't make me."

"Women are less reluctant to admit they're disorganized," Winston said, "but they apply a heavy overlay of guilt: 'I'm bad. I'm lazy. I'm no good.' Men admit disorganization less readily, and take it as a failure of competence not morals."

Winston recalled being organized, even as a child, in the sense of knowing where everything was. But she admitted to a tendency to leave her clothes thrown around her room— then, and now. "I know where each garment is but, even so, there comes a point every few days when I have to go through it all."

Anyone Can Do It: "Every piece of paper must be tracked. Each one goes someplace. It's getting stuck in indeterminate locations that causes the problem," Winston explained. If you have a paper you just don't know what to do with, give yourself "one legal postponement." The first time it's O.K. not to make a decision (which itself is a decision, albeit a passive one); the second time, you're obligated to make the decision active. Throw it out, act on it or file it. One, two or three. That's all there is to it. Living and functioning, getting organized and functioning. . . . For $200 a day, Stephanie Winston will help you find a way. The Organizing Principle, (212) 533-8860. She also has a book on the subject: *Getting Organized*, published by W.W. Norton.

PRISCILLA ADAMS is a freelance writer who falls into Stephanie Winston's category of those who are neat but not organized. "I'm neat because I throw things out like mad," Adams said. "Then when I want them, they're gone."

PERSONAL PUBLICITY: GETTING YOURSELF KNOWN

by Anne Marie Riccitelli

Personal publicity means bringing yourself to the attention of others. The importance of appropriate personal publicity to an ascending career woman cannot be stressed enough. Perhaps at the very top of the ladder you can afford the luxury of a low profile, but until then, you'd do well to cultivate your public image. (On page 298 you'll find what you should know if you need to hire a publicist.)

Why Me?

Personal publicity develops and sharpens your image, draws attention to your activities and achievements and invites opportunities for advancement by making people aware of you.

Everyone—from chief executives of major corporations to volunteers in community organizations—can be accessible to public attention. The secret is to have an interesting story, something to say. Women executives can offer advice on the pitfalls of success or the stress of a top position; volunteers can discuss how community activity develops skills that lead to lucrative jobs; seniors may be able to tell how retirement has led to a second career.

Who Wants To Know?

Once you have something to say, ask yourself who would be interested: the business community? specific professionals? college students? the nation? home-town folks? When the "who" has been defined, determine where this audience goes for information. Do they turn to the *Wall Street Journal*? a weekly newsmagazine? a local radio call-in show? You then can focus directly on your target for tone, content, even length.

Story and audience determined, the next step offers several options. If you are an executive with a large corporation, contact your corporate public-relations department—the in-house publicity professionals who will be able to advise you and your firm, and might even do the legwork for you.

If your company is too small to have its own publicity department or if it simply doesn't have one, you may have to develop your own contacts. Ask yourself, whom do I know? If you have friends in the media, they may be able to help. Perhaps they can introduce you to or simply name an editor of a newspaper or magazine who might be interested in your story.

In approaching an editor, think of the general content of your story: Is it something for the homes-and-gardens section? Would it be a business feature? a news story? Find out the name of the person in charge of that section and call with a brief description of the idea. If there is any interest, you'll be asked for some printed material (a press release or brief descriptive letter with a photo usually will suffice). If you've sold a publication on the idea, its staff either will write the story from the material you send or will interview you for more information.

More Than Media

When considering publicity outlets, do not overlook alumni associations, professional societies, community organizations—especially those groups that recognize achievements. Alumni associations always are proud of successful graduates. Inform your alma mater of your accomplishments—your success contributes to the school's prestige and invites recognition in the form of awards or appearances.

Successful graduates always are needed to lecture to students—and such appearances usually receive advance announcement in the college or local paper.

Professional societies are most important, because active participation in one helps create an image of authority and generates recognition.

Awards Win Respect

Remember that organizations frequently present awards to outstanding members. Thousands of awards are presented every year, calling attention to quality and excellence, and earning respect for the recipient.

According to Denise Burke, manager of awards for ABC Television, "A person must seek out an award, go after it. Awards are not just handed out!"

Burke suggested that women interested in learning about awards consult the book *Awards, Honors, Prizes,* by Paul Wasserman, published by the Gale Research Company, Detroit. "The winner of an award has worked hard to get it," Burke said. "She's initiated, applied and fought for it. The honor has not just been handed to her; she's earned it."

In pursuing a prize, there are guidelines to follow: Define what you are doing now, whom it interests, whom it benefits and who will recognize the achievement and why. Would your accomplishments be of interest to national, local or special-interest groups, such as teachers or doctors? (*Awards, Honors, Prizes* has lists of the interested groups.) Get in touch with these organizations and follow up with meticulous attention to the details of requirements and deadlines. Remember, when you win an award it's news—an making news is the whole idea of personal publicity.

PERSONAL PUBLICITY
THE PROFESSIONAL APPROACH

If those who do the honoring, hiring or promoting don't know about you and your talents, and you aren't the type for self-promotion, you might consider hiring someone to do the promoting for you.

Personal publicity can be anything that calls attention to you in a favorable way. Unlike some entertainment personalities who cannot always control what is written about them, a working woman should take great care in creating a positive image.

Good publicists can be expensive, charging $1,000 a month or more, and finding the right one may be difficult. Generally, the safest approach is to call the Public Relations Society of America in New York City (212-826-1750) and ask for the chapter closest to your area. The national or district office can provide information on firms suited to your needs.

In considering a firm, it helps to know what you'd like to accomplish through publicity. Do you want to reach potential clients for your business? present yourself as a professional in the community? call attention to your accomplishments? You should approach the firm with clear goals. Before you hire a publicist, discuss whether attaining these goals is realistically possible. Beware of anyone who promises everything. Ethical publicists will allow only *reasonable* expectations—not miracles. You won't make the cover of *Time* if your story really belongs in the home-town gazette or a trade publication.

You can expect a publicist to set out a program of what she can do for you, but do not expect a detailed program with rigid timetables. Your publicist is dealing with the whims of editors and producers; she could get you placed in three publications one month, nothing the next; this doesn't indicate she's not working hard. Publicists and press agents usually get paid a monthly retainer and bill you over and above that for any services they commission on your behalf (printing up photos, for example).

When an interview has been set up for you, your publicist should brief you as thoroughly as possible on what you should do and say. If the interview is with a newspaper reporter doing a general story on women in banking, she'll expect you to cover your work experiences and financial background. If you're on a panel discussion about the state of the economy in general, you'll be expected to give your input on economics, not your life story in banking.

In presenting yourself, think of the impression you'd like to create. Remember, those who complain that they are misquoted or who seem inarticulate on talk shows usually haven't done their homework.

Think about what questions you would ask

you if you were a reporter. Write down your answers. If you are preparing for a television or radio appearance, remember that the written word is different from the spoken; practice speaking into a tape recorder. Do you sound articulate? warm? well informed? On television, you must use not only your voice but your eyes, face, entire body to communicate your message. Speaking persuasively is an art that requires confidence, and preparation helps gain that confidence.

The assessment of a great publicist? When you are approached to speak and appear at functions, when your opinions are sought after, when the world comes after you rather than your going after it, that's when you know you have a good publicist. For more information see *Publicity: How To Get It,* by Richard O'Brien, Harper & Row, Publishers, Inc.

ANNE MARIE RICCITELLI *is a press representative for the American Broadcasting Companies, Inc. Based in New York, she is also a free-lance writer whose articles have appeared in numerous national magazines.*

HOW TO LIVE (WELL) WITHIN YOUR MEANS

by Gail Dinkel

When you live from paycheck to paycheck, not only do you end up spending more money than you should, you do yourself out of a luxury that money can't buy: peace of mind.

I know a young professional woman who's making $25,000 a year, which she spends as if she were making that amount per *month.* She is carrying car and mortgage payments, food, utility and clothing expenses, plus all those easy-to-overlook bank-account "killers" such as auto insurance, life insurance, car maintenance, house repairs, health and dental care. . . .

In addition, she is up to her ears in debt to Master Charge and to a department store. With less than $300 in a savings account, she still can't resist buying expensive clothes, jewelry, more makeup than she needs and little "extras" for her house.

By the end of her two-week pay period, this woman has to write checks that she knows will bounce if they beat her paycheck to the bank—and to do without milk because she's run out of money.

When asked about her spending binges, she says, "I deserve it. Besides, I could die tomorrow, and what good would money in the bank do me?"

The fact is, most of us are *not* going to "die tomorrow" and our futures—particularly our financial futures—should be prepared for today.

Make Your Budget "Your Business"

The people who have money, people who are in the business of finance, usually are very strict about how they spend it.

"Anyone who does not operate on a budget is fooling herself," said Lance Morton, president of the California Coastal Bank. "Especially today, with inflation eroding your income, you've got to keep track of where your money is going."

That applies whether you're single and self-supporting or responsible for a family; whether you make $15,000 or $150,000 a year. You *need* a budget. Since women spend and control most of the money in this country, the budgeting challenge rests with us. Veryl Mortenson, chairman of the board of the California Coastal Bank, suggests you make your budget "your business" and challenge yourself to make a profit.

To set up a budget, you need to know your monthly income, both gross (before taxes) and net (after deductions). Then, make a list of your expenses. (Go back through your checkbook if you can't remember them all.) Your list should look something like this:

1. Housing
   a) rent/mortgage
   b) gas and electric
   c) water
   d) telephone
2. Food
3. Clothing
4. Medical
   a) doctor and dentist
   b) insurance
5. Savings

These are considered the Five Basic Needs. Add other categories, such as transportation, as your circumstances demand.

Housing usually is the largest item in your budget. While the average person spends an estimated 25 percent of his or her income on housing, a recent survey by the US League of Savings Associations indicates that approximately one-third of the people in the US spend more than that yearly on housing. This trend reflects the fact that paychecks have not kept up with inflated housing costs.

Food is a variable, depending upon how many mouths you have to feed, what types of food you prefer (vegetarians pay less than meat-eaters) and how much you entertain. You should be able to estimate what you spend *on the average* for food per week. Multiply that figure by four to get your monthly expenditure.

Clothing is another variable. Put yourself on a *sensible* allowance.

The medical category of your budget will depend on how healthy you are and whether you're covered by a group policy through work. Include life and auto insurance in this category.

Last, but far from least, is savings. Many people overlook it as an important monthly payment. The truth is, a savings account is the backbone of your security, your emergency reserve. A rule of thumb, according to Morton is to have the equivalent of three months' salary in the bank—six, if you're the head of a household.

Making A Budget

Using the above guidelines, the following three budgets were planned for differing incomes and situations.

I. SINGLE WORKING MOTHER WITH ONE CHILD

Gross Monthly Income	$	1,300
(Gross Annual Income	$	15,600)
Net Monthly Income	$	900
Monthly Expenses		
1. Housing		
a) rent	$	270
b) gas & electricity		12
c) water		4
d) telephone		25
	$	311
2. Food	$	160
3. Clothing	$	150
4. Medical		
a) doctor/insurance	$	50
b) life insurance		25
	$	75
5. Savings	$	100
Total Month's Expenses	**$**	**796**

Left over is $104 to cover miscellaneous—haircuts, movies, car fare. It's a tight budget, but the variable areas of food, clothing, doctor and dentist permit flexibility. In a month when she saves $20 on food and $100 on clothing and incurs no medical expenses, this working mother can wind up with $274 for extras. It's a matter of listing priorities and making choices.

II. SINGLE WORKING WOMAN

Gross Monthly Income		$	2,096
(Gross Annual Income		$25,000)	
Net Monthly Income		$	1,330
Monthly Expenses			
1. Housing			
a) mortgage		$	239
b) taxes & insurance			50
c) gas & electricity			35
d) telephone			20
		$	344
2. Food			
a) groceries for one		$	80
b) eating out and			
entertaining		$	60
		$	140
3. Clothing		$	200
4. Medical			
a) health insurance			
(paid by her company)			
b) life insurance		$	16
5. Savings		$	100
6. Additional			
a) auto: insurance		$	17
gas		$	50
maintenance		$	30
		$	97
b) house furnishings		$	100
c) debts: charge card		$	50
dept. store		$	50
parents		$	50
		$	150
Total Month's Expenses		**$**	**1,147**

This woman could be a model for the spendthrift described at the beginning of the article. For tax purposes and as an investment, she has bought a small house for $35,000. Her parents loaned her $7,000 as a down-payment on the house, which leaves her with a $28,000 mortgage at 9½ percent interest. The $183 she has left after expenses goes for theater tickets, presents, etc; it will increase as she pays off her debts.

III. MARRIED COUPLE WITH THREE CHILDREN

His: Gross Monthly Income		
	$	2,500
(Gross Annual Income	$30,000)	
Net Monthly Income	$	1,900
Hers: Gross Monthly Income		
	$	1,500
(Gross Annual Income	$18,000)	
Net Monthly Income	$	1,075
His Monthly Expenses		
1. Housing		
a) mortgage	$	625
b) gas & electricity	$	150
	$	775
2. Medical		
a) kids' medical	$	15
b) health insurance		
(paid by his company)		
c) life insurance	$	45
	$	60
3. Auto		
a) gas	$	60
b) car payment	$	156
	$	216
His Total Expenses	**$**	**1,051**
Her Monthly Expenses		
1. Food	$	240
2. Transportation		
a) commutation		60
b) gas for her car		40
	$	100
3. Child care	$	300
4. Furniture payment	$	53
Her Total Expenses	**$**	**693**

In addition to dividing up the financial load proportionately to their earnings, this couple has a joint savings account in which money is earmarked for anticipated expenses.

His Monthly Savings		
1. Auto insurance	$	21
2. Vacation		100
3. Additional medical		75
4. Children's clothes		75
5. Household misc.		100
6. College for the kids		50
His Total Savings	**$**	**421**

Her Monthly Savings
1. Auto insurance $ 21
2. Vacation 50
3. Kids' clothes 75
 Her Total Savings **$ 146**

After expenses and savings, he has $428 and she has $236 left over in their respective accounts to spend on their own clothes and car maintenances, on extras or on investments.

Making it Work

No matter how tight your budget is, you can make it work to your advantage. Mortenson, who started out raising three children on a "very strict budget," said: "Women who live on a budget are able to take much better care of themselves and their families and to have a far better life style than women who don't."

People who are budget-conscious spend their money more wisely, saving up for one "good" pair of shoes that will last much longer than two cheap pairs. They're more careful about the kinds of food they buy, passing up such items as chocolate bars that may lead to expensive dental bills. Most of all, when money is not free-flowing, adults and children appreciate more the things they do have.

Even if you tend to be impulsive, to blow your budget on a new suit or an expensive dinner immediately upon getting paid, remove some of the temptation. Sign up for a payroll savings plan and have a set amount from each paycheck automatically deposited into a savings account. Many banks will deduct your monthly mortgage payment from your checking account and send it to your loan carrier. Some will pay your utility bills. Insurance companies often will give you a break on your premium if you allow them to be paid directly from your account. Still, you have to budget for these expenses, even though you're not writing the checks.

The real key to sticking to a budget is to have a goal—something that is more important to you than buying clothes or splurging on a restaurant. It can be a long-term goal—such as sending yourself or your children to college, buying a house or simply having $5,000 in your savings account—or a short-term goal, such as a vacation or a new piece of furniture.

"If you have a goal, you know what you want to do," said Mortenson. "If you put a certain amount of your money into it that you feel will pay off, then whatever immediate sacrifice you make becomes worth it to you." Morton goes so far as to say, "Without a goal at the end of a budget, the budget itself is meaningless."

Sticking to a budget takes discipline, but the reward is great: It is the unshakable knowledge that you are in control of your life.

GAIL D. DINKEL *is a television anchor woman and reporter for KCST-TV, the NBC affiliate in San Diego. She has a hard time balancing her checkbook.*

THINK BIG ABOUT MONEY
Start Your Six-Figure Nest Egg

by Ruth Halcomb

Money. Everybody wants it, but few—especially women—actually get to a place where they're commanding large salaries or accruing sizable returns on investments.

What differentiates the women who do get into "bigger money" from those who continue to slave away for little? After talking to successful women in a variety of fields, I'm convinced that some women have a "mindset" that enables them to take stock of their needs, tap their abilities and fit those abilities to the marketplace. They think big and they think ahead.

It's a mindset that can be acquired, a kind of up-shifting of your mental gears. Although a few fortunate women never have conceived of being modestly paid, many of today's high earners had to take a hard look at the way they had been programmed in order to see their working lives, financial needs and abilities in a new way.

Assessing Your Needs

Although your needs are not what you should mention when asking for a raise or specifying a starting salary, your awareness of them can lead you to the following conclusion: "I simply cannot work for the kind of money women traditionally have been getting." Suddenly you know that you must formulate some hard-headed money goals along with your career goals.

Gone are the days when women considered their earnings as mere pin money to tide them over until Prince Charming came along. Money is a serious matter to most women who work and yet many women's incomes still aren't much beyond the pin-money level.

Phyllis Haeger, president of her own Chicago company, P.M. Haeger and Associates, Inc., one of the largest professional-association management firms in the country, looked back at the change in her own thinking: "Like so many women I was a victim of what Margaret Hennig and Anne Jardim call the 'tooth fairy' syndrome. Women used to believe that if we were good girls and worked hard, someone would tap us on the shoulder and reward us. By the time I

reached my 30s, I'd been getting the usual small raises. I needed more things. I realized that I couldn't afford a house or a car and that if I kept going at the same pace, I might never be able to afford them. I began to see my work as a career and not just a job, and I became aware of the fact that I'd have to go after what I wanted aggressively."

Venita VanCaspel held a degree in economics but had been a homemaker until she was in her late 30s, when her first husband was killed in a plane crash. "I felt a certain stewardship toward the insurance money," she said. She considered various careers, including church work, then went back to school to study investments and was hired by a brokerage firm. Some years later she opened her own investment firm, VanCaspel & Company, in Houston.

Tragedy or other serious life changes, such as divorce, can be the catapult that launches women into new ways of looking at money. For a woman who is married, the transition may occur after her first child is born, when she and her husband decided to buy a house or when the children reach college age. Assessing your needs helps firm up future goals.

Sometimes the needs that impel women to go after more money are less tangible but no less real. Sherren Leigh, president of her own marketing firm in Chicago, Leigh Communications, said, "Being well compensated is important. We may work for many different reasons, but the bottom line, in most instances, is money. It's a gauge of our corporate worth."

Thinking about the Future

Women today are far less willing to live like second-class citizens or to count on someone else to take care of them financially. "It used to be that it wasn't *nice* for a woman to talk about money," said VanCaspel. "But that's changing. You'd better believe it's nice to talk about money or you're not going to have any!" Her definition of financial independence is having $200,000. "That's how much you'd need to draw $1,000 a month at 6 percent," she explained. "And by next year, you'll probably need more to live that well."

Most of us find it hard to conceive of $200,000, and our definitions of financial independence may be quite different. For people who don't want to think about it at all, there are some startling statistics on the elderly who live in poverty: For instance, in 1977, almost two million women over age 60 had annual incomes below $2,898. Van-Caspel maintained that it's not unrealistic to plan for a six-figure estate if you don't procrastinate. If you start when you're 25, using a diversified portfolio of investments, she said, it will take only $20 a month and an average return of 12 percent to have $200,000 at age 65. When you're 35, it will take $60 a month. And at 45, $200. "Remember, you have to keep ahead of inflation and the tax man. That's why most people need financial counseling." VanCaspel's message is this: You should *think big*—even if you have to start small—and don't put off starting.

Mercie Butler, now an account executive with Merrill Lynch, Pierce, Fenner & Smith in Sherman Oaks, a suburb of Los Angeles, remembered putting $5 in a savings account under her own name back in 1968. "Don't laugh," she said, "but I was beginning to research real estate and other investments then." She was looking for a way that she and her professor-husband could finance the education of their three children, and although she'd always worked, she began searching for a career that would demand her full commitment.

Butler maintained that there are many good investment channels open to the small or average investor. "Call any brokerage house for free information. Get on a mailing list. If you don't like to read, go to lectures and seminars. Just start learning and you'll see that there are numerous investment vehicles that yield more than a savings account," she said. Her own self-education began when she was in her late 30s. "I had to start with algebra; then I studied business math, which is much easier," she explained. Working at home, Butler paved the way first to become knowledgeable about investments, then to launch her own investments career.

Matching What You Have with What They Want

Just as it's hard to think about a six-figure sum for future security, so it's often difficult for even a well-qualified woman to conceive of a good five-figure salary for herself. Achieving one's money goals demands being positive *and* realistic about one's career, and it's a challenge to be both at the same time.

Women who are positive about their careers are absolutely convinced on some inner level that "Yes, I can do it" and "Yes, there is money *out there*." But if they're realistic, they also know what the obstacles are because they've made a detached assessment of themselves and of the job market as well.

"The trick is to find a match between the abilities you're offering and the demands of the marketplace," said Anita Lands, East Coast director of the National Association of Bank Women. "If there's a direct match, fine. If there isn't, find out what you can do to meet those demands."

Although the phrase "selling yourself" still has negative connotations, many women have learned from experience that the concepts of marketing apply to career planning. Haeger recommended that a woman look at herself as a product. She said, "The first thing you consider with any product is its basic design in relation to its use or purpose. Find out what you are and what you need to become. There are excellent tools available to help you assess your abilities, but select carefully from the books, courses and career seminars you see advertised." She advised women to pay careful attention to the packaging they present: "Every product has a package and so do you. Dress *up* so that people at higher levels will feel comfortable with you, and you'll find your own confidence bolstered, too.

"Next, make your market plan and mount your campaign," Haeger continued. Some jobs are in a direct line with an organization's top-paying positions, while others, such as technical specialties and clerical spots, lie outside the pyramid. Not all organizations today are pyramidal or hierarchical in their structure, Haeger pointed out, adding that companies with participatory or team management offer greater opportunities. "Be sure to find out about the size of the job field. If there are only a few jobs in your specialty or organization that pay $30,000, $40,000 and up, you'll have a much tougher climb."

Pricing Yourself Right

Finally, there's the pricing of the product, a difficult task when the product is you. Traditionally, women have greatly undervalued themselves. So greatly, Leigh pointed out, that some large corporations have deleted "minimum salary requirement" from employment applications. Women were putting in such low figures!

"Do your homework," Haeger advised. "Salary surveys are available for positions in all the major industries.

"The largest industries publish their own reports and there are government surveys, too." In addition, some women's associations have studies on the differences between men's and women's salaries in a given field.

Haeger is talking about two kinds of homework. The first involves hunting down the official figures; the second—making contacts—is essential if your industry is small or if what you're doing is unique and there's no job description for it. "We used to say, make friends with the bookkeeper," she said. "Now we say, make friends throughout your company and your industry. Join professional associations and networks. Ask your boss—and others—what salary range you can expect in the job you're reaching for."

Lands emphasized that networks and professional associations provide informal as well as formal help. "Women compare salary ranges within different companies," she explained, "and although there's still some resistance to asking or revealing exactly how much one earns, I've heard women say, 'I'll tell you my salary if you'll tell me yours.'"

Affiliating with professional societies and networks also lets you see yourself alongside others who are doing what you do or what you'd like to do. There's a "we're in this together" spirit in women's groups that helps individual members set their sights higher. But not all women feel they need the support a women's group offers. One woman in a male-dominated field said she had found that it was the meetings of mostly males she attended that spurred her confidence. "I realized that male competition wasn't as keen as I used to think. I began to see myself as a viable candidate for a promotion. The men were sharp, but I stood out well among them."

Needless to say, the fact-finding and ego-bolstering activities outside one's own company lead to broader visibility, especially if you take an active role in the associations you join. Your efforts may convince your boss that you're ready for a big jump in salary. Even if they don't, once you yourself are convinced that you're ready for bigger money, you'll only have to tap the industry grapevine to find out where the openings are. In most industries, switching to another company is the surest way to land a sizable increase in earnings.

Leigh added, "If you go to a job interview with a definite idea of what you feel you're worth, they'll respect you for your convictions. And you may be surprised at the ease with which your salary requirements are met."

Whether you're talking money with your old company or with a new one, you should keep in mind that supervisors, personnel people and other company officials are there to keep salary costs down. In an effort to justify paying you less, they may point out experience or skills you don't have. "Don't let them sidetrack you or undermine your confidence," said Haeger. "Stick to the point, list all the credentials you *do* have plus the ones you're working on. Remember, too, that salaries are negotiable, although they'll try to give you the impression that they're fixed. There's rarely a frozen salary!"

Taking the Plunge

Be firm, be positive, believe in what you're worth. The homework you do to reach this point may reveal the bad news that the track you're on doesn't lead to the kind of money your goals require. Some careers that are otherwise fulfilling simply do not pay well, and some women find that underlying discriminatory attitudes, despite existing laws, are stalemating their progress. A shift in career direction may be the quickest route to where the money is.

"Look ahead, not back," said Lands. "Of course, it's difficult to think of tossing away experience you've accumulated over the years, but a carefully planned career change means gaining far more than you lose. If you're 35, you probably have 30 more years of working life ahead of you. Ask yourself, 'What do I want those 30 years to be like?' It may be worth a step backward in the short term to gain several steps ahead in the long term.'

Butler, who had taught art in a community college before joining Merrill Lynch, said, "I don't feel that I threw away my past experience. Instead, I built on what I already had. What I do now is an educational process—organizing facts so that they're easy for people to understand, and there's that same satisfaction in seeing people learn, then seeing the results." Butler also built on experience she'd had as a fashion model in developing an image that would see her through business contacts and public appearances. "Unfortunately, teaching and art aren't among the things our society rewards right now. And modeling isn't something that's rewarded after you're 40. If I have only one life, I want to spend it doing what society rewards," she said.

Many women feel the same way. They want to be where the rewards are given out, where the money is. There's no treasure map with an X marking the spot; the route is different for each of us. The ones who do find rewards are those who believe beyond a doubt that there is a place for them in the mainstream and are willing to search it out.

RUTH HALCOMB *is a writer based in California. Her most recent book is* Women Making It, *published by Atheneum.*

MAKING YOUR LIFE WORK
A Life-Planning Counselor Tells How To Stop Fighting Change and Start Managing It

by Jill Severn

Where Dr. Spock left off, the academics and their popularizers finally have stepped in: Adults continue to change after the age of 18, and the ages and stages of adult development can be gauged with almost as much predictability as those of childhood.

What's even more revolutionary than this recognition of continuing change and growth is the idea that we can *plan* for these changes; we can anticipate our future needs and capacities when we plan our families and careers.

After all these years of approaching our crises through every new form of therapy that came along—from Freud to Gestalt to the Primal Scream—it is refreshing to find an alternative that puts our problems in a larger perspective and teaches us to manage the changes in our future rather than dwell upon the past. As James Hugh Lurie concluded in an article on life planning that appeared in the *Journal of American Psychiatry:* "Life planning for many people caught in a developmental crisis offers an alternative to psychotherapy and can be a useful tool for helping the individual who does not wish to define herself as 'sick.' "

One person who's done just that is Alene Moris, co-founder in 1972 of the Individual Development Center in Seattle. Through classes and seminars in life and career planning, Moris has worked extensively with both individuals and corporations and now is considered a pioneer in her field. She's also helped design affirmative-action plans that take into account problems special to women in management jobs, and she spends a good deal of her time traveling and speaking about her work. An eminently practical woman who has raised four children while keeping her own career afloat, Moris is

amused by the "pioneer" label. She describes her work simply as "organized common sense."

Moris began as a career and lifeplanning counselor at her own kitchen table. The wife of a clergyman, she was "thrown willy nilly into advising women who had been divorced or widowed. I got really tired of hearing the same litany: 'I never thought I'd have to work.' I would look across the kitchen table and ask, 'Where did you ever get the notion that you wouldn't be working?' "

Financial reliance on a man still creates problems for women, Moris said, and women in dependent situations are frequently "just one man away from welfare." Moris observed that, even now, most high-school girls believe the same things their mothers did about the future: "The heavy message is still that, if God is good to you, if you're beautiul enough and if you play the games well, your work life will be a very short one. After that, your basic security will be provided through your relationship with a man. You can keep a little job going to amuse yourself if you like, but," she maintained, "it is still the rare woman who counts on work for a large portion of her happiness."

Before starting the ID Center, Moris had an idea for a life-planning program at the Women's Center for Continuing Education at the University of Washington, but she couldn't find a sympathetic ear. "It was suggested that I teach the women flower arranging, even in Continuing Education. I insisted that women needed a different kind of help; that, in fact, everyone needed help in life planning. We have to be taught skills to assess what's going on within ourselves and our environment. We must continually be making appropriate plans and adjustments so that we don't just go along blindly until we hit a crisis, such as losing a job or a husband. That kind of severe trauma, and the reorganization that comes in its wake, can be most painful. People need to be managing change and accepting the inevitability of change. A 'Plan B' should be designed so that all our life and career plans are not in one basket."

Originally, Moris focused on counseling women because their needs seemed to be greater and because she felt women were urgently needed in positions of public policy-making. "Women have been kept out—and have allowed themselves to be kept out—of the decision-making system. Economists talk about the growing scarcity of resources and all that, but the biggest scarcity is the scarcity of intelligent, gutsy, creative, risk-taking leadership. Half of the world's resource for that kind of leadership lies in women. It's not scarce, really, it's just underutilized."

With all her clients, Moris starts by raising the question of time and what to do with it. In the well-planned life, Moris sees life time divided into thirds: "One third of our life energies, and not more than a third, should be invested in relationships; one third of our energies ought to go toward simply growing and becoming mature human beings and the remaining third can be invested in something I call a 'lifework'—that something you do with your unique set of talents and assets. With such a plan, it would be reasonable to expect life satisfactions to come from many different sources. A person could design a balanced life that would be both strong and flexible."

This doesn't preclude mothers from staying home for a few years with young children, only that they not let children rule out all other activities. "It will be nice when we get to the point where men will stay home, or when couples will jointly decide who stays home," Moris said.

"Ideally, it would be nice for both parents to have part-time jobs. But I don't think we need to see child raising as drop-out time. It is time we can use to build career skills or finish our education. It can provide a security base preferable to what I see among young women who have small children, full-time jobs and are also trying to keep a marriage going. The word that keeps popping up when I work with these women is *fatigue*. A human being has just so much energy. Relationships take a great deal of psychic energy, and if you're exhausted, these relationships are really put in jeopardy."

Rather than dropping out of view altogether, Moris would like to see women with small children using their time in some carefully chosen volunteer work—work that will build new skills and develop good contacts for later jobs. Moris doesn't think volunteer work need be a waste of time. "Volunteerism is one of the genius marks of our country. I don't like the way it's being shoved off onto women; I think every human being needs to contribute to their country and that teenagers and men should be more heavily involved. Men have generally been saved for the power spots and women have been doing the mechanics, and that makes me angry. But I think it's ridiculous to jump from there to being mad at volunteerism. Most work done by volunteers simply wouldn't get done any other way. We can't get funding for things that need to be done because of our crazy national priorities.

"Volunteerism gives you a kind of power a paid position doesn't. You can be a very effective agent for change if you're not depending on someone for a paycheck. I see volunteerism as absolutely essential. But you have to choose your area carefully and do it with style. Go after it just as seriously as if you were being paid. I want women in every position of power they can possibly muster, and pay or no pay is a matter of what is appropriate to your own personal situation."

Moris sees volunteer work not only as an arena in which women can build contacts and job skills but also as a valuable tool for teenagers and young people who want to investigate various career possibilities. A variety of volunteer experiences would help young people choose the focus of their education and allow them to come out of high school or college with a clearer sense of what they want to do with their education. "Then, I'd like to see both men and women heavily involved in career building in their 20s. I'd like to see them feeling free to try different things and to risk failure and not to be too centered on success too early. I'd like to see them continue to do volunteer work because that's where you can risk even more."

In Moris's ideally planned life, childbearing would come in the late 20s or early 30s. At that point, women would most likely stay home for a while. "Depending on a woman's style and the kinds of things that satisfy her, she might be able to stay in that role for ten or 15 years. Or she might be able to cope with that and stay sane and happy for only two or three years." During this period in a woman's life, volunteer work would keep her in touch with the professional world and build toward her eventual return to work. Then, when kids are in the very expensive teenage years or in college, both parents would be bringing in full-time salaries.

The next big change would most likely come when the kids are grown and gone. "I'd love to see the man have some options then," said Moris. "This would be his time to hang loose. If the woman was very heavily involved in her career, he could take up a supportive role in the same way that she was supportive of him when he was beginning his career. Men in their 40s often feel trapped. It is a time for them to do some reassessing, and often they find themselves locked into vast responsibilities. It isn't that their lives have been bad; it's just that they may not want to continue doing the same thing for another 20 years. They're getting a very strong sense of their own mortality and the preciousness of time. Now is when they must do whatever it was they really wanted to get done in their lives. I see it all the time among very fine, sensitive men who are feeling a lot of pain. If the wife hasn't been growing and the husband hasn't been supporting her growth, she can't really be helpful at this point because she's scared herself. Many men discourage their wives' careers because it's more convenient to have a wife who sits at home waiting to do whatever he wants her to do. Men don't realize they are building their own trap when they do that."

When couples reach their 50s, Moris sees the possibility of both men and women working part time and, again, having time to invest in the needs of their communities. Part-time executives and leaders may not be the norm now, but Moris thinks such a plan would solve one of the country's leading health problems: "Think of the demands we place on our top executives. We put them on the board of trustees of a college, on the board of a hospital and ask them to head up the United Way—at the same time that they're holding their most demanding jobs—because it's that executive job that gives them the prestige for those other positions. And then we are surprised when they die at 53 of heart attacks. Well, I'm not surprised. We overload them; we overload our best men."

Those heart attacks and ulcers visited upon male executives have started to show up among successful women as well. But Moris doesn't think that ruined health has to be the price of success. Rather, she said, we must learn to decentralize our leadership, and spread the load more equitably so no one is terribly pressured. The benefits of such a plan are manifold. Aside from an improvement in the physical and emotional health of our top executives, there would also be more leadership positions to fill, thus creating more opportunities for more people. And, said Moris, "If we've got people working half time in these areas, we'll also have more people with free time to think creatively and start new projects."

Ultimately, Moris would like to see life- and career-planning courses available to everyone so that the skills of self-assessment and planning for change become as much a part of our education as reading and writing. As the rate of change in our society accelerates and as the life expectations of women grow beyond former boundaries, this sort of education may become more and more of a necessity.

JILL SEVERN *is a free-lance writer living in Seattle and the author of* Growing Vegetables in the Pacific Northwest. *Recently, she began work on a novel, an undertaking she had put off—before she met Alene Moris. "Talking to her made me resolve to risk spending a year writing a book. A career doesn't have to move in a straight line. She sees time in bigger chunks than most people do, and can plan better for the future because of that."*

Part Six

Thinking Ahead

Chapter Sixteen

Hang ups

FEAR

by Marlene Cimons

Several years ago, Linda Spivak, president of her own greeting-card company, suddenly realized that she was terrified of flying.

"We have trade shows all around the country, and they are very important," she said. "I had to get there, but I couldn't. I didn't want to take the time to drive or go by train, but every time I got on a plane, the anxiety was so great, I couldn't deal with it. So I stopped flying for about a year."

Wilhelmina Schendeler, who several years ago was a saleswoman and bookeeper for a construction-materials supplier, found herself unable to drive on super highways. She discovered, over a period of several days, that she virtually became paralyzed behind the wheel of her car while traveling on a Washington, DC, beltway. Normal city streets did not affect her.

"After I got off on an exit, I'd be fine," Schendeler said, "but while I was on the highway, it was awful. Every time a truck drove by, I felt as if I was being drawn into it.

I thought I would lose control. Every truck was a monster. Then I became afraid of other cars. I felt like a hazard on the beltway, so I stopped driving on it."

Fortunately, Schendeler did not need to use the beltway to get to work—but she feared for her job. "I thought if my boss found out, he would know I could never get another job and would take advantage of me by holding back raises and promotions," she said. "I was boxed in. I couldn't change jobs—I was afraid I'd have to use the beltway to get there."

Merle Baboyian, president and owner of Dental Power, a dental employment agency, and of Health Careers Institute, a school that trains dental assistants, could not be in an enclosed space. Her problem first surfaced when she had a panic attack during a college exam and fled the classroom. Later on she manipulated her work life to accommodate her phobia.

"We have a big dental convention every

313

year in the underground parking lot of a large hotel," she said. "They just clear out the lot and set up the booths. There is a freight entrance that leads into the convention area. I used to arrive at the hotel at least an hour early—just so I could park my car right near that door. I had to have that spot. I had to know exactly where my car was, so I could get to it fast if I had to. I also combed the hotel, checking out the location of every possible exit."

Each of these women had a phobia, an abnormal fear of situations that usually are not considered to be anxiety producing. But these three—and countless other women like them—do not fit the almost universally held picture of the typical woman phobic. They work.

"One of the cruelest and most misleading stereotypes is that all women phobics are housewives," said Robert L. DuPont, MD, a Washington, DC, psychiatrist who runs one of the approximately three dozen phobia clinics that have sprung up across the country in the last several years. "This is not true at all. And the myth makes it harder for working women to deal with their problems."

Jerilyn Ross, director of clinical services and a therapist with DuPont's program, agreed. "Working women are independent women, and it is more difficult for them to admit that they have phobias," she said. "They see it as a weakness. It's the one area of their lives they cannot control. They feel inadequate, phony. 'Here I am, managing 50 people—and I can't get into an elevator.'"

Doctors have identified numerous phobias, among them fear of cats, insects, snakes, pigeons, water, public speaking, writing, injections, blood, elevators, and the most common phobia of all—the one often labeled "the housewives disease'—agoraphobia. Literally translated from the Greek as "fear of the marketplace," agoraphobia is an all-encompassing term used to describe a variety of ailments, including fear of leaving the home, of open spaces, of driving, of crossing bridges, of tunnels or of a specific territorial boundary.

Almost all phobics—including men and nonworking women—share some characteristics. According to Manuel Zane, MD, a psychiatrist who founded a phobia clinic in White Plains, New York, "Phobics automatically become afraid in situations that one wouldn't expect to be fear producing, and they are afraid that once the fear comes up, it will get out of control.

"They panic," Zane said. "They fear loss of control—of mind and body. They feel so afraid that they either have to escape the situation—or avoid it completely."

Having a phobia, DuPont said, is different from having a fear. "A momentary twinge of fear is not the same thing. There are lots of little fears in peoples' lives. For it to be a phobia, there has to be avoidance, a serious disruption. The response has to be out of proportion to the stimulus. If you're in a parking lot and someone comes bearing down on you at 90 miles an hour, that's a fear. But if going to the supermarket fills you with dread, that's a phobia."

Spivak, Schendeler, Baboyian and other women like them have been successful in overcoming their phobias through the work of phobia clinics, which have taken a new approach in treating these afflictions. Therapists in these clinics are not concerned with finding the underlying reason for the phobia, if in fact, there is one. They deal with the here and now, working with patients within the daily situations they fear.

"Traditional psychotherapy does not deal with phobias in a practical sense," said Natalie Schor, a psychotherapist and director of the Roosevelt Hospital phobia clinic in New York City. "Conventional therapy goes back to Freud and the analytical position that a phobia is only the symptom of a deeper underlying conflict. So the conventional therapist deals with the patient's early history and relationships, trying to uncover the conflict—never dealing with what is happening now. The person still can't fly, go to work—or go out."

The clinics use a method known as "contextual therapy," a term coined by Zane, who is considered to be a pioneer in this new approach to treatment. With this method, phobias are studied and treated within their context—in the actual environment where the phobic reactions take place. Thus, a key part of the program is practice.

Patients, accompanied by therapists, or "helpers," deal directly with the situations they fear the most. In some clinics, therapists make initial house calls to the homebound—but the phobic is expected to leave the house as the program continues.

Progress is made one small step at a time. "If you can't go into a restaurant, we have you try to look at a picture of a restaurant first, and we work from there," said Susie Kent, a group assistant at Terrap (for "Territorial Apprehensiveness" groups), established by Arthur Hardy, MD, a Menlo Park, California, psychiatrist who has set up about 20 phobia clinics throughout the country.

"Each goal leads to another in the hierarchy," Kent said, "but always retreating when we reach a level of anxiety. Retreating is very important. Some people try to push their way through—and suffer. The next time, all they remember is the suffering. If you retreat at the point when all you have are butterflies in your stomach, then all you remember next time are the butterflies—not a nightmare. That gives you courage."

Although working women may have greater problems than nonworking women accepting their phobias, they seem to have a distinct advantage in overcoming them. "The working woman has to do what she has to do," DuPont said. "She can never really give in to the phobia. She is never as dependent or helpless as the agoraphobic housewife."

DuPont went on to point out that this does not mean that there is no disruption in the working woman's career. In his Washington clinic, for example, he treated a stewardess who, not long after the fatal Pacific Southwest Airlines crash in San Diego, found that she could not get back on an airplane, and also a researcher who couldn't use a telephone.

"A working woman may avoid a certain job or turn down a promotion because it involves flying or public speaking," DuPont said. "A phobia also may protect you from something. One of the problems in overcoming phobias is dealing with the issues that are exposed once the phobia is gone. For working women, this often means dealing with success. Sometimes there is a related fear of failure—'The higher I get, the farther I have to fall.'"

Not all experts in the field believe that women create these phobias in order to avoid work situations, including promotions or success.

Jerilyn Ross, for one, disagreed. "If that were the case, a woman who is afraid to fly, for example, should be able to fly again once she's lost her job or lost the promotion she was supposed to have feared."

Most phobic-clinic patients first are taught the following six points, originally developed by Zane:

- Expect and allow fear to arise and accept that you have a phobia.
- When fear appears, let it be.
- Label your fear level from zero to ten—watch it go up and down.
- Focus on and do manageable things in the present.
- Function with a level of fear and appreciate your achievement.
- Expect and allow fear to reappear.

Phobics, DuPont said, should expect setbacks. "Nine times out of ten, there won't be a problem. Then, the tenth time, you'll get that old twinge. Instead of feeling that you've failed, you should say to yourself, 'Here it is. I can cope. I'll use my techniques, and the feeling will go down.' Success in overcoming a phobia is measured in terms of living a normal life."

There are millions of phobics in this country. Medical experts say that the precise number is difficult to estimate. "We have now redefined a large class of problems, such as agoraphobia, that used to be called other things," said Alan Goldstein, PhD, director of the phobia clinic at Temple University's Medical School. "A few years ago, there wasn't an awareness of the syndrome. Agoraphobics tend to be depressed; consequently, many had been diagnosed as depressive personalities."

Although the number of male phobics has increased in recent years, women still make up the majority. Natalie Schor explained why: "There are social reasons. In general, more women than men request treatment for emotional problems. Traditionally, women and girls have been protected. They usually aren't encouraged to face unpleasant situations, unlike men who are told to go fight it out, and therefore, many women never really learn how. Women also have a great deal of conflict about home and staying home. They have a lot more opportunities to become immobilized. They also have been taught that being weak and vulnerable is feminine. There are dozens and dozens of explanations."

Now there is also hope. Spivak, Schendeler and Baboyian not only have conquered their phobias, they now work as phobia therapists.

"I can't say I don't have the fear anymore, but now I don't avoid flying," Spivak said. "I'm getting to the point where I almost enjoy it. My business is stronger. I have more energy. More important, I have peace of mind."

Where To Get Help

Treatment at a phobia clinic runs anywhere from eight to 20 weeks, and costs range from about $400 to $1,000. For information regarding phobia clinics in your part of the country, send a stamped, self-addressed envelope to Dr. Alan Goldstein, who runs a clearinghouse for phobia clinics at Temple University, Health Sciences Center, Department of Psychiatry, 3400 North Broad Street, Philadelphia, PA 19140.

You can get a year's subscription to *Lifeline,* a monthly newsletter for phobics, by sending $10 to: Lifeline, Phobia Resource Center, 525 East 89 Street, New York, NY 10028.

MARLENE CIMONS, *a former flying phobic, is a reporter with the* Los Angeles Times *Washington bureau.*

IN THE HEAT OF ANGER

by Terri Schultz

Recently a friend told me that when she'd bragged to her therapist that she'd never been angry with anybody, her therapist replied, "Well, then, you've never loved anybody either."

The story touched a sore spot. If anger is a key to good loving, I realized I was in a lot of trouble. When I was married, I seldom showed anger toward my husband. Over the years, I never fought with my closest friends. And my silence extended into my professional life as well. When I worked in an office, I rarely got angry on the job.

But the marriage ended, and so did the jobs and a lot of the friendships; and thinking back on them now, I think that a little more honest anger could have salvaged at least some of them. During those times when the marriage, or job, or friendships seemed sour, I remember crying and feeling hurt or depressed. But angry? Never.

A lot of women seem to have trouble expressing their anger. And I also know a lot of women who are just the opposite: my friend, Miriam, for example, blows up all the time. At the slightest provocation—real or imagined—her voice rises, she begins to protest or accuse, and the anger skims off her surface. Once, I admired the way she could shout. But eventually, I came to realize that she and I faced the same dilemma: our anger was not coming out right. It was ineffective. In my case, no one even knew I was mad until it was too late, and my anger had turned into self-pity or spite. In Miriam's case, people turned off; they simply would not listen to her verbal abuse, especially since it flowed from her so often. "My anger is like a sheet of fire. It drives people away," she says. Yet, she seems powerless to stop it— just as I feel unable to rev myself up to a point where I can get angry at all. "We need to find a middle road," Miriam suggested to me one day after her latest blow-up, "so that we don't block up anger, but we don't just fling it around either."

By now, the experts agree that anger is a basic, healthy instinct. Why, then, is it so difficult for women to use it in healthy ways? Many men have trouble showing anger too, but they aren't as likely to feel guilty about its existence. They acknowledge it, even if they don't always do something about it. Women, however, often feel they have no right to be angry; they punish themselves with it. They seem to be more prone than men to ignore it entirely or to brandish it like a lethal weapon. In either case, anger closes them off from the people around them.

Psychiatrists tell us that when anger is repressed, it does not disappear. Instead, it goes underground. It may reappear in psychosomatic symptoms: headaches, arthritis, diarrhea, colitis, allergies, hives, sleeplessness, over-eating, over-drinking, sex problems, or hypochondria. Repressed anger can even be deadly. Medical researchers in America and England now believe that women who cannot show anger in appropriate ways are more susceptible to cancer. *Medical World News* recently reported that among suspected cancer patients tested for personality traits, women who did have malignant tumors "showed a strong correlation with extreme suppression of anger . . . Tumor incidence also correlated significantly with the opposite trait, 'a history of frequent temper outbursts.' " Doctors warn that women who grimly suppress their emotions, and women who vent every emotion, are more likely to end up with cancer than women who are moderate but consistent in expressing how they honestly feel.

Repressed anger sometimes converts to mental illnesses as well: depression, phobias, anxiety, withdrawal. "There is a tremendously higher rate of depression among women than among men, and it is certainly related to repressed anger," says Dr. Alexandra Symonds, a psychiatrist and training analyst for the Karen Horney Psychoanalytic Institute. "When you try always to be good and nice the anger doesn't disappear. You think you're controlling it, but you're not— it's controlling you."

But, as destructive as they may be, we can't change our emotional habits overnight. Like all habits, no matter how bad they are for us, there is something in them that brings us comfort. Those of us who have trouble getting mad, for instance, do have compensation. We spend days, even weeks, plotting little victories in our imaginations. We rehearse, in retrospect, our perfect comebacks: that combination of intelligence, irony, and condescension that will wither the objects of our wrath, who unfortunately remain blissfully unaware of our stunning successes. In fact, they probably forgot about the incident in question five minutes after it occurred, while we relive it again and again.

I realized the absurdity of this charade one evening when I telephoned a friend I hadn't heard from for a couple of weeks. I was stunned to learn she was angry with me for something she heard I had done, nursing a grudge without telling me how she felt, or checking her information with me. For once, I didn't pause to be sure I was right or wrong, justified or overreacting. I felt angry, and I said so for the next ten minutes. After hanging up, I sank to the carpet and sat there feeling delighted with myself.

The point was not, in the end, who was right or wrong. Nothing was resolved, but by the end of the conversation the air had been cleared between us. I had gotten angry at a friend—and she was still my friend, after all. The world hadn't caved in. I hadn't been rejected. None of those awful things I had always feared would happen had happened. In fact, I had to admit I felt good. It was a breakthrough for me. By the next morning, I had put the incident in the back of my mind. In the past, I would have kept my anger to myself, and brooded over it for weeks.

Since that time, however, I have learned that, while it is important to recognize your anger, it is not always wise to show it. Timing is a factor and so is tact. The important thing is to know that you're angry. Then you can choose what to do about it. Sometimes it is wiser to postpone dealing with it, or to release it on the tennis court, than it is to go charging in with emotions blazing. As one psychologist pointed out to me, "Anger is, after all, an impulse, like sex. I don't believe every impulse should be acted out. If you're aroused in a restaurant, you don't jump on the table with your boyfriend and make love. It's the same with anger—there's a time, and a place."

Anger used wisely can get you what you want. Used unwisely, it can compound the feelings of being unappreciated, unloved, and misunderstood. When you feel angry with people you work with, and indulge in a temper tantrum or a screaming match, it could cost you your job. And in love, the stakes are even higher.

Dr. Mary Cox, a New York psychologist, says, "Anger is simply energy—the energy we experience when we have a need and confront an obstacle to fulfillment of that need. That energy has a lot of potential, a lot of survival value. We can use it to overcome obstacles, if we learn how to handle it right. If you're angry with your boss, it might be constructive to stay in touch with your anger and say things that need saying. But shouting and tears will not usually get you what you want. In business, there's no room for blind rage. An emotional outburst is just a 'problem' to the boss, and he doesn't want another problem. Men in business know that, and so they don't get angry; instead they get ulcers."

At work, women often serve men, which puts them in a double bind when they feel angry: not only must they struggle against worries of losing their job, but the boss is often a benevolent (or tyrannical) father figure, and they must also fight off their childhood fears of displeasing a man.

This double dilemma makes women do strange things. One woman, a bank executive, breaks down in tears when superiors criticize her; another, an executive editor, acts cute and seductive when her work is rejected; another, a college professor, sulks when she doesn't get her way with her department head. Crying, sulking, flirting all can be twisted forms of anger—forms a dependent child might use to get what she wants from her parents. It may work for "Daddy's girl," but it doesn't work for a working woman who wants respect.

Sometimes, women who feel they are being discriminated against at work are being stepped on not because they are female, but because they are people who won't stand up for themselves. "The refusal to get angry, the tendency to cry and feel sorry for yourself, is simply neurotic adjustment to life," says Mildred Klingman, a New York therapist. "If the only way you feel you can get what you want from your mother or father is to be meek, good, passive, then you grow up with these responses. As an adult, they work against you, but they're familiar and very difficult to give up."

A woman who was repeatedly passed over for promotion in her job came to see Dr. Symonds one day, complaining about how "the System" was abusing her. It soon became clear, however, that "they"—her boss and co-workers—were not mistreating her; she was undermining herself. She could not speak up to her boss and tell him how she felt. Instead, she let him take her to lunch and felt flattered he had invited her; she was pleasant all through the meal, rather than running the risk of being honest with him.

"If she were honest, she would risk her image of being a 'nice girl' and perhaps he would not like her," Dr. Symonds said. "Women have been pressured from early childhood into the dependent, submissive role in life, and by and large they have accepted it . . . To be lovely and unaggressive, a woman spends a lifetime keeping hostile or resentful impulses down. Even healthy self-assertion is often sacrificed since it may be mistaken for hostility," she later wrote in the *Journal of the American Academy of Psychoanalysis*.

This, of course, applies to love as well as work situations. And in love, the fears can be even deeper: a woman may be afraid that if she blows up she will be left—alone and unloved. "I was taught that once you've said something in a moment of anger, things will never be the same—like fine china which, once broken, can never be mended to its former perfection," one woman told me. "I have this fantasy that anger equals destruction, that anger is like an atom bomb inside me, and I save the world by holding in that rage. It is a fantasy that gets passed along from generation to generation. I don't know anyone whose parents knew how to have good healthy fights that were simply part of an intimate loving marriage."

In my own marriage, I was constantly afraid to rock the boat. I hid my anger so well that my husband didn't even realize it was there until it was too late. Dr. Symonds says this phenomenon is not uncommon among married women who feel dependent on their husbands for the love and reassurance they desperately need to feel good about themselves.

Such women often have romantic illusions about how a man can save them. If women see marriage as a refuge from the world, or a form of personal salvation, they may build up rationalizations for not getting angry and deaden any emotion, such as anger, that might endanger the relationship. "When faced with the ordinary difficulties of marriage, the possibility of friction and the need for self-expression, they react with enormous rage, and underlying this, a profound despair," Dr. Symonds reports. Many women caught in this position feel depressed much of the time.

They may take their anger out on their children, or their neighbor, or they may turn it inwards—and feel guilty. "When you feel like a traitor for being angry, or when you can't put your finger on what you feel angry about, then it turns into guilt," says Jean Mundy, director of the Women's Institute for Psychotherapy in New York. Some women end up manipulating the people around them with covert forms of hostility. One psychiatrist calls this "horizontal aggression"—an attack from a lying down position. This can take several forms. Some women become extremely critical, resentful, and envious of other people—which can end up in man-hating or racism. Others complain and act like martyrs. Rather than fight back, they show the world how hurt they are by other people's aggression. In this way, they can get back at people while still maintaining the facade that they are powerless, helpless victims. Others become passive-aggressive: instead of expressing an opinion, or standing up for themselves, they become unenthusiastic, noncooperative, apathetic. They block whatever the other person does. If asked "What's wrong?" they will often reply "Nothing." They get back at the person with silence and inertia.

In the end, of course, all of these techniques are equally self-defeating because they are dishonest; you're not getting your real message across in a way that people can understand and respond to. "When women cry because they're angry, it's a detour of feeling. If you're crying, you can't talk. It's a message without words. People don't understand the message, so they can't deal with you realistically," says Hester Eisenstein, coordinator of a Barnard College program to help women overcome conflicts that prevent them from making desired changes in their lives.

Once women become aware that they are doing these things simply to cover up anger, then they can begin to fight fair and effectively. Eisenstein suggests that women practice putting their anger into words. "You don't have to do it all at once. First, just train yourself not to cry. Bite your tongue for one minute. Think it all over for twenty-four hours. Give yourself space, and then go back and say to your boss or your husband: 'You know what we were discussing the other day, well I felt very annoyed because. . . .'"

Some of the anger that women feel on the job is built into the social and economic system. Men are often the doctors and supervisors, women are the more expendable nurses and secretaries. Dale Bernstein, a psychotherapist with the New York Association of Feminist Psychotherapists, suggests women become aware of this, and, if they feel frustrated, form groups with other women, friends or co-workers where they can release their anger in a safe and supportive way.

Women who explode in anger all the time should learn to differentiate between pointless, childish rage and the reality of each situation. "I used to scream and yell and it didn't make me feel any better," one woman told me. "Now I focus inside and see where the anger is coming from. I try to pinpoint it. I say: 'A. I'm angry. B. What am I angry about?' If it's tied in with my old anxieties, then I don't express it; if it's a reaction to something a person did which was inconsiderate or hostile, then I tell that person how I feel."

It is also important to say how you feel without blaming the other person. It's your response that counts, not his intention. "If you blame the other person, his or her first reaction is to defend himself, and then you defend yourself, and you're off and running. It's better to say: 'I feel angry' than it is to say: 'You make me angry'. In true anger, you have to make yourself vulnerable. If the other person is interested and concerned, he or she will respond," one psychiatrist explained.

Women who don't want to get angry because they prefer to be "liked" often end up having their "niceness" backfire on them: the boss thinks he can't give her any responsibility, because she won't stand up for herself; the husband does as he pleases, because he feels she doesn't really care about him. Moreover, unexpressed anger festers like a sore and spreads into a general hatred against others, and finally a contempt for yourself. Anger is part of intimacy, and has its place in love. It is part of self-respect, and has it place in work. You don't even have to be *right* to be mad. You just have to care enough about yourself and those around you to take that step into an anger that can end in mutual understanding and respect.

TERRI SCHULTZ *is a freelance writer and the author of* Bittersweet: Surviving and Growing from Loneliness.

AMBITION—IS IT A DIRTY WORD?

by Elizabeth Elliot

Jean Welty is a top trial lawyer and an associate in a firm known throughout the Northeastern United States for its aggressive and successful practice of criminal and family law. She recently bought a rundown, ten-room house in an inner-city neighborhood, which she plans to renovate.

Marjorie Weinreb graduated with a master's degree in psychological counseling. After one look at the lack of opportunity in today's educational establishment, she decided to take advantage of her BS in merchandising and went to work as a management trainee in a Washington, DC retail store. Today she is a systems analyst and all-around troubleshooter for one of the world's best known department stores, Bloomingdale's in New York.

Nancy Young quit college after her freshman year to help her husband through medical school. One year, one baby and one divorce later, she took a clerical job at a major women's magazine. Today she writes a regular column for that magazine, edits the work of many of its freelance writers and recently was put in charge of a whole section.

All three women are in their middle 20s.

Florence Haseltine is a physician who holds an additional degree in biophysics from MIT. She has written a novel that was published in hard-cover last year and will be appearing in paperback this fall. She is an assistant professor of obstetrics and gynecology at the Yale University School of Medicine and one of the few women on the staff of Yale New Haven Hospital who regularly performs surgery. She is in her middle 30s.

Sigrid Holland, a widow with seven children, is the manager of a prestigious New Haven eating club that has become a popular gathering place for local business and professional men. On the side, she runs a catering business that is used by many of the top firms in New England and New York for VIP entertaining. A cookbook she wrote will appear next year, and she recently has auditioned for a regular spot on a TV network news program as a food commentator. She is in her middle 40s.

All of these women are, of course, outstandingly successful in their work. All are ambitious, but there is a difference in the way they think, feel and speak about their goals. The three younger women regard ambition as a simple fact of life. If asked whether they consider themselves ambitious, they look a little surprised at being asked such an obvious question, then answer: "Of course." The two older women also say, "of course," but with an explanation. It is evident from their carefully thought-out comments on goals and lifestyle that they grew up in a time when a woman who admitted freely to family, friends or even teachers that he was ambitious might be referred to a psychoanalyst rather than to a graduate school.

"Ten years have made a decisive difference in the way young women feel about their own ambitions and goals," said Mary Albro, who, for more than two decades, has been counseling students at Smith College on career planning. The name of the department she heads was changed about five years ago from "Vocational Office" to "Career Development Office," a new name that in itself describes much more accurately what Albro is expected to do these days. "Formerly, students came to me late in their senior year," Albro said. "Usually they were looking for some kind of job they might hold until they married and had children. Very few had any serious, long-term career plans.

"That's completely different now. Some of the students come to see me early in their *freshman* year. They want to know exactly where the best career prospects are, so they can plan their course schedules accordingly. They drop in regularly during their four years here to discuss career plans with me. They make absolutely no bones about the fact that they intend to work most of their lives and that they want and expect the appropriate personal and financial rewards a successful career will bring."

There has been one other drastic change: Many women now admit not only to themselves but to anyone who cares to listen that, if at all possible, they would like to make a lot of money. "Of course, I still get an occasional student who is clearly committed to some kind of service to humanity," Albro said. "But now I get a great many more who want to know, as accurately as possible, what kind of income they may expect from their chosen profession within five or ten years.

"What's more, many of these women do long-range career planning. Formerly, when a student wanted to work for a few years to help buy a home or put a husband through graduate school, she was most interested in the immediate financial rewards of a job. She might also have been concerned about whether the job she chose would be one she could leave for a while when she had children and reenter after they were in school. That's why so many chose teaching or social work. Today's young woman will take a lower-paid job if the advancement opportunities are right. She may plan to take a leave of absence during her early childbearing years, but that's not her principal motivation for choosing a career. Many women expect to keep on working, even while their children are young.

"Not only that, but women who graduated five or ten years ago ask about opportunities for additional training. Business, along with ambition, is no longer a dirty word to women," Albro said. "As a matter of fact, the degree toward which many of them are aiming is a Master in Business Administration. Formerly, the most popular post-graduate degrees were in social work or education." Her statistics bear her out. Twelve Smith students, many of them graduates of five or more years standing, applied to the Harvard Business School last year. Over half of them got in.

Another popular program with recent graduates is offered at a Chicago bank. It provides training, a relatively modest salary, a chance to attend the University of Chicago's School of Business Administration for a master's degree with tuition paid and time off given by the bank. "That's the kind of organization that, ten years ago, would have sent recruiters to Amherst and Williams, not to Smith," Albro said. "It wasn't

just that the bank would not think of hiring women trainees, it was also that few women were ambitious enough to commit themselves to a three-year training program that combined employment with graduate school, thus leaving very little time for any kind of social life."

Other career counselors support Albro's impressions. "We have more women than men planning to go to graduate school," a counselor in a Midwestern state university said. "And they are aiming for careers that demand a high degree of commitment and time: law, medicine, business administration and, within recent years, engineering and aerospace technology. We now have almost as many women interested in degrees in economics as in English."

Haseltine agrees that the attitude of women toward ambitious careers has changed drastically since she was a student in medical school. "Not only have the women changed, attitudes of society have changed as well," she said. When Haseltine went to medical school, she was still a frequently isolated exception: the only female in a classroom or laboratory full of men. When she chose obstetrics and gynecology as her specialty, she became even more isolated. "Most women in those days were expected to go into such fields as pediatrics, psychiatry and dermatology," she added. "If we wanted to specialize in a field that was considered a male bastion, we had a fight on our hands. Any undue show of determination and ambition often led to our being labeled 'aggressive,' 'bitchy' or 'unfeminine.' And that kind of label could hurt one's career.

"Today's female medical students do not have similar worries. They are no longer isolated . . . as a matter of fact, this year's first-year medical-school class at Yale is about 30 percent women. The same is true of many other top medical schools, I understand. Women no longer have to worry about fighting their way into a specialty either. They expect to be able to practice in any field of medicine for which they can qualify. Now they tend to worry about the quality of their post-graduate lives, rather than a specialty that they may or may not be allowed to enter.

"Today's women are working for different goals: for the right to take part-time residencies, for instance, so they can have children and still continue their careers. We had to fight to have any kind of career. Women today don't have to hide the fact that they are ambitious and goal-oriented. It's simply assumed that *every* physician has ambition. Otherwise, why choose such a demanding profession in the first place?"

Sigrid Holland faced even more formidable obstacles. She grew up in Germany where ambitious women were regarded with dislike and distrust not just by men but by other women as well. She wanted to go to medical school; her father prevented her from attending a university. Instead, he allowed her to apprentice herself to the food purchasing and processing business he ran, since buying and cooking food were regarded as feminine activities.

When, in the late 1950s, Holland married an American engineer and moved to Oklahoma, she found Oklahoma City to be about as hospitable to feminine ambitions as Berlin. Only after a meal of chicken-fried steak did she realize she had a skill that was sadly lacking in the community: gourmet cooking. She began neighborhood cooking classes, first as a volunteer, and later, for a fee. She continued working, even during repeated pregnancies.

When the family moved to New Haven, Connecticut, Holland began a small, local catering service, which expanded first throughout the Greater New Haven area, then into New York City. When her husband became ill, she took a full-time job as a chef in an outstanding new restaurant that soon became the gathering place for New Haven's university crowd. After her husband died, she took the job she now holds at the prestigious eating club because she had to have a clearly-defined income, but she continued her catering activities as well.

As a young, exceedingly attractive and independent widow with seven children, Holland achieved a certain modest fame. An appearance on Barbara Walters' *Not for Women Only* TV show (discussing the importance of careers for mothers of large families) resulted in some freelance magazine work and a book. "I wonder what I would have done if I had not been ambitious . . . if, in spite of all the pressures to keep me in my place as a happy *hausfrau*, I had not insisted on making and following long-term career goals?" she asks today. "How much does welfare pay a widow with seven kids?"

Financial necessities aside, Holland likes her independence and intends to keep it. "I've not let myself become too involved with men who would like nothing better than to lock me and my pots and pans up in their kitchens," she said. "I know now that I can make it on my own, as I had always imagined I could."

By the time Marjorie Weinreb started her career in retailing, the climate for ambitious women had, of course, undergone the drastic change noted by Albro and Haseltine. "When I graduated from college, it was just as great a status symbol for men to have ambitious wives or daughters as it always had been for women to have ambitious husbands or sons," she said. "Nobody tried to stop me from getting the best job I could find. I had all the support from my parents and from my husband that anyone could ask for."

As a matter of fact, when Weinreb and her husband both graduated from Syracuse with masters' degrees in the same year, they moved to Washington, DC because that's where *Marjorie* had the best offer. Her husband, of course, found a good job in the area, too . . but in the meantime, he had passed up several other opportunities in order to go where his wife's chances looked brightest. When Marjorie Weinreb reached a point where her career seemed stalled, the couple moved into the New York area where jobs for women in retailing are most plentiful. "When we talk of moving, we consider *both* our careers equally" she said. "Neither set of parents thinks it even slightly peculiar." As her main interests lie not in systems analysis, where she is now, but in merchandising, Weinreb has so informed her employer. She is willing to take a step backward (such as working as an assistant buyer) in order to move two steps forward later on. That's the kind of decision that formerly might have been expected from a career-minded man, not from a woman, who was supposed to put limits on her potential career growth.

Jean Welty, too, looks on her law practice as a life-time venture. "There are a great many women going into law now," she said. "I hear that in some law schools women make up half or even more than half of the student body. But there are still very few women in *trial* law in this part of the country. Many of the older women lawyers still seem to prefer the quiet office or law library to the direct, person-to-person competition of the courtroom. I find that in a courtroom, the fact that I'm a woman actually helps . . . opponents tend to underestimate me and, of course, that can only benefit my client."

Welty serves on several important State Bar Association committees, and she gives her reasons frankly for assuming so much time-consuming volunteer activity. "Every committee meeting gives me a chance to make important new contacts," she said. "A man joins organizations in order to further his career, so why not a woman? But just accepting volunteer responsibility in and of itself is, of course, not helpful. One has to do a good job, too. . . . ."

Welty bought the house she is renovating not only because she liked it, but because she wants to put the kind of financial-planning advice she gives to her women clients into practice for herself. "So many women just don't know anything about money . . . even women who are accomplished and successful in all kinds of professions," she said.

One of Welty's volunteer activities was undertaken not out of personal ambition, but simply out of a commitment to a cause. In spite of her incredibly busy professional schedule, she leads a Girl Scout troop. "When I was growing up in Pittsburg, Kansas, being a Scout helped me develop the qualities I now need as a lawyer: competitiveness, self-reliance and ambition," she said. "I want to help other young women gain the personal qualities and skills that will help them to set and achieve their own high career goals."

Obviously, this kind of professional schedule leaves only a limited amount of time for social life. "You have to make some sacrifices for everything you gain," Welty said. "I realized that a long time ago. I would like to get married and have children some day. But I also expect to go on working for the rest of my life, and at the moment, my career takes first priority." She does not mind telling this to anyone . . . and that includes the many successful young men she dates.

Nancy Young also realizes that a successful career demands sacrifices. "I take work home with me," she said. "I pass up social engagements when they interfere. But I have another important responsibility, and that's my daughter, Amy. She is a terribly important part of my life . . . and I can't afford to shortchange her." Young lives with a young graphics designer with no immediate plans for marriage. She considers the relationship a stable and permanent one and has, occasionally, considered going into business with him. "My parents are a very traditional Chinese couple," she said. "And in China, it's common for a woman to work alongside of her man. As a matter of fact, my parents worked together in Chinatown. They ran a small shop for tourists. I worked there, too, from the time I was about four years old. I just stood on a box and waited on customers."

Young simply assumes that Amy (who is now attending a special school for gifted children) will want some kind of career, too.

"But I don't believe in pushing children," she said. "That's one of the problems that many of today's women have. In reaction to the way they themselves were raised, they often pressure their daughters too soon to become super career women. That's a good way to produce a backlash. I'm letting Amy proceed at her own pace. But, yes, I do indeed expect her to be ambitious, although there's no way to tell as yet what her ambition will be."

It would seem as if the younger generation of career women have few problems with striving for success and excellence. But are there still problems under the surface that may not have emerged? Elizabeth Phillips, a psychiatric social worker who is also an assistant clinical professor at Yale University's department of psychiatry, feels there may well be. "The obvious, open barriers to ambition and success may no longer be present for some women," she said. "But there still are subtle, subterranean influences and attitudes that may cause conflicts and tensions. Even the younger women who openly strive for professional recognition probably have detected from people closest to them signals that an overly ambitious woman makes a man uncomfortable. How many young girls have been told by their mothers: 'You'll be so successful he won't be able to touch you.' The choice of the verb here is telling. How many young women really want to remain untouched and untouchable? Perhaps the daughters of the Jean Weltys, the Marjorie Weinrebs and the Nancy Youngs will really be free of conflicted feelings about ambition. I certainly hope so, but I still see entirely too many young women who are torn between ambition and the fear of being untouchable to feel that the problem has been solved."

Psychiatrist Rima Brauer also thinks that the ambitious career-oriented women who seem to have no doubts about their future may, later in life, develop more ambivalent feelings. "Most women still want to marry and have children," she said. "When you are 20, it's easy to postpone such decisions . . . the future seems endless. When you hit 30, and you realize that your childbearing years are limited, you may be in for some problems and tensions." Still, she thinks today's young women seem better able to cope with such ambivalence than their mothers were, or even their older sisters.

How does the business establishment, which, of course, is still male-dominated, feel about today's ambitious young career women? A recent business survey showed that it's good strategy for a woman to verbalize her ambitions to her employer, even when that employer might react *adversely to a similar indication from a man.*

Betty L. Harragan, a management consultant and author of the excellent paperback book, *Games Mother Never Taught You: Corporate Gamesmanship for Women,* sums up this astonishing fact in one paragraph: ". . . We've come upon one of the unwritten codes of etiquette in the (corporate) game. This admonition reads: 'Don't verbalize high ambition.' Men have little need to violate this injunction because an ambitious man's superiors instinctively know that he expects to move steadily forward and act accordingly. A woman player elicits no such response. It will be assumed that she *doesn't want* to progress, so blind adherence to the male etiquette code will destroy her chances. A woman must convince superiors that she expects to advance as steadily as ambitious male cohorts."

This means that it's not only fine for a woman to *be* ambitious, but that she may *talk* about her ambitions, even more freely than a man. This is what all five of the women interviewed for this article have done, as have many others who also discussed their plans and goals. An ambitious woman is no longer looked upon as a freak, a fit subject for psychoanalysis or an undesirable employee. If she finds the right professional environment, she'll be encouraged and, if all other factors are right, promoted.

There's one story that illustrates this

point as well as any we've come across. A successful female writer, in her middle 30s, applied for admission to a top-rated law school that turns down 25 applicants for every one admitted. When asked why she wanted to change careers so relatively late in life, she said: "I want to be the first female Chief Justice of the US Supreme Court." Most of her friends knew she was only half kidding. So did the law-school dean who ad-

mitted her . . . over several equally qualified, younger males.

ELIZABETH ELLIOT was ambitious long before it became fashionable for women, a result of a strong belief that "the only thing you can count on is what's inside your head. Other things are ephemeral." Elliot is a free-lance writer who specializes in psychological and sociological subjects as well as in law.

WHY THE PURSUIT OF HAPPINESS IS A WILD GOOSE CHASE

by Enid Harlow

I think it's important for working women to accept their assertiveness and competitiveness and to get out of their psyches the idea that somewhere out there is a woman who can handle everything—job, kids, husband—and be perfectly happy doing it all. There is no such woman out there." This reassuring news comes from Willard Gaylin, MD, who is a psychiatrist and psychoanalyst as well as a teacher and writer.

"Get rid of the notion that there's a way to do it all and be happy. That's a laid-back, mellow, California concept of happiness that in no way corresponds to reality.

"If you think that you can solve your problems in half an hour—as the working wife in the situation comedy does—or that you can find happiness by going off somewhere to howl and scream for a weekend, you're going to be dreadfully disappointed."

Gaylin, who is on both the law and psychiatric faculties of Columbia University in New York City, is also president of the Hastings Institute of Society, Ethics and the Life Sciences and adjunct professor of psychiatry at Union Theological Seminary. His books include *In the Service of Their Country: War Resisters in Prison* (Viking Press, 1970),

Caring (Alfred A. Knopf, 1976) and, most recently, *Feelings: Our Vital Signs* (Harper & Row, 1979, $10.00).

A premise Gaylin holds basic is that pleasure and happiness do not come to us unalloyed. "There's a peculiar concept of happiness being circulated, as though it were a state something akin to a cow's," he remarked, "with no pain at all. That's a disastrous concept. Because if you think that others feel no pain, you're going to begin to think that your own pain is somehow neurotic or inappropriate. There's almost no extremely pleasurable experience that doesn't involve pain."

When asked about the most pleasurable thing in his own life, Gaylin replied without hesitation: "It's raising children. There's just nothing like it." Coming from a woman, that would not be a particularly startling statement, but coming from a man—especially an American man over the age of 50—it certainly is.

Raising his two now grown daughters, Gaylin said, was not without pain. "It was the most agonizing as well as the most joyous experience of my life. The pain I felt as a father when the children were hurt . . . my anxiety over their well-being . . . it's incomparable."

But what about the smaller pleasures, such as having a nice cold drink on a hot day? "That's the simplest kind of pleasure," Gaylin said. "It's pleasurable to eat a good meal or to look at a beautiful table. It's much more pleasurable to have the capacity to make one. But an intense amount of very demanding work goes into that. Pleasure means, 'I did it.' "

Feelings: Our Vital Signs was written, in part, to counteract the "pop"-psychology movement that advises people to rid themselves of their "useless emotions."

"There are books that tell you to get rid of feelings such as anxiety and guilt because they're useless emotions. This is stupid," Gaylin said. "There are no useless emotions. Emotions serve purposes. The books that try to lead you into that state of cowlike happiness are false prophesies. It's a strange psychological wisdom that compares a human being to a cow in the cow's favor."

Gaylin's new book presents a descriptive account of common, everyday feelings, and it makes a clear distinction between feelings and emotions. "Emotion is a complicated mechanism for alerting an organism," he said. "It involves psychological changes." It involves what we call in psychoanalysis *affect*—that part of your emotion that's visible to me. Then there's the part of the emotion that is the feeling, which speaks directly to you. It's a signal from you to you.

"That's why I call feelings our 'vital signs.' They're indicators. They get you going. It is not particularly necessary that you express them. If a woman has a sexual feeling for her boss, let's say, it isn't necessary that she demonstrate it by seducing him. She can learn to live with her feelings or to express them in an appropriate way."

Grand and Small Passions

"Most of us don't win Nobel Peace Prizes or declare war or commit murder," Gaylin continued. "A therapist deals on a day-to-day basis with the smaller feelings—feeling hurt, for instance, touched, bored, envious, humiliated, ashamed.

"In the theory and writing of academic psychology and psychiatry, feelings have been neglected. This has happened because psychologists, in our country at least, have been behaviorally oriented, which means that they don't quite *believe* in feelings; or else they've been animal psychologists, and animals don't have a wide range of feelings. Psychiatrists, for the most part, are involved in treatment; theirs is a medical orientation, and, as such, it has a scientific bias.

"There are no statistics in my new book. You cannot measure or quantify feelings. Many of the people who have written about feelings have not been the best trained. Some unfortunate nonsense has come out as a consequence."

Gaylin believes that feelings such as guilt, jealousy, anxiety, feeling used or feeling moved are common to both men and women, but the ways in which each sex articulates them are culturally determined.

Biology is Not Destiny

"In the human animal, biology gives very little direction," he explained. "We have very few biological imperatives. We were not born to fly, and yet we fly. We were not born to swim underwater, and yet we have scuba divers. We were not born to have birth control, and yet we have it. One of the intriguing things about the human species is that we are born incomplete, but with the capacity to complete ourselves. The uniquely human characteristic is the ability to be the designers of our own state.

"There is absolutely no question that our attitudes toward feelings are culturally determined. If you walk the streets of Palermo, you know you're in a different city from Stockholm simply by the level of noise and the emotional effect that is being generated.

"In our own society we have, in addition to an ethnic, a gender difference. We encourage in girls a freer expression of emotion than we do in boys—except for anger, assertion and aggression, which we do encourage in boys. It's considered tough and cute for a little boy to show aggression, and somewhat threatening (especially to the male parent) for a boy to get teary or flirtatious. We make these distinctions right from the start. Children are conditionable from the time they're one or two weeks old."

Gaylin sees the gradual breakdown of gender stereotypes as one of the best products of the women's movement. "This doesn't mean that there may not be different biological directives toward feeling," he cautioned. "As the women's movement matures, women involved in it will learn to be unafraid of biological differences. In the early days of the movement, activists felt that in order to defend a 'right' psychological or emotional position, they had to deny biological fact. You don't have to do that. Biological facts may mean that we should die of pneumonia. We weren't born with penicillin in us. Still, we're free to use our moral judgment about how we want to be.

"It wouldn't surprise me to find that there are biological differences in the expression of emotions between men and women. But *most* of the differences you see—the incapacity of men to express tender, affectionate feelings with other men—are culturally determined. We *breed* that into our kids."

Emotion is not the opposite of intelligence but a correlate of it. Throughout his book, Gaylin stresses that, as human beings, we have a highly developed intelligence and therefore lots of choices. He sees feelings evolving as quick guides to choice.

Guilt is Not a Dirty Word

Gaylin defines guilt as "the failure of an ego ideal. Somehow not measuring up to your own image of what you should be. There are no 'good' feelings and 'bad' feelings. Guilt is as good a feeling as joy or pride, in the sense that *all* feelings serve our purposes."

As an example of how guilt can work for us, he offered the following scenario: "Sup-

pose a working woman comes home feeling tired and humiliated. It's a dehumanizing, brutalizing world out there. Normally, the home is a source of nourishment; if we are drained of self-pride and self-confidence in the working world, we come home to the love of our children, our spouse or lover, and that restores us. But suppose the woman comes home and the first thing she does is to take it out on her husband or children.

"If she doesn't feel guilt, she will continue to behave that way. The husband and children who take the brunt of her anger will become estranged. Gradually, she will convert them into enemies, and they will then retaliate and be punishing toward her. If you convert your family into a camp of enemies, where are you going to get the strength to face the hostility and indifference in life?

"When you rage at your husband or smack your child inappropriately, you will feel, *I hope,* a rush of guilt. What that guilt does is stop you from doing something that not only is unjust to them but also does not serve you. On the other hand, if you feel guilty and say you're sorry or do something that means you're sorry, your husband and children will realize that you're in pain, that you love them, and they will then begin to supply the nutrients you need in order to get back on the right track.

"So guilt serves an enormously important function—not just to protect *others,* but to protect ourselves because we need those others. In that sense, it's a self-serving emotion."

Dual-Role Guilt

Another kind of guilt is suffered by the working woman who feels torn between commitment to her job and devotion to her husband and children.

"We're in revolution today," said Gaylin. "Or at least a transition. I feel enormous compassion for a woman trapped in a revolutionary period such as this one. She has all the guilt endowments of a previous generation, which have been given to her in childhood. She still has an ideal of behavior that she is trying to change but is stuck with. She probably does not have a partner who has been adequately trained to value his responsibility to the children and the household. I don't know what the solutions are.

"I'll tell you what the solution is *not*. It's not to decide that a child doesn't need a primary caretaker. That would be the easy solution. And it's patent nonsense. Every piece of evidence points to the fact that a child requires a primary caretaker and that it *demands* full time.

"Now, can that job be split between two adults? I don't know. It's conceivable. Could that primary caretaker be a man? Yes. But that would just turn the problem around. Women, of course, are as entitled to their careers as men are, but somebody has to stay at home with young children. If we respected the value of raising children, and indicated our respect by paying for it, that might be a whole different kettle of fish."

Gaylin holds our society partially responsible for depriving men of an identity in fathering. "We've allowed men to be lousy fathers without making them feel guilty about it," he said.

As an example of the kinds of social pressures that can prevent men from structuring their lives to give fathering a more prominent place, Gaylin presented the hypothetical case of three people applying for a job at a law firm.

Number One is a tough, aggressive young man, just graduated from a prestigious Ivy League law school at the top of his class. He says he's dedicated, tireless and prepared to work 70 or 80 hours a week. Number Two is a woman, also from a prestigious law school, also at the head of her class. She says she's raising children and wants to be at home for them, but she can give the firm a hard 40-hour week. Number Three is a young man whose credentials equal those of the first two applicants. He says he's a father who wants to help raise his children. He's bright, hardworking and offers 40

hours a week, but not more.

"I'll tell you what happens," Gaylin continued. "Number One will get the job. Number Two will be hired in a great many firms, because we have laws and social pressures now that demand women be taken in. Number Three had better go jump off a bridge somewhere. No one will give him the time of day. So, even if men wanted to change, the pressures against it in our society are very, very tough."

Feeling Used—For Good or Ill

"We live in a world where many of us feel used—both at home and at work. I think the first thing you have a right to ask yourself is, are you indeed being exploited? If you find yourself feeling used in a number of ways all the time, then you ought to examine yourself. You might ask yourself if you haven't come to a state in life where you're *ready* to feel exploited. But in many ways I would say that being used occassionally is not the worst thing that could happen to you. I would rather be taken advantage of once in a while than go through life so armored, so protected, that no one could ever hurt me. That kind of person is never going to experience anything."

How Stereotypes Hurt Women and Men

In his chapter on feeling tired—which is often a mask for an underlying depression— Gaylin wrote: "More men commit suicide over the loss of a job than over the loss of a wife or child." Asked to elaborate, he said: "From birth, a man's system of pride is built on what he does. His work establishes his manhood, not just his earning power. A woman's pride, until modern times, has been established in the dependency relationship, by the kind of man she's involved with.

"If a woman loses her love object, she hasn't just lost the love object, she also has lost her feeling of self-worth; she has a sense of herself as a failure. A man feels that sense of failure if he loses his job. Failure is defined in terms of being lovable for the woman, and of being successful for the man. All of this is changing as women change.

"I am thankful for the women's movement for what I feel it will do to liberate us all from impossible gender stereotypes. I'm not sure that what the women have lost has gone to the men. It isn't as though life were a bowl of soup, and the less you have to drink the more I have. We've both been shortchanged in this deal.

"If it's a concept of liberation to convert the typical stereotyped woman into the typical stereotyped man, we're in *terrible* trouble. What we want is to modify the gender roles, to soften the rough edges of both.

Sexual Liberation—a Mixed Blessing

"Just as sex can be used to relieve anxiety, it also can be an incredible source of tension," Gaylin said. "This is an irony that has given rise to one of the clichés of psychiatry: When sex is good, it's 10 percent of a successful marriage; when it's bad, it's 90 percent of a failed marriage.

"For years a woman's sexual role was defined as a pleasureless one. Sex was a service a woman performed for her husband. Since she was not expected to feel pleasure, she was relieved of the distressing sense of failure when she didn't. In those days, women were free of the agony of proving themselves sexually. Now they're getting into that agony. The human condition is always a mixed blessing. Once you have choice and freedom, you have pain, ambivalence, confusion, guilt and shame. I don't think that's dreadful. It's part of the complexity of human life."

Is it Honest or Cruelty?

Far from being an advocate of the "let it all hang out" philosophy, Gaylin believes the need to impose one's honesty on others is "more often an act of violence and aggression than the generous sharing of knowledge that it purports to be.

"We are public creatures," he said. "We work in a public space. I think all of this venting of spleen in public is the product of a peculiar kind of self-indulgent individualism that this country has promoted, and I think we're coming to the end of it. Often it's only a rationalization for cruelty."

The Rewards of Involvement

"Working women may be suffering the strain of taking on too many roles," Gaylin commented. "In return for this, they're paying an enormous price. On the other hand, they're reaping the rewards of those roles that they didn't have before. Living is involvement. The more you're involved, the more pain (and pleasure) you'll feel."

Feelings, Willard Gaylin would remind us, serve our purposes not only as individuals but as members of the human race. We are dependent upon the social good not only for our survival but also as the source of our joy and pride in life. Since pleasure and pain are inextricably bound, easy prescriptions for happiness can only be seen as fraudulent.

"We all share the existential complication of being human," Gaylin concluded, with a very human grin.

JOB BURNOUT

by Dick Friedman

● It was her first job out of college, and the public-relations executive at a major corporation threw her entire self into it. "During one seven-week stretch I worked seven days a week," she recalled. "I ate breakfast and lunch on the job, and I wouldn't take a break." Then, the excitement and the adrenaline wore off. "I was at the office on a Saturday night, and I thought, why? I'm too young, work too hard and get paid too little."

- The 33-year-old owner of a design firm had devoted five years to making her business a success, putting in 60-to-70-hour weeks at the expense of the rest of her life. But now her world seemed to be falling apart: A big client was threatening to leave, she faced a sales-tax audit and the firm was beginning to lose money. "I love design, but I had lost my inspiration," she said. "Every day at the office was a struggle. And I worried: What else did I have if the business failed? One day, I just decided I couldn't stand it anymore."

- Appointed to the faculty of a prestigious university, the new PhD decided that she had to prove herself not only as a teacher but in counseling (her field) and as a scholar as well. "I got overinvolved with everyone and everything except myself," she said. A back problem—which she now realizes was stress related—drove her to a doctor, who warned her, "Slow down or you'll be in the hospital."

What the three women above were and still are confronting is a phenomenon once thought to be the hallmark of the hard-driving three-martini male executive: job burnout. Maybe you have had it, either in mild or acute form. One day, it seems you're happy enough with what you're doing—or at least as happy as you were the day before. Then, suddenly, you're "tired of it all," mentally and physically. Maybe you have "battle fatigue." Perhaps you're so sick of the job that you don't want to go to work in the morning. Or you seem to be working harder but getting less done. Or you're bored with work but feel guilty about being bored.

You feel trapped, but you don't know what to do about it. Besides, you're worried about how you've neglected your hobbies, family, friends or love life. And for what? You have vague feelings about leaving your job to do—

something, anything, as long as it isn't what you're doing now. Beyond that, there is a feeling of panic and helplessness that makes all of the above add up to considerably more than the sum of their parts. In short, like the designer, you can't stand it.

Job burnout is not an affliction merely of the successful, those who at least get some return for the high price they pay. (In fact, according to many experts, success might be just the elixir to help withstand burnout.)

Teachers, counselors and others in the "helping" professions—many of which are heavily female—have jobs that make them susceptible to burnout. Other people may be vulnerable because of their personalities or upbringing or because of their expectations. What are the real causes of job burnout? And is there anything short of escaping to a tropical island you can do about it?

Why Now?

One of the most frustrating aspects of job burnout is trying to pinpoint its origin. Burnout is a highly personal, emotional and, at times, vague process. "The mystery is, what's the straw that breaks the camel's back? What sets it off?" mused the designer. In her case, all she can say is, "One day I was fine, then it started."

That's not so, declared James P. Smith, PhD, associate professor of counseling psychology and director of the Vocational Counseling Clinic at Philadelphia's Temple University. "You're probably talking about a whole bunch of stuff that's been bothering you," he said, adding that it's most likely been vexing you for a long time whether you know it or not. In other words, one bad day at work or an argument with your boss will not a case of job burnout make.

On the other hand, said psychiatrist Sidney Lecker, MD, president of New York's Executive Health Examiner's StressControl Systems, Inc., and author of *The Money Personality, The Natural Way to Successful Stress Control* and *Family Ties*, even a week filled with such problems can be a warning.

"Look at each day," advised Lecker, "and ask yourself, 'Was there a purpose to my work? Did I get a payoff from my job?' If the answer is no a few days in a row, then you may be in the earliest stages of burnout." This is the time to start rectifying the situation, noted Lecker, because your standing with your employer, your energy level and your self-image usually still are high. Later, he added, "you'll have no bargaining power. I've seen too many people live in a burnout stage for ten years, just waiting until their pensions are vested." The designer put it another way, "Don't let the situation get too desperate."

Why Me?

Some situations seem to set you up for burnout. The roots may lie in your job, your nature, your goals or some combination of these factors.

Superwoman. For the sake of self-image, this person, as the new PhD we spoke of earlier put it, "wants to do everything, all equally well. For me, that means working constantly, six days a week, 12 to 15 hours a day." Superwoman must have a hand in every project. "I felt I couldn't let anyone down," said the designer. Superwoman thinks that if she doesn't do the work, nobody else can or will—and she'll get blamed. "I didn't have a choice," recalled a former office manager of a radio station. "It was either get the work done or not get it done and get fired," although she admitted that her boss knew she was holding the station together.

Superwomen who are married or have families are doubly susceptible to job burnout—unlike supermen, who generally give their careers top priority. The burnout of married superwomen, said L. Warwick Coppleson, MD, medical director of Chicago's Coppleson Medical Center, is akin to the burnouts he's seen in men with two jobs. The married superwoman tries to hold two jobs, too—one at home, one at the work place.

The Good Little Girl who does her work

and expects to be rewarded. Said Lecker, "Too many people think, 'I'm a good person, so somebody will take care of my destiny.' That's not the way things work." Work must yield benefits—emotional *and* monetary. Sometimes—maybe because of the system, perhaps because you're not forceful enough—they don't come through. For many women, the knowledge that they are being inadequately compensated can simmer into bitterness. "They wouldn't pay me, but they'd keep patting me on the back," said the PR executive. "When you see that the guy next to you is making three to four times what you do and you have to bust to do it, that's very frustrating. You begin to ask why you're putting yourself through this."

Helpful Counselor. As Smith defined it, counselor burnout in the health profession means "you're seeing a lot of clients all the time, always giving to everybody—and nobody is giving back to you. Also, you're dealing with such troubled people that you realize the enormity of the task and your contribution seems so small that the whole thing becomes meaningless."

You don't have to be a teacher or a social worker to get into this syndrome. The radio-station office manager remembered that she was considered "the core of the station. The job deals with everybody, and everything lands on your shoulders. A salesperson was hassled, so he'd come over to talk. I knew everyone's problems, everyone's story. I wanted to scream, 'Is there any time for me?'"

The Workaholic. A well-documented phenomenon. The biggest problem the workaholic has with burnout is not necessarily fatigue; rather, it's depression when she realizes that she has no life outside the work place. That often compounds the difficulty: "It's a vicious cycle," said the radio-station office manager. "You know your home life is lousy, so you decide to work more, and so your home life gets lousier...." The workaholic tries to meet her social needs at work rather than by developing other contacts.

Workaholism often leads to weekend anxieties. On Saturdays, said the designer, when she needed to relax, she'd find herself thinking, "I really should be doing something productive."

The Challenge-aholic. Some people, noted Smith, can do the same thing for years without getting bored, while others always need something new. "It might be healthy," he said, "or it might be pathological." When it's the latter, a sense of emptiness sets in. "When I first started my job," remembered the radio-station office manager, "I loved it. But after a while, I knew how to do it and there was nothing left." Again, said Smith, self-image is bound up in each new challenge. Challenge-aholics say, "Hey, if I just learn that, I'll be a great person." But he warned, "The feelings about themselves don't change when the smoke has cleared."

The Misplaced Person. Just because you've been doing something for a while doesn't mean you're suited for it or you like it, even if you're a success at it. "I was a bright, shining star at 24," said the PR exec. "That's what I needed—then." Her reappraisal of what she really wanted to do was thus even more agonizing. Similarly, the radio-station office manager was seduced by the apparent glamour of her fast-paced business. "I was 18 when I started working there," she said. "I didn't think about what would happen to me eight years later."

Few Easy Answers

After you've figured out what is causing your job burnout, what can you do about it? Even when the answers sound easy, applying them isn't. Your solution might involve changing long-entrenched habits or having a tough confrontation with your boss. But, reassured Smith, "People can do a lot more risk taking than they think." Lecker compared the process to a high-wire act. "You have to let go of one trapeze before you catch another, but you do have a safety net—your talent."

The best way to deal with physical fatigue is to start taking care of yourself. Slow down and, as the designer advised, "Work as hard at your personal life as you do at your business." Both Lecker and Smith tell patients suffering from burnout to list how they've spent their time recently in order to see how they might profit from a schedule change. "You never stay home on Saturday or Sunday?" asked Smith. "You need to do that." The designer always had arrived at work at 9:30 AM and stayed late, eating lunch on the job. "Now, I sometimes come in later in the morning," she said. "I discovered that life went on there without me. I try to go out for lunch every day—which was very difficult for me to make myself do at first. And now, when it comes to working late, I draw the line—I do it only when I'm compensated for it financially and esthetically." Proper diet, rest and whatever stress-reduction techniques (jogging, yoga, meditation) you prefer can help, too.

Changing your job to alleviate psychological fatigue is a little trickier. You may not have the leverage to get your superiors to give you a raise or new responsibilities, but resist the temptation to quit in a huff. Precipitous leave taking, said Smith, only means "you haven't thought about things constructively. 'I can't stand it anymore' is not a solution." If the situation is really bad, he added, you might request a leave of absence. Even if you do so with trepidation, a three-month breathing spell might take the pressure off, removing the feeling that you're going to be there 16 hours a day for the next 40 years.

If only temporarily, try to refresh yourself by assuming new duties, or at least by concentrating on those you like. The designer decided she enjoyed the esthetic aspect of her business more than the job of selling. "I was good at both, but I didn't like to sell," she said. So she's devoting herself to graphics in hopes of "bringing the fun back into it." If the job is getting dull, tell your superiors rather than risking enervation and stagnation. "I've worked with men who think that because I'm such a nun about my job it's valuable to leave me on a boring project," said the PR woman. "But now, I walk into my boss when I'm bored and say, 'I'm being wasted on this work.' " Try not to be superwoman. If you're overworked, see if you can get an assistant. And if you have an assistant, delegate. "Once, I supervised five people but I didn't trust anyone," said the PR exec. "I finally learned not to do it all myself."

Above all, don't keep your feelings to yourself; they'll just build up inside and exacerbate the problem. "Trying to protect my coworkers, friends and parents and also to keep up my image was unfair," said the designer—meaning it was an injustice to them and to herself. Talk things over with a friend or relative; if you think the situation is serious enough, get professional counseling.

If these suggestions don't snap you out of your burnout, or if, for some reason, you can't implement them, you may need to make some major and difficult decisions about your life. If the job demands long hours, said Smith, you may have to change jobs or negotiate for a lesser job. "Some people can go for 16 hours a day," he said,

"and some can't. Maybe it then becomes a question of your limitations—or a choice between success and happiness." This may require, warned Smith, some painful admission to yourself—such as, "I've peaked and I'm going to be in middle management for 25 more years."

The younger you are, the more you can do about it. The radio-station office manager, for instance, decided she wanted to move into a high executive position but didn't have the educational credentials. She's planning to attend business school, sacrificing two years of income.

You never may be satisfied with the sacrifices you are forced to make. But, unless you are very driven, you probably shouldn't make perpetual burnout the price of success. Her new perspective has allowed the designer to feel that "even if the business did go under, I'm not going to go under. My needs are different from the company's." Asked if she has any regrets about seeing people promoted above her whom she considers less talented than she, the PhD pondered before answering: "One side of me says, 'Wouldn't it be nice if that were me?' Then, the other side says, 'I'm not so sure.' "

ARE WE STILL AFRAID OF SUCCESS?
YES

by Elizabeth Elliot

It all started with Anne who, about ten years ago, found herself at the top of her medical-school class. From that day on, it was downhill all the way for poor Anne, at least in the eyes of a majority of the 90 young women and 88 young men who read about her successful academic career and were asked to speculate on her future.

Anne was an acne-faced bookworm, they concluded. She studied 12 hours a day, lived

at home to save money and never had a date. She was worried that perhaps she wasn't normal, particularly since all her classmates (male and female) despised her.

Then there was John, who also was at the head of *his* medical-school class. Everything came up roses for him. The same group of men and women, who apparently considered Anne a disaster, characterized John as a conscientious young man who worked hard. He didn't worry about being abnormal . . . he was pleased with himself. Not only was he bright, he was also handsome and dedicated, and eventually became a famous surgeon.

Anne and John are not real people. They are imaginary characters, invented by a distinguished American research psychologist, Matina Horner, PhD, who is president of Radcliffe College. Horner was exploring the basis for sex differences in achievement orientation. So she gave groups of students one unfinished sentence containing a single clue. The sentence read: "After the first-term finals, Anne finds herself at the top of her medical school class. . . ." Then she asked her research subjects to write a short paragraph finishing the story. That's where Anne met with all those misfortunes. When the word "John" was substituted, the reaction was exactly reversed.

The test results led Horner to this conclusion: "A bright young woman is caught in a double bind in achievement-orientated situations. She worries not only about failure, but also about success. If she fails, she is not living up to her own standards of performance; if she succeeds, she is not living up to societal expectations of the female role. Men in our society do not experience this kind of ambivalence because they are not only permitted to achieve, they are actively encouraged to do so.

"In recent years many legal and educational barriers to female achievement have been removed, but it is clear that psychological barriers remain. The motive to avoid success has had an important influence on the educational and professional lives of the women in our society," wrote Horner.

Ten years have passed since Horner's research results were completed, widely publicized and labeled "the fear of success" syndrome. Of course, the label was never entirely accurate. . . . Horner's theory encompasses many other emotions than fear (guilt and ambivalence, for examples) that may hinder a woman's striving toward suc-

cess. But after a decade of the Women's Movement, do her observations still apply? Do women still feel uncomfortable with success? Does their anxiety quotient still rise, right along with their salary bracket and the size and location of their private office?

The answer is a qualified "yes." Success is still often hard for women to take for a number of basic causes that have not changed very much. One additional observation has been made: Today, there are also a great many *men* who fear success, a problem their fathers and grandfathers probably did not have.

Alexandra Symonds, MD, is a training and supervising psychoanalyst at the Karen Horney Clinic in New York City, and an associate clinical professor of psychiatry at New York College of Medicine. She has studied the problems of professionally successful women and has many of them among her patients. In a paper she gave at a recent meeting of the Association for the Advancement of Psychoanalysis, she reported a dream one of these patients had recounted.

The woman dreamed that she was hanging out of a window, holding on by her fingernails. Meanwhile, her husband was calmly walking across the room, and all she could do was whisper inaudibly: "Help me."

Symonds concluded that the patient, like many other successful women, had "deeply buried dependency needs" she might have been denying for years. Outwardly, she seemed to be living an almost ideal life: She was doing brilliantly at a job she loved; she seemed to have a fine marriage and her children seemed to be doing well. Underneath the veneer of success and composure, this woman was feeling overwhelmed.

Psychiatrist Karen Horney, to whose work Symonds pays close attention, described three main character types: self-effacing, dependent and detached, and expansive. "Both men and women can fall into any of these categories," Symonds said, "but women have, over the years, experienced tremendous cultural pressures to conform to the self-effacing or the dependent role." When they don't . . . when they strive to excel and succeed, they may get into emotional trouble. . . . almost exactly the kind of double bind that Horner described.

Expansiveness, the quality that makes success possible, is not inherently undesirable. Symonds said: "It's part of a healthy self-actualizing process of growth and autonomy . . . the kind of development that is expected of a man. But 'expansive' women often feel that they have to suppress tender feelings and normal dependency needs that all of us carry with us throughout our lives. Often these women are the ones who did not want to be like their mothers, whom they perceive as 'passive, dependent and second-class citizens.' " The daughters cultivated qualities of strength, courage and intellectual achievement from early childhood on. They strive, above all, to be self-sufficient and frequently they are. If the mother could be honestly supportive and loving in spite of her daughter's rebellion against a traditional lifestyle, the daughter might achieve success with few problems. But many of the mothers were just not able to do this. The self-effacing, silently suffering mother—even if she says to her daughter, "Don't get caught as I did, amount to something," may feel resentful and threatened by the daughter's rejection of her role model, and she lets the daughter know this in many subtle ways. If the mother becomes frankly hostile, the problem for the daughter can become even more severe, Symonds has found.

The result of this conflict characteristically produces three types of neurotic patterns in women who are apparently doing exceedingly well in their professional lives, according to Symonds. "Some women become chronically depressed. Their feelings of sadness are pervasive but often are not even evident to co-workers, friends or family. Such women usually become totally involved with their work and are overly concerned with giving to others. They expect very little joy and happiness for themselves.

To a psychiatrist they would seem emotionally malnourished," Symonds said.

The second syndrome Symonds designates as "a confusion in feminine identity. Such women tend to feel real panic when they perceive aspects of their personality that they consider masculine," she said. Yet, they must keep up a facade of self-sufficiency . . . they cannot ask for help because they feel that such a plea would destroy their autonomy. The woman who dreamed she was hanging out of the window by her fingernails and was unable to call out to her husband was expressing these feelings symbolically.

Then there is the third kind of woman who feels the only way she can relieve her ambivalence and guilt about having and enjoying a career is to be superwife and supermom as well. Such women tend to run themselves ragged. They are the ones who, in spite of demanding jobs, cannot bring themselves to curtail entertaining their husbands' business associates and who somehow manage to become secretaries of the PTA and chairmen of the local Heart Association Campaign on top of all their other duties. "They have the feeling that they must prove their femininity by overcompensating in their roles as wives and mothers," Symonds said.

She pointed to a recent study that showed women psychiatrists tend to have more children than male psychiatrists, and to another that indicated that 87 percent of female doctors questioned in a survey did all their own housework, despite full-time professional commitments and incomes that would easily allow them to employ household help.

Many of these women refuse to allow their husbands to help, even if assistance is freely offered. "Their unshared burdens take their toll with such psychological dysfunctions as depression and repressed rage, which in turn can result in severe insomnia and sexual problems," Symonds said.

Some of these women are very difficult to help because they consider asking for professional counseling a sign of weakness.

Even if they do come for therapy, they may find it rough going because it is too painful to look back into their childhoods for clues to their present troubles.

What's even sadder is that some of these women transmit some of their own conflicts to their daughters who, in turn, will have problems in their own adult lives. "Often it's the daughter of a highly trained, successful, professional woman who doesn't want to go to college, doesn't want to prepare herself for a career and wishes nothing more than to fulfill the traditional role of her grandmother," Symonds said.

Will today's more liberated woman be able to relate more positively to a daughter who does not choose to follow the same lifestyle she has chosen for herself? Symonds said she certainly hopes so . . . but that the evidence will not be in for many more years.

Helen Singer Kaplan, MD, associate clinical professor of psychiatry at the Cornell University Medical School and head of the Sex Therapy and Education Program at the Payne Whitney Clinic has a more optimistic view. In a paper she gave to a meeting of the American Psychiatric Association, she indicated that, sexually at least, the liberated woman seems to have fewer, rather than more, problems that her unliberated sister. She also maintains that there are simply no statistics to prove a theory currently popular in some quarters: that there has been a sudden rise in male impotence, due to the fact that women have become freer, more assertive and more self-confident.

"Of course, there are some successful women who can cause potency problems in their partners . . . but they probably would be doing so whether or not they had careers," she added. "I have one couple in therapy because the man is apparently having trouble with erection. He is married to an incredibly aggressive woman who demands intercourse no matter how he feels and who berates him if he can't comply. She happens to have a PhD in physics. The chances are this couple would have the same problem if she had failed to graduate from high school."

Another case Kaplan cited was that of a gentle, beautiful, young career woman married to a man whom Kaplan described as "restless, pushy and agitated," who "yells at his wife in front of other people and interrupts her every time she tries to talk." On top of all that, his lovemaking is so rough that she has chronic cystitis. The couple came to see her because the husband insisted his wife was frigid due, according to him, to a demanding and successful career. "There is nothing wrong with that woman sexually," Kaplan insisted. "There *is* something drastically wrong with the man and with the relationship . . . and it has absolutely nothing to do with what and how well either does in his or her profession."

Kaplan maintains that a bright, ambitious woman who wants to establish herself in a profession will probably be a happier person and a better sex partner if she follows her desires. "A martyr is not much fun to have around . . . in the home or in bed," she said. If such a woman marries a secure, loving man, her career should be an asset to a good relationship, on a sexual as well as any other level."

Leon Tec, MD, is a psychiatrist who practices in Westport, Connecticut, a community where success is as prevalent as flawless green lawns. Recently he has published a book called *Fear of Success* (New American Library), which deals almost exclusively with men who get into emotional trouble as they climb the career ladder.

"Success means change and uncertainty," Tec said, "and a great many people feel very uncomfortable when they have to leave their accustomed groove."

He tells of one patient, a politician, who would go to sleep worrying about losing a campaign and who would wake up in a cold sweat in the middle of the night thinking: "My God what will I do if I *win?*"

Another patient was a research scientist whose brilliance had earned him high status and a large income early in life. But he was feeling very unhappy. "Every time I get a new thought, every time a hypothesis presents itself, I get scared and depressed," he told Tec. "I don't understand this at all. . ."

As it turned out, both men were fairly rigid individuals. Both excelled in their professions but felt real discomfort in intimate personal relationships. In a way, they were similar to the picture Horner's research subjects had of Anne: all work and no play. Once they realized what was bothering them, they were able to relax and take their successes (and occasional failures) in stride.

Tec has also seen some men who seem to suffer from a problem very similar to Dr. Symond's superwife and supermom. They want to be superhusbands and superfathers because they are becoming increasingly aware that they will miss something important. This is a development that we owe to the Women's Movement and the human potential movement, and in my opinion, it is a very healthy one," Tec said. "Of course, I don't want my patients to feel guilty and anxious, but more concern on the part of professionally successful men for a healthy and loving family life has been long overdue. Usually these men appear to cope very well once they understand what has been happening."

So where does all this leave us? Is their own emotional ambivalence still a problem to today's ambitious young career women? The chances are that this generation of working women is still going to have some guilt and anxiety about success. Perhaps our daughters will be free from these problems and will be able to cope with career and family, femininity and assertiveness, happiness and success. Even among Horner's students, there was at least one young woman who foresaw a happy future for Anne, and by extension, for herself. This is what she wrote:

"Anne is quite a lady . . . not only is she tops academically, but also she is liked and admired by her fellow students . . . quite a trick in a male-dominated field. She is brilliant . . . and she is also some woman!"

ELIZABETH ELLIOT *first became intrigued by Matina Horner's ideas about women and success when she interviewed her over ten years ago. "The label of fear in relation to success may be oversimplifying, but I've had those feelings, I know they exist," she added. For now, Elliot, a freelance writer who specializes in psychology and travel, feels, "I don't have any fear of success anymore."*

Chapter Seventeen

At the Top

WHAT POWER IS AND ISN'T:

An Interview with Jane Trahey

by Jacqueline C. Warsaw

"I think I started working when I was around two," Jane Trahey will tell you with a half-serious smile. What might seem like a life sentence isn't. For Trahey, "it's been a gas most of the time." Certainly the mind-print she left on Madison Avenue is traceable to her laser-beam copy and outspoken bid for the summit. From a retail copywriter in Chicago to founder and president of Jane Trahey Advertising, she never once forgot her mother's warning that she, alone, was going to have to hack out her own living. So she made up her mind early on that if she had to work, she was going to do what she wanted to do.

Trahey's formulas for working women who want power aren't based on bio-rhythms or ritual magic. Her tips are real. Her ploys are power veterans, used and tested by herself or other female executives she knows. The result is her book, *Jane Trahey On Women and Power*, that shows you what real power is and what it isn't. Its honesty quotient often comes too close for comfort. But it's that Trahey willingness to see things as they really are that inspires the reader to see how they can be.

Q. *In the opening of your book you state that it's about women and power; that only if they really want it and know how to get it, will it come their way.*

A. Yes. We've been told a hundred times what's keeping us down. We need ways to change the situation.

Q. *Is that why you wrote the book?*

A. Honestly, I started because I've always been pro-female. When the editors came to me about doing the book, I thought I could knock it off in about three months. Ten months later I was still at it. When it was finished, I came out of the experience a raging revolutionist. I could kill because I think we're so mistreated.

Q. *Do you think other women will react with the same rage to your candid lowdown on the male-power structure and the road-*

blocks it puts in the way of women's advancement?
A. I really don't know what's going to happen. I think women who are working, especially in middle management, ought to get a lot out of it. If nothing else, they're going to see what the game is all about.
Q. *Is the corporate world men have built the only viable environment in which women can do business? Or is there a way for them to step outside the circle and set up a workable "third world" alternative?*
A. Today's work force is, unfortunately, a very unfeeling world. Men build it, thrive on it and pass it on— usually to their sons. It perpetuates itself. The Sulzberger family of *The New York Times* capsulizes this system. All the sons-in-law went into the business knowing nothing about publishing. The daughters didn't. Yet they grew up in a family where probably little else but publishing was discussed. So you have to ask why none of these women wanted in. I think it's because we've been conditioned to play a different role.
Q. *Yet there are some highly capable women who have penetrated the corporate structure. Why would they accept the status quo of a dead-end career or even stay and function within it?*
A. Unless you have your own business, you have to face the reality of being part of the job force. Like many others, one capable woman I know stays in a male-dominated company for two reasons. She knows that eventually the corporation will be forced to recognize the token female executive, and she may be it. And secondly, the benefits available to her—health and life insurance programs, etc.—are far superior to those packaged in companies employing many women. This woman happens to be the sole family supporter, which is the case more and more today, and benefits to her family are very important—just as they have been to men over the years.
Q. *You come to the conclusion that corporations promote women to so-called execu-*

tive spots as part of their tokenism campaign and that these women really have no power.
A. Lots of corporations have developed ways to lull a woman into thinking she's winning the war. She wants to be upwardly mobile. Okay. Give her a title. The president's secretary becomes his "administrative assistant." The corporation has gilded the cage but kept her as powerless as ever. And the ploy works!
Q. *Are you saying that all the press coverage about women executives becoming board members, cabinet members and committee members is a deliberate smoke screen?*
A. Yes. In the appendix to my book, I did a study of the top 50 corporations to see how they envision women today. I started with their annual reports and it's pretty clear that women are nowhere. If you figure an average of 16 people on each board, you get 800-plus seats. But of that total, only 14 belonged to women. And, since some of those same women sat on more than one board, the real number was more like 11. The cruelest blow was the obvious absence of women in power jobs at the chief executive officer level.
Q. *In your book, you interviewed nine female executives who've made it to the top. Four were in publishing where the "power of the press" is real. Do women gravitate to situations where the power is already vested in the profession?*
A. I think they do. It's because they're acceptable in publishing. Such is not the case in steel, for instance. Yet, when you look further, you see that most publishers of women's magazines are men. Again, I have to ask why. Even in retailing, where we find so many women, there's only Gerry Stutz as president of Henri Bendel.
Q. *But in your book you said you really have to want power to get it. Could it be that not enough women realize it's okay to want a top position?*
A. Women get shunted into dead-end jobs and they don't even know it. If they get com-

partmented they'll go nowhere, especially not to the top. In his fascinating book, *Ways of Seeing,* John Berger says that women see themselves through other people—a kind of second-hand reflection. When a boss asks her opinion, her tendency is to figure out subconsciously what he wants to hear. What she really wants to say gets lost in second guessing. Women don't respond as a man would. If a man goes for a job interview, both he and the boss say up front what salary bracket they're talking about. But when a woman comes in, the boss asks, "Dorothy, what do you think you're worth?" Dorothy freezes and asks herself what she thinks he'll pay. And the cycle begins again.

Q. *So women defer to the opinions and direction of the boss.*

A. Sure. Men expect to run and edit things. Women expect to be run and edited. Women are so hungry to get "daddy's" approval they don't care how or from where it comes. They don't even feel they are being used because they are so used to serving.

Q. *Many women express anxiety about taking charge, which, according to sociological and psychological studies, is because they're afraid to confront their self-worth. True?*

A. Women have an incredibly hard time converting worth into money. They sit back and say they've made it once they hit a certain salary bracket, say $37,000. But that's nothing compared to the salaries paid for comparable jobs held by men. Once, when I asked a client for a certain fee, he told me he could not in good conscience pay a woman that much money. So we hacked it out, and finally he paid me what I had asked for but in other ways, such as travel expenses. I didn't care about the method, as long as the agency got paid. But it was important to *him* to be able to say he got Jane Trahey for less.

Q. *Didn't you feel that taking such a stand involved risk?*

A. "No" isn't the worst thing that someone can say to you. Neither is taking a risk the worst thing you can do. And there's nothing

wrong in being fired, either. Firing makes you take stock. My only recommendation is to direct your own move before it's done to you. If changes are happening in the office, be alert to them. And if you have to, go through the exit gate before someone points to it.

Q. *Winston Churchill said that only when you risk more than you can afford to lose do you know what the game is all about. Playing by such rules does provide a sense of freedom and exhilaration, but doesn't it also dissolve the buffers that people, especially women, tend to hide behind?*

A. In part, that's because women in business don't have the life support system men have. Female executives are fragmented all over a company, and their chances at clustering are slim. When a man loses his job, he asks why and immediately springs into action—setting up lunches, interviews, contacting buddies. A woman gets fired and never asks why. She goes home to cry, turn off her answering service and hide.

Q. *Many of the women you interviewed equated power with control. Only Jacqueline Babbin, executive producer at Universal Studios, connected it strongly with money. Why, even at this level, do women not associate financial savvy with clout?*

A. First, there is no mystery about money. Only mystique. The reconditioning starts early. Every effort should be made to encourage girls to learn math and science. When they come home with first-year high school schedules, a parent should see red at the recent history and music courses listed. They should take the kid back to the school authorities and tell them that these are not the only subjects they want their daughter to learn. They should say: "I want her to have four years of science and four years of math. I'll take her myself to the art museum and symphony on Saturday afternoons." The payoff to this kind of parental response will come at college entrance time. Math and science courses will give a young woman a 40 percent better chance to pursue the kind of career she may want. If she has none of the basics, her options are already cut.

Q. *If women ever hope to play the power game well, don't you feel that attitude-overhaul has to start even earlier than high school?*

A. Absolutely. We have to start with the lower grades. By high school, children's sights and minds are already set.

Q. *Children today are a media generation. Does this reinforce for them society's traditional view of women as second-class citizens?*

A. Sure. Kids are bombarded with television's image of women, which is terrible. Plus porno, which is cruel.

Q. *Haven't women had any role models or champions in the media?*

A. We had one in Mary Tyler Moore, but she's gone. And you can't recondition attitudes successfully with satire. Just look at *Mary Hartman, Mary Hartman.* People take it seriously—they don't get the message at all. I think our image is worse now than it was 20 years ago.

Q. *How do you think men will react to your book?*

A. One of the saddest comments already came from my lawyer, a longstanding personal friend. After reading it he said, "You really don't like us, do you?" Liking or disliking men had nothing to do with it. What I don't like is the society that supports a system of exclusion. That's what I'm against.

Formulas for power might be seasoned differently. But when you look closely, as Trahey does, you'll find some basic cell structures without which power can't happen. She sums it up this way: "It's a combination of timing, luck and hard work. Plus one ingredient women often overlook. *Wanting* power."

Trahey's Laws on How to Get Power

Job Hunting

Don't fool with the folks at the bottom. Head for the top guy. You can't go wrong and can't do better.

Interviewing

Sell your uniqueness. Write a "Position Paper" on yourself, as you would on a product. That tends to knock out competition.

If asked how you would make changes in the company, keep your plans to yourself, at least at the interview.

Ideas

Ideas are power because ideas are money.

Never dump a good idea on the conference table. It will belong to the conference.

Don't dish at meetings. Listen at meetings.

Chivas & Chivalry

With boozing and sex, men usually land on their feet. Women on their seat. You don't have to give a kilo of your flesh for any job unless you want to. If you do, remember that the market price goes down fast, but not as fast as your reputation.

Claim Staking

Race, don't walk, when you see a good job opening you can fill. Wanting power is half the secret of getting it.

Your Office

You are where you sit. Don't let anyone tell you it isn't important to have a power office. And the best investment you can make is to improve the looks of your terrain.

Image

It's power. Most people are not born to the purple. They mix their own colors.

Build it with clothes, PR, volunteer work, public speaking and contacts.

Clothes

Forget the fantasy wardrobe. No woman executive should ever look like her secretary.

Firing & Being Fired

Go through the exit gate before someone points to it. Search for what you did wrong. Ask everything. Maybe it's not your fault. Maybe it is. But at least make your exit a growing experience as well as a going experience.

Don't equate being fired with failure.

Activate your contact network.

Growth

Learning how to learn is essential. Knowing what to learn and doing it early can mean the difference between moving up or getting on.

Money

There's no mystery to money. Only mystique. It's power. Learn math, finance.

JACQUELINE C. WARSAW *took the entrepreneurial route after she decided that staying a corporate ad director meant staying a paper tiger. As president of her own advertising company, Warsaw Associates, she appreciates the risks and rewards of orchestrating her own career.*

THE LEADERSHIP CRISIS: NEW ROOM AT THE TOP FOR WOMEN

by Michael Maccoby

Leadership has two interrelated aspects. One concerns the functions of leadership. The second involves presenting an image, a model of an ideal character that others want to emulate if not imitate. This image draws out and integrates shared character traits of the leader's constituency (the social character). Through this image, the ideal leader brings out the best in people. When an individual in a position of leadership has the wrong traits or presents a discordant image, he or she will not be able to inspire people to copy that image.

Today, even when a woman is fully qualified to exercise the functions of leadership, she may have problems with the image. This is not only because she is a woman, but because the image of both the leader and the ideal character is itself in question—a problem for men *and* women.

For the past 20 years, the dominant model for leadership in America has been the gamesman, an image that appealed to Americans who had become more concerned with individual rights and abilities and less respectful of traditional authority than in earlier years. The coming of the gamesman coincided with the election of John F. Kennedy as President. His New Frontier energized the electronics and aerospace industries, which were discovering they needed gamesmen to lead teams of specialists in research and development.

With a boyish, informal style, the gamesman controls subordinates by persuasion, enthusiasm and seduction rather than by heavy and humiliating commands. Fair, but detached, the gamesman has welcomed the era of rights and equal opportunity as both fair and efficient for moving the "best" to the top. He is not a hardhearted power seeker, but he can be ungenerous and uncompassionate, feeling that emotion may cloud strategy and weaken the will to win.

The positive traits of the gamesman fit America in a time of unlimited economic growth and hunger for change. The negative traits of manipulation, seduction, super-careerism and the perpetual adolescent need for adventure always were problems, causing distrust and unnecessary crisis. They have become serious liabilities in a period of limited resources and intense international competition, when the team no longer can be controlled by promises of more. Without carrots to offer, it is hard to seduce. Many people are turned off by the gamesman's careerism and lack of compassion for those who are not winners in the meritocratic game.

The problem of leadership in both business and government today is how to bring out the best in people who are becoming increasingly self-affirmative and skeptical and more concerned with enjoying life than any other generation in American history. The problem will not be solved by regression to the Godfather as leader. The "new breed" of employee, as Daniel Yankolovich, president of Yankolovich, Skelly and White, a national polling company, calls it, seeks security in contractual rights, not paternalistic protection, and responds to tough treatment with protests or sabotage.

When the image of the protecting father is gone and people don't trust the ambitious brother, what kind of leader can inspire trust and create a spirit of interdependence? There is yet no generally accepted model, but the confusion about leadership and the absence of clear models sanction experimentation. The stage is set for a new leader to bring out the best in the changing American character. Ironically, at a time when women have the opportunity to design new images of leadership, the most popular book for women who aspire to leadership, *The Managerial Woman*, urges women to be gamesmen.

By so doing, the authors, Margaret Hennig and Anne Jardim, also contradict the most interesting part of their book, based on Hennig's comparison of 25 highly successful women with another group of women whose managerial careers ended at the middle level. Growing up, both groups differed from most girls of their generation in the 1930s. Close to their fathers, they felt free to experiment with male activities and were rewarded for it. Women in both groups entered the corporate world as pioneers and struggled against male discrimination. But the most successful women reassessed themselves in mid-career, usually in their 30s, when they had become successful middle managers.

"For the first time a preoccupation with femininity emerged." These women took "a moratorium on career striving." About half married, and their husbands were older men who were widowed or divorced with children. When they returned to the executive race, they approached management with greater openness to the views and ideas of subordinates. By concerning themselves with their emotional development, they became more complete, more confident and more effective. One woman said, "I began to realize that my goal at work had been to be something like a well-oiled machine running at top speed—nothing more human than that. Now that I had accepted myself I began to enjoy people as well as tasks." By contrast, the women who remained at the middle levels "maintained and strengthened further a behavioral style which sought to deny that they were women. . . . They saw themselves as cold and domineering people who had been forced by painful experience to become what they were."

It is well known that relatively few women have risen to the top in big business or government. Three years ago, the *Wall Street Journal* reported that only 4 percent of top management, vice-presidents and above, were women. Those who do reach the top appear to experience significant strains on their marriages, if any. Besides the data from *The Managerial Woman*, the *Wall Street Journal* (February 20, 1979) reported a survey of 13 women chief executives of relatively large firms: 23 percent had never married and another 31 percent had been divorced. In polls of males, almost all were married, and few had been divorced.

The families of the male top executives we interviewed for *The Gamesman* usually served as support teams for their careers, even though the wives were, on the average, extremely intelligent and well educated. Some did volunteer work; others had jobs that were secondary to their husbands' careers. Unlike most of the women we interviewed, men were further supported by "old boy" networks, which not only help careers but humanize the high-pressure contest at upper levels. Women who are leaders in the gamesman image may find the experience more painful than men because of this lack of support.

In *The Gamesman,* I reported a repetitive dream told by a woman near the top of a large multinational company. In her interview, she continually emphasized that her job was an interesting challenge for her, one that gave her a great deal of independence and self-development. She said, "I really enjoy my work. I moan and groan, but I've had some fantastic opportunities and challenges."

What were the challenges she enjoyed so much? The major challenge she mentioned was the competition with other executives for top positions in the corporation. What she claimed to value—challenge and independence—appeared to be anxious struggle and lonely careerism. As she said, "The main thing is the ability to survive in this environment." Although she talked about being open and trusting and emphasized the importance of cooperation to get the work done, she described a suspicious and unfriendly environment.

Despite her conscious satisfaction with work, on the symptom list, she checked troublesome anxiety and severe headaches. She also said she lacked hope, did not know what she wanted and that it was too often necessary to give in to circumstances.

The woman's recurring dream seems to express her unconscious experience of work. She dreams that she is buried alive and all she she wants is a telephone in her casket. It sounds like a joke, but such a dream is all too serious: It symbolizes the experience of emotional deadness in her work and her acceptance of her fate (as long as she can continue to stay in the executive competition). Rather than rebelling at being buried alive and fighting to become free, she asks only for a telephone so that she can communicate with others, presumably in their own casket-offices.

This dream expresses feelings about competitive work common to men as well as to women managers. Anxiety about being judged, guilt about self-betrayal for the sake of career and depression are the common symptoms reported by successful managers. Given the added pressures on women managers, some have taken the lead in attempting to balance competition and pressure to produce with responsiveness and a concern for people. These are the kinds of traits needed to lead today's skeptical employees in this period of limited resources and incentives.

Women managers have been in the forefront of experiments to improve work based on a better understanding of human needs, particularly in the federal government. This effort began with flextime but has developed into programs in the Commerce and State departments and at ACTION, the agency that directs VISTA and the Peace Corps.

What could this new model of leadership be like? Elsa Porter, assistant secretary of commerce for administration, is a good example:

1. She cares about people and resents the wastage of human life in work that mechanizes people. This conviction gives her a sense of security (to balance the insecurity of the job) and a basis for pragmatic experimentation. It also supports pati-

ence, the ability to bounce back from failure and satisfaction from step-by-step gains, in contrast to the gamesman's need for perpetual drama.

Porter is willing to stand back and let others take control, but she is able to assert authority strongly on issues of principle.

2. Porter is a student of the organization she leads, able to evaluate both its mission and the way performance is controlled and measured. In government, where the product often is service, measurements of productivity may distort the mission—for example, auditors either can collect instances of fraud or mistakes (easily measured) or help people avoid trouble (hard to measure). If policy is to promote minority businesses with little experience in constructing financial systems, the most easily measured productivity may contribute less well to the achievement of the mission. If the organization of government work and the way employees are evaluated does not reinforce qualities of cooperation as well as competence, service and mission will suffer.

Bureaucratic systems in business and government that are built on assumptions of control and competition are inadequate to the requirements of our time. To change them, we need new kinds of leaders who can involve employees in the study and transformation of work according to the emerging ideals of our society. Although this requires technical understanding, the task is not merely technical but, in the fullest sense of the term, political. The new image of the leader depends on the success of such people as Elsa Porter, who are developing the new functions of leadership.

MICHAEL MACCOBY, *director of the Project on Technology, Work and Character of the Kennedy School of Government at Harvard University, is the author of* The Gamesman *and* The Leader.

THE NEW LOOK OF CORPORATE BOARDS: WOMEN DIRECTORS

Women Directors are Making Their Presence and Influence Felt as They Join Corporate Boards in Unprecedented Numbers

by Ann Curran

"Being a corporate board member is an increasingly serious commitment that involves time, thought and responsibility."
—Marina v.N. Whitman

There are some new faces in the board rooms of corporate America. They belong to talented, successful people; people who, in spite of reaching the top levels of their professions, were—until recently—rarely asked to serve as directors on the boards of corporations: women.

The women's movement, affirmative-action legislation, government pressure on corporations to increase the number of outside directors (directors who are not employees of the company), the fact that 12 million women have entered the work force in the last decade alone and the entrance of women into management and executive ranks—all these factors have contributed to creating a climate receptive to the woman director. Today, 427 companies of the top 1,300 listed by *Fortune* magazine have at least one woman serving on their boards—boards that can influence the nation's economy as they oversee management and set corporate policy.

Tokenism Controversy

"When I first started sitting on corporate boards, everyone told me, 'You're only a token,' " said Jewel S. Lafontant, a prominent Chicago attorney who took on her first corporate directorship in 1971 and now serves on six boards. "That may have been the intent, but once we get our foot in the door, it's up to women directors to turn tokenism into something real."

With only 300 women serving as corporate directors—compared with an estimated 15,000 men—the issue of tokenism still is a live one. There are those inside and outside the business community who still see women directors as mere window dressing—a gesture made to soothe the corporate conscience. Others disagree, saying that women directors are being selected for board service on the same basis as men are—their professional credentials.

Eleanor Elliott, director of Celanese and the CIT Financial Corporation, deals with the tokenism issue in a straightforward, no-nonsense manner. "Let's face it," she said, "at this stage, a woman on a corporate board *is* a token. In 99 percent of the cases, she wouldn't be there if she were not a woman. But in a sense, can't most outside directors be called tokens? Board composition is pretty stereotyped these days, as the business journals are fond of pointing out. You have a lawyer or investment banker or two, a couple of corporation presidents, perhaps a retired government dignitary and your university president, your black leader or your woman—or all three."

The tokenism controversy has died down considerably in the past few years not only because more women have joined corporate boards, but also because of the high caliber of women being selected for board service. Women like Hanna Holborn Gray, president

of the University of Chicago; Carla Anderson Hills, former secretary of the Department of Housing and Urban Development; former Congresswoman Martha Griffiths; and Marina v.N. Whitman, vice-president and chief economist of the General Motors Corporation have impeccable professional credentials.

How They Got There

"The first group of women who went on corporate boards, and that includes me, were largely not from the corporate world," explained Whitman, who has held several senior government advisory posts, including serving on the President's Council of Economic Advisers during the Nixon administration, "What you got was women from education or from nonprofit institutions who had significant government service, or whose reputations and experience had been obtained—or at least polished—in high-level government jobs."

The correlation between government experience and corporate directorships goes both ways, as demonstrated by President Carter's selection of Patricia Roberts Harris, HEW Secretary, and former Secretary of Commerce Juanita Kreps—both experienced corporate directors—for his cabinet.

Whitman serves on the boards of the Manufacturers Hanover Trust Company and Procter & Gamble. She believes that there are so few corporate women on boards because not many women have reached the senior management levels that would qualify them for corporate-board service. "I don't mean to say that there are no women from the corporate world on boards—there are. But that's not where the majority of them came from initially. I suspect the balance may change a bit as women come up through the corporate ranks. Eventually there will be more women at those management levels in a corporation that make joining boards appropriate."

Constituencies

Women directors agree that they do not sit on corporate boards to represent women—they are there to represent the stockholders.

"I never have the feeling that I'm sitting at the board table to present the woman's viewpoint," said Barbara Scott Preiskel, senior vice-president and general attorney of the Motion Picture Association of America, Inc., "because I really don't know what the woman's viewpoint is." Preiskel serves on three boards—Amstar, Textron and Jewel Companies, Inc., a diversified retailer that includes four grocery companies. "I do think I'm more sensitive than other directors on certain issues," Preiskel continued. "For example, whenever we have an affirmative-action report, I think I listen more carefully than some of the other people on the board—and probably I'm asked more questions about it. On other problems—on the Jewel board, for instance, when we're talking about changing buying patterns—I'm more sensitive to the fact that there are a lot more women working today than ever before and that, therefore, their buying patterns at the supermarket are somewhat different than they have been."

Officially, the woman director may not be representing women, but frequently she can find herself advocating women's issues—with frustrating results. Eleanor Elliott told this story as an example: "After a meeting one day," she said, "I brought up the subject of maternity benefits to a couple of fellow directors. My point was that in the future, with so many more young women joining corporations and planning to work during childbearing years, management probably would have to improve maternity policies. One guy said, 'Ridiculous. I'd never vote for that. Childbirth isn't a disease, an incapacity. And it's voluntary. We don't have to treat it like an illness.' I answered, 'I'm not saying that we should treat it like an illness. I'm saying that we are going to be asked to improve maternity benefits by the young

women in college now and those who come after them—the very women we want to hire.' My friend grumbled, 'Well, not today, anyway.' Later I said to him, 'You know, most companies pick up the tab for tennis elbow, for heaven's sake. Talk of things voluntary, some companies pay for vasectomies.' He replied, 'What's a vasectomy?' "

Responsibilities and Liabilities

The overriding responsibility of all corporate directors—men and women alike— is to the investors.

"We are elected by the stockholders, essentially as stewards of their investment in the corporation. We stand in lieu of them; we represent their interests," said scientist and educator Cecily Selby, former national executive director of the Girl Scouts, USA, who serves on the boards of RCA, NBC, Avon Products, Inc., and Loehmann's, Inc.

"Basically we're there to monitor the manner in which the corporation handles the stockholders' funds. It's our job to choose a CEO [chief executive officer] to manage the assets in a way that's best for everybody. We have no direct responsibility for the operations of the company except through the CEO. So, first last and always, the hiring and firing of the CEO is our main responsibility; second, we're there to aid, abet and counsel the CEO, again in the best interests of the stockholders."

Corporate boards once were considered "rubber stamps" for management policies. This seems to have changed. In a 1978 Touche Ross & Company survey on the changing nature of the corporate board, directors who had served for five years or less believed that greater involvement by directors in company management and policy making has been the most significant change of the past decade. Long-established directors—those who have served for more than five years—cited greater director liability, account ability and responsibility as the major changes.

Corporate directors take their responsibility to the stockholders seriously—they have to. If they don't, they may find themselves facing a lawsuit. Lawyer Lafontant, underscoring the extent of a director's liability, said, "It used to be that you would be criticized for making a wrong decision. Now, if you are found negligent you can be fined. If you are found grossly negligent, you could go to jail. I think it makes people more aware of what they are doing when they take on a board membership."

Marina V.N. Whitman agrees. "Being a corporate board member is an increasingly serious commitment that involves time, thought and responsibility. You don't have to get served in suits very often to have it brought home to you—if you haven't realized it already—that you'd better be paying attention and taking your board responsibility seriously."

In response to the increasing responsibilities of boards, most corporations provide their directors with liability insurance to protect them in case of legal action.

Inside, Outside

The average size of a corporate board is 13—nine outside directors (those who are not employees of the company) and four inside directors (usually the CEO and members of the senior management staff), according to a 1979 survey by Korn/Ferry International, which describes itself as the world's largest executive-search firm. At this point, most women corporate-board members are *outside* directors. There are a few—a very few—who are inside directors, women who have worked their way up the corporate ladder to the highest rungs. Juliette Moran, executive vice-president in charge of communications services at the GAF Corporation, is one of them. Moran started as a chemist with GAF in 1943. She was elected to the board of directors in 1974.

Moran said she sees little difference between inside and outside directors. "There is not the kind of cleavage between inside and outside directors that people seem to think there is," she said. "They ought to be the same—totally reliable people who are interested in the corporation and its shareholders." But she did admit that "there's no way someone who has spent 36 years with a company doesn't know a great deal more about it than it is reasonable to expect an outside director to know. Each director brings different strengths and weaknesses to the board—my years of experience with the company is one of my strengths."

Outside Money

There *is* one substantial difference between outside and inside directors: compensation. Most inside directors receive no pay for their board activities beyond their company salaries. Outside directors, on the other hand, receive substantial payment for their board work. Of the 542 companies surveyed by Korn/Ferry in 1979, 72 percent paid outside board members on an annual *and* a per-meeting basis. The average board meets eight times a year, the total average yearly fee to these board members was $11,250. Among the companies that paid an annual fee only, the average fee was $11,600. Among companies paying a per-meeting fee only, the average was $572 per meeting.

Each outside director receives additional payment for service on board committees such as the audit committee, the nominating committee, and the compensation committee.

No Time

The Korn/Ferry survey found that an average outside director spends approximately 89 hours a year on board matters, usually while carrying on a high-gear, demanding career. Ironically, the women already serving as directors—whose time commitments already are stretched to the limit—are the ones who are asked repeatedly to join other boards. Like many of her colleagues, Preiskel has had to turn down directorships because she had no time. "After joining my third board, I decided that I couldn't handle any more as long as I had a demanding full-time job," she said. Women directors often feel that they must spend more time on board matters than men directors do. "Most women directors think they have to be more informed," said Preiskel. "I guess it's the old syndrome—you don't want to fail, so you work harder. I feel I have to read everything that comes through, so that I know what's being talked about—some men directors may not feel strongly about it."

Preiskel is quick to point out that the tax on her time is easily offset by the advantages of board service: "I once said to the head of one corporation that I should pay him because it's been a terrific learning experience. Also, it opens other doors—like everything else, once you get in the door, other doors seem easier to open."

Corporate View

Corporations are quickly discovering the woman director. In 1978:

- Each of the top ten industrial companies had a woman director.
- Of the top 100 industrial companies, 48 had a woman director.

These were some of the findings of a study of major corporations with and without women directors conducted by financial analyst Marilyn Brown for the Financial Women's Association of New York (FWA), an organization of over 350 women who work in finance and related fields in the New York City area.

One of the FWA's study's more fascinating—though questionable—discoveries surfaced when the sales and earnings records of companies with women directors were compared to those of companies without women directors. (The figures used were from the five-year period 1972-1977.) Brown reported: "We found that, on average, Fortune 1,000 industrial companies with women directors showed financial results superior to those companies without women directors."

The financial advantages to a company of a woman director—if there are any—may not be clear, but CEOs who have worked with women directors see other advantages. Coy Eklund, president of Equitable Life Assurance Society of the US, which has four women sitting on its 30-member board, said, "I think the main benefit we get is simply the unique quality that each of them brings to our board by virtue of her own professional experience. But in addition, I must concede, we get the public-image value of having four distinguished women on our otherwise all-male board." The four women now serving on Equitable's board are Jewel Lafontant, Nancy Hanks, Eleanor Sheldon and Marion Stephenson.

Jewel Companies, Inc., has two women serving on its board—Barbara Preiskel and Helen LeBaron Hilton. To Donald S. Perkins, chairman of the board and CEO of Jewel Companies, Inc., having women on his board is just plain common sense. "In the first place, most of our customers are women, so I don't want to miss an opportunity of having some bright women looking at all the challenges of the business. There are other advantages, too: It is a way of saying that we're serious about wanting women in management."

Neither Eklund nor Perkins subscribes to the theory—mainly advanced by companies with all-male boards—that corporations would have more women directors if only they could find them. "That's sheer nonsense," said Eklund. "There are plenty of qualified women available across the nation."

Perkins agreed: "I think anyone who looks can find. The number of women who can contribute is much greater than the number who serve."

Eklund believes—and the numbers are beginning to show—that women's participation on corporate boards is a growing trend. "Many boards are only now looking for their first woman director," he said. "I predict that as they add one woman, they will rather promptly add two or three. The day is sure to come—although it's still far off—when boards will be composed rather evenly of male and female directors."

FALLEN IDOLS
by Jane Adams

Was 1980 a bad year for women executives? It was a year in which three women came as close to real corporate power as women ever have, the kind of power symbolized in America by carpeted jets and mahogany board rooms, thick management contracts and thin lines of newsprint in the *Wall Street Journal.* It is 1981 and, as I write this, only one is left at the top. Sherry Lansing is still president of 20th Century-Fox, but Jane Cahill Pfeiffer is gone from NBC and Mary Cunningham has left Bendix; neither, at this writing, has taken a new job. Sherry Lansing is a model of female corporate success, but it is on her two female peers that I want to dwell. Because it may be that in their experiences, buried under the barrage of publicity, hidden behind the carefully worded press releases, camouflaged by the "psychohistories" of journalists, some truth might emerge, not just about the women on top but about the men who have been there all along.

Jane Pfeiffer did not come, or go, quietly. "One of the messiest firings in recent corporate history," said one *Wall Street Journal* article. "Firing Method Makes Some Wince," headlined another. Nor did Mary Cunningham leave quietly; her departure from the post of vice-president of Bendix was accompanied by even more ink than Jane Pfeiffer's, including a much ballyhooed series of articles in which Cunningham bared her psychological and corporate soul, to the delight of millions of newspaper readers and the dismay of a few who felt that perhaps she had been too candid, too open.

Jane Pfeiffer took the NBC job from the man she had persuaded to be the company's head of programming when she was a consultant to NBC's parent corporation, RCA. She was the president, he was the chief executive officer, but in fact the power was all his. Fred Silverman was not Pfeiffer's mentor. He hired her, say high network executives, to divert attention from the risky game he was playing to bring NBC out of the ratings cellar. It was "a no-win job," according to an NBC consultant, and if Pfeiffer made an error in judgment, it may well have been in accepting it in the first place.

Moving from the squeaky clean corporate environment of IBM, Pfeiffer devoted herself at NBC to rooting out scandal—a thankless task in an industry where it is allegedly commonplace and often taken for granted. She did so with with a high-minded, morally superior attitude that offended and threatened not her superiors, but her peers and subordinates. "She was chewed to death by gnats, and brought down by them because she had no corporate support when Fred got rid of her," is the way one executive at a rival network described the situation. The complaints of those on whose toes Pfeiffer trod reached the ears of corporate higher-ups, and provided Silverman with an excuse to fire her, a diversion he still needed two months before his new programming brought NBC back to the top, at least for a while. It wasn't hard to fire Pfeiffer; her tactless handlings of peers and subordinates already had earned her their enmity, as reflected in the sobriquets they gave her, of which "Attila the Nun" and "Mother Superior" were the kindest.

Pfeiffer was "had" by a man more skillful in manipulation and corporate gamesmanship than she was. But once she realized just how had she'd been, she left NBC with her head held high, her honor and integrity unsmirched, and in the end, with some admiration even from her enemies for the cool, tough way she played hardball with the big boys. I doubt she will pound the pavement long; when she says she's considering offers, it is certainly the truth.

Cunningham's case is different. She was not as powerful as Pfeiffer, though she enjoyed greater support from her CEO, who, unlike Silverman to Pfeiffer, was also her mentor. Cunningham's power was, however, derivative. It was given by Agee and, in a sense, taken by him when he raised the issue of their personal relationship in a speech last October to Bendix employees.

The other difference between Cunningham and Pfeiffer was the implication that Cunningham's rise to second in command at Bendix was influence by her youth, attractiveness and relationship with Agee. No such implications attended Jane Pfeiffer's departure from NBC—not just because she was a 47-year-old, respectably married lady, but because she got the NBC job after having proven herself throughout a superlative 25-year career. And because her personal conduct was above reproach as well.

That is neither an afterthought, nor a judgment, on the relationship between Cunningham and Agee. Executive women, like Caesar's wife, must in fact be above reproach. No matter that their male peers and bosses may not be; they must be. It's not fair, but that is the way it is in 1981 and I daresay, in 2000—at least until women equal men in the board rooms of America.

Women in high positions can't sleep up, said one Fortune 500 CEO, but they can sleep down. That is because their peers see even the mere suggestion of such activity as an unfair advantage in the corporate game. Most women on top are astute enough to know this, and I think Mary Cunningham was too. As columnist Ellen Goodman said in her provocative column on the subject, "If women can sleep their way to the top, how come they aren't there?" If Mary Cunningham had had an intimate friendship with a junior vice-president, or even with the guy in the mailroom, her career at Bendix still might be rolling along in high gear. And whether or not she had one with Agee is irrelevant. Their constant personal appearances together in nonoffice situations—despite the fact that they were legitimate appearances for a trusted adviser to make with a corporate chieftain—might have been problems in themselves. Combined with Cunningham's looks, brains and unsettled marital situation and Agee's recent divorce, they made such gossip inevitable.

Pfeiffer was fired like a man; the issue of her sex was totally irrelevant to the circumstances of her departure. Cunningham resigned like a woman; she left under a cloud of doubt about whether her personal closeness to Agee had influenced her rapid rise at Bendix. And in the eyes of many of her female peers in the business world, in so doing she bore out all the stereotypes about women buckling under pressure.

She felt she had no choice, that her effectiveness at Bendix was compromised by the publicity attendant on Agee's public discussion of their friendship. I think she did have a choice; I think she had the power to dissuade Agee from going public at all. I wish she had used it.

In agreeing to cooperate with Agee's own candor, she allowed to be brought to the boiling point an issue which had been simmering for months at Bendix headquarters. Southfield, Michigan is hardly a bastion of liberal behavior or attitudes. Their going public was the most powerful ammunition she could have handed to her enemies, to those same subordinates and peers ignored by Jane Pfeiffer at NBC and discounted by Cunningham at Bendix. She threatened them, she angered them and she allowed them to destroy her. Only in that respect was her situation analogous to Pfeiffer's; they both operated at the top without a safety net, a support group of people who believed, trusted, liked and admired them.

Cunningham asked for, and was denied, a temporary leave of absence from her duties at Bendix. The Bendix board which gave her a full vote of confidence, denied this. Some say a deal was made, that they gave her that vote to whitewash the issue. But I don't think so. I think that vote was in fact a test to see if she could take the pressure. If she had been able to, her own continued excellent performance would have been the proof of her fitness for her high-level job. And if she and Agee did have a romantic friendship, they might have continued to work together until such time as both were able to make some decisions about their individual and joint futures. She might have used that time to locate another position, from which she, not he, could then announce that relationship. And if they were no closer than mentor and associate, their continued professionalism ultimately might have made that clear.

Published interviews with Cunningham make it appear that she saw herself as a test case. Perhaps now she has learned the problem of being one—you set the precedent, and while others capitalize on it, you find another job. If her resignation was symbolic, it was an empty gesture, for it diverted attention from the real problem, which is recognizing that men must take equal if not greater responsibility for situations such as the one at Bendix, instead of ghettoizing it as "a woman's problem." For the problem was as much Agee's as Cunningham's; it is the problem of every corporate manager who must deal with the new reality of female peers—of women who are promoted because they are able and talented, of women threatening men who may not be as able and talented. For, while there have been substantive changes in women's progress to the top, there have been few, if any, in the men already there.

Agee's motives appear unquestionable; he wanted to defend his judgment of Cun-

ningham and did so by commenting publicly on questions that had been raised privately. That she cooperated with him in allowing him to do so is the clearest indication that idealism or ambition clouded her own judgment. Cunningham was schooled in a time and place—Wellesley, Harvard and the late seventies—that was seemingly free of overt discrimination against capable women. Nothing had prepared her for the hard reality, which is that behavior may have changed, but attitudes have not. Because she had never suffered sex discrimination, she believed it did not exist. In her efforts to get and stay ahead, she ignored the issues that affect and move the people behind and below her. She believed that her performance put her above the innuendo, the malice and the envy. Some sensitivity to others might have shown her that she was not immune.

What of the men who refuse to cope with today's corporate reality—women in the board room? They live in a world that churns out Mary Cunninghams every June, at Harvard and Wharton and Stanford and dozens of other graduate business schools. Yet they still refuse to do what they must; what one successful woman executive characterized as "taking responsibility for their own involuntary erections." And so they blame the women who engender those feelings by putting women in what many still regard as their rightful role—sexual objects.

There are more differences between Cunningham and Pfeiffer, differences in experience, wisdom, clout and style. Pfeiffer left under no cloud; she made it clear to her superiors and subordinates, to the media and other corporate executives, the exact circumstances of her firing. Cunningham, despite reports of numerous job offers, left under a very dense cloud indeed. She did not use the vote of confidence given her by the board; she left the board members looking like idiots.

Agee had little to lose by going public. He did, in fact, stimulate a public dialogue. Cunningham, though, will always be "that lady from Bendix." And that will doubtless influence what height of corporate power is accessible to the person James Heskett, former chairman of Harvard's MBA program, once called "the one woman in America who can become CEO of a Fortune 500 company any time in the next ten years, on her ability."

Were there ways Mary Cunningham might have deflected the potentially explosive impact of her relationship with Agee? Perhaps. Perhaps if she'd worn dowdy clothes, pulled her blonde hair back in a bun, gone to lengths many women go to "pass as a man," she might have. Perhaps if she'd never appeared with him at tennis matches or political conventions, if she'd cultivated relationships with other mentors and peers, if she'd controlled her own hubris, or her in-

stinct for martyrdom. Those seemed like sellouts to her.

But like it or not, that's still the way the game is played. Women who choose to play by their own rules are advised to have both ammunition to fight with and a taste for the fray.

Mary Cunningham may have blazed a trail, but whether she actually accomplished anything—for women, for corporate values or for herself—is much less clear. There still are not enough women at or near the top for Cunningham or Pfeiffer to be more than isolated cases. In 1980, they brought the changing corporate world to public attention. If in 1981 some attention is given to how men as well as women can attempt to deal with those changes, then 1980 was a very good year for all of us.

WORKAHOLICS
by Dawn Raffel

Marilyn M. Machlowitz became interested in workaholics when her father accused her of being one, while she was an undergraduate at Princeton University. She conducted the first extensive study on the subject for her master's and doctoral theses at Yale University. After hundreds of interviews and several years of research, perhaps her most important discovery is that workaholics often are quite happy. "They are doing exactly what they love—work—and they can't seem to get enough of it.

"The word workaholic has such negative connotations," Machlowitz said. "It seems somehow un-American, despite the Protestant work ethic, to live for your job. Unless you're an artist, you're supposed to live for the weekends, for vacations, for fun." But workaholics prefer labor to leisure—they enjoy their work. They find inactivity intolerable and pressure preferable. They regard

rest, relaxation and especially retirement with disdain and dread. Most probably would agree with the late Margaret Mead, who said, "I may die, but I'll never retire."

While most people wouldn't view a lunch hour typically spent eating with the left hand, while dashing off six memos with the right and cradling the phone on the neck as fun, a workaholic thrives on the challenge. She is the one who will use any means to get to her office during a blackout, devise a new sales strategy at her sister's wedding and avoid vacations like the plague.

"Workaholics make the most of their time," said Machlowitz. "Saving time becomes a goal in itself as they put to good use the spare seconds others seem not to notice." They use lists, appointment books and gadgets (dictating devices, lighted pens for darkened rooms, car telephones) that enable them to work wherever they are—to master every minute. They like to do two things at once, whether it's learning a foreign language by cassette while commuting to work, or talking on the phone and writing a memo while at the hairdresser.

With so much going for them—energy, drive, efficiency, enjoyment and enthusiasm—why have workaholics earned such a bad reputation? Machlowitz explained: "The prejudiced beliefs about workaholics have less to do with the people themselves than with other factors. First, there is the word itself—a takeoff on the word alcoholic. Second, the little research literature largely is based on case reports from psychologists and psychiatrists who treat troubled individuals who happen to be workaholics. Third, we hear about them from their fellow workers—envious and anxious people concerned with competing with them at work. Fourth, the anger of those at home who have to cope with an compensate for what the workaholic won't do. The workaholics themselves are not unsatisfied with their sex lives or their social lives. Other people project that unhappiness onto them, because *they'd* be miserable following a workaholic's schedule.

"Part of what motivates workaholics is insecurity," Machlowitz admitted. "They may feel that they have to work double time to succeed or, as one workaholic put it, to make up for lack of talent with sweat. But they find their work fulfilling and gratifying. Their reward isn't money or success; it's the thrill of the chase."

Although the women's movement has encouraged more women to strive for success, often in traditionally male fields where they may feel somewhat insecure, Machlowitz feels that workaholism is based on deeper factors: It is ingrained in your personality from childhood. If you're a workaholic, there's a good chance that one of your parents was one, too, and you probably took your lemonade stand more seriously than any other 6-year-old on the block.

A workaholic shouldn't be confused with that byproduct of the feminist movement known as a superwoman. "Superwomen are those who run conglomerates by day and Cuisinarts by night. Women workaholics are more apt to let the domestic side of things slide a bit," Machlowitz said. "The women I interviewed wouldn't hesitate to spend the money to hire cleaning help or to eat out. One woman had a set list of groceries delivered every week in order to save her precious time.

"These women are not consumed with petty details on the job or frustrated in their efforts to reach the top. Most are successful and can delegate responsibility, even to the point of hiring *two* secretaries if one can't keep up with all the work.

"The biggest problem for workaholics," Machlowitz stated, "is the problems other people have relating to them."

At home, the workaholic's family may feel that there's no time for them in her 25-hour-a-day schedule. In the past, when practically the only outlet for married women with workaholic natures was housekeeping, the spouse caught up in a career was the husband. The wife then dutifully bought the workaholic husband's shirts, ran the home and raised the kids single-handedly. There always have been women workaholics; it is simply more apparent now that more women are in the work force.

Nowadays, if the wife is the workaholic in the family, quite often she'll decide not to have children, Machlowitz said. For one thing, even with husbands beginning to share in the housework, it's the wife who bears most of the domestic responsibility. "Furthermore workaholics are perfectionists, and a woman may realize that it's easier to have a perfect career than to raise a perfect child," she said.

"There's no need to feel sorry for the person a workaholic is married to. Spouses usually know what's in store. In many cases, they met at work—where else would you expect a workaholic to meet someone?" Machlowitz said. "If not, the mate usually finds out soon enough. One woman told me she should have known what she was in for when her husband called his office the second day of their honeymoon."

Of course, there *are* problems. Often, the spouse expects the workaholic to slow down after getting established in a job or settling down in the marriage and is surprised and upset when this doesn't happen. For example, one workaholic Machlowitz interviewed would take work-related calls until 1:00 AM when she was single. After marriage, she wouldn't take any calls after 11:00 PM. That's not much of a change!

Spouses sometimes feel pressured to keep up with the workaholic, a competition that can be destructive. Independent interests and pursuits are absolutely necessary for anyone who wants to live with a workaholic—and like it.

Workaholics sometimes are accused of using their jobs as an escape from any kind of intimacy—with a husband, children, lovers or friends. "While a workaholic's job usually comes first it's the quality of the time she spends with her husband, her lover or her children that's the telling factor," said Machlowitz. "Whether a workaholic can have a good relationship with a man depends on whether she can keep him from feeling that whenever she's with him, her mind is elsewhere, that she'd rather be at the office." In such cases, it's not the workaholic, but the lover or spouse who suffers.

What about health and stress-related problems? Workaholics, according to Machlowitz, seem to have a physical need for the healthy stress of hard work. Long hours do not necessarily cause medical problems; it's one's attitude toward work that is important. "What's more," claimed Machlowitz, "a workaholic is less likely to succumb to an ulcer or heart attack than someone who's being pressured from the outside—perhaps by a workaholic boss—rather than setting her own pace." According to a 20-year study by the American Cancer Society, people who

refuse to retire live longer. There is one potential problem, though: The workaholic may not realize when enough is enough and may not take time to visit a doctor to check out any early warning of physical illness.

"Workaholics are 'racehorses,'" said Machlowitz. They're not overworked, they're going at the speed that's best for them. They are extremely energetic and enthusiastic. They'll say such things as, "If I didn't have to pay the rent, I'd do my job for free," or that their 16-hour workday seems only six hours long. Or, as one woman who works in a department store put it, "I wish I could sleep in the model rooms."

"Workaholics definitely are not well-rounded people, but they've found their niche and love it."

Some Tips for Workaholics

1. Make sure you're doing work that suits you, because your career is going to claim most of your waking hours. Since workaholics tend to be rather rigid, some prefer jobs where they can be their own boss; others do fine within large corporations.

2. Try—even if it hurts—to expand your horizons a little. One danger of being a workaholic is that you may miss out on activities you'd enjoy, if you'd give them a chance. You're never going to be a dabbler, though. If you do hit on a hobby or sport that interests you, be prepared to go at it with great fervor.

3. Eventually, you may be forced to go on a vacation. Don't torture yourself by scheduling a week in a chaise longue in Barbados—you'll drive yourself crazy. Instead, plan an active vacation that engages your mind, maybe a tennis camp or archaeological dig.

4. Don't marry a man who can't accept the fact that you're a workaholic or who expects you to change. Workaholics don't change.

5. If you have kids, include them in your life by sharing and explaining your job. Let

your children see where you work and what you do.

6. Don't allow the negative press about workaholics to faze you. Said Machlowitz, "Of all the questions I've been asked about workaholics, the one I like best came from a young professor who asked, 'How do I become one?' "

"I'm compulsive. Whatever it is, I must do it today. And must do it over until it's right."   Barbara Walters

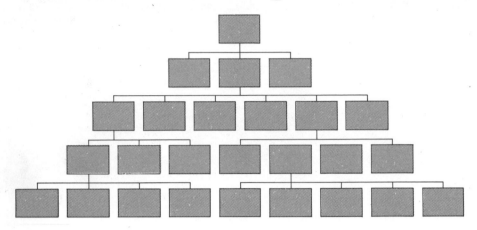